Inside the Cell

INSIDE *the* CELL

THE DARK SIDE *of* FORENSIC DNA

Erin E. Murphy

NATION
BOOKS
New York

Copyright © 2015 by Erin E. Murphy

Published by Nation Books, A Member of the Perseus Books Group
116 East 16th Street, 8th Floor
New York, NY 10003

Nation Books is a co-publishing venture of the Nation Institute and the Perseus Books Group.
All rights reserved. Printed in the United States of America. No part of this book may be
reproduced in any manner whatsoever without written permission except in the case of brief
quotations embodied in critical articles and reviews. For information, address the Perseus Books
Group, 250 West 57th Street, 15th Floor, New York, NY 10107.

Books published by Nation Books are available at special discounts for bulk purchases in the
United States by corporations, institutions, and other organizations. For more information,
please contact the Special Markets Department at the Perseus Books Group, 2300 Chestnut
Street, Suite 200, Philadelphia, PA 19103, or call (800) 810-4145, ext. 5000, or e-mail special
.markets@perseusbooks.com.

Designed by Jeff Williams

Library of Congress Cataloging-in-Publication Data
Murphy, Erin E. (Law teacher) author.
Inside the cell : the dark side of forensic DNA / Erin E. Murphy.
pages cm
Includes bibliographical references and index.
ISBN 978-1-56858-469-0 (hardcover)–ISBN 978-1-56858-470-6 (e-book) 1. DNA finger-
printing—Law and legislation—United States. I. Title.

KF9666.5.M87 2015
363.25'62—dc23

2015020264

10 9 8 7 6 5 4 3 2 1

To Quinlan and Crosby,
for sharing the first years of their lives with this book,
and most of all to Jeremy, for sharing the rest of his with me.

CONTENTS

PART IV
BUILDING A BETTER DNA POLICY

INTRODUCTION

Forensic DNA testing has been hailed as a savior. It has led to over three hundred exonerations, including for over twenty innocent men sentenced to death.[1] DNA testing has also resulted in the apprehension and conviction of some of the nation's most dangerous repeat offenders, including serial attackers identified through DNA testing long after the trail from their victims had gone cold. And finally, by offering the criminal justice system a way of proving identity with unprecedented degrees of certainty, DNA analysis has closed innumerable cases that otherwise might have gone unsolved.

Yes, to be sure, DNA testing is a savior. The trouble is, no one likes to admit that even a savior can have flaws. Popular understanding of forensic DNA testing, also called DNA typing, paints it as an all but infallible technique. In the crime shows that dominate prime-time airwaves, forensic investigators work with the steely precision typically associated with surgeons or navy pilots. Technicians study crime scene evidence, fortified by sleek instruments galvanized by strikingly plausible technologies. *Of course, the ridge line of the nail indicates whether the victim was left-or right-handed. Just look at the creases along the edge: they reflect the particular brand and size of nail clipper. A quick search reveals that this clipper was only sold in six shops in this city in the mid-1990s—I think we can find our man!*

There is something deeply reassuring about the sophistication and certainty depicted in these shows. Perhaps the comfort they offer traces to our longing to believe that we leave an impression on the world. It seems right that the microscopic traces of self left behind by criminals should be both so evident and so individualized. It affirms two of our own innate, but conflicting, desires. We can see *ourselves* as unique and complex—as complicated as the whorls on our fingertips or the flecks in our irises—and yet at the same time, intelligible. Despite our complexity, we are all still capable of being *known* and *understood* by others. I leave fingerprints, therefore I am.

Whatever the reason, it is clear that forensic science is a popular dish, most often served without garnishes. But cracks have been slowly accumulating in this facade of scientific perfection. First, in September 2005, the Federal Bureau of Investigation (FBI) announced that it would stop offering bullet lead analyses. This method purports to match bullets recovered from a crime scene to those in possession of a suspect. But after having conducted roughly 2,500 of such tests since the 1980s,[2] the FBI desisted when a major study of its reliability exposed the dubious basis for claiming such matches.[3]

Then, in 2009, the *New Yorker* published an article about Cameron Todd Willingham. Willingham was sentenced to death in Texas for setting a deadly fire, and the conviction rested largely on the conclusions of the fire investigators. Most of those conclusions were grounded in disproven bits of folk wisdom that actual fire science has since disavowed.[4] But by the time that science had earned wide acceptance, Willingham had already been executed. The field of hair analysis has likewise come under close scrutiny, causing the FBI to announce an unprecedented attempt to reexamine the hair evidence in over 2,500 cases in order to check for errors. Review of just the first 160 cases showed so many major problems that the process temporarily ground to a halt.[5] By the time investigators finished 342 cases, they concluded that the FBI examiners offered inaccurate and unsupported testimony in 257 of 268 trials—95 percent of the cases, including in 32 death penalty cases.[6]

Lastly, the wave of exonerations across the nation—over half of which are attributed at least in part to faulty forensic evidence—brought to light systemic problems with familiar forms of expert testimony, such as bite mark evidence, fiber and hair analysis, and other pattern evidence.[7] These issues were comprehensively addressed in a 2009 report by a blue-ribbon panel of the National Academy of Sciences. That report condemned nearly every traditional forensic discipline as insufficiently grounded in science, finding that "With the exception of nuclear DNA analysis, . . . no forensic method has been rigorously shown to have the capacity to consistently, and with a high degree of certainty, demonstrate a connection between evidence and a specific individual or source."[8]

But even with increasing awareness of the problems that plague conventional forensic science, DNA typing has largely emerged unscathed.

It has even been lionized in *Science* magazine in 2005 as the "gold standard" for forensic evidence.[9] The casual contact that people have with DNA testing likely affirms this view. Expectant parents who rightly trust a DNA sample to tell them whether their fetus is a boy or girl, or has genetic abnormalities, are unlikely to think that the government's tests are unreliable. The people who send a swab from their cheek to 23andMe .com or Ancestry.com—companies that perform genetic testing for recreational purposes—are unlikely to believe that much harm can come from sharing their DNA sample with strangers interested in historical or medical research.

Generally speaking, this enthusiasm for DNA typing is not misguided, and it is not wrong. DNA typing *is* a marked advance over more primitive forensic methods. It *does* rely on scientifically established principles and mathematically sound statistics. And studying DNA *has* in fact revolutionized how we judge all scientific evidence in the criminal justice system.

But revolutionary does not mean infallible, and better does not mean faultless. Forensic DNA analysis is technical and it is complex. Yet it feels familiar and trustworthy because we encounter it in pop culture and in the medical context on a regular basis. Most people have little understanding of the difference between medical and criminal justice DNA tests, or what the government currently does or may in the future do with DNA. But as Peter Gill, founding father of forensic DNA testing—currently a professor of forensic science at Oslo University and formerly a leading scientist with the United Kingdom's Forensic Science Service—has acknowledged, "There is little doubt . . . that misinterpretation of DNA profiling evidence may cause miscarriages of justice."[10]

This book aims to complicate the narrative surrounding forensic DNA analysis by telling the tales of mistake, abuse, and misuse. It intends to situate DNA testing in the forensic context, to show how even a reliable scientific discipline can be pushed beyond its limits, corrupted, or fall prey to ordinary error. The exoneration cases have set the tone for popular views of DNA analysis in the criminal justice system, which is to view it as an unmitigated good. But, in fact, two lessons might be drawn from them. The first, well received, is that DNA testing is a transformative technology breakthrough—a definitive way to separate the criminals from the wrongly accused. But the second lesson, too often overlooked, is that the same broken criminal justice system that created mass incarceration, and that has processed millions through its machinery without catching even egregious instances of wrongful conviction, now has a new and powerful weapon in its arsenal.

Forensic DNA methods are entering the same criminal justice system that we now know got away for decades with peddling faulty "science" as truth. We have learned that our criminal justice system has a propensity to push science beyond its justified limits, to neglect to adequately safeguard the integrity of evidence or the forensic testing process, to ignore systemic failures in the training and supervision of analysts, and to dismiss problems that arise as incidental or unrepresentative in the hope that they will simply go away. And while DNA science is better than traditional forensic techniques, the corrupting forces of the criminal justice system have little changed. Nearly all of the pathologies that led to the unfettered embrace of now-discredited bullet lead, arson, and hair methods are still in place in our criminal justice system today. Police, prosecutors, and public laboratory officials still shroud their methods and mistakes in secrecy, and defense lawyers still all too often lack the skill and resources needed to effectively challenge scientific evidence in court.

By exposing its dark side, this book inevitably tarnishes the halo that surrounds forensic DNA analysis. But its intention is not to call for an end to forensic DNA testing. That approach would be foolish, and would forfeit the innumerable benefits that DNA testing has to offer the criminal justice system. Instead, this is simply a call to proceed with caution. To trust less, and think more. To recognize that the value of a DNA match is not just the product of abstract science, but rather must be measured by the performance of a long chain of human actors—from crime scene collector, to lab analyst, to lawyer.

In calling for caution, this book undoubtedly puts a damper on the current unbridled enthusiasm for DNA testing. But there are no shortcuts in the criminal justice system. No free passes, and no cure-alls. DNA analysis may be many things, but it is not an antidote either to crime or all that ails the criminal justice system. What is more, DNA testing comes with a cost. If used unwisely, forensic DNA typing will exacerbate some of our system's greatest dysfunctions, such as racial injustice, boundless government power, and a propensity for overly harsh prosecution and punishment. This book cannot fix the systemic problems in our criminal justice system, but it can help steer the reliance on DNA typing down a different, and better, path.

PART I

When a Match Isn't a Match:
How DNA Testing Goes Wrong

CHAPTER 1

The Basics: DNA Typing for Dummies

DNA TYPING HAS resulted in the exoneration of hundreds of wrong-fully convicted people, and the conviction of innumerable guilty ones. It seems like every day, the media reports a verdict overturned after new evidence exculpates the accused, or recounts the spellbinding tale of the use of science to net an elusive killer. But the stories rarely say *how* exactly the DNA tests helped identify the guilty or free the innocent. It would be easy to believe that DNA analysis works like a home pregnancy test—simply swab a suspect's cheek and then read the result: *guilty* or *not guilty*.

But DNA testing is not that simple. If it were, then sending the same DNA samples to different analysts would always yield identical results. Yet studies have shown that is not always the case. For instance, in one 2011 study of subjectivity in DNA interpretation,[1] researchers sent the file from an actual case that occurred in Georgia to seventeen different DNA analysts, all experienced caseworkers at an accredited government lab in the United States. The sample derived from an alleged gang rape. Given the charge, it could be assumed that the DNA samples would include at least the victim's DNA, but it was unclear how many additional contributors might be found.

The file included the typed DNA profile of the victim along with those of three identified suspects. The analysts were asked to draw one of three conclusions for each suspect: excluded as a possible contributor to the crime scene sample, "cannot be excluded" as a possible contributor (that is, a possible participant), or "inconclusive." One suspect in particular was considered critical: he claimed innocence, but another suspect who had confessed to the crime implicated him in exchange for more lenient treatment in his own case.

Instead of a uniform response, there was marked variation among the analysts' findings. One examiner found that the suspect could not be excluded, and therefore his genetic material could plausibly be part of the DNA evidence. Twelve reached the opposite conclusion and excluded the suspect from having contributed to the sample. Four found the evidence inconclusive. The Georgia analyst in the actual case agreed with the lone examiner in the study who found the suspect a possible contributor—and this evidence was used to convict the real-life suspect of the crime.

Although this study was the first of its kind to be published, it simply crystallized what had long been known: interpretation of DNA from crime scenes can be incredibly complex. As Peter Gill, one of the world's leaders in forensic science, once said, "If you show 10 colleagues a mixture, you will probably end up with 10 different answers."[2] Why were the expert's conclusions all over the map? How is it that DNA testing allows doctors to confidently predict fetal traits, yet when DNA is studied in connection with a criminal case, even experienced, trained analysts may disagree about something as basic as who contributed to a sample?

There are five key differences between DNA science practiced in the criminal justice system—*forensic* DNA testing—and DNA science practiced in the medical or research context:

1. Forensic DNA testing involves a kind of *shortcut DNA test*, not the sequencing tests more typically performed in the research context.
2. The *quantity* of DNA recovered from a crime scene limits forensic analysts to what is available, whereas clinicians or researchers can take optimal quantities of samples and redraw a sample or retest if anything goes wrong.
3. The *quality* of DNA samples taken from a crime scene is often much poorer than that taken in a clinical environment or from a known individual; crime scene DNA may have degraded due to environmental exposure or contain a mix of biological material from an unknown number of people.
4. Forensic analysts seek to answer a question that is usually of no import to medical or clinical researchers. Namely, who is the source of this crime scene sample and how confident can we be in that attribution?

5. Clinical and medical researchers perform their work openly, and their results are subjected to layers of critical review before they impact individual lives. In contrast, forensic DNA testing endures far less oversight, and the DNA databases used to match suspects to crime scenes remain wholly sheltered by the government from any external critical review.

In sum, forensic DNA typing departs radically from DNA testing in the medical, clinical, or academic context. It can be a far more complex and nuanced operation than might appear at first glance. And many of these nuances and complexities are unavoidable; they arise as a matter of course in an ordinary criminal case, not just as the product of lack of training or analyst error. To truly appreciate the nature of interpretative subjectivity, one must first possess a basic understanding of the fundamentals of forensic DNA typing.

DNA TYPING: THE BASICS

Although the exact number of cells in the human body is unknown, one estimate places the number at 37.2 trillion, composed of more than two hundred different cell types.[3] There are blood cells, skin cells, sperm cells, and saliva cells, among others. People shed those cells constantly. Every two minutes, in fact, we shed almost enough skin cells to cover an entire football field.[4] A typical human fingerprint, barely visible to the naked eye, contains roughly one hundred cells.[5]

Inside nearly every one of those cells lies a nucleus,[6] and inside that are twenty three sets of paired chromosomes that form the human genome. One chromosome in each pair is inherited from one's biological mother, and the other from one's biological father. The sex chromosomes that make up the final pair determine whether a person is genetically female (XX) or male (XY).

Unfurled, these DNA strands stretch roughly three feet long in the form of the characteristic double helix structure that won James Watson, Francis Crick, and Maurice Wilkins the Nobel Prize in 1962.[7] You can imagine the DNA strand as a twisting ladder, in which each rung is a step joining two base pairs. There are only four possible bases—abbreviated A, T, C, and G—and they always pair off in the same way: A joining with T, and C joining with G. In the 1990s, the Human Genome Project started a global race to assemble the human genome: participating scientists tested one person's DNA sample to figure out every single letter along each side of that ladder. There are 3.2 billion such rungs, so it is easy to see why the project to discover, or "sequence," them all did not finish until 2003.[8]

At first, researchers assumed that the human genome would differ dramatically from that of other organisms. But as scientists sequenced more human and nonhuman genomes, it turned out that huge chunks of the human genome were identical to those of cows (85 percent), dogs (84 percent), and chickens (65 percent). Indeed, we share half of our genes with the common fruit fly, and a quarter of them with a grain of rice or a wine grape![9] Given how much we have in common with plants and animals, it is perhaps not surprising that the variation in the human genome is incredibly slight—roughly 0.1 percent.[10] But although it is slight when expressed as a percentage, it still is significant in absolute numbers. That percentage encompasses roughly 3 million base pairs of difference.

It would be easy to assume that because so little of the genome varies from person to person, the parts that do differ must all be critical in determining any one person's makeup. In other words, you might think that this 0.1 percent is packed wall to wall with *genes*. Genes, as most people know, are the identifiable stretches of the genome that we know have a clear function in the human body. Typically thousands of base pairs in length, genes determine characteristics as superficial as eye color or as profound as an increase in susceptibility to breast cancer.[11]

But the 0.1 percent is not full of genes. It is estimated that there are only about 25,000 genes. The purpose of the base pairs contained within the remaining areas of variation is currently unknown; indeed, huge stretches of the genome do not seem to play any role in the actual function or appearance of the body, even though they differ from person to person. In some ways, this finding nicely dovetails with another recent realization: that even parts of the genome that *are* identical may nonetheless have different manifestations when actually put to work.

Researchers interested in medicine and human biology typically study the working—or *coding*—parts of the genome, for obvious reasons. Academic and medical researchers are interested in finding clues that might prevent or treat disease or disabling conditions, or even just help understand why some people lose their hair while others do not. That means that, for the most part, these researchers also engage in *sequencing* of genes. They want to learn the specific letters that make up the ladder rungs of the double helix, along with their order, because the letters are like the instruction manual to the rest of the body. If scientists can un-cover how to read the instructions, they will be able to rewrite them when they go awry.

Forensic DNA testing, in contrast, deliberately ignores the genes, an-alyzing only those regions of the genome that vary for no discernible reason. That is, forensic DNA methods focus on the *noncoding* regions of the genome—the parts that do not send any orders. That choice is made intentionally, most notably to protect privacy and ensure accuracy. Looking at the noncoding parts also gives forensic scientists greater con-fidence that each place they look is disconnected from the other places studied. Think about it in terms of coding genes: we know from experi-ence that blue eyes, blond hair, and light skin tone tend to go together more than do blue eyes, brown hair, and dark skin tone. That means that there may be genetic connections between those traits—such that having blond hair makes it more likely that one will also have blue eyes. If they are connected, they are not independent of one another—and that diminishes their value in distinguishing one person from the next. To maximize the use of genetic information to identify people, we want as many disconnected data points as possible; otherwise the value of each point is compromised by its connection to another piece of information that predetermines its result.

The other important way in which forensic DNA typing differs from medical or academic research is that forensic DNA typing usually ignores sequence variation. That is, it does not differentiate among people by typing the base pair sequences. Instead, forensic DNA typing studies a different kind of variation—specifically, *length variations*.

FORENSIC DNA TESTS: A PRIMER

Since forensic DNA methods first emerged in the 1980s, several tech-niques have been used. Most common today is an approach that looks at short, tandem, repeat sections of the genome—known as STR typing. To understand STR typing, some basic vocabulary is essential. First, recall that the word *gene* denotes a section of the genome that has some purpose or function—each gene regulates the body in some way. A more general term for these sections is the Latin word for "place"—*locus*, or *loci* in the plural. The word *locus* is the preferred way of referring to identifiable chunks of the genome that have no purpose but are distinguishable for other reasons (most pertinently, because they vary from person to person). Forensic DNA typing typically uses thirteen loci as its core set of identifiers, although that number will soon be raised.[12]

Here is the tough part. At each of these loci, known sequences *repeat* in different combinations in different people. These known sequences are short—typically around four base pairs—and they are the same in every person. The only difference is that they repeat a different number of times in each individual in predictable increments.[13]

The more the sequence repeats, the longer that fragment of DNA. Thus, by measuring the length of the fragment, an analyst can identify the genetic "signature" of a person at that locus. This is done by analyzing two repeat lengths, one from each biological parent. Some loci have as few as eight commonly observed patterns of repeats (for example, the sequence repeats anywhere from ten to seventeen times), whereas others have as many as twenty-seven. By counting the number of repeats present at each pair of the thirteen loci, an analyst can thus obtain twenty-six discrete measurements, or variations, for an individual.[14]

These variations are called alleles. So, if a suspect has a "5, 8 allele pattern at the D3 locus," this means that at the locus D3, the suspect has five repeats of a known sequence on one of the chromosomes, and eight repeats on its partner chromosome. When all the alleles of the selected loci are compiled, the result is the individual's *genetic profile*—a composite of traits that identify that person. Because each of the thirteen loci has anywhere from eight to twenty-seven different allele possibilities, and each person has two alleles at each locus,[15] the genetic "signature" becomes highly discriminating. Only identical twins share an entire genome, and so examining a sufficient number of snippets of the genetic strand typically distinguishes one person from another.

FORENSIC DNA TESTING

How is DNA obtained and tested forensically? It starts, of course, with a sample. For controlled samples, such as those from known persons, the most common approach today is what is known as a *buccal swab*. This is simply a painless scraping of the inside of a person's cheek to collect skin cells, using a cotton swab–like sampling device. Uncontrolled samples, such as crime scene evidence, are usually collected in either of two forms:

a swab or a cutting. Swabs are simply the rubbing of those sampling devices against a surface (say, of a light switch or bloodstain), whereas a cutting is a piece of an item likely to contain biological material (for instance, fabric or upholstery). Often referred to in shorthand as *stains*, these swabs or cuttings most commonly hold biological material such as blood, skin (epithelial cells), sperm, or saliva—but any human cell with a nucleus can yield a result (even sweat, tears, etc.). That means that a wide array of objects can yield DNA results: predictable things, such as guns, bloody clothing, or an intimate swab containing ejaculate; but also unexpected sources, such as a sweat-stained hat brim, a half-eaten burger, a used facial tissue, or a disposable razor.

In the early days of forensic DNA typing, an analyst needed a significant amount of biological material to conduct a test likely to yield a useable result. For instance, if you can picture a dime, the forensic sample would have needed to take up about half of the dime's surface. Today, however, much less is needed; a sample the size of just one of the digits in the minuscule year printed on a dime can reliably produce a profile. Techniques for maximizing the recovery of genetic material from crime scene stains continue to evolve, and some newer methods even extract genetic material from as little as a dozen or fewer cells.

Once an analyst has a crime scene stain in hand, the next step is to figure out what kind of sample it is and whether it contains human DNA. In a process called extraction, the analyst separates the DNA from all the other cellular materials that make up the sample. The nucleus of the cell is broken up and all the extraneous bits washed away (there are several different methods for this, most involving chemical washes), exposing the DNA left behind. This reduces the stain to a DNA sample. Because extraction is highly sensitive, it has been described as "probably the moment where the DNA sample is more susceptible to contamination in the laboratory than at any other time in the forensic DNA process."[16] Due to this risk of contamination and the difficulty of uncovering it after the fact, it is crucial that labs take care not to unintentionally introduce foreign material to the sample. Good labs will use different stations for processing evidence samples (for example, the murder weapon) and reference samples (such as the suspected killer's buccal swab), and sequence and separate the testing process so that the entire area may be thoroughly cleaned, and so that at worst any problems arise in a sample of known origin as opposed to a crime scene sample.

Special methods of extraction help produce results in difficult cases. One method was proposed in 1985, by Peter Gill.[17] Known as differential extraction, this process solves a problem common in rape cases: intimate swabs from sexual assaults often contain a mixture of material. For instance, a vaginal swab may contain traces of the attacker's ejaculate, but may be overwhelmed by cells from the victim. Differential extraction allows the analyst to segregate the sperm portion of the sample from the skin cell portion of the sample, so that the analyst can distinctly see the male portion of the mixed sample. If there is no sperm in the sample, another way of separately examining the male fraction is to look for markers specific to the Y chromosome.

The next step in the testing process is known as quantification. Different biological sources carry different amounts of DNA—liquid blood or semen has a large quantity (roughly 20,000 to 40,000 nanograms [ng]), whereas urine or bone contain much less (roughly 1 to 20 ng).[18] Before testing, the analyst must ensure that the sample contains an appropriate quantity of DNA. The amount matters because DNA testing machines are sensitive: too much or too little DNA will compromise the results.

Next comes the core of forensic DNA testing—two processes known as amplification and capillary electrophoresis. Amplification accomplishes two things: first, it reduces the 3.2 billion base pair genome down to the particular fragments that the forensic analyst is interested in, and second, it copies just those segments so that they may be examined more closely. Some people liken this process to genetic Xeroxing, but it actually trims down the sample first, before building it up again in as section-specific replicates.

To illustrate, imagine you went to watch your friend run in a marathon. You want to make sure you see her when she passes by, so you can meet her at the end of the route. If your friend is going to be running on her own, it might be easy to miss her in the crowd. If you turn away for a minute, or if your attention is captivated by someone else along the route, she might jog by without your noticing. But if your friend plans to run with a large team dressed identically, she would be almost impossible to miss. Even if you did not see her specifically, you would know for certain when she passed because her group would be hard to overlook.

DNA testing works along a similar principle: the pertinent fragments of DNA are so tiny that measuring them correctly, if you looked at just

one, might be difficult. Indeed, this problem would be particularly vexing in forensic cases, because not only are the fragments small, but the
number of available fragments may be few. With amplification, however,
a small amount of DNA can be trimmed down to the relevant bits, and
then replicated to millions or even billions of copies that make studying
those little fragments possible.

This genetic photocopying technique, known as polymerase chain reaction, or PCR for short, so revolutionized molecular biology that its
inventor received the Nobel Prize.[19] In forensic typing, commercial kits
are available that contain *primers*, tiny chemical scissors that help cut the
whole genomic strand into just those tiny fragments of interest to the
analyst. The PCR process then applies alternating cycles of heating and
cooling (typically 28 to 32 cycles[20]) that copy those fragments. During
the amplification, the samples are also tagged with fluorescent labels in
different dye colors to separately identify each part.

Amplification thus achieves several goals: it cuts the genomic strand
down to just the parts the analyst is interested in measuring, copies those
parts so that there are more of them, and tags the genetic material so that
it can be measured. Scientists continue to improve upon amplification
techniques, such as improving the ability to amplify multiple spots on
the genome at one time. Known as multiplexing, these methods permit
a scientist to use a small amount of genetic material to create a large
amount of selectively copied regions all in one round of PCR. However,
multiplex processes also introduce added sensitivities, as the ideal conditions for amplifying one region of the genome may not perfectly mirror
the conditions needed for amplifying other regions.

Other problems can arise during PCR that result in the loss of genetic
material. Just as the quality of an image declines as you make photocopies
from photocopies rather than from the originals, so, too, can the quality
of genetic copies lose their integrity. Pieces of the DNA strand may slip,
leaving genetic replicates close in size to the original material but slightly
shorter. Or a mutation in the parts of the genome adjacent to the portion
of interest can cause the primers—those genetic scissors—not to work,
leading to a failure to amplify that region. The primers may likewise fail if
some non-DNA material manages to infect the sample and inhibit their
proper functioning.

Contamination at this stage is also a real concern; the addition
of even the tiniest amount of extrinsic DNA to the sample before

amplification will result in the extra DNA being copied many times over, making it seem like part of the original sample. In fact, the risk of inadvertent contamination is so great that most labs maintain databases with the genetic profiles of staff members and even crime scene investigators, so that accidental contamination with their material will be immediately apparent.

Once the DNA sample has been cut up into the relevant pieces and those chunks have been reproduced, the next step is to measure the size of the resulting DNA fragments. This is typically done through a second process, capillary electrophoresis. Electrophoresis accomplishes two main tasks. First, it separates out clusters of like material from the soup of DNA fragments that was created in PCR. Separation is a delicate process because large multiplexing systems can process so many fragments at the same time. It is akin to throwing a large family's laundry into one basket—it not only makes it easy to lose a sock here and there, but also may lead to mistakenly putting Big Sister's leggings in Little Sister's drawer. These dangers are particularly acute given that some alleles differ very minimally.[21]

The second major task of electrophoresis is to measure the fragments to determine the allele that is present. This measurement is accomplished by effectively entering the fragments in a race. Again visualize a marathon with hundreds of entrants. Some runners are small and sprightly and will finish quickly; others are larger and move more slowly. If you are not wearing a watch, but want to find out how long it takes for certain runners to cross the finish line, you might look for pace setters. Those runners, planted in the race to run at a specific speed, offer a point of comparison for determining the rate of the unknown entrants. Because you know that a certain pace setter will finish in three hours, you know that the unknown runner that finishes next to the pace setter also must have run the course in three hours.

Electrophoresis operates much the same way. To get the DNA fragments started, a negative electric current is applied to the sample. That current causes the DNA to move toward a positive current at the other end of the capillary, or tube. Along with the material that is being tested, the analyst runs a sample called an allelic ladder, which functions as the pace setter. As each of the strands get to the positive side, a detection window makes a note of the point at which the fragment crossed and the color of the fluorescent tag that was attached during the amplification stage. The fragments are then measured against the allelic ladder, which contains known size markers (the pace setters). To make sure the process runs smoothly, the analyst also runs several controls, including a "negative control" that ensures that there are no contaminants in the capillary, a "positive control" that contains DNA with a known profile to ensure that the test yields accurate results, and an "amplification blank" to ensure that no extraneous material compromised the amplification stage.

The next chapter and the Appendix both provide more detail about the capillary electrophoresis process, and the kinds of challenges an analyst may encounter when testing a sample. But this overview gives sufficient foundation in the basic testing technique. The machines most commonly in use today take about thirty minutes per run, but more rapid machines capable of returning results within 90 minutes, measured from swab-in to the profile output, are increasingly available.[22]

DATABASES

Once a DNA sample is typed, it may be put to any of several possible uses. The most low-tech version of forensic DNA typing is simply to compare the profiles from evidence collected at the crime scene with that given by a suspect in the offense. These "confirmation cases" simply link known suspects to evidence. A match does not conclusively prove that the person may have left the crime scene stain—more on that later—but it can be strong evidence of that kind. An exclusion proves that the known person was not the source.

But most DNA profiles are not just used in a single case. Instead, the government retains indefinitely the samples taken from known persons. The retention of the physical DNA sample is an area of controversy, as it gives the government access to the entire genetic code of all the persons it has tested, raising serious concerns about privacy. The government claims that it needs these samples in case it wants to confirm a crime scene match, or so that it can apply the latest kinds of genetic tests as the technology evolves. But, of course, matches can and ought to be confirmed by taking a new sample from the individual, and the state's ability to subject the samples to new kinds of genetic tests without any prior permission is precisely why privacy advocates object to sample retention.

In a cruel twist of logic, most states lack policies regarding the retention of *evidence* taken from crime scenes even though they all retain known persons' samples. In fact, most states routinely discard crime scene evidence after a finite period of time. Although crime scene evidence may be bulkier to store and thus more difficult to maintain, it is also possible to take cuttings or swabbings from such evidence that could be more readily kept. As a result of current practices, the federal and state governments have in their possession over 13 million biological samples from known persons, even though most of those persons could easily be located for retesting if necessary, whereas condemned prisoners have lost the ability to challenge their convictions using the latest DNA technology because the state threw out the crime scene evidence.

In addition to physical sample retention, the typed profile from known persons and crime scene samples are also uploaded to DNA databases. This allows law enforcement to search and share DNA data. The DNA databases grew from a pilot project initiated in 1990 by the FBI. The goal was to develop software that could store DNA profile data that would in turn be searchable. The result was CODIS, the Combined DNA Index System. "CODIS" is often used as shorthand for the DNA database, but in fact it refers to the software program used to search files held at three different levels: national, state, and local.

At the highest level is the national DNA index system (NDIS). Below that is the state DNA index system (SDIS), and below that are the local DNA index systems (LDIS). The LDIS feeds into the SDIS, which in turn feeds into the NDIS. The NDIS is overseen by the FBI, whereas state and localities control their own SDIS and LDIS. At the national level, submissions must follow specific rules. For instance, NDIS labs must be affiliated with a criminal justice agency, be accredited, comply with quality assurance requirements issued by the FBI, and undergo periodic auditing for compliance. State and local indexes, in contrast, need only comply with any state or local rules, and thus often contain profiles that would otherwise be ineligible for upload to the national database, including samples examined at nonaccredited labs.

DNA databases are organized by discrete subindices. At the national level, these include a *forensic* index, with DNA profiles developed from crime scene evidence; a *convicted offender* index, with profiles from persons convicted of crimes; an *arrestee* index, with DNA from persons sampled pursuant to state laws authorizing sampling at arrest; a *missing persons* index, an *unidentified human remains* index, and a *biological relatives of missing persons* index. There is also a *legal* index, which includes profiles from persons whose samples are lawfully collected, but who do not fit in another category (such as a voluntarily provided elimination sample), and a *detainee* index for those lawfully detained for immigration reasons.

When police or analysts talk about a "DNA profile," they are referring to the profile that reflects the set of loci that are the standard identifiers used for criminal forensic purposes. Without a standard set, it would be difficult to set up a database. Every jurisdiction would be looking at its own preferred part of the 3.2 billion base pair genome. So, early in the history of DNA databasing, the FBI selected thirteen loci that became the reference set for criminal cases. Because there are two alleles at each locus, the typical forensic DNA profile contains twenty-six pieces of information.[23] The thirteen loci are known as the CODIS loci, and the whole profile is known as the CODIS profile—each after the FBI software.

So, for instance, suppose a theft occurs in Baltimore, Maryland, and the suspected thief is arrested. Local law enforcement collects a sample from the crime scene, such as a bit of DNA from blood found on a glass shard from a broken window, as well as a swab of the suspect's cheek. Each is sent to the county lab for testing. The results might be stored locally, in a city or county database, as well as in the statewide index. If eligible, they might also be uploaded to the national index—say, if the state allows arrestee sampling.

It is important to understand that the national DNA database is not a single computer server that contains files; instead, it operates like a pointer system. NDIS stores only the basic data necessary to make a match —such as the numeric digits in the profile, and a case file, lab, and analyst reference number. The full case information, including the name and identifying information of the sample donor, is retained at the state level.[24] In other words, the database files are decoupled from identifying information and the physical sample, both of which are retained at the state or local level.

There are several reasons for this; the most prominent are expedience and privacy. The national database now contains over 10 million known individual profiles. If all were stored in one centralized place, it would be incredibly complicated to keep that information current and accurate, because in theory each of the nation's nearly 20,000 law enforcement agencies would be entitled to enter and change information for a single entry. Moreover, a centralized system would be more vulnerable to hackers or other bad actors.

Instead, FBI officials wisely conceived of the national system as a kind of clearinghouse. Each entry in the NDIS database contains an identifying number linking it to the lab and technician that processed the sample, another number linking it to a particular person or piece of evidence, and a third number linking it to the actual DNA profile itself. When a connection is made between pieces of evidence or a person and evidence, the laboratories that processed those samples must get in touch with one another to obtain more information about the match, such as the name of the person who contributed the sample or details about the case that the sample came from. Once a match occurs, standard practice is to re-test the individual whose sample was in the database, to ensure that the profile does in fact match the crime scene evidence.

The story of DNA databases has generally been one of steady expansion since their inception. The NDIS was authorized by Congress in the DNA Identification Act of 1994.[25] Four years later, in 1998, CODIS went online. By 2004, all fifty states had actively joined. Today, roughly 190 public law enforcement labs across the United States participate in CODIS. In addition, more than seventy labs in forty nations use CODIS software to organize and search DNA profiles within their respective countries.[26]

Today, CODIS contains over 11 million convicted offender profiles, almost 2 million arrestee profiles, and over 600,000 crime scene profiles.[27] Widespread DNA sampling of persons at the time of arrest, the most recent direction in which DNA testing has expanded, may generate dramatic increases. Sampling all arrestees could nearly double the size of the database—in just the year 2013, there were over 11 million arrests. Notably, fewer than 5 percent of those arrests were for violent crimes; the vast majority were for misdemeanors and other low-level offenses. Indeed, the three largest categories of arrest were for drug crimes (1.5 million), theft (1.2 million), and driving under the influence (1.2 million).[28] Sadly, legislators and law enforcement advocates have *not* been as zealous about collecting DNA samples from crime scenes, and so all those known profiles get compared to only a tiny fraction of crimes.

In sum, the criminal justice system has built, and continues to build, an enormous repository of physical DNA samples and searchable DNA profiles. As a result, DNA serves an ever more important role in our criminal justice system. But what does that mean on the ground? Which set of headlines about DNA in the criminal justice system will we read most in the future: the ones that rejoice in the capture of a serial killer that had long eluded police, or the ones that reveal systematic fraud or malfeasance in a government forensic laboratory? The remainder of this book lets you decide for yourself.

CHAPTER 2

The Dirty Business of Crime: The Challenge of Forensic Samples

A LAY PERSON who only watched television or read news reports might easily believe that DNA typing is as simple as swab in, profile out. Amazingly, the technology is creeping toward that reality when it comes to samples taken in controlled conditions from known persons. But obtaining results from forensic samples—the bits and pieces collected at crime scenes—is a far different matter. Human intervention is not just incidental to DNA testing in those circumstances; it plays an indispensable role.

Think about it: When a known person gives his or her DNA, the sample is taken and tested in clinical conditions. A clean, pristine swab is typically rubbed against the inside of the cheek, painlessly gathering some of the cells that line the mouth. That swab is then placed into a sterile container, where it remains sealed until it is opened in a sterilized testing laboratory. There, an analyst wearing protective gear, and following protocols to minimize the possibility of contamination, subjects it to numerous tests. Although the specific genetic markers of the person may not be known in advance, the contours of the expected outcome is. The resulting electropherogram should show a clean and well-balanced profile of that individual's genetic markers. If that does not occur—if test results indicate that something went wrong—then the analyst can simply request another sample and repeat the test again. DNA testing in this environment is akin to going to a doctor's office, where samples are taken in a controlled environment designed to safeguard their integrity. A doctor would never just say, "Bring in an old, bloody Band-Aid and we will run some tests!"

Crime scene testing, however, is like seeking results from that dirty Band-Aid—after it has been in the trash for two weeks. Crime scene samples may contain only faint traces of DNA, yet they cannot be re-collected if anything goes wrong. Before the time of collection, the DNA may have been exposed to light, heat, moisture, or chemicals that can compromise the ability to get results. Indeed, some very common sub-stances contain inhibitors—including feces, urine, certain plant materi-als, certain components of blood, and even the dye used in denim—that can prohibit DNA tests from working at all, or produce partial results that are unreliable.[1]

And, of course, crime scene samples are, by their very nature, un-known samples. Sometimes an evidence swab clearly relates to the perpe-trator of the crime, such as a vaginal swab from a rape victim that shows traces of sperm that could only have been left by the assailant, or a cut-ting from the deployed air bag of a car crashed by a thief after hot pursuit.

But other crime scene stains are more like shots in the dark—they do not come certified as "deposited exclusively by the alleged offender," but may contain the DNA of a mélange of contributors. For instance, a swab of the light switch flipped on by a burglar might seem logically to contain only the burglar's DNA, but may be compromised by DNA left on the switch by other people who touched it. Maybe one person who touched the switch had nothing to do with the crime, or maybe ten peo-ple touched it, one of whom is the perpetrator. If interpreting the sam-ple is straightforward, and the case contains a lot of other evidence that suggests that a person who matches the sample committed the offense, there may be little cause for worry. But if a DNA match is the only real evidence in the case, it can point to multiple individuals who may or may not be innocent.

For these reasons, in all but the most undisputed cases, the actual typing does not end the testing process, it begins it. DNA test results do not arrive in the form of a printout of numbers labeled according to each contributor's particular profile. Instead, the output of a DNA test is a kind of graph with different peaks that represent the presence of ge-netic material in certain places and quantities, but without any further information about the who, when, and why of the contributors. The interpretation of that graph is the most important, and difficult, part of the DNA analyst's job, and the area where that analyst's judgment and training most comes to bear, against a backdrop of established rules and protocols. The Appendix provides a more detailed description of the mechanics of forensic DNA testing, but the remainder of this chapter gives an overview of the kinds of problems that may arise.

HIDDEN SUBJECTIVITY IN DNA TESTING

A political showdown in Washington, DC, illustrates just how controversial these judgment calls can be. In 2012, the city opened a state-of-the-art facility for its Department of Forensic Sciences (DFS). But in 2015, the chief prosecutor for the District of Columbia announced that its office planned to stop sending the DFS lab crime scene samples, and the director of the lab and two senior officials eventually resigned under pressure.[2] The prosecutor alleged that the lab's DNA methods led to erroneous conclusions about the probability of a DNA match, including, in at least one case, a finding that the defendant might have left a DNA sample on a gun magazine, despite an independent expert's determination that the defendant's DNA was absent from the magazine.[3] In another case, the DFS told the prosecutor that the profile shared by the defendant and the crime scene evidence was as uncommon as 1 in 3,290 people; in fact, it could be seen in as few as 1 in 9. That defendant was convicted on the basis of other evidence, but it led prosecutors to question the accuracy of the lab's results.

As a preventative measure, the prosecutor referred over one hundred cases to another lab for review, and stopped the pipeline for testing. In response, the head of DFS acknowledged that other experts might reach another conclusion, but contended that "different[ ] isn't wrong."[4] John Butler, a leading figure in DNA testing and scientist at the National Institute of Standards and Technology, agreed that "You can have the same data, and scientists at different labs—or even within the same lab—can interpret that data differently."

In an effort to resolve the conflict, the mayor of Washington, DC, ordered an independent audit of the crime lab. Eventually, the lab's accrediting agency found that analysts "were not competent and were using inadequate procedures," and ordered all testing suspended until additional training and validation could take place.[5] Some hailed the decision as a rare exercise in accountability. But Bill Thompson, a leading DNA scholar and professor at the University of California at Irvine, wrote in an op-ed that the response was out of proportion to the complaint. He observed that the new DC lab was among a very few in the nation to have full independence from the prosecutor's office, and worried that the political underpinnings to the incident constituted a "serious setback for efforts to protect the scientific independence of crime laboratories."[6]

The story of the DC crime lab underscores the depth of complexity in forensic DNA testing, and the dangerous way in which that complexity interfaces with the politically charged task of testing crime scene evidence. To minimize the human subjectivity factor in interpreting DNA samples, labs develop and validate interpretive protocols, or standard operating procedures (SOPs), that set baseline rules to guide every analyst's discretion. These protocols ought to be keyed to the laboratory's specific equipment and methodologies, because different machines or typing kits can have peculiarities that the lab must take into account. The purpose of such protocols is twofold: to help ensure that different analysts reach the same conclusions when interpreting ambiguous results, and to prevent analysts' deliberately or inadvertently tilting their readings in a particular direction as a result of external pressures—such as from a prosecutor or defense attorney in search of a particular result.

Recall that the results of a DNA test look like a graph with pointy peaks. (Figure 2.1 depicts one line of a typical DNA result; for a complete image, see the Appendix.) Across the very top are the names of the loci being tested. Thus, you can read across the top of the figure to see names of the five loci for which there appear results. This particular color channel is green; a full DNA profile shows different lines in different colors for each channel. Each channel in turn contains several different loci. The peaks tell the analyst which alleles were present in the sample. (The number in the little box below the peak is the actual allele—the number of repeats that were observed.) Some people assume that the *height* of the peak corresponds to the number of repeats—that fewer repeats would create a short peak, and more repeats, a tall one. But, in fact, the height of the peak indicates the *quantity* of genetic material present. That is what the numbers on the left of the graph indicate: the amount of genetic material detected, as measured in RFUs, or relative fluorescence units. If the instrument detected just a little bit of DNA, the peak is small; in contrast, a taller peak indicates that a greater quantity of material was observed in the testing.

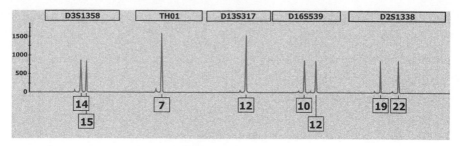

Figure 2.1. Single-source DNA electropherogram excerpt.
Source: Image courtesy of Dr. Simon Ford, Lexigen Science & Law, San Francisco.

Following these principles, it is easy to see why a single-source, clinical-quality DNA sample will typically produce a nice, clean graph with tall, even peaks, each of which represent a true report of the sample's genetic material. At every locus in Figure 2.1, there is either one or two peaks—one very tall peak if the person had two copies of the same allele at that locus, or two peaks half that size if the person had two different alleles. And the peaks are roughly the same size across the loci, indicating that all the genetic material amplified and was detected evenly. There are not a lot of extra peaks that must be explained, or missing peaks that would otherwise be expected, or loci with greater or lesser genetic material. Because the original DNA sample was precisely the right quantity and good quality, testing produces predictable results.

Unfortunately, samples taken from crime scenes do not always produce the tidy results seen in Figure 2.1. Common conditions that compromise the ability of the test to produce easily interpreted results include the degradation of the sample due to the elements, the presence of more than one person's DNA, or the presence of low amounts of DNA. And yet, in the words of one expert, "Due to the success of DNA testing . . . many laboratories are seeing an increasing number of poor quality/quantity samples being submitted."[7] Even a sample from a single source—say, the DNA retrieved from a cigarette butt smoked by one individual—can generate contestable results if only low levels of DNA could be recovered, or if the sample was subject to environmental insults, such as rain or heat, either of which degrade the sample or inhibit testing. Even a single-source, high-quality sample can behave unpredictably at times, such as when an unexpected genetic mutation prevents the testing process from working properly or if a portion of the DNA profile simply drops out.

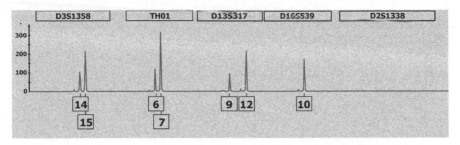

Figure 2.2. Single-source electropherogram excerpt illustrating low-quantity or -quality testing conditions.
Source: Image courtesy of Dr. Simon Ford, Lexigen Science & Law, San Francisco.

If the sample is of low quantity or quality, then the test results may look more like Figure 2.2 than like Figure 2.1. The hypothetical DNA sample tested in Figure 2.1 is identical to that in Figure 2.2, and yet now the results are not as easy to read. First, rather than reflect material measured in RFUs in the thousands, the detected material hovers in the low hundreds. That means that even small blips that would have been dwarfed in the results of Figure 2.1 now may register as meaningful.

Moreover, each of the loci illustrates a different kind of ambiguous result. Were this an unknown crime scene, however, we would not know what results to trust. Here, because we know the true profile, we can explain what happened. At the first locus, nicknamed D3, the 14 and 15 peaks are different sizes; but we know that they still both reflect the presence of true genetic material. At the second locus, THO1, we know that the 6 peak is not true genetic material; it is just material left over from slippage that is known to occasionally occur. At the third locus, D13, material "dropped in" that makes it appear that there is a 9 allele present, when in fact we know that the true profile is 12, 12. At the fourth locus, D16, one peak "dropped out" entirely—the 12 allele simply failed to amplify or show up in the testing. And at the last locus, D2, all the genetic material seems to have disappeared, a phenomenon known as locus dropout. When there are peaks that may vary dramatically in size, or extra missing peaks, or even missing loci altogether, the job of the analyst is to make sense of it all, determining which peaks to trust and which to disregard.

Ordinary challenges such as these present interpretive difficulties when a sample clearly contains only one person's genetic material, but they become unbelievably problematic when a sample contains DNA from multiple

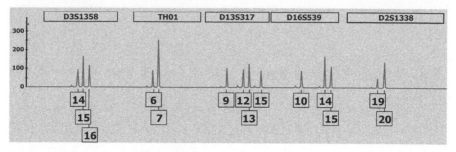

Figure 2.3. Mixture electropherogram excerpt.
Source: Image courtesy of Dr. Simon Ford, Lexigen Science & Law, San Francisco.

contributors. Such samples are called *mixtures*, and they raise some of the most vexing issues in forensic DNA interpretation. For instance, the concerns that shuttered the Washington, DC, forensic laboratory stemmed largely from conflicts over the rules for mixture interpretation.

Figure 2.3 is a good example of the results from testing a mixture, as compared to the single-source results in Figures 2.1 and 2.2. It is clear that the tested sample contained DNA from more than one person, because there are more than two peaks at each locus. Contrary to many people's expectations, DNA testing cannot determine the number of persons who contributed to the sample, or even indicate the proportions that each person contributed. As Figure 2.3 shows, the peaks are not associated with a person and do not indicate the number of persons in the sample. Yet those two pieces of information provide the backbone of forensic interpretation.

Ascertaining the number of contributors to a mixture can prove difficult. In Figure 2.3, it appears that there are at maximum four peaks at any one locus, which might lead one to assume that only two people contributed to the mixture (each with their respective two alleles). But, in fact, even that determination might not be that simple. One study showed that roughly 3 percent of three-person mixtures are misidentified as two-person mixtures, and over 70 percent of four-person mixtures may be mislabeled two- or three-person mixtures.[8]

Even where the number of contributors is known, an extraordinarily broad range of conceivable single profiles may be derived from the results.[9] Notice in Figure 2.3 that the peaks are very uneven—some are very small, suggesting only a little bit of DNA was present for that allele, but others are much taller. That suggests a wide variety in the amount of DNA that each person contributed to the sample, or that some other problem compromised the test results. It also raises the likelihood that one contributor's DNA may mask the presence of DNA from another contributor, due to the individuals' having overlapping genetic profiles. Disparate peak heights also adds to concern that it will be more difficult to detect missing material or identify as spurious peaks that may be there as a result of glitches in the testing process. There is no way to know for certain that *this* peak came from one person's genetic material while *that* peak came from another, or that this peak is reliable but that one is not.

Finally, because the amount of DNA that is loaded for testing remains fairly constant regardless of the number of contributors in the sample, the ratio of each person's contribution to the mixture may matter a great deal. If both parties contribute equally, then a sample may have half the amount of DNA that would otherwise ideally be present. If parties contribute in wildly disproportionate quantities, then some of the contributors may have their contribution dwarfed by others in the testing process. If contribution levels fall low enough, then some contributors' share may qualify as officially "low quantity," and produce erratic or unpredictable results.[10] As one eminent group of forensic scientists has observed, "[i]n real life, crime-stains will show additional complexities across multiple loci. Mixtures will be common, with varying amounts of drop-out levels per contributor."[11] And of course, as in single-source testing, mixture samples exposed to environmental or other degradations may also suffer from interpretive problems attributable to those conditions.

There are no definitive estimates of the number of forensic samples that contain DNA from more than one person. In one of his authoritative texts on DNA typing methodologies, John Butler asserted:

> At the turn of the 21st century mixtures did not represent a majority of cases in forensic DNA laboratories, especially if a good differential extraction was performed in a sexual assault case. . . . In more recent years, however . . . an increasing number of mixtures are being observed.
>
> . . .
>
> [In addition,] based on feedback the author has received from discussions with forensic laboratories around the world, the number of complex mixtures (those containing three or more contributors) appears to have risen significantly. . . . [12]

This increase is attributed to several factors: advances in technology increase the probability of gleaning DNA results in a wide array of cases, and police and prosecutors put pressure on analysts as juries increasingly expect genetic evidence. But whatever the cause, it is undisputed that forensic samples from unknown persons are often fraught with not just one but several confounding conditions, all of which may compromise the analyst's ability to discern the true profiles of the contributors.

Significantly, exculpatory testing often does not raise quite these same problems. It is far easier to tell that a suspect does *not* have a genetic profile than to assign meaning to the possible inclusion of a suspect in a DNA test. By analogy, you may have a hard time telling the difference between a "6" and a "G" on a license plate as it speeds by, but you can be certain it was not an "X."

The primary way that analysts attempt to account for all the things that might complicate DNA testing is to use rules of thumb to help narrow and guide their subjective interpretations of DNA test results. These rules of thumb are like presumptions derived from testing and experience—such as guessing that the larger shoes belong to the taller of two people. But all of these principles provide only rough guidance. One of the most common practices is to draw inferences about DNA profiles from the size of the peaks in the test results and their relationship to other peaks.[13] Other rules of thumb reflect anticipated idiosyncrasies that arise in the testing process. For instance, in its protocols every lab must specify rules like (1) how big a peak must be to be considered evidence of genetic material worthy of interpretation, (2) when a peak may be discounted as a predictable artifact of the testing process rather than deemed indicative of true genetic material, (3) and when the absence of expected genetic material can be explained as understandable versus treated as evidence that the DNA sample lacked that trait (thereby excluding, for instance, a person who is known to have that material).

The discrepancies among different labs in setting these rules of thumb explain some of the variation seen in the conclusions reached by forensic analysts. Each analyst assesses the profile by crediting some information and discrediting other information, and incautious analysts can often "see what they want to see" in DNA results. Even well-meaning analysts often find themselves operating in a wide berth of uncertainty, because interpretation is more an art than a mechanical application of predetermined principles. But the rules are nonetheless important. Without them, a lab and its analysts are unmoored from any guiding principles at all. They can simply choose to credit results that they favor, while discounting results that they disfavor, with no objective basis for those conclusions. And a lab that does not make its rules transparent deserves criticism for shielding itself both from scrutiny about the accuracy of its principles, as well as from attacks for departing from those principles without justification.

The difficulty in assigning meaning to forensic profiles, and particularly to mixtures, has led to increasing efforts to develop probabilistic software to aid the forensic analyst. A major advantage of these programs is that they may incorporate more subtle and fluid ways of interpreting complicated DNA samples, relying on predictions based on simulations and probabilistic models, and completing calculations that would be largely impossible to do by hand. But these programs are only as good as the science upon which they are based and the algorithms upon which they are run—both of which are far from perfect.

The inherent subjectivity of DNA testing of crime scene samples explains why the training of DNA analysts, and the supervision of their work and conclusions, plays such a crucial role in maintaining a fair and accurate justice system. It is also a reminder that forensic DNA science must know its own limits. Analysts should refuse to accept cases where testing is technically feasible but likely to produce unreliable results. As John Butler remarked, "It is important to keep in mind that increased complexity in sample results can lead to decreased confidence in the interpretation of the evidence. . . . Laboratories may want to consider increasing the stringency of their case/sample acceptance policy in order to avoid a 'garbage in, garbage out' situation."[14]

The subjectivity involved in DNA testing is also why DNA profiling should never be considered infallible. In some cases, DNA evidence simply adds to existing evidence, reducing the dangers of erroneous results. In others, the purported DNA match bolsters otherwise borderline evidence, such as a thin motive or shaky eyewitnesses. Increasingly, a DNA match may be the only real evidence against the defendant at all, or may even contradict strong evidence of the defendant's innocence.

Without awareness of the problems that can arise in DNA testing, jurors may place such stock in a DNA match that they fail to give due weight to contrary evidence. That is what happened to Timothy Durham.[15] Durham spent three and a half years in prison, serving a 3,220-year sentence for raping a young girl. At trial, Durham offered eleven witnesses who placed him at a skeet-shooting contest in another state at the time of the rape, along with credit card receipts for purchases he made out of state on that day. But the jury believed the prosecutor, who produced DNA and hair evidence that purported to match him. Years later, retesting of the material showed that the analyst had misinterpreted the initial results. Redone, they exculpated Durham, and other evidence pointed to a convicted rapist who had moved to town. Durham, who had maintained his innocence throughout, endured physical brutality while in prison; as punishment for having raped a child, other inmates beat him bloody and broke his ribs. When he was finally released, he returned home to work in his family business, but the shadow cast by his conviction continued to hang over him. In the words of the founders of the Innocence Project, "How do you unring a bell?"[16]

CHAPTER 3

Phantom Suspects:
The Prevalence of DNA Transfer

IN THE EARLY days of DNA testing, examining samples was not unlike determining a person's blood type. An analyst usually tested large drops of blood or semen stains, all visible to the naked eye. But forensic DNA testing can now yield results from samples with just a few cells, and routinely handles samples of several hundred cells. When you consider that over 10,000 cells can fit on the head of a pin, it becomes clear that the days of testing only large, visible stains are long past.

The ability to discern a DNA profile from a tiny amount of material is an indisputable benefit. No one wants a rapist to go undetected simply because he wore a condom, or a burglar to evade detection by wearing gloves. But with the ability to test the scantest of evidence comes a responsibility to recognize the limits on what inferences can be drawn from that evidence. It is one thing to base an accusation on the smudges of blood on a windowpane broken by the robber; it is another to do so relying on cell residue on a doorknob that was turned to get inside.

The difference, of course, is that the blood on the glass shard almost certainly came from the perpetrator, whereas any number of persons might have touched a doorknob. That is because of a phenomenon about which little is known: *DNA transfer*.

Some people might consider DNA transfer a form of contamination. But that is not really a fair way to look at it. *Contamination* implies that a sample was somehow compromised along the way from collection to testing—that an *uncontaminated* sample would not have contained extraneous biological material. *Contamination* connotes lack of care on the part of a crime scene technician or laboratory analyst. With care and preventive actions, such as wearing protective gear or cleaning a work station, true contamination can be reduced or eliminated.

Transfer, on the other hand, is inevitable. It is not the product of accident or inadvertence, or sloppiness or malfeasance. It is simply life. Transfer is unavoidable unless we are all going to live in a bubble. It cannot be stopped through better training or education. And concern about transfer is the natural by-product of our ability to test samples so small as to be invisible to the human eye.

Researchers often distinguish between *primary*, or *direct*, transfer and *secondary*, or *indirect*, transfer. *Primary* transfer occurs when a person transfers his or her own DNA to another person or object by coming into contact with that person or object—for instance, when you kiss your spouse, your DNA is likely transferred via a small amount of skin or saliva cells. Similarly, when you pack your kid's lunchbox, you leave your DNA all over it—from your handling of the items placed inside to the cells you deposit as you close the latch.

In the first decade or so of DNA testing, criminalists focused their attention on only the most obvious cases of primary transfer—on examining clear and unambiguous stains left directly by the perpetrator, such as the bloodied knife or semen-stained sheets—rather than looking for other, invisible cells left behind. It was not until 1997 that a study first suggested that DNA typing might be capable of recovering a profile from skin or other DNA-carrying cells on objects merely handled by the perpetrator.

Such trace, or touch, evidence, quickly garnered great attention. Since then, a series of studies has shown that DNA transfers quite readily based on even brief amounts of contact (see Table 3.1). Moreover, the amount deposited can range from just a few cells to a sizeable amount (recall that each cell contains about 6 pg of DNA, and most ordinary DNA typing methods today return reliable results with roughly 500 pg, or .5 ng, of template).[1]

If primary transfer is the engine that turns the wheels of justice, by identifying perpetrators based on the DNA they leave behind, then secondary transfer is the cog that causes that wheel to grind to a halt. *Secondary* transfer occurs when DNA from one person is transferred to a person or object, even though the person never came into contact with that

TABLE 3.1 Quantities of DNA recovered from bare hands or surfaces once touched with bare hands, as published in the scientific literature.

Surface	Length of contact	Nature of contact	Quantity (ng)	Reference
Direct swabbing of hand	–	–	2–150	van Oorschot and Jones (1997)
Plastic knife handle, mug, glass	15 min	Holding	7–34	van Oorschot and Jones (1997)
Direct swabbing of hand	–	–	0.1–6.4	Bright and Petricevic (2004)
New lower bed sheet on foreign bed to sleeper	1 night (8–11 hr)	Sleeping	0–8	Petricevic et al. [37]
Various paper types (and extraction techniques)	30 s	Pressure	0–110	Sewell et al. (2008)
Door frame	1 min	Grabbing	0–>0.2	Raymond et al. (2008)
Melamine-coated board	10 s	Pressure	0–160	Kamphausen et al. (2012)
Glass	1 min	Holding	0–5	Daly et al. (2012)
Fabric	1 min	Holding	0–15	Daly et al. (2012)
Wood	1 min	Holding	0–169	Daly et al. (2012)
Cotton	10–15 s	Rubbing	6–12	Goray et al. (2010)
Plastic	10–15 s	Rubbing	0.4–0.5	Goray et al. (2010)
Infant's clothing	1 min	Rubbing	0.3–9	Goray et al. (2012)
Toy plastic building block	1 min	Rubbing	0–2.5	Goray et al. (2012)

Source: Reprinted from Georgina Meakin and Allan Jamieson, "DNA Transfer: Review and Implications for Casework," Forensic Science International: Genetics 7, no. 4 (July 2013): 434–443, Table 1, with permission from Elsevier.

other person or object. Instead, the transfer occurs via an intermediary person or object. The problem is that what looks like primary transfer, and leads investigators to believe that the suspect was there, might in fact be secondary transfer.

Returning to the earlier example, suppose you give your spouse a kiss on the cheek. Later that day, your spouse meets an old friend, who plants a kiss on the same cheek. Secondary transfer may occur: *your* DNA may now be on the face or lips of the *friend*, even if you have never seen or met that person. The same scenario can happen with an object. For instance, when you send your child off to school with the lunchbox you packed, your DNA goes to school, too, and may end up on the teacher who collects the lunchboxes to put them away, or on the shelf where they are stored, or on the table where your child eats—even though you do not come along personally or interact with any of those persons or surfaces.

The transference is called secondary because the original depositor of the DNA did not come into direct contact with the place where the DNA was found. Using ordinals can also help illustrate degrees of remove from the initial DNA donor. For instance, it constitutes tertiary transfer if your DNA starts on the lunchbox, goes from the lunchbox to your child's teacher, and then is passed from the teacher to her aide. *Tertiary* helps signify that the DNA ended up in a place three steps removed from the initial owner. The ordinals used in the forensic context tend to start from the original *source* of the DNA sample, always defining its journey in reference to that originator.

But this language is also a bit confusing. DNA that transfers between persons or objects away from the originator is also, in a sense, directly transferring. Imagine that a source leaves a pool of blood on the floor. I step in it, which transfers that blood to the bottom of my shoe, which in turn rubs onto a rung of a chair where I prop up my feet, which then transfers to the pants leg of a person who later sits in that chair. Each of those contact moments was *direct*, albeit at increasing remove from the original DNA depositor. Or if I speak, and tiny bits of saliva deposit my DNA on the ground in front of me—or I do my laundry and the mingling of the clothes distributes the shed cells contained therein—in both cases the transfer is *direct*. But, in the saliva example, the transfer is *primary* because the DNA emanated directly from the source, whereas in the laundry example it is *secondary* because it is moving among objects with which I initially came into contact.

Another important concept to grasp when considering transfer is the notion of *persistence*. Once DNA is deposited on a surface, be that surface a person or an object, how long will it stay there? How easily might it be erased or overwritten by contact from a subsequent person? Is the last person to come into contact with a person or item always the one to leave the dominant DNA profile in a sample? Such questions can be further complicated by asking whether the quality and duration of contact by each person influences the amount of transference to or from each party in the chain.

To illustrate these concepts, consider a high-profile crime with a little-reported dimension. In 2009, a horrific murder occurred in a place rarely associated with violence: a Yale graduate scientific laboratory. On what was to be her wedding day, a graduate student's body was found head down within a small mechanical chase behind a wall in the laboratory. As she fell, her underwear snagged and entangled on a vent pipe that spanned the length of the chase. Extensive DNA samples were taken from the victim, her clothing, and spaces around the chase. Testing revealed two profiles, one of which matched a co-worker later implicated in the crime through other evidence. But a second person's DNA was also found, ominously recovered in significant quantities from samples that included the waistband of the victim's underwear. When the profile was submitted to the DNA database, a match returned the name of a convicted offender living nearby.

Further investigation, however, turned up something mysterious. The database match suspect had died two years prior to the Yale attack. Stumped, investigators first ruled out an identical twin or other relative, as well as laboratory contamination errors. Ultimately, however, they learned that years earlier the offender had worked in construction. Specifically, he had spent one long, hot summer building the very mechanical chase in which the victim was found—and he had even made errors the first time around that required him to effectively rebuild it a second time. Even though the victim did not encounter that chase until years later, the fact that it was a space that was closed from ordinary traffic or regular cleaning, coupled with the building's strict temperature and environmental regulation (as a result of its role as a scientific lab), helped preserve in pristine condition the large quantity of DNA the worker had left behind as he sweated in that space during the construction.

Amazingly, these cells rested undisturbed until the moment that they transferred to the victim as she fell through the cramped space. In other words, there was a primary DNA transfer—via skin and sweat cells, most likely—from the worker to the walls and pipes within the chase. And then, when the victim encountered those objects and that space years later, there was a secondary transfer from those objects to her skin and underwear.

Stories such as that vividly illustrate the importance of appreciating the prevalence, ease, and persistence of secondary transfer. Absent a good alibi—in this case, the irrefutable proof of his prior death—the worker might have ended up implicated in the crime. His familiarity with the space, along with his prior record, might have been used against him to prove that he had special knowledge of a good place to dispose of the body.

The Yale story illustrates how important it is, now that we have the capacity to link perpetrators to an offense by the presence of their DNA in criminal evidence, to understand completely how easy it is for such cells to appear somewhere that in fact the DNA donor has never come into contact. But unfortunately, we still know very little about DNA transfer, and one major entity that funds DNA studies—the National Institute of Justice—has not expressed much interest in learning more.

The small array of existing transfer studies paint conflicting pictures. Early observations of the different rates with which people seem to transfer their DNA led researchers to posit two categories of persons: "shedders" and "nonshedders."[2] These categories emerged after researchers engaged subjects in a series of exchanges of an object, and then tested the object. They found that the ensuing genetic profiles did not always reflect the time or intensity of the touch of those who had handled the object. They concluded that some people simply transfer DNA more readily than others: that shedders tend to leave significant amounts of DNA on whatever they touch, even when they have recently washed their hands, whereas nonshedders tend not to.

For instance, in one experiment, researchers asked two or three people to hold a plastic tube for roughly ten minutes each, passing it to one another. They found that not only did the profiles of previous holders show up in tests of swabbings taken of the tube, but "[t]he strongest profile obtained was not always that of the person who last held the object." Interestingly, they also observed that profiles from a prior holder of the tube showed up in swabbings taken from the *hands* of those who had later held that same tube. Thus, a prior holder of an object could both dominate a DNA sample of that object, despite its later passing through other hands, and also leave enough DNA for the person who later handled the object to show traces of that prior holder on his or her own skin, despite never having come into contact with the prior holder. In other words, a DNA test might mistakenly leave the impression that two people had come into direct contact, when in fact they had only in common having touched the same item.

A 2002 study attempted to further understand this dynamic of shedding by testing another variation of the tube experiment. Researchers first classified subjects as "good" or "bad" shedders and then conducted a series of experiments.[3] Using two sets of good shedder/bad shedder pairs, researchers asked the good shedder to hold hands with a bad shedder for one minute, then asked the latter to hold a plastic tube for ten seconds. To add some variation, they also repeated the experiment with added delays between the hand holding and tube holding: thirty minutes and then an hour. The goal was to determine whether the good shedder's DNA would show up on the tube, even though the person had never held the tube at all, but had only shaken hands with the person who did hold it. Each test was repeated five times.

In the one-minute-delay test, in one pair the good shedder's complete profile appeared four out of five times, including one occasion when it was the *only profile* to appear on the tube, even though the good shedder had never held it. The bad shedder had consistently transferred the good shedder's DNA from his or her own hands to the tube, and even did so without leaving behind on the tube any trace of his or her *own* DNA. In the other pair, the good shedder profile showed up only two of five times, and never as the sole profile. Under the thirty- and sixty-minute-delay conditions, the object tended to produce DNA mixtures. The ultimate conclusion was that not only can good shedders routinely transfer their DNA to objects or people that they touch, but their DNA can then transfer to a third party or object with which they *never come into direct contact*. Moreover, a bad shedder who *does* actually come into contact with an object or person may leave very little DNA, or even none. In short, these studies showed that it is possible to test an item and recover a profile for a person who never touched it, while also yielding no evidence whatsoever that it was handled by someone else.

In another study, researchers asked three individuals to sit together at a table for twenty minutes, using a communal jug of juice to fill individual glasses from which they drank.[4] New glasses were used for each test, but the jug was cleaned and reused between tests, as were the chair arms and all test surfaces. No restrictions on interaction were imposed, and the test was recorded and replicated four times with different persons. Samples were taken from parts of the table, the chair arms, jug handle, glasses, and hands of the participants.

The study revealed interesting results. A quarter of the glass samples returned a profile for a different participant than the person who had held the glass, and a third of the samples returned the profile of a person *who was not one of the participants*. In fact, a single phantom person turned up not just on the glass, but also on the hand of the person who had held the glass, the table area, and even a glass that had never been touched by that participant directly.

One of the jug handle samples returned the profile of an unknown person not involved in the experiment; the same person also appeared in samples from a chair both before and after cleaning. Most jug handle samples, however, matched to participants—although unexpectedly, the participant who last came into contact with the jug was not the one who left the majority of DNA. Researchers surmised that the last person with contact had likely "picked up" the DNA profiles left by others on the jug, which then was deposited along with his or her own sample, leading the overall contribution of another person to dominate the samples.

Nearly two thirds of hand samples returned profiles to persons other than the person swabbed or other participants; one third of hand samples showed the profile of another participant. Intriguingly, one unknown, nonparticipant profile that was detected in a hand sample showed up on an area of the table never touched by the hands, and thus was likely transferred through the touch of the jug.

DNA was also detected on the chair arms from individuals who were not involved in any of the testing, notwithstanding the earlier cleaning. Roughly a third of chair samples and a quarter of table samples returned a DNA profile for a person who never came into contact with those surfaces; and roughly half of chair and table samples came from persons other than the participants in the experiments. Perhaps most shockingly, in a quarter of the table mixtures that were detected, there were profiles that did not match any participant, but did match unknown profiles also detected on the hands of participants, glasses, and chair arms. In other words, unknown super-shedders had left traces of themselves so strong that their profile appeared on an array of surfaces with which they had never come into direct contact.

In sum, as the study reported, "in some instances the participants acted as vectors for foreign DNA transfer, possibly present on their hands, via multi step transfer." And although "in the majority of situations the holder/sitter was the major contributor to the DNA detected and the transferred DNA profile was detected as [a] minor component, there were several samples where the transferred DNA was a major component." Moreover, identifiable persons not part of the experiment repeatedly surfaced on items and surfaces, which might leave a mistaken impression that they had been present when in fact they were not.

These two studies both seemed to suggest that shedder status was a powerful determinant of both the probability of DNA transfer and its persistence once transferred. But later experiments complicated this picture. Namely, when other scientists attempted to replicate these results, they discovered that "shedder" status was not as static as it initially appeared to be. Instead, it seems that a single person varies in his or her "shedder" status throughout a day as much as one person may vary one from another. Even different parts of the body can shed at different rates.[5] Nevertheless, there is still some indication that some people may have a background "shed" rate that hovers higher than others'.[6]

These controlled experiments were recently unintentionally replicated in a real-life case in California. A millionaire was strangled by invaders who also blindfolded and beat his wife and ransacked his home.[7] DNA tests of scrapings from beneath the victim's fingernails—precisely where one might expect to find evidence left as the victim struggled against his killer—revealed a DNA profile that matched in a database to Lukis Anderson. Anderson fit the profile of a killer: he was a homeless alcoholic, had a prior conviction for residential burglary, and had been incarcerated in the same facility as members of a gang suspected of setting up the home invasion.

Unfortunately, Anderson had no recollection of his whereabouts on the night of the killing, due in part from a brain injury he had once suffered. Fortunately, however, his attorney relentlessly pursued exculpatory evidence—despite the seemingly damning DNA evidence found on the victim. Even more fortunately—especially for a homeless man with few reliable social connections—his lawyer eventually found conclusive proof of his innocence. Medical records showed that Anderson had spent the night of the killing detoxing in a local hospital to which paramedics had taken him after finding him passed out drunk on the streets of San Jose. Faced with incontrovertible proof that Anderson had never come into contact with the dead man, much less been the one to take his life, prosecutors then had to reverse course to explain the presence of his DNA under the millionaire's nails.

After five months in prison, held pretrial on the murder charge, Anderson was finally released when further investigation showed that the same paramedics that responded to the crime scene had earlier treated Anderson. More important, the paramedics had clipped a common oxygen-monitoring device to the finger of each man—and the device had apparently transferred some of Anderson's cells to the fingernails of the dead man. Anderson was cleared, and eventually the state accused a sex worker who had long counted the millionaire as a client, who allegedly aided her brother and his associates in the home invasion.[8]

In hindsight, the incriminating nature of the fingernail samples probably deserved closer scrutiny, although such evidence is routinely offered in criminal cases. In a study of two hundred fingernail scrapings from one hundred volunteers from diverse backgrounds, researchers found foreign DNA in 15 percent of samples (30 of 200).[9] Of those, a third (5 percent of the total) yielded results that were typeable under most casework standards. A follow-up study tested forty individuals and found foreign DNA in 45 percent of samples; of those, roughly a quarter were reportable (in other words, about 1 in 10).[10]

A similar test of skin samples showed background levels of foreign DNA in a quarter of tests from twenty-four adult volunteers.[11] An experiment to determine transfer based on a projection of cells from a person's mouth detected DNA on the surface in front of the individual after only thirty seconds of talking.[12] Conversely, a study in which five volunteers were tested after having another person lick their neck, revealed that although a full profile transferred in two cases, no DNA transferred in two others, and a partial profile in the final case. The only clear conclusion that can be drawn from these studies, then, is that intimate, direct contact may yield full results or none at all—and the same is true when a person had no contact whatsoever.[13]

The unpredictability in transfer rates emerged clearly from a 2002 study.[14] In this experiment, two lab co-workers simulated strangulation twenty-nine separate times, under different conditions. Swabs were taken from both the "victim" and "strangler." Researchers tested the victim's neck and strangler's fingers, both areas that had touched and those that had not. In some cases, swabs were also taken up to ten days after the incident.

The results were all over the map. Swabs from the condition most likely to produce results—immediate sampling after a one-minute friction contact—produced no DNA profiles. At the same time, swabs taken as many as ten days after the mock strangulation returned profiles of both the victim and the offender. In fact, not only did swabs from the victim's neck show the offender's DNA, but those from the offender's fingers showed the victim's profile. Shockingly, one swab from a site on the victim's neck that the strangler had *not* touched returned the strangler's profile ten days after the simulation, even though there had never been direct contact and so much time had elapsed. Another surprise was the presence of DNA from an unknown third party on both test and control sites for up to ten days after the incident. In other words, the DNA of a person totally unconnected to the experiment appeared on *both* the fingers of the strangler and neck of the victim, and on both parts that had come into contact and those that had not. Researchers speculated that "the finger pads of the offender may not only transfer offender's DNA onto the skin of their victim and vice versa but also transfer[] third party DNA from objects or the third parties themselves, which the offender handled prior to contact with the skin of the victim."

Transfer may occur at greater rates than expected nor just in person-object studies, but under other conditions as well. For instance, one study endeavored to determine whether transfer occurs more readily when saliva, rather than skin, serves as the primary source of the DNA.[15] Saliva is rich in DNA, and so experiments had the subjects lick their thumb or chew the end of a pen, and then engage in a series of tests and behaviors to gauge primary, secondary, and tertiary transfer rates. The findings showed that saliva has a much stronger capacity to transfer than did ordinary skin cells. Thus, DNA is less likely to transfer from simply a handshake than from a handshake by a person who had previously bitten her fingernails.

Even ordinary cleaning does not eradicate every DNA trace. Several studies have proved this inadvertently, when unknown profiles popped up in the results despite efforts to create a clean initial surface. But anecdotal glimpses into the persistence of DNA also arise in the context of criminal investigations. For instance, after a housekeeper at a fancy hotel accused then head of the International Monetary Fund Dominique Strauss-Kahn of sexual assault in 2011, crime scene detectives took extensive samples from the hotel room in which the alleged assault occurred, including portions of the carpet and wallpaper. In addition to a sample that showed a mixture of the housekeeper and Strauss-Kahn's DNA, analysts also found three separate semen stains on the carpet from unrelated men, and a fourth stain with a mixture of DNA from at least three individuals.[16] A stain on the wall revealed a mixture of semen and DNA from another unknown male. It was uniformly acknowledged that these stains were wholly unrelated to the case, meaning that they had been deposited and remained at the very least before Strauss-Kahn had checked into the room, and likely in several distinct episodes, despite routine cleaning of the room.

In fact, not only does cleaning not necessarily eliminate DNA traces, it might even serve as a conduit for transfer. For instance, in a 1996 study of laundry, researchers wanted to test whether ordinary clothes washing might distribute sperm cells from one article of clothing to the other items being washed. They deposited a single semen stain on a pair of underwear, and then washed it with pristine clothing.[17] When nine of those items were randomly sampled and examined microscopically, all nine showed signs of sperm.

A follow-up study attempted to further probe the probability of laundry transfer.[18] Experimenters first replicated the earlier findings, and determined that cuttings taken from new underwear washed with a sperm-stained item could yield a full genetic profile that matched the sperm depositor. The researchers then attempted to determine whether cuttings from pristine underwear washed with underwear that had been worn by a woman could yield a profile, and results showed that cells from vaginal secretions on underwear worn in an ordinary way not only could transfer in the wash to an unused pair, but that genetic tests could then generate a complete DNA profile from the cells on that unused pair. As a result, it might seem as though the laundered pair of pristine underwear had been worn by the woman.

As a final inquiry, the experimenters sought underwear samples from two- to eleven-year-old girls in families with no evidence of child sexual abuse. This underwear was not new but clean; it had previously been worn but was clean from having been laundered with the families' other dirty clothes. Twenty-four pairs were collected from eleven families; in eight families, sperm could conceivably be present on the clothing but in three it could not (the male was vasectomized). Sperm was detected in multiple places on one child's panties, when the washing occurred five days after the parents had engaged in intercourse. In 45 of 168 samples taken from the underwear, the genetic profile of the brother or father was detected in combination with those of the girl and the mother, although at very low levels. Interestingly, the mother's profile was frequently detected on the various articles of clothing; researchers surmised that was likely due to the mothers' taking primary responsibility for dressing the children or laundering their clothes.

THE MORE WE LEARN, THE LESS WE KNOW

Although more experiments need to be done, DNA transfer seems more likely to occur under some conditions than others. Porous surfaces appear to more readily retain DNA cells than nonporous surfaces, and wet materials more readily transfer than dry materials.[19] This perhaps comes as no surprise to any person who regularly does laundry—a damp cloth absorbs detergent better than does a dry cloth, much less a dry tabletop. Rubbing and friction enhance the likelihood that DNA will transfer as might also be expected, and a freshly scrubbed body is less likely to transfer DNA than one even a couple of hours dirty.

That said, many of the conditions that increase the probability of DNA transfer may diminish the likelihood that DNA persists. For instance, cells deteriorate more quickly when deposited on a wet, porous surface as opposed to a dry, nonporous surface.[20] Of course, the extent to which profiles may be recovered may also turn on the efficiency with which the analyst conducts the laboratory tests. For instance, different methods of extraction yield greater or lesser rates of success.

Naturally, the more that conditions facilitate the transfer of DNA, the farther that DNA may be expected to travel. Ultimately, one set of tests suggested that the highest rates of secondary transfer occur when a nonabsorbent item carrying a wet DNA sample comes into contact with an absorbent item. Imagine a knife with a smear of saliva, which then comes into contact with a towel; it is highly likely that due to its absorbency the towel will test as having been in direct contact with the person who had left that saliva on the nonporous knife. In fact, one study indicates that the right combination of biological material and receptacle can lead to DNA's being transferred all the way through at least six contact events, so that a profile is still recoverable from the sixth item.[21]

Despite numerous studies and efforts to track the transfer behavior of DNA, no set of rules can predict with certainty when and how it will occur. One recent review of the state of the science on DNA transfer, which looked at the existing scientific literature to date, concluded that there were so many contradictions and inconsistent findings that the studies simply did not back up most predictions or "rules of thumb."

Take the conventional wisdom that finding a lot of DNA likely indicates direct contact, whereas small quantities of DNA suggest transfer. Or the corollary that the most DNA found on the object is most likely from its last or most enduring contact. As it turns out, neither assumption finds scientific support. Studies have shown that a person in direct contact can leave *no* DNA trace on the object, whereas a significant quantity might be present through indirect means. It is not even decisively true that once DNA quantities fall below a certain threshold, test results are likely to be erratic. Some high-quality profiles emerged from very low quantities of material. Accordingly, the review of the state of DNA science concluded that "The experimental data . . . shows that neither the quantity of DNA recovered nor the quality of DNA profile obtained can be used to reliably infer the mode of transfer by which the DNA came to be on the surface of interest."[22]

Unfortunately, these findings are in keeping with the one principle that does seem to be true when it comes to DNA transfer: that the more we learn, the less we know. Not only do too few studies attempt to capture the real-world conditions under which DNA transfers, but those that try seem to generate more questions than answers. Findings are further complicated by subtleties in the way in which DNA is collected and processed. Methods with greater success are likely to return more sensitive results, yet those variables are not always clearly reported in the literature.

In a 2011 investigation into three mock case scenarios, one of the leading research teams in this area "attempt[ed] to evaluate the application of DNA transfer percentages generated in previous studies and better understand the nature and effects of different variables on transfer rates."[23] But instead of the experiments' producing the results predicted, they yielded "mixed results." The first scenario involved a homicide victim whom police alleged, based in part on DNA recovered from her pajamas, had been strangled by her ex-husband. The ex-husband, who claimed to have not been in contact with the victim for months, alleged that his DNA must have transferred inadvertently; most likely through their child or the child's toys. The scenario derived from a real case in Australia, in which the issue of transfer was raised to the court, which concluded that it "cannot exclude contamination or indirect transfer as a reasonable possibility," and on the basis of that finding and other evidence, acquitted the defendant.[24]

When the researchers conducted an experiment intended to replicate possible scenarios of transfer, using both plastic toys and new baby onesies, they found that all but one of their forty samples contained DNA, most often in a mixture of the role-playing perpetrator and victim. Moreover, DNA from an unknown person was found in nineteen of thirty-five tests, including on half of the *otherwise new* toys and onesies that had been purchased and handled only pursuant to the experiment.[25] Significantly, those quantities of DNA were sufficient to create a profile. These results depart significantly from what transfer models, built on limited earlier research, would have suggested. Stumped, researchers had no option other than to conclude that there must be more to transfer than their previous research suggested and that if it is even possible to get a handle on when DNA is likely to transfer and when it is not, they have to do a lot more research.

IMPLICATIONS FOR CASEWORKERS

The risks of inadvertent transfer have serious implications for crime scene processors. Care must be taken at all steps in the collection and testing process to ensure that samples are not accidentally contaminated with the DNA of law enforcement or laboratory officials, or even unknown third parties. In one notorious case, police in Germany hunted for fifteen years to find "the country's most dangerous woman."[26] Dubbed "the Phantom of Heilbronn" and the "woman without a face," she was suspected in six murders, including that of a police officer, along with forty other crimes ranging across two countries. At one point, police offered a €300,000 reward for any information leading to her capture. In the end, police found their mysterious killer. It turned out she was no killer at all—just a factory worker who had inadvertently tainted a whole line of swabs sent out in DNA testing kits. Her DNA profile had popped up in crimes across

Europe because it was on the swabs analysts had used to recover DNA from evidence. In fact, the crimes had no connection to one another—except that in each case the swab used by the different investigators came from the same batch.

Countless studies have affirmed the need for meticulous care when handling DNA evidence, and called into question the adequacy of standard cleaning practices. The best practice for a laboratory is to conduct the testing of evidentiary items in an area entirely separate from that of known, reference samples in the case, and at a period in time prior to testing the reference samples. That way analysts minimize the chance that the DNA from the suspect or victim inadvertently contaminates the crime scene evidence. Yet many labs still allow the same analyst to conduct both sets of tests in the same place, or give only token gestures toward maintaining separate areas—such as defining adjacent lab benches as "separate."

Most labs maintain elimination databases with the profiles of analysts, and even some police officers, precisely so that they can double-check unexpected results. But even a lab operating with the utmost care may still encounter instances of contamination, whether due to its own actions or those who collected the evidence. In one case from the United Kingdom reminiscent of the millionaire murder, a forensic scientist examined fingernail clippings from a woman murdered in London.[27] DNA testing revealed a match in the national database; the problem was that the suspect had been killed three weeks before the victim's death. Confounded, investigators searched everywhere for the source of the contamination, but no obvious solution presented itself. Eventually, a manager at the laboratory realized that the clippings had been collected at the morgue. Records showed that the suspect-victim had been kept in the freezer for weeks as the investigation unfolded, and that clippings from her nails been taken the day before the second victim's body arrived.

Although the nail scissors used to take the clippings had been cleaned between uses, the manager suspected they were the source of the transfer. Sure enough, a test of the scissors revealed three different DNA profiles, and further tests found that other autopsy instruments had been similarly contaminated. The manager responded by sending an urgent memo requiring that clippings be taken with disposable scissors. The lesson was shocking enough at the time, even though DNA testing then still relied on relatively large sample sizes. Today, the manager observed, the need for special care has only risen, "since DNA retrieval techniques are now so sensitive that simply lightly touching an object—such as a doorknob or knife handle—can leave enough of a trace to carry out a successful DNA analysis."

As technology continues to evolve, and these issues continue to be studied, it is hoped that crime scene technicians and scientists will be able to devise improved frameworks that incorporate what scientists have learned from transfer experiments. Already there are some positive steps in that direction. For instance, given the studies that show remarkable persistence of DNA over time, some investigators have encouraged sampling from persons long after it might otherwise be assumed that such trace evidence would be left. For instance, a rape victim who reports a week after the alleged assault might still be sent for examination, because evidence may exist that corroborates the victim's claims. DNA used this way, to bolster otherwise strong evidence, raises fewer transfer-related concerns.

Newly devised tests that aim to identify the biological source of DNA through analysis of associated RNA also may help mitigate transfer concerns. These tests can ascertain whether a DNA sample came from saliva, blood cells, or seminal fluid. For example, suppose a rape victim alleges vaginal sex, but the defendant claims they only kissed. The presence of the victim's DNA on the defendant in such a case will offer little evidence in support of either version of the encounter, given what is known about transfer and the allegations of the offense. But if the defendant's clothing shows signs of the victim's vaginal fluid, then that finding could lend significant support to the victim's claims.

Until more is known about DNA and how it transfers, criminal justice actors should be extremely circumspect before drawing conclusions related to the presence or absence of DNA, particularly low quality or quantities of DNA, on a person or physical object. DNA may be found in places where you would not expect it, and does not appear where you would. This unpredictability led one research team to conclude that "unknown DNA profile components may originate from innocent sources, unconnected to the event being forensically investigated, and may therefore provide false intelligence that may hinder the investigation."[28]

Consider a case in which the victim was bound and raped on a stairwell landing in 2004. Evidence technicians collected the ligature used to bind the victim, as well as three strands of hair—one of which was a pubic hair with the follicle attached. In 2010, DNA testing revealed that the pubic hair matched to an inmate shortly due for release. Some investigators wanted to move promptly to ensure his continued detention in light of the match, but the lead investigator urged caution. Although the evidence inventory report made it appear that the pubic hair had been found on the ligature, closer inspection of other documents in the case, including sketches and photographs from the scene, made clear that the hair had simply been found near the scene.

Further investigation revealed that the man was a known marijuana seller who not only worked that area back in 2004, but also had the habit of storing his "stash" down his pants for safekeeping. As a result of careful investigation, investigators concluded that the pubic hair must have fallen from a bag of marijuana that he traded in that stairwell back in 2004, or even been carried there by one of his customers.[29] By letting the DNA test inform, but not overcome, their work as investigators, they were able to avoid a false accusation and potential miscarriage of justice.

IMPLICATIONS FOR CASES

This caution in collection extends to caution in court. As prosecutors and forensic investigators continue to push the envelope of DNA typing, DNA testing kit manufacturers have complied by supplying increasingly sensitive instruments capable of gleaning results from minuscule amounts of DNA. "Touch DNA" samples purport to identify a suspect from cells left behind after an object has been handled, and "low copy" methods are capable of returning results from no more than a handful of cells. Sophisticated software programs likewise use complex algorithms to fit incomplete or imperfect DNA test results to various scenarios involving the defendant's guilt.

In general, more sensitive techniques represent a positive advance in the science. But as technology evolves to permit testing low-quality or -quantity samples, care must be taken not to overstate the conclusions from those tests. When the location or quantity of the DNA sample does not strongly suggest direct deposition (e.g., 100 cells versus a large bloodstain), there is always the possibility that transfer, rather than actual contact, explains the presence of the suspect's DNA.

Accordingly, lawyers and testifying analysts should draw their conclusions with caution in cases where transfer is a significant concern, lest they find themselves unwitting handmaidens to injustice. Specifically, the testimony and argument in such cases ought to resist the temptation to declare that the presence of DNA on an object indisputably signifies contact. Because many lawyers may lack awareness of the problem of transfer, analysts should flag the issue in their reports whenever the testing process indicates that transfer may explain the findings. Indeed, the safest course is for an analyst simply to report the results of the DNA test, alert both counsel and the jury to the possibility of transfer, and leave the jury or factfinder to assess its implications. Attorneys, for their part, should take care not to misrepresent the confidence with which conclusions can be drawn from DNA evidence, or push the analyst to state opinions that are unfounded.

Finally, full sensitivity to the risks of transfer requires far more concerted efforts to study the phenomenon than are now in place. The National Institute of Justice has funded very few studies of DNA transfer, and the industry has little reason or incentive to undertake such studies. Most of the work on the issue has been done by analysts in forensic science labs in other countries.[30] Without such work, prosecutors, investigators, and the general public may easily be carried away in thinking that a DNA finding represents conclusive proof—that the defendant handled an item, or was present at the scene, or even committed the offense—when the presence of DNA may instead be the result of innocent transfer. What looks like degraded sample may in fact be secondary or other transfer. But whereas in the studies researchers know what to look for, transfer does not come labeled in real life.

CHAPTER 4

Contamination, Mistake, and Outright Fraud

IN MAY 2004, Juilliard student Sarah Fox went for a jog in a park near her Manhattan apartment. Her decomposed body was found a week later in a remote area of that park; she had been strangled. Police had a suspect, but no evidence. The case remained unsolved, but analysts recovered a foreign DNA sample from the CD player Fox had carried. They uploaded it to a forensic database, and waited.

Eight years later, there was a hit. Police had lifted a DNA sample from a metal chain used at a political protest associated with the group Occupy Wall Street. Although officers had not yet identified the donor of the DNA sample, surveillance showed a group of hooded protesters wrapping the chain to hold open an emergency door at a subway station, enabling passengers to avoid the fare stalls. A DNA profile from the chain sample had matched the DNA sample from Fox's CD player.

After the news leaked, police were careful to note that the connection could be innocent. But the city was still tense from the protests, and factions on both sides were invested in maintaining a certain image of Occupy members. The idea that a violent killer might be among Occupy's ranks would call into question the protesters' claim to legitimacy, and certainly distract from—if not entirely undermine—their efforts to effect political change. On July 11, 2012, almost every major news outlet reported the story. The *New York Post*'s led with the headline "OWS Shock in Unsolved '04 Sarah Slay."[1]

Just a day later, the media had to publish a retraction. For the *Post*, it was a short item titled "Cold-Case Slay DNA Match the Result of Lab Contamination: Sources."[2] In hindsight, it was lucky the identity of the protester remained obscure; otherwise, a Google search might have forever wrongly linked him or her to a brutal killing. Although neither the lab nor the police ever revealed precisely how the mistake happened, or explained what steps had been taken so that a similar misattribution would not occur again, news accounts suggested that the DNA in fact came from a worker who handled both pieces of evidence.[3] Today, police reportedly believe another man—the initial suspect in the crime—committed the murder, but lack the evidence to prove it.[4]

As it turned out, that 2012 mistake was just a glimpse of what was to come. The lab responsible for the testing, the Department of Forensic Biology within the Office of the Chief Medical Examiner (OCME) in New York, had long been recognized as among one of the finest DNA testing units in the country. It occupied state-of-the-art facilities constructed for it in 2007, and considered itself a leader in forensic research. Its staff had even promoted a new, hypersensitive DNA test that it claimed could reliably coax results from even just a few cells.

Although the Occupy scandal besmirched this stellar reputation, it did not destroy it. After all, it seemed as though the error occurred outside of its confines—an unprofessional leak to the press coupled by poor handling practices by a police evidence technician. Plus, the OCME had long been held out as the paragon of laboratory integrity. Indeed, New York boasted one of the nation's few legislated oversight structures for forensic laboratories. Prompted in part by the fallout from the first major challenges to DNA evidence, the state had adopted what was intended to be a rigorous system of supervision. In 1994, legislators created the Commission on Forensic Science.[5] The commission is tasked with comprehensive oversight responsibilities, including setting standards, assessing accreditation, ensuring the qualifications of key personnel, and approving new testing methodologies in forensic laboratories. It also convenes a subcommittee specifically assigned to superintend DNA laboratories. That subcommittee possesses exclusive power to "grant, deny, review or modify a DNA forensic laboratory accreditation" by issuing a binding recommendation to the commission.[6]

New York's OCME was accredited under the most rigorous standards, and subject to the state's full panoply of oversight mechanisms, when, in the first weeks of January 2013, the *New York Times* revealed that the laboratory had reopened eight hundred cases due to irregularities in the testing process. As the full story unfolded and the extent of the malfeasance sank in over the course of several weeks, it became increasingly clear that the commission's trust in both the OCME and its accreditors had been misplaced.

The seeds of the scandal were sown on January 3, 2000, when the OCME hired Serrita Mitchell as a second-level criminalist.[7] Her job was to analyze and interpret DNA results. But Mitchell had a rocky start. She finished training, but could not pass the next stage—an oral competency exam. Displaying patience unfamiliar to most in the working world, supervisors gave her two years to pass, during which she took and failed the test five separate times.[8] In addition, a review of her work during that time resulted in a conditional overall rating, which was uncommon among personnel. Specifically, the report cited "'lapses in maintaining a chain of custody . . . numerous instances where [she] has not properly followed prescribed guidelines for laboratory analysis,' and disorganization."[9] Finally, supervisors concluded she was not capable of passing the exam necessary to ensure an analyst was capable of testifying in court.

Rather than terminate Mitchell's employment, officials instead ordered her to perform tasks suited only to a criminalist one step down. Those responsibilities included conducting blood and DNA analyses that precede actual testing. This juncture is critical. An analyst who is careless can contaminate samples and then pass them on to another person to test, who will have no way of knowing that the evidence has been compromised. An analyst can also fail to detect the presence of biological material, thereby foreclosing further testing. Without such testing, the analyst not only may fail to exculpate a person wrongly accused, but may also overlook evidence that could have kept the true offender from committing another offense.

Perhaps most shocking of all, despite her demotion in responsibilities, Mitchell retained the title and higher salary of the job she was originally hired to do, not the one she was demoted to based on her lack of skill. She continued this way for six years, during which she received "subpar" evaluations for all but one year. Throughout, her reviews noted her lack of care in her work, such as "the incorrect naming of samples (i.e., the victim's name instead of suspects [*sic*] name) or not clearly labeling samples both of which led to confusion and unnecessary fixing of paperwork."

Despite supervisors' continued efforts to force her to exercise greater care, Mitchell failed to improve. A highly critical evaluation of her work in 2008 cited "typographical errors and improper labeling of samples that led to the misinterpretation of samples."[10] Throughout this time, Mitchell continued to work on cases, and the OCME kept her record of shoddy performance a secret from the lawyers and court officials who counted on the integrity of her work.

Remarkably, after discovering irregularities with Mitchell's performance while testing two rape kits, supervisors still did not terminate her employment. In one of those cases, the quality assurance leader had been particularly troubled by what appeared to be an effort by Mitchell to hide mistakes in her work. Specifically, Mitchell had cut away a portion of the special sealing tape used by an analyst to denote that an item had been opened and resealed, so that it would instead look as if it had never been opened.[11] As a result of this and another incident, Mitchell was first suspended and then, as of late 2008, she was restricted to one basic task: measuring the amount of DNA that another analyst had managed to extract from evidence, before passing it on to a different analyst to test. In this role, "the OCME removed Mitchell from any contact with original pieces of evidence"—almost eight years after she had begun working at the lab.[12]

Just over a year later, the Human Resources Department finally determined that Mitchell could not be titled and paid for a higher level of work than she performed. In response, the OCME sent her to a three-month training program for the second time in her career. In January 2011, eleven years into her tenure as a "Criminalist II," and nearly at the end of her second go at the training program, Mitchell was permanently suspended from working on cases.[13] Given her history, the lab decided to review two of her cases that had led to citations for wholesale failure to identify DNA on evidentiary items, along with "falsification of evidence testing results"—she had "reported as negative" stains that "showed no signs of ever being tested."[14] Despite a law that requires labs that receive federal funds, as did the OCME, to report allegations of serious negligence or misconduct to an external monitor, the lab failed to report any of these incidents.[15]

These incidents prompted directors in July 2011 to initiate further review of Mitchell's work and a move to terminate; a month later, she resigned. In a later press interview, Mitchell denied having made errors and claimed she was unaware of any problems with her work.[16] But an initial review of her work by those within the OCME indicated that she got it wrong in about one in four of her cases.[17] Eventually, an exhaustive review of her work in 877 cases found pervasive error.[18] Of 147 cases subjected to full reexamination of the entire file for inventory or testing errors, thirty-seven cases were shown to have DNA that Mitchell had failed to recognize. Nine of those cases produced a profile that proved useful to later investigation.[19] In one case, a minor accused a man of rape, but Mitchell had wrongly reported that the rape kit lacked DNA. When it was retested, analysts found DNA that confirmed the victim's accusation, which in turn led to the man's indictment.[20]

Alarmingly, the process of revisiting Mitchell's cases revealed the gravest cause for concern for injustice. Twenty-four cases had evidentiary discrepancies, fifty had documentation errors, and in eleven cases, the inventory of the evidence kit was clearly compromised. In some cases, items were missing. In others, items had been transferred among kits. That meant that Mitchell had violated a central precept of maintaining evidentiary integrity—to only work on one kit at a time. It also meant that evidence from different crime scenes had been handled simultaneously, which could easily have allowed for biological material from one scene to migrate to another without anyone's noticing. The OCME asserted there were no wrongful convictions, but there is no way to know that for certain. Whereas contamination across cases might be more readily discernible—DNA from a person clearly not a suspect can often be identified—the same is not true of contamination within a case kit. If Mitchell was so careless as to work on multiple kits at the same time—and to misfile the evidence when done—then who is to say that she clearly took care to ensure that a suspect's reference sample never came into contact with the evidentiary samples in a kit, or that she meticulously cleaned her workstation?

If Mitchell's case sounds outrageous—well, it is. The OCME tried to pass off her failures as a costless error, but those across the country who have suffered directly as a result of mistakes of this kind would probably disagree. A man named Marlon Pendleton, for instance, spent ten years in prison before a DNA sample exonerated him—the very same DNA sample that a Chicago lab analyst had wrongly claimed could not be tested.[21] And Pendleton is not alone; among others, he is joined by a Massachusetts man imprisoned for seventeen years, and a New Jersey man, for sixteen and a half years, all before retesting uncovered exculpatory evidence that had been there the entire time.[22]

Sadly, what happened at the OCME is far from the only story of its kind. By now, tales of forensic science failures are as common in the newspapers as tales of forensic science successes. In fact, there are tales even more egregious, in which analysts perpetrated elaborate and long-standing fraud. The most notorious of all is forensic scientist Fred Zain, who worked first in West Virginia and then in Texas, and left behind a trail of wrongful convictions in both states. Among a long list of cases in which he falsified evidence and perjured himself is that of Gilbert Alejandro, who was convicted of violently sexually assaulting a woman in her apartment. During the attack the victim's face had been covered with a pillow. Although she could provide only a threadbare description, and failed to identify Alejandro in a number of photo lineups, he was ultimately convicted based in significant part on Zain's testimony, which claimed that DNA found in a semen stain on the victim's clothing could "only have originated from him."[23] Four years into his twelve-year sentence, postconviction testing revealed that the DNA in fact excluded Alejandro, and that Zain had not even finished the testing he claimed inculpated Alejandro.

In fact, nearly every major DNA unit—from the most applauded and sophisticated to the most amateur and haphazard, has endured a scandal of some kind. Some have resulted in wrongful arrest or conviction, such as the case of Dwayne Jackson. He accepted a plea deal, despite proclaiming his innocence, because the evidence against him seemed irrefutable: a Nevada lab technician claimed his DNA matched that from a kidnapping and robbery.[24] In fact, the technician had accidentally switched his DNA sample with that of another suspect—who unfortunately had actually committed the crime. The mistake was only caught when a technician in California tried to upload the DNA profile of the true perpetrator. That man had gone on to commit a violent crime in California, and when his DNA sample was uploaded it appeared to match to the crime scene sample that had been attributed to Jackson. Confused, the California authorities reached out to the Las Vegas police, who initiated an investigation. When the sample switch was revealed, Jackson, who had spent nearly four years in prison, was exonerated. The actual offender was never charged, seemingly because the statute of limitations expired, but he was also already serving a lengthy sentence for the other offenses in California.[25]

Shockingly, that sample switch was not the only one to happen at that crime lab. Around the same time as the mix-up in Jackson's case, a technician at the lab mistakenly switched the DNA samples collected from an alleged rape perpetrator and his accuser. The perpetrator's sample—wrongly attributed to the victim—then matched two unsolved rapes in the DNA database. As in a horror story, the victim became a wrongfully accused defendant when prosecutors charged him with those crimes, but fortunately the victim's lawyer managed to uncover the error.[26] Unfortunately, the list of DNA laboratories that have been involved in a serious error along these lines touches nearly every major DNA laboratory in the nation.[27] And, of course, these are only the mix-ups that are caught; not every accused will be so lucky.

In addition to these common lapses, audits of the DNA database have revealed that labs have not always adhered to quality assurance benchmarks in choosing which profiles to upload. As a result, partial profiles or those not clearly associated with the perpetrator of the crime have been entered into the database, raising the likelihood of an erroneous accusation. A 2007 review of the UK database of 4 million entries discovered around 550,000 errors, such as duplicate entries and false or wrongly recorded names. Moreover, the database contained samples that ought to have been purged.[28]

In early 2014, the FBI admitted that a software upgrade had revealed 170 errors in the database, although many more likely exist. Far from a comprehensive audit of the database, the FBI had simply switched on a more sophisticated searching method, thereby turning up a number of supposed matches that in fact represented error. By way of illustration, imagine a searchable database of names. If the software only returns exact matches, then a search for "Lawrence Stroud" will only hit if it finds that name. But more sensitive software might also turn up "Larwrence Stroud" and "Lawrence Strout." It takes only minimal investigation to determine that all are in fact the same person (the first representing a typographical error, and the second an interpretive error in which the scribe heard the *d* as a *t*). Similarly, in the case of the FBI's search, the vast majority—166—of the mistakes consisted of entries that were off at a single point, which an official speculated was largely the result of "interpretation errors by DNA analysts or typographical errors introduced when a lab worker" entered the profile.[29]

Understandably, given the large size of the database, the chief of the biometric section announced that she was "pleasantly surprised" there were not more errors. But what is truly surprising is that she did not indicate any intention of instituting a system of regular checks of that kind. Nor did the federal government mandate that states using its software conduct the same searches to check for errors within their own state-level databases, and most states have shown little initiative in undertaking their own review.

To be sure, there are some exceptions. In the wake of the national revelation, New York state police conducted the same test on its state database, and uncovered several more errors beyond the six that had contributed to the national total.[30] For instance, in two cases analysts seem to have misinterpreted the results of testing, believing the profile to be one thing when in fact it was something else. But rather than view such basic aspects of quality control as central to the mission of forensic testing, many state lab officials just sweep such concerns to the side. Even the FBI did not announce a thorough review of the 170 cases, so that the source of the discrepancy was clear for each one and measures could be implemented to prevent further mistakes.

Entering an erroneous profile in a DNA database can result in wrongful accusation, which is not always easy to catch. For instance, in one California case, the police in Sacramento collected a DNA sample from a victim alleging sexual assault, and a technician analyzed the sample and entered the profile of the perpetrator into a DNA database.[31] The database returned a match to a man living nearby, and police went to conduct further investigation. Fortunately for the man, it became clear that the suspect could not have been the perpetrator of the assault, and the lab was asked to reexamine its finding. Further inquiry revealed a number of mistakes. The analyst had inadvertently discarded the evidence swab, failed to follow protocol requiring that only data above a certain threshold be interpreted and that every sample of that kind undergo review by a supervisor, and had uploaded a sample that did not meet the minimum standards. In addition, the analyst "made assumptions reading and interpreting the profile . . . that were incorrect."[32]

Another high-profile database transcription error occurred in the United Kingdom. In a scene that could have come from a novel, Gareth Williams, a British spy, was found dead, locked in a sports bag in the bathroom of his own apartment.[33] DNA tests on the bag and lock revealed a mixture of his DNA and another person's. That profile did not match anyone in the national database. At a coroner's inquest, it was revealed that the profile ought to have matched an elimination sample belonging to a police scientist; the failure to catch the mistake was due to a transcription error made when entering the reference profile.[34] The current best guess of the authorities, based in part on reconstructions of the scene, is that the spy took his own life.

One undisputed cause for all these problems is the simple ease with which contamination may occur. Study after study has shown that DNA has a way of ending up where it should not be. And as labs process more low-quantity samples, even the slightest amount of contamination may compromise the entire test result. Analysts have contaminated evidence by talking over it during testing, inadvertently brushing such objects as lamps or other surfaces, or even handling exhibit packaging with less than meticulous care. There are even concerns that the customary practices of bleaching a workstation to eliminate residual DNA may ultimately not be sufficiently effective.[35]

One of the most mystifying cases involving contamination started with the murder of a young woman in Michigan in 1969. Jane Mixer's body was found strangled with pantyhose, shot, and left in a cemetery. Authorities initially ascribed the death to a serial killer later apprehended, but the slight differences in modus operandi convinced them to reopen the case in 2002. DNA tests were conducted on three drops of sweat found on the pantyhose and a single drop of blood found on Mixer's hand.

Test results in 2002 showed two separate DNA profiles, each producing a hit in the DNA database. The problem was with the matches. DNA from a sweat stain matched Gary Leiterman, a sixty-two-year-old nurse. He had to submit DNA to the database after he was caught forging a prescription. DNA from the blood spot, however, belonged to a man named John Ruelas, a murderer serving time for beating his mother to death. The mystery was that Ruelas, who was forty, would have been only four at the time of the killing. He also lived in Detroit, far from the scene of Mixer's death.[36]

The logical explanation for the finding was laboratory contamination. But prosecutors, likely hoping to preserve the perceived integrity of the Leiterman hit, insisted that the evidence had not been compromised. Instead, and incredibly, they argued that Ruelas was a "chronic nose-bleeder" who, while not the murderer, had somehow bled at the scene.[37] The only other significant evidence against Leiterman were creepy photographs found in his house of a sixteen-year-old exchange student his family had hosted, who appeared naked and unconscious. The strategy apparently worked: Leiterman was convicted.

It is certainly possible that Leiterman was guilty. But it seems equally possible that lab contamination simply led investigators to the wrong men. Significantly, as noted by a defense report, both Leiterman and Ruelas's samples were processed in the same laboratory at the same time as the original sample from the 1969 Mixer case.[38] Leiterman's sample came into the laboratory on February 22, 2002; the evidence in Ruelas's case was processed the day before. Leiterman's sample was first analyzed between July 17 and July 23; Ruelas's reference sample was submitted on July 19 and then sent to an outside lab for testing. The Mixer evidence was processed at the lab between March 26, 2002, and April 9, 2002.

Given the timeline, it certainly is conceivable that Leiterman's sample ended up in the crime scene evidence through contamination, just as Ruelas's did. Both samples had entered the lab at the same time. And Ruelas's sample was not even processed by the lab—since it was sent out—yet somehow it made its way to the crime scene evidence. Moreover, a forensic report by a defense expert noted that the first attempt at getting a profile from Leiterman's sample failed—only part of the profile showed up. That is an unusual result for a sample taken in controlled conditions, where a large amount of DNA is obtained and preserved in a way that makes processing so easy it can be automated. The missing material, the expert speculated, may indicate that some of Leiterman's sample went somewhere it should not have gone. Also strangely, the DNA sample from the crime scene evidence that matched Leiterman seemed remarkably well preserved, despite the passage of years and the degraded condition of all the other DNA recovered from that evidence, including that of the victim—who presumably would have left the strongest trace of all.

Furthermore, the lab analysts admitted that, due to time and space pressures, they routinely processed samples from different cases at the same time. They also did not keep a centralized error log at the time, and thus an accurate picture of the established error rate would require combing through all the files from that period. Finally, it was discovered that one of the negative controls processed at the same time that a pantyhose sample was processed had become contaminated, but the analysts had attempted to hide that fact.

For obvious reasons, most reported cases involving known mix-ups, transfer, or contamination involve suspects who can prove their innocence. In the Mixer case, one suspect, Ruelas, could conclusively establish his innocence. He was simply too young to have committed the crime or even have been at the crime scene. But Leiterman was not so lucky; he remained a plausible suspect. Still more unfortunately, Mr. Leiterman's lawyer raised almost none of these issues at trial. The result, as a later expert concluded, was that the jury was left with the impression that "the finding of DNA consistent with Gary Leiterman was . . . reliable," even as "[t]he laboratory and the State viewed the finding of DNA consistent with John Ruelas as either an unreliable, or perhaps inconsequential, result given the attribute of his age."[39]

INADEQUATE SAFEGUARDS

If the justice system is willing to convict despite clear evidence that the sample was corrupted, accountability for good practices must come from somewhere else. With regard to other critical services, the public expects as close to a zero error rate as possible, including through the identification and correction of problems that may arise, and external checks that penalize institutions that fail to comply with protocol or prevent further problems from occurring. Airlines and hospitals, for instance, are closely regulated by government monitors. They also compete in a marketplace where fatal mistakes can cause consumers to flee from their business or generate insuperable legal costs. The combined societal, governmental, and commercial commitment to aviation safety or public health drives strong systems of accountability and error correction. But even though forensic scientists also hold liberty—and sometimes even lives—in their hands, current accountability systems governing collection, analysis, storage, and use of DNA evidence either fail to exist or keep faltering in a systemic, not just idiosyncratic, fashion.

With regard to DNA laboratories, three models of accountability dominate. The first is the accreditation system—requiring labs to undergo some kind of external review to ensure they follow certain established standards. The second is proficiency testing—requiring individual analysts to undergo regular examinations intended to gauge their competency to complete their work. And the last is the oversight board model, wherein a panel of distinguished or learned persons convene to superintend the functioning of the laboratory. These three models are not incompatible; in fact, some regulatory systems draw from all three. But sadly, few are implemented with the rigor necessary to make them fully effective.

ACCREDITATION

Accreditation can be a vague word. Generally speaking, it denotes the stamp of approval given by an authoritative body after an institution demonstrates its capability to meet a set of predetermined standards. Schools are often accredited—for instance, a state may only allow students who graduate from accredited schools to take the bar exam or sit for a medical license. In general, accreditation works because an independent expert sets a list of standards, and then measures the performance of the institution against them.

Accreditation standards might require a laboratory to have certain protocols in place to ensure that the testing environment remains sterile, and to minimize variation among analysts in exercising their discretion. A lab might need to keep logs of any mistakes or errors, ensure that employees possess certain qualifications or backgrounds to perform particular tasks, or follow certain supervisorial and oversight models. Standards might also demand regular proficiency testing to gauge each employee's abilities.

For most of their history, forensic laboratories operated without any accreditation requirements. Even today, only eleven states require that at least some of their all-purpose crime labs be accredited,[40] although a number of states have imposed accreditation requirements on labs offering DNA test results conducted by the defense.[41] However, because the FBI rules that govern access to the national database impose accreditation standards, accreditation is nearly universal among DNA testing laboratories as a practical matter. The FBI also conducts its own checks to ensure compliance with its quality assurance standards.

A handful of states, including Maryland, Texas, and New York, have oversight bodies that by law are responsible for accrediting their labs.[42] But many of these states do not have the resources or expertise to engage in direct audits. Instead, they outsource that task to other organizations. For instance, New York law compels the Commission on Forensic Science to ensure proper accreditation of any DNA labs under its supervision. The commission, in turn, chose an accreditation program run by the American Society of Crime Lab Directors/Laboratory Accreditation

Board to fulfill this requirement. Known by its acronym, ASCLD/LAB, this entity emerged as an offshoot of a major professional organization for forensic scientists.[43] On its website, it describes itself as the "first organization in the world dedicated to accrediting crime labs," and states it is still the "only accrediting body that focuses 100% on laboratories performing testing for criminal justice."[44] As of December 2014, ASCLD/LAB accredited 397 crime labs—190 state labs, 130 local labs, 31 federal labs, 20 international labs, and 26 private labs.

Despite the seeming rigor of the accreditation system, in fact, it has long tolerated unacceptable levels of inadvertent mistake and outright malfeasance. The total failure of the current oversight system is well illustrated by a tale of two laboratories. The first involved a scandal that engulfed the North Carolina crime lab in 2010. In 1991, Gregory Taylor was accused of murder after police found him returning to get his truck unstuck from mud nearby the home of the victim.[45] He was convicted of murder in 1993, but maintained his innocence. A critical piece of evidence used to connect him to the victim was the supposed presence of blood in his truck. The lab report stated that tests showed "the presence of blood," and another analyst testified accordingly at Taylor's trial. Despite subsequent testing that revealed the spot was *not* blood, this critical fact was neither included in the written report given to the defense lawyer as discovery, nor brought out during the testimony at trial. Its only record was in bench notes that were never shared with either the prosecutor or defense lawyer.

Shockingly, it was standard practice in many jurisdictions then, and remains so even today, not to disclose an analyst's bench notes. It is also standard practice for lab reports to omit any mention that later confirmatory tests reached conclusions contrary to initial indications. In fact, in North Carolina this practice was enshrined as formal lab policy in 1997.[46]

As a result, Taylor spent seventeen years in prison serving his life sentence before his exoneration, which was based in part on the discovery of the errors in the forensic evidence. Appalled by his case, the state attorney general opened an investigation into the forensic biology section of the lab. That review, conducted by two former FBI officials, criticized the lab's practices, singling out "poorly crafted policy; lack of objectivity[;] the absence of clear report writing guidance; inattention to reporting methods that left too much discretion to the individual Analyst[;] lack of transparency; and ineffective management and oversight of the Forensic Biology Section from 1987 to 2003."[47]

Investigators found 230 other cases that contained misleading reports similar to the one that wrongly convicted Greg Taylor. Those cases included four inmates on death row, three who had already been executed, and five who died in prison.[48] In all of those cases, reports described a positive presumptive test for blood, but then failed to disclose the results of later, more sensitive tests. Of the 230, 190 resulted in charges; all but 25 of those ended in convictions. The lab reports ranged in the severity of the misrepresentation, but fell into four general categories. Each described a positive finding of blood, and:

1. Failed to add that a confirmatory test was conducted that showed that the substance was not blood (85 cases, including 23 still incarcerated, 3 on death row, 1 who died in prison, and 1 already executed);

2. Failed to document in the file one or more negative or inconclusive confirmatory tests, thus leaving the file incomplete (105 cases, including 43 with currently incarcerated defendants, 1 on death row, and 4 who died in prison);

3. Lied and obfuscated, by stating that no further tests were conducted, when in fact one or more confirmatory tests were conducted with negative or inconclusive results (36 cases, including 3 still incarcerated and 1 already executed);

4. Flatly stated that confirmatory tests either affirmed the presence of blood or were inconclusive, when in fact those tests were negative for the presence of blood (5 cases, including 1 execution).[49]

Moreover, the subsequent investigation into the scandal revealed that a dangerous laboratory culture persevered. That report found "anecdotal evidence that some Analysts were not objective in their mindset," and that they had actually been trained to discount and withhold negative test results.[50] Investigation also revealed additional significant errors in the DNA testing unit, including a case in which the analyst "inadvertently switched" the DNA samples, "causing a report to be issued linking the victim's body fluid to the defendant"; the misrepresentation of the sex of the defendant in the DNA profile report, including an erroneous report of a match; and revelations of poor storage and evidence handling policies, among other improprieties.[51]

Amazingly, during all of this time, the North Carolina laboratory was accredited by ASCLD/LAB—the same organization that accredited the OCME right up and through the Serrita Mitchell scandal.[52] In fact, North Carolina and New York hardly stand out in this way on ASCLD/LAB's rosters. One review of DNA laboratories from 2005 to 2011 documented fifty instances of significant failures; of those, more than half (28) were clearly accredited by ASCLD/LAB at the time.[53]

Although ASCLD/LAB recently tightened its accreditation process, three main areas of criticisms of the organization endure, relating to: the rigor of their standards,[54] the manner in which they are measured, and ASCLD/LAB's professionalism in its role as an auditor. For instance, although accreditation requires that analysts pass proficiency tests, labs are granted a wide latitude regarding the difficulty of those tests. Nor do ASCLD/LAB's standards impose a requirement of independent investigation into lab malfeasance, whether intentional or inadvertent. Thus, a laboratory can simply hide its dysfunction for years, as many have done, while claiming it is self-policing. Indeed, because audits are essentially exercises in document review—verifying the existence of required protocols or qualifications rather than conducting unannounced spot checks, pulling casework files for reexamination at random, or otherwise ensuring that a lab actually follows the protocols it announces on paper[55]—a laboratory that excels at looking good on paper can pass all its tests.[56] As Bruce Budowle has stated, the auditor will "go in and they'll check and see if you have a protocol, if you've done a validation study. . . . But what they don't do is they don't evaluate the protocol . . . [or] validation studies."[57]

The difference between a document review and an in-depth probe is perhaps evident in the disparity between the outcomes of the two FBI audit components of its DNA database. The FBI examines national database (NDIS) compliance and quality assurance. In the past five years, twenty-two labs have been audited. The NDIS aspect includes a document review, along with reexamination of one hundred random files associated with NDIS uploads. The quality-assurance review rests largely on documents alone, and does not entail any retesting or reanalysis. Of the twenty-two labs, almost half have been found in noncompliance with the more-rigorously reviewed NDIS standards, whereas only three have been found noncompliant on a largely paper review of quality assurance measures.

Finally, the ASCLD/LAB audit process has been criticized as too chummy. All accreditation inspections are announced. Janine Arvizu, an experienced and certified independent inspector, has described ASCLD/LAB as "essentially a trade organization of crime laboratory directors." She notes that this "peer-to peer composition of ASCLD creates the potential for conflicts of interest in the insular forensic community. ASCLD/LAB inspectors are required to be employees of (or retired from) ASCLD/LAB accredited laboratories (although there is a special provision for ASCLD/LAB to invite an inspector from a non-accredited laboratory)."[58] In other words, in February an inspector from lab A goes to lab B to conduct an audit of its functions, knowing that in May someone from lab B may be coming to check up on lab A.[59] This system creates powerful incentives to overlook errors or "go along to get along."[60]

So, what was ASCLD/LAB's response when it learned of the North Carolina scandal? Did it reopen its files to see what went wrong? Did it announce a plan to revamp its accreditation standards to ensure that malfeasance of this magnitude would never occur again under its watch? Did it express concern that the current lack of standardization in reporting language would invite future such errors? No. It simply argued that the disputed wording was used by all labs during that period.[61] That assertion, however, was later contradicted by a survey of laboratories, at least eight of which stated that it did not report results in this potentially misleading manner.[62]

At the same time, ASCLD/LAB appeared to minimize the problem, proclaiming that "[j]ust as a physical examination and good report from your doctor does not guarantee that you will not have any further health issues, an accreditation certificate from ASCLD/LAB or any other accrediting body does not guarantee no further issues will arise."[63] It defended its practices by arguing that "[m]istakes can and do occur in every profession, including forensic science." Rather than take a critical and hard look at its own accrediting practices and the systemic deficiencies that enabled North Carolina's problems to go undetected, ASCLD/LAB instead chose to circle the wagons and tell the public, "Hey, stuff happens."

This blasé attitude is underscored by a visit to the ASCLD/LAB website. Prominently displayed are opportunities for continued education and training, as well as instructions on filing an accreditation application—all highly lucrative aspects of its work. There are also lists touting the number of accredited laboratories, showcasing ASCLD/LAB's dominance in the field and underscoring its reputation as the preeminent accrediting body. But even basic data on compliance is absent. As one critic observed, despite advertising itself as the "self-proclaimed largest forensic laboratory accrediting body in the world[,] it has not published nor revealed in any literature the empirical extent of laboratory break-downs."[64] Audit documents are not publicly available, so consumers of laboratory services—including prosecutors—cannot easily check a lab's history or the records from its most recent audit. In fact, auditors pledge confidentiality in all aspects of the process.

Considering that ASCLD/LAB's sole responsibility is to vouch for the proper functioning of a forensic laboratory, the organization shows very little interest in documenting or exploring instances of laboratory failure. ASCLD/LAB asserts that "the organization doesn't track" how often probation or suspension occurs, much less document lesser problems. It provides no easy means for lodging a complaint against or seeking an investigation of any of its accredited labs, and keeps no public repository of complaints filed by others. The only available information is found in drop-down menus on the website that indicate which laboratories are on probation, have been revoked, or are under suspension. Yet it is rare to find a lab on that list; none is there at the time of this writing, and one could count on one hand the labs that have had their accreditation revoked in the organization's thirty-year history.[65]

In light of all this, ASCLD/LAB's response to the North Carolina situation was probably to be expected. Consistent with complaints about chumminess, it is worth observing that three of ASCLD/LAB's leaders at that time were former leaders at the North Carolina lab.[66] On a positive note, however, even if ASCLD/LAB did not take the allegations seriously, North Carolina officials clearly did. A series of meaningful legislative changes imposed more demanding standards on the lab, and the attorney general cleaned house. When the inspectors interviewed the former lab section chief, he stated that he "considered the primary consumer of the lab reports to be law enforcement." In contrast, the current chief and analysts all identified their customer as "the criminal justice system as a whole."[67]

Still, the road to excellence remains rocky. Among the newly enacted standards at the lab was one that dictated its analysts pass a state-mandated certification exam. Unfortunately, a third of the seventy-five analysts responsible for testing blood and DNA failed their first time at the exam, despite being a supposedly "experienced and qualified" group. This time, the lab director notified district attorneys and the public—although only after "a glitch" caused a delay in the information release.[68] In addition, a number of district attorneys had to fight to win release of the names of those failing analysts in the face of the laboratory director's claim that such information was "private."[69] A judge sided with the district attorneys, one of whom voiced his belief in the obligation to "live in sunshine as much as possible."

North Carolina may be able to turn its lab around, but the problems within some crime laboratories are so pervasive and entrenched that even a fully operating justice system may be incapable of meaningful remediation. The poster child for a problematic lab of this kind is the Houston crime lab, whose DNA division has been plagued with severe problems that come with the regularity of a leap year.

The most dramatic episode took place in the early 2000s, with the case of Josiah Sutton. Sutton spent four and a half years of a twenty-five-year sentence in jail for a rape he did not commit, largely on the basis of a wrongly interpreted DNA sample.[70] He was sixteen years old and walking to the store one day with a friend, when the police stopped him and placed him under arrest. The victim of a rape had just driven by and identified the two boys as her attackers, based on their hats. DNA tests excluded the other boy, but prosecutors claimed that they still matched Sutton.

At trial, the analyst told the jury that Sutton's DNA matched that found in the rape kit, and in reports placed the likelihood of a random person match at 1 in 694,000. In fact that profile could be found in as few as 1 in 14 black men.[71] Moreover, serious questions were raised about the reliability of the tests performed and the competence of the analyst. Unfortunately, even though Sutton's mother gave his lawyer over $600 for an independent test, the lawyer never followed through.[72] The family claimed that he said that the crime scene sample had been consumed in testing and that retesting was futile in any event; the lawyer contends that he had told them he would need more than twice what they had offered to pay for the test, and that he doubted there were samples available for testing.[73]

Whatever the case, the DNA evidence entered the case essentially unchallenged. Sutton's lawyer did point out that Houston's lab was unaccredited and operated according to unacceptable standards, but not

much more. Generally speaking, everyone had faith that the lab's technicians spoke scientific truth. The jury found Sutton guilty in less than two
hours, and the judge sentenced him to twenty-five years in prison. While
incarcerated, Sutton wrote to the Innocence Project, seeking review of
his case, but his request was turned down because, at the time, even the
Innocence Project presumed DNA-based convictions reliable. The organization has since changed its policy, and now counts faulty DNA typing
among the cited contributors to erroneous conviction in cases that have
been overturned.

When a new Texas law provided for postconviction DNA testing,
Sutton filed a request to reopen his case. It was during this period, three
years later, that the Houston crime laboratory would be shut down
after an independent audit revealed deeply troubling systemic flaws.
That report showed "widespread deficiencies related to virtually every
area covered by the FBI standards, including the lack of an established
quality assurance and internal auditing system, inadequate resources,
a technical leader with inadequate qualifications, an inadequate training program for DNA analysts, insufficient educational backgrounds
for analysts, inadequate SOPs, and poor documentation in case files."[74]
When Sutton's mother saw the news story on the closure, she reached
out to a reporter, who secured an expert to examine the evidence in the
case.

Even without retesting, the expert caught evident mistakes. Ultimately, independent testing confirmed that the crime scene samples did
not contain Sutton's DNA, and he began the path to full exoneration.
And then, three years after Sutton's release from jail, his story achieved
final closure. The DNA profile developed by a competent laboratory retesting the evidence in Sutton's case turned up a match in the DNA database to a convicted offender named Donnie Young. A year later, Young
pleaded guilty to aggravated sexual assault and received a ten-year sentence. He also provided the name of the man he said joined him in the
crime, who turned out to have already died in prison.[75]

A later systemic audit of Houston's crime laboratory found that errors in evidence handling and documentation, and interpretation and
reporting of test results, were "prevalent in the Crime Lab's DNA work
during the 1990s and early 2000s."[76] The report also identified "staggering" discrepancies between the statistics used by the lab to express the
significance of a match, and the accurate statistics for those cases. In one

table of twenty-three cases, the report gave examples in which the lab calculated the rarity of the profile as 1 in 11 million or 1 in 6.3 million, when in fact the real probability was 1 in 113 or 1 in 9, respectively.[77] Indeed, a review of 135 DNA cases analyzed by Houston's crime lab prior to 2002 revealed "major issues in 43—or approximately 32%—of these cases."[78] As in the case of the North Carolina lab, one major shortcoming was a "pattern and practice of avoiding the reporting" of exculpatory results.[79]

But Suton's case was not the end of the lab's troubles. Just four years after Suton's exoneration, Vanessa Nelson, the head of the DNA division hired after the lab reopened in the wake of the scandals, was forced out. Her offense? Nelson had fed DNA technicians the answers to their proficiency exams. DNA testing was suspended once again, although Nelson's career path did not seem to suffer. She was hired to direct the DNA lab at the Texas Department of Public Safety in McAllen—a laboratory with its own record of scandal and closure.[80]

Then, just six years later, yet another scandal broke.[81] DNA technician Peter Lentz confessed to colleagues during a happy hour that he "knew he was not following lab protocols after one of his test results was found to be faulty."[82] In an encouraging sign of progress, one of his co-workers immediately called a supervisor to make a report. The subsequent investigation revealed that Lentz had tested a switchblade and clothes for DNA in an aggravated assault case, but the results matched a co-worker in another part of the lab, indicating that the test was contaminated. When ordered to complete a retest, he deliberately used an improper combination of chemicals; the lab director speculated that it was to "get out of extra work associated with reporting a contamination."[83] Shortly after, an internal investigation was instigated and Lentz resigned; his attorney denied any deliberate wrongdoing and wondered whether he was being used as a scapegoat. As the old saying goes, the more things change, the more they stay the same.

PROFICIENCY TESTING

As the Houston crime lab experience suggests, in some cases, a DNA lab's blunders can take on a more sinister character. Although the most common kind of laboratory error involves inadvertent or unintentional acts, there are also far too many stories of deliberate fraud. These acts tend to derive from sheer laziness, a desire to appear industrious, or an attempt to mask incompetence. It is hard to know which of those desires animated an FBI scandal involving a DNA analyst named Jacqueline Blake. One day, a colleague realized that all of Blake's negative control results shared a similar blip. Further probing revealed that the similarity was because Blake had falsified them all. Rather than actually run a sample to ensure no contamination, she had copied the results from one particular run and passed them off as a new file in each case. Deception of this kind— suggesting work was performed that actually was not—has occurred so many times that there is a word for it: *dry-labbing*.

Another quite common form of overt malfeasance has arisen with regard to the testing of analysts to ensure they are competent to perform their jobs. These tests, known as proficiency tests, can vary widely in their difficulty. Proficiency tests are like performance evaluations; analysts are given a known sample to examine and the results of their work are then reviewed. They can be either "blind," meaning that employees do not know that the file they are working on is in fact a test, or "open," meaning employees know that their work is being judged. Proficiency tests can also replicate casework, in the sense that the materials simulate forensic conditions, or they can involve single-source or other high-quality samples that present few of the challenges that analysts face in actual day-to-day operations.

For obvious reasons, then, the most rigorous form of proficiency testing involves "blind" tests in casework conditions. In other words, the analysts are unaware that the work they are doing is a performance evaluation, and the work itself closely simulates the kinds of conditions (in terms of the quality and complexity of the sample) that an analyst regularly confronts. Conversely, the least rigorous form of test is an open, or declared, test, or one that involves only simple, single-source samples. In that case, analysts know they are being tested, and their work simulates only the most straightforward of tasks they might ordinarily perform.

Some accreditation standards further simplify open proficiency tests by specifically allowing that they "should not be subject to policies adopted by the laboratory for efficiency or expediency of casework," but that "all parts of a proficiency test provided by an approved test provider should be examined as completely as the laboratory's procedures allow."[84] In other words, the testing conditions do not replicate real-world conditions, where analysts might employ certain shortcuts or otherwise compromise best practices. Instead they take place completely by the books. But what use is a driver's test taken only on empty roads?

In a 2009 survey of crime labs across all forensic disciplines, 97 percent of labs conducted some form of proficiency tests, but 97 percent of those tests were done with the analysts' full awareness that the test was taking place. Only 10 percent of labs also conducted some form of proficiency testing through blind examination.[85] Resistance to blind testing is to some extent understandable. Blind testing, in true casework conditions, is both cost- and labor-intensive. At the same time, blind tests are the best way of measuring how analysts perform in true casework conditions.

Implementing better proficiency testing is not without significant challenges. First, even under the current model of proficiency tests, which afford all possible advantage to the analyst, some analysts still resort to cheating in order to pass.[86] And the risk of cheating does not dissipate simply because the tests are blind. A 2003 study commissioned simply to determine the feasibility of implementing blind testing of DNA uncovered that, in one of five labs that administered blind tests, a contact person had "revealed the plans for the blind test to laboratory management," thereby compromising its secrecy.[87] Similar cheating scandals have besieged other labs, as in the Houston case. Nonetheless, it should be the goal of every lab to conduct some degree of blind testing of its analysts. If blind testing of this kind proves too difficult or resource intensive, then random case reanalysis offers a less intensive alternative. This method requires only that a monitor randomly pull cases completed by examinees and subject them to reanalysis, thereby checking the quality of their actual work.

OVERSIGHT BOARDS

The final major model of DNA lab oversight is the one pioneered in New York in the early days of forensic DNA typing. In the wake of large-scale scandals, some states turned to standing commissions to superintend the forensic laboratory system. These commissions take an array of different forms, but sadly they, too, have largely failed to fulfill their promise.

Some are ongoing entities tasked with general oversight and standard-setting, whether for all forensic science disciplines or specific to DNA labs. Other versions of this kind of commission may outline a narrower role for the oversight body, such as to address database issues.[88] Some states have convened temporary task forces charged with specific objectives, often in response to an acute concern. Groups of this kind tend to operate for a finite period, after which they issue a report of their findings.[89] Significantly, only a handful of states even describe the purpose of their oversight board to be active monitoring of compliance and laboratory integrity, as opposed to setting basic standards.

Although commissions of this kind play a critical role in oversight, most are ill-equipped to conduct the kind of ongoing scrutiny that forensic DNA testing laboratories require. Most commissions meet only two to four times a year, for a day or two at most. They rely entirely on the material prepared for them by others, often by the very laboratory personnel whose work they are supposed to be scrutinizing. And even if those documents are complete and objective, commission members can effectively conduct only a paper review of a laboratory's processes. Such bodies are therefore poorly positioned to ensure that laboratories actually do the things they claim to do, or follow the rules that they put in place. These structural infirmities reveal why, in the wake of a major lab scandal, many compromised labs are shown to have managed not only to maintain accreditation but also to have appeased oversight entities.

Even if state commissions were willing to intensively scrutinize the functioning of the state's crime labs, most lack the manpower and resources to do the job properly. Boards typically contain a mixture of lawyers, academics, and lab scientists—thus at best only a few persons in the group would even be qualified to conduct a detailed laboratory audit. A rare exception is the New York DNA Subcommittee, which comprises eminent members of the forensic and research science community. But given their very eminence, those members are not tasked with on-the-ground investigations of lab performance. The subcommittee generally does not conduct random spot checks of labs or probe behind a director or supervisor's self-serving assertions.

Instead, oversight boards focus their attention on questions of methodological and scientific soundness as judged by a laboratory's own attestations about its work. In a recent judicial hearing about the reliability of a new scientific technique, for instance, one former member of the New York DNA Subcommittee testified that he had changed his mind about the reliability of a method that as a board member he had voted to approve. In describing his change of heart, he explained that the subcommittee met for roughly two hours, three to four times a year, and members occasionally missed meetings due to scheduling conflicts.[90] Committee members were not paid for their time, and yet the materials given them to review the adoption of the new method were so voluminous that they could only be provided on CD-ROMs. Not surprisingly, the members did not undertake any independent verification of the assertions by the lab. The picture painted was one of a nominal review—more "are your ducks in a row?" than standardized test.

Due to their lack of capacity to conduct independent audits, oversight boards entrusted with quality assurance tend to look elsewhere for support in that task. And the primary place to outsource that job? ASCLD/LAB. Even the FBI, which requires that labs meet quality assurance requirements to participate in its national DNA database program, recognizes accreditation by ASCLD/LAB as a suitable proxy for compliance. Yet, as explained earlier, ASCLD/LAB's audits have left much to be desired. Both North Carolina and New York used ASCLD/LAB to monitor the performance of their DNA labs, and both states paid the price for that misplaced trust.

Finally, oversight boards tend to suffer from political imbalances that may predispose them to show leniency toward other government officials. Most boards are composed of a "balanced" group representing all the important constituencies engaged in DNA testing. Thus, members include representatives of the testing laboratories, the prosecutor's office, law enforcement agencies, victim's rights advocates, innocence protection advocates, and defense attorneys.[91] Although on paper those factions accurately represent the important constituents, the net result can be a board that heavily favors the entrenched interests of the laboratory, and permits members to advance their own agendas.

Even if some members are inclined to be skeptical, institutional concerns may cause them to check that instinct. Prosecutors, police, and even victims rely on laboratory goodwill to perform their jobs. Prosecutors, in particular, must routinely stand up in court and defend those same laboratories from the attacks—at times spurious or petty—of defense lawyers. To expect any of these vested interests to turn a critical eye on the laboratory's representations—potentially generating material that will come back to haunt them in court, or inviting disfavor that may hinder their future requests for assistance—seems at best optimistic, and at worst foolish. Concerns of this kind ring particularly true in states that centralize DNA testing in one or two labs, such that the members of the commission directly rely on, and may even have personal relationships with, the lab personnel that they are supposed to regulate.

Political problems of this kind were on display recently in California, when the state's Crime Lab Task Force suddenly disbanded itself. Created in 2007 to address increasing awareness of the troubled state of forensic science, the group issued a 2009 report that contained forty-one specific recommendations to improve lab science. The task force itself had seventeen members, and its composition reflected just the kind of interest-based imbalance common to these kinds of commissions.[92] Eleven members were affiliated with police, the district attorney or the attorney general's office, or labs affiliated with one of those groups; three were criminal defense lawyers;[93] two were academics; and one was a representative of the court system.

The inevitable absences that plague such groups were evident in June 2010, when only nine members of the task force were present when it voted to disband at what turned out to be the final meeting. Of those, two were public defenders, two academics, and the rest were representatives of labs and the government. Some members argued that the task force should continue in an oversight role, but the representative for the California Association of Crime Lab Directors, Bob Jarzen, argued that would be "improperly duplicative of ASCLD/LAB . . . programs currently in place."[94] Jarzen later proposed the motion to disband the group. Public defender Jennifer Friedman offered an amendment that would invite task force members to draft written proposals for oversight, which could be discussed at the next scheduled meeting, but her amendment was voted down. Ultimately, by a vote of 6–3, the motion to suspend the commission carried.[95] The members voting against were the two representatives of the defense community present, along with one of the academics—a leading scholar of forensic science who has criticized the lack of rigor in the field.

Certainly an oversight board with no members representing the very institutions under scrutiny would be a mistake. But is it any surprise that a group so heavily tilted toward lab personnel might happily go along with recommendations for greater funding, salary increases, more reasonable and flexible workloads, and ongoing education opportunities, and yet fail to embrace more rigorous oversight standards? In the end, thirty-nine of the forty-one recommendations in the written report addressed these kinds of noncontroversial demands that, while sure to improve the state of forensic science, also do little to correct systemic dysfunction.[96] As attorney David Lynch, who voted against disbanding, later commented, "this means that things will just continue the way they've been. . . . The people who voted to suspend the proceedings are essentially crime lab directors, and they are of the opinion that 'we regulate ourselves just fine.'"[97] Unfortunately, history tells a different story.

CHAPTER 5

Single Cell Samples:
Low Copy Number DNA

ONE AUGUST NIGHT in 1978, fifteen-year-old Barbara Nantais zipped herself into a sleeping bag with her boyfriend on Torrey Pines State Beach in San Diego. At some point that evening, they were attacked. An assailant beat her boyfriend unconscious as he slept. As he regained bare consciousness the following morning, Barbara's body was found naked. She had been viciously beaten and strangled, and one of her nipples had been sliced off.[1]

Six years later, on another August night, fourteen-year-old Claire Hough decided to take a walk on the same beach. She never came home. Witnesses reported seeing a group of people hanging out in that area that evening. A beachcomber known for collecting cans from the beach found Claire's body the next morning. Her condition matched Barbara's—nearly naked, badly beaten, with one breast removed.

The FBI concluded that the same killer committed both offenses. The beachcomber was an early suspect, particularly after he sent eerie letters to Hough's parents for a month after the killing, but police ruled him out. The case went cold. In 2012, partly in response to pressure from Barbara's childhood boyfriend, police retested the evidence in both cases and gleaned some DNA results. They ran two profiles in the national database, and found two hits.

Blood found on Hough's clothing matched to a man named Ronald Tatro. Apart from the match, he fit the profile. A former police officer,

Tatro had convictions for two violent sexual offenses that had triggered his state's compulsory DNA sampling law. He had also lived in the area at the time of Hough's killing, although he was incarcerated in Arkansas at the time of Nantais's death. Because he died in a boating accident in 2011, further investigation stalled.

The other match—a small amount of DNA recovered from sperm found on a vaginal swab from Hough—was more surprising. The sample traced to a lab technician named Kevin Brown, who had retired in 2002 after working for San Diego's crime lab for twenty years. Investigators attempted to determine whether Brown had somehow inadvertently contaminated the sample, but ruled it out. Although the precise scope of their investigation is unclear, they stated that Brown had never been assigned to the case, nor associated directly with any of the handled evidence.

Brown's widow, however, claims that Brown's workstation was adjacent to the desk where the evidence was processed in the 1980s. At that time, the idea of testing for a DNA signature was still some years away, and analysts routinely let samples dry in the open air or left swabs uncapped. Moreover, because commercial samples of blood and semen were less available, it was not unusual for lab technicians to use their own samples as controls and references. And while analysts surely took care to avoid contamination of evidence even back in 1984, surely no one appreciated that even a few cells from a stray sneeze or passed pencil might be enough to type and test for a DNA sample thirty years later. As one British forensic scientist described it, "Back then the idea of being able to identify someone from a few tiny drops of blood seemed like something out of science fiction. In those early days, we rarely wore protective clothing at crime scenes or worried about potential contamination because there was no method to analyse any biological material that was as small as the eye could see."'

But as DNA testing methods have become increasingly sensitive, the possibility rises that seemingly "iron-clad" evidence condemns an innocent person. It is one thing to examine a large bloodstain left during the course of a struggle with an assailant, but quite another to find a handful of cells on an item of evidence and try to adduce their meaning. Yet an increasing number of forensic samples are from samples of this low template kind. As scientist John Butler has proclaimed, it is the penalty for DNA's triumph: "Due to the success of DNA testing and its value to the criminal justice system, many laboratories are seeing an increasing number of poor quality/quantity samples being submitted."[3]

Even what appears to be a sizeable sample of biological material can raise concerns if more than one person contributed to the sample. The reliability of the test may turn in part on the ratio of each person's contribution to the mixture. Interpreting such profiles accurately requires at minimum that the laboratory have extensively experimented with its own instrumentation to gauge performance variation. John Butler has remarked, "In my opinion, a laboratory cannot run a single two-person mixture series . . . and feel confident that minimum requirements for 'mixture validation' have been met."[4]

These issues have recently come to a head in courtroom battles over the admissibility of a DNA testing technique known as low copy number, or LCN, testing. This novel, ultrasensitive method of DNA typing was developed around the turn of the twenty-first century, and is capable of coaxing a DNA profile from even a single cell.[5] Although there is some dispute as to what precisely LCN is—a testing method or an interpretative approach—at base the term refers to the results from very low-quantity samples, which tend to produce DNA profiles of questionable reliability.[6] LCN is also sometimes referred to as "low template" DNA (LtDNA) or "touch" DNA. New York City's Office of the Medical Examiner (OCME)—the US laboratory most invested in this technique—even started calling it "high sensitivity testing" in a realpolitik move, hoping to cloak the method in a more positive moniker.

LCN testing involves the same basic steps as conventional DNA testing—extraction, quantitation, amplification, detection, and interpretation—but because so little genetic material is analyzed, those steps must be radically transformed. Think of the difference between building an actual house and a playhouse; some of the basic tasks and concepts are the same, but the methods and materials differ dramatically.

There are two major concerns raised by LCN testing. First, when low quantities of DNA are tested, the potential for contamination runs high. Suppose the crime scene collector sneezes, or the analyst misses a tiny speck when cleaning her station. While a couple of cells that inadvertently contaminate an ordinary DNA sample will be dwarfed by the true genetic material in the testing process, the same is not true if the sample is small. Five stray cells have a much bigger impact on a low copy sample of ten cells than on a regular sample of 150. The slightest compromise to the sterile testing environment can wreak havoc in the context of a low template test.

Second, with so little material to test, failures in the testing process are often harder to catch, or lead to misleading results. Peaks that seem real may not be, or others that should be present may inexplicably disappear. Chunks of DNA can buckle, creating false peaks that are easily interpreted as real, or the two peaks at a single locus may have asymmetrical heights, indicating the presence of dramatically different amounts of DNA, all of which confounds analysis. In essence, the rules of thumb that help analysts interpret ordinary samples do not work as well in the low copy number context, and guided subjectivity risks becoming little more than self-justifying guesses.

In addition, because LCN testing requires tweaks in the customary process of testing and interpretation, laboratories must test whether their instruments, which already have quirks and sensitivities, behave predictably with such low quantities of material. These idiosyncrasies exist for larger samples, too, but low copy testing intensifies the distortions. By analogy, this process is akin to cleaning the photocopier and testing that it reliably churns out spotless pages when there is nothing to copy. While such safeguards are not so important if you are just copying pages from a book, they become essential if you want to copy the single pencil-point dot on an otherwise blank page.

Advocates of LCN methods find the uncertainty in the testing and interpretive process simply a magnified version of the kinds of problems that arise when typing an ordinary forensic sample, and thus prefer proceeding with caution in place of abnegating the technique altogether. Critics, however, charge that the method strains the bounds of scientific understanding and dangerously invites forensic analysts to see what they want to see, which runs a serious risk of wrongful conviction.

Nearly every lab in the United States, including the FBI lab, has declined to pursue low copy number testing.[7] Only one public laboratory aggressively pursues it in criminal casework: the Office of the Chief Medical Examiner (OCME) in New York City. Around the time of the attacks of September 11, 2001, OCME started preparations for low template testing.[8] By 2004–2005, OCME had renovated its facility to create a dedicated hypersterile section for LCN testing and begun validating its techniques. In 2006, it accepted the first case. By 2012, the lab had processed over 6,000 low copy number samples from 2,500 cases, and was marketing its services to crime laboratories around the country.[9]

Notwithstanding this large number of cases, very few courts have actually confronted the question of whether LCN testing is sufficiently reliable to use as evidence of a defendant's guilt (as opposed, for instance, to simply using it to generate an investigative lead to a suspect, who then might be convicted based on other evidence). The lack of judicial intervention is probably due in part to the high rate of plea bargaining in the American system, coupled with the lack of a right in many jurisdictions to discovery prior to the tendering of a plea. A prosecutor might let leak to a defendant that "we have DNA," thereby precipitating acceptance of a favorable plea offer, and obscuring from the defendant that the supposed conclusive evidence was in fact a LCN test result of dubious reliability.

Moreover, the vast majority of defendants are indigent and receive appointed counsel, and systemic problems with the quality of representation in the indigent system have been well documented. Defense attorneys may be either ill-equipped to challenge the evidence, or else choose not to for strategic reasons. Even well-meaning public defenders may lack the time, resources, or knowledge to mount a challenge to a technique as novel and complex as LCN. Like most lay persons, they may simply see a purported "DNA match" and assume all DNA is reliable and unimpeachable.

Even in those cases in which defense lawyers have attempted to challenge the reliability of these tests, judges have often proven reluctant to take on the task of learning a complex new science. In the handful of cases where defendants asked courts to hold a hearing to determine the reliability of LCN testing, most either refused or undertook only a superficial or cursory review. Judges often trust at face value the government's unsupported assertions that LCN is no different from ordinary STR testing. One often cited opinion remarkably declared: "The same analysis that is utilized in [high copy number] DNA testing and which has been admitted nationally in our Courts for years, is basically the same type of DNA testing that is used when LCN DNA testing is performed. . . . "[10] The court's reasoning is akin to concluding that because a cake bakes properly for thirty minutes at 350 degrees, it is the same thing to bake it for fifteen minutes at 700 degrees. Even advocates of LCN testing acknowledge that it is not the same as STR testing. As one federal district court put it diplomatically, the assertion that LCN is not a "novel scientific technique" is at best a "questionable finding."[11]

The sloppy way in which the criminal justice system has handled a cutting-edge method like LCN bodes poorly for the future of DNA testing. But it is not too late to correct course. After extensive hearings, three trial courts—state trial courts in Brooklyn and Los Angeles, and a federal court in New Mexico—excluded LCN test results as insufficiently reliable.[12] In the Brooklyn hearing, a leading DNA expert and member of the New York DNA Subcommittee—the group responsible for approving new methods of forensic testing—testified that he would vote no today if asked whether to approve use of the method.

The hearing also brought to light serious problems of lack of transparency in LCN testing methods. Protocols set out the rules that labs must follow in testing and interpreting evidence. Validation studies and reliability tests are experiments that show that those protocols and the associated testing instruments actually reach accurate results, and can do so on a consistent basis. But labs have tended to shroud all of this material in secrecy. As former FBI scientist and leading critic of LCN Bruce Budowle has charged, "The scientific community does not know how LCN typing is being used in actual casework by the LCN laboratories. Part of the problem has been proclamations that LCN technology and interpretation are proprietary." In other words, labs have refused to disclose the protocols and studies, claiming that such information was legally protected as their own intellectual property. But without access to that information, Budowle rightly argued, "The forensic science community does not know what the practice of LCN laboratories are and whether they are valid and reliable."[13]

Of course, even full disclosure of a laboratory's protocols and validation studies would not alone appease all concerns. That is because in practice the formal rules are too often bent or broken. As Budowle observed, "There is a significant and problematic discordance between practice, publication recommendations, and reliance which calls into question the reliability of the interpretation of results of LCN analyses in current casework."[14] In other words, "[t]he specific practice in actual LCN casework is very different than what is recommended in the scientific literature." Budowle even named names, calling out the New York City lab, among others, for significant departures from the scientific literature or their own protocols in the standards actually applied in reporting the profile allegedly seen in the evidence.

Budowle's criticism turned prescient when, in April 2013, in the middle of the Brooklyn LCN hearing, one of the government's critical witnesses unexpectedly resigned her position. A top deputy at OCME, Theresa Caragine was a major champion of the technique and architect of the New York practice. But she eventually became embroiled in questions regarding improprieties at the lab.[15] OCME had just weathered a scandal involving a lab technician's gross incompetence and mismanagement, but Caragine seemed unscathed; a December 2012 story in the *New York Times* painted her work in glowing terms.[16] Less than six months later, however, it was revealed that she had changed a subordinate's DNA results in LCN cases on at least two occasions, using her authority to override the analyst instead of having a third party resolve the dispute as required by laboratory protocols.

In one case, the criminalist used LCN typing to recover a mixture of at least two people's DNA from the handle of a gun. He drafted his report, which his supervisor approved, and sent it to the assistant district attorney assigned to the case. When the lab later received a sample from a suspect to compare to the gun evidence, the analyst found that the suspect's DNA was not present on the gun, and a supervisor signed off. But Caragine disagreed, and without consulting the analyst, rewrote the report. When the analyst confronted her, she explained the basis of her disagreement, but then orchestrated the reassignment of the case to a new analyst. Caragine then met with that analyst, who drafted a new report consistent with Caragine's view.

An investigation by the inspector general regarding malfeasance at the lab concluded that Caragine's actions departed from both custom and policy at the OCME in several ways.[17] First, OCME protocols dictated that disputes of that kind should be resolved by a neutral supervisor. Second, as a matter of custom, it was highly unusual to simply rewrite a report when a dispute arose, not to mention to reassign a case when the dispute could not be resolved. And third, although the DNA findings report—the document sent to the prosecution and disclosed to the defense lawyer—was rewritten no fewer than six times, each rewrite overwrote the prior draft. Thus the only external indication of the tremendous ongoing dissent about the interpretation was an obscure internal document that records each review by initials and dates. This case marked the most egregious of Caragine's actions. In another case, she simply reassigned a case where analysts disagreed with her, and in a third case, she asked an analyst to run an analysis but not include the results in the case file.

These documented improprieties at OCME confirm Budowle's intuitions. Even if a lab establishes protocols for testing and interpreting low copy cases, and even if those protocols are accurate and validated, there are simply too many opportunities for departure when it comes to reporting results in this highly sensitive arena. Contrary to assertions that the lab always "follows its protocols," actual investigation showed evidence of uncomfortable departures.

As for the evidence in Kevin Brown's case? When confronted, he denied knowing either the victim, Hough, or his supposed associate Tatro. But some circumstantial evidence exists. Brown admitted to having belonged in the 1980s to a group that took nude pictures of young women and strippers, although always with their consent. Some co-workers also described him as "creepy."

Brown offered to take a polygraph to prove his innocence. He passed one independent test administered by a former police officer. A separate police-administered polygraph showed deception when he was asked about having had sex with Hough or awareness of her death, but no deception when asked about having killed her or hurt anyone. Police also claimed that Brown made a plausibly incriminating statement during a casual conversation at the polygraph, and another to a friend he knew back in those days, to whom he reached out after the police investigation began.[18]

But on the other hand, Brown had worked in New Mexico at the time of Nantais's killing. Moreover, a surprise search warrant was executed at Brown's home, and an enormous volume of material seized. None of it appeared to include what might be considered the smoking gun—a purse that Hough had in her possession at the time of the killing but had not been recovered from the scene. His wife describes Brown as "a quiet good man who devoted his life to helping people—and helping, he thought, by putting away bad guys and doing his job."[19]

Was Brown a sick killer and rapist who eluded capture until trace DNA techniques finally identified him? Or did he have consensual sex with a girl who later turned up dead, and feared admitting his involvement when he learned she was underage? Or did Brown just have the misfortune of having coughed at the wrong time while the lab technician next to him worked on a gruesome new case?

It is unlikely we will ever learn for certain the answer to these questions. Just before authorities moved in to make an arrest in October 2014, Brown committed suicide. His wife and lawyer say he had been "hounded" for two years by police investigators, who questioned and searched him and his family, friends, and neighbors. He suffered from anxiety and depression, which his wife says overcame him as a result of "the fear that he would be falsely accused and imprisoned."[20] So much time had elapsed, perhaps he felt it would be impossible to prove his innocence. Perhaps he felt it would be hopeless to fight against evidence as damning as DNA. Eventually, a jury may have a chance to pass on the evidence to some degree—Brown's widow filed suit. But even still, the truth may never be known.

PART II

Misunderstood Matches:
How DNA Statistics Mislead

CHAPTER 6

Brave New World of Probabilities

SUPPOSE YOU READ about a terrible crime in the newspaper, then learned that a suspect had been apprehended and his DNA matched evidence left from the scene. You would probably be relieved, believing that the perpetrator had been caught and powerful evidence existed to ensure a conviction. But that relief might be unwarranted. Many jurors, and even legal officials, hear the word *match* as synonymous with *case closed*. However, not all matches are created equal.

A DNA match between a suspect and crime scene evidence has value, but without more information about the quality of the match, its value is indeterminable. Jurors and lawyers cannot rely on their personal knowledge or experience to assess the significance of a DNA match. They can intuit the frequency of visible traits, such as being female or having brown eyes, but not how often a person has a 12 allele at the D4 locus. Ordinary life experience does not include lessons in how common certain unobservable genetic profiles are, or how many places on the genomic strand should be tested to make a match meaningful.

That is why the last step in a forensic DNA analysis is always to assign a probability to the existence of a match. The analyst must assess statistically the likelihood that particular genetic characteristics, or genetic profiles, occur. This step is so important, given that very few people have an intuitive sense of the frequencies of a particular profile, that it is well accepted that to speak of a "DNA match," without assigning it a statistical significance, is to actively mislead lay persons.

There are several ways to make an assessment of statistical significance. The most common is to assess the rarity of the profile: the analyst calculates how often one might expect to encounter that exact profile in the population at large. Suppose that 1 in 3 people have brown hair in your city. If you closed your eyes on a busy street and grabbed the first person who walked by, there would be a 1 in 3 chance that he or she has brown hair. On the other hand, suppose that only 1 in 60 million people have brown hair, brown eyes, a nose piercing, and are carrying foreign money. You might close your eyes and grab a person off the street, but it is now much less likely that your random choice would have those characteristics, because though some pieces of the profile are common (brown hair, brown eyes), some other parts are less likely (nose piercing, foreign money), and all four together may be somewhat rare.

The common term for the calculation of the rarity of the profile is the *random match probability,* or RMP for short. The RMP captures how likely it would be that a person picked at random would match a particular profile—if, say, we plucked a name from the phonebook, what is the probability that the person would have the genetic profile seen in the crime scene evidence?

The RMP is sometimes confused with other things. Most commonly, people assume the RMP expresses the chance that the defendant is guilty, or that someone other than the defendant left the crime scene stain. They hear "1 in 20 trillion" as a "1 in 20 trillion chance the defendant did not do the crime" or maybe even a "1 in 20 trillion chance that it was not the defendant's DNA." But the RMP is neither of those things. It is simply an expression of how rare the profile is within the population at large—just as the likelihood is probably a little over 1 in 2 that the person standing behind you in line at the coffee shop is a woman. In DNA typing, RMPs commonly range from ratios as low as 1 in 10,000 to those as rare as 1 in billions, trillions, or more.

To compute the RMP, the analyst first looks at the frequency with which each of the twenty-six individual genetic traits occurs, and then multiplies those frequencies together to come up with the final statistic. Multiplying each frequency together works because of a mathematical principle known as the *product rule*: the idea that the overall probability of an event with multiple components is the product of the individual probabilities for each component, so long as those events are unrelated, or independent. For instance, the probability of flipping a coin and landing "heads" is 1 in 2; that same probability repeats for a second flip—nothing about the first flip influences what happens on the second flip. What makes five straight "heads" results unusual is not that the probability of any one flip landing "heads" has changed, but that it is difficult to get the same result when you repeat five times an action that has a 50 percent probability of coming out a different way each time. The *cumulative* likelihood of five straight "heads" flips requires multiplying 50 percent by the five times—which produces a much rarer probability than multiplying 50 percent one or two times.

Unlike a coin toss, which has only two possible results per throw, there is much more variation—statistically speaking—in a forensic DNA profile. You will recall that the standard DNA profile looks for two genetic variants at thirteen different places—or twenty-six discrete identifiers for each individual.[1] There are only a finite number of variations at each of these twenty-six places (just as, by analogy, only a handful of hair colors occur naturally); the precise number of the genetic variants in forensic DNA testing runs from roughly eight options to twenty-seven. But even this limited diversity still affords sufficient range to provide a fairly strong identifier, especially as not all variants are equally probable. Just as red hair is rarer than brown hair; so, too, are certain genetic variants in forensic DNA typing less common than others.

To underscore the potential diversity in profiles, consider that, mixing and matching all of the known variations at the thirteen observed loci, in theory there are 3,645,313,799,703,916,475,520,000 (or roughly 3.65 × 10^{24}) possible DNA profiles.[2] That means that the theoretically imaginable DNA profiles, also known as genotypes, far exceeds the total population of the planet, which is around 7 billion. It even exceeds educated hunches about how many people have ever lived on earth since the dawn of human time, which some speculate to be around 108 billion.[3]

Given the enormous number of possible genotypes, it is easy to see why a complete DNA match proves such powerful evidence: it generates spectacularly small probabilities—such as 1 in 235 quintillion—that a person picked at random would have had the same genotype as the DNA evidence in the case. In theory, whereas a profile RMP of 1 in 1 billion would suggest that at least six or seven people on Earth probably have that same profile, an RMP of 1 in 235 quintillion leaves only a small—albeit still nonzero—chance that any other person on Earth, other than the person who left it at the crime scene, shares it.

In reality, however, some of those profiles are far more likely than others; and others, while theoretically possible, may never be seen. Some therefore doubt whether these spectacular numbers are justified, pointing to several important ways in which they can mislead. First, these statistics assume that one can do a sampling of DNA profiles and from that determine how often certain traits appear, when in fact that sampling may not be entirely accurate. For example, some genetic traits may be rare in some populations but more common in others; thus a sampling that picks up only one member of that subgroup (or none) may result in researchers' believing a trait is rare when in fact it is not so uncommon in that group. Second, even seemingly rare profiles may arise multiple times in the population, given a large enough pool of persons. Both of these issues are of less concern when other strong evidence implicates a defendant, because the probability of guilt then hinges on both the independent evidence *and* a DNA match. But with the rise of DNA databases, many more cases begin and end with DNA alone. On those occasions, the existence of one or two other potential matches to the evidence matters a great deal.

This concern that the statistics reflect the sampled groups, rather than actual observations of the frequency of genetic traits, is magnified by the social tendency of people to mate and reproduce within racial, linguistic, or geographic subgroups. For the RMP to work, people must mate with sufficient randomness to ensure that the traits are randomly assorted in later generations.[4] This concept of random mating is known as Hardy Weinberg Equilibrium, after the two scientists who separately discovered the principle. RMP models assume that a population is in equilibrium—in other words, that all persons in a group have an equal chance of inheriting a particular genetic characteristic, because random mating leads to random inheritance. But, of course, genetic inheritance often does not occur with true randomness.

Rather than genetics being as random as a roll of the dice, they instead may be weighted in ways that reproduce traits at a higher rate within subcommunities. Long-standing geographic and socio-cultural divisions within society mean that people in the United States still tend to marry and reproduce within defined demographic subgroups. Recall, after all, that some states outlawed marriage between persons of different races until the Supreme Court ruled it unconstitutional in 1967,[5] and school, housing, and other long legalized forms of segregation resulted in high concentrations of reproduction within subpopulations.

As a result, groups with high rates of marriage within that group—for instance, communities bound by religious affiliations or geographic isolation—have different rates of certain genetic characteristics than do other groups. The scientists' term for this kind of genetic clustering is population substructure.

Statisticians have pointed to population substructure as a reason to differentiate between a theoretical profile probability and an actual match probability. The theoretical probability is the number captured by the RMP. But, as noted, not every profile that exists in theory exists in actuality; instead, a much smaller subset of variation likely appears. Viewed this way, the RMP statistic is not quite right; the better statistic is one that provides the probability of a suspect's having the profile observed in the crime scene evidence, given that its existence in the evidence affirms that at least this particular profile has occurred at least once in the world.[6]

By way of crude analogy, it is like computing the probability that there is someone in the world who is one-quarter-Turkish, one-quarter-Swedish, half-Japanese, and has red hair and blue eyes. In *theory*, the probability may be very remote. But if such a person is shown to exist, the probability that there are others like him or her increases dramatically. Relying on the theoretical RMP for such a genetic combination while disregarding evidence that this one example has been observed in the world, may overstate the profile's rarity, although it is difficult to know to what degree.

In the end, two complementary approaches to address these concerns about population substructure emerged. The first approach was to introduce a statistical figure (known as the theta correction) to deflate the RMP and offset the possibility of inaccurate numbers as regard suspects belonging to highly insular groups, such as some Native American populations. The second was to break down the statistical tables into categories that reflect some of the most prevalent dimensions of segregated patterns of reproduction in the United States.[7] The groups commonly used by the FBI are Caucasian, African American, southwestern Hispanic, southeastern Hispanic, and Asian. But there are also data sets that cover a wide array of other populations, and some labs construct their own data to meet the specific demographic needs of their geographic area. Doing so helps ensure greater precision in statistical estimates.

At the same time, the use of racial and ethnic classifications in forensic DNA analysis has led to criticism.[8] Reporting match statistics in these terms may leave the impression that there is a direct connection between race (largely a societal construct) and biology (the more subtle genetic phenomenon that reflects generalized notions of ancestry). Genetic traits map onto geographic and socio-cultural signifiers; but they do not *create* racial classification—just as being blond does not make one Swedish, even though Swedes may be more likely to have blond hair. The fact that socio-cultural factors created biological difference, rather than the reverse, should be particularly clear when reflecting on the Hispanic category. "Hispanic," of course, is a linguistic category created in the 1970s, not a biological or genetic category that somehow predisposes one to speaking Spanish.[9]

The reservations of racial justice advocates were exacerbated by the rather haphazard way in which the frequency tables were composed. Rather than relying on objective studies, researchers based their tables on individuals' self-report of their race. As one scholar observed, although government scientists took meticulous care when researching the technical aspects of DNA testing—such as the validation of the instruments or the selection of the core CODIS loci—they seemed satisfied with a subjective foundation for the statistical tables when it came to racial categorization. It appeared that, to the researchers who drew up the tables, "race [was] seen as easy and obvious; DNA [was] seen as difficult and complex."[10]

As an alternative, some statisticians have advocated using the most popular frequencies at each locus when computing the random match probability.[11] This would be the equivalent of saying that, because we do not know the true frequency with which blue eyes appears in a population, we will use the very high rate at which it appears in the United Kingdom when we calculate the probability for any other person in the world. This approach strikes some as unduly conservative, because in effect it might make blue eyes seem common in a place like China, where brown eyes dominate. But it also would ensure accuracy when applied to a group where a precise rate is unknown. This approach has the benefit of minimizing the likelihood that the predictive tables understate profile frequency when applied to an unusual subgroup. It also does not too terribly diminish the statistical power of DNA evidence overall, because good evidence typically returns a profile well that produces very low probabilities.

Finally, it must always be remembered that naked match statistics assume the absence of error. They do not factor in the possibility of problems in the collection, testing, analysis, or interpretation stages. Critics charge that failing to include error rates artificially bolsters confidence in the reliability of the match. For instance, your physician's statement that you have a 1 in a million chance that you will live to see tomorrow sounds pretty bad, until you learn that the doctor's predictions have a 99 percent error rate.

This overview of probability calculations provides a little taste of how much must be taken into consideration when determining the significance of a DNA match, even in the simplest case of a large crime scene stain—such as a pool of blood—that clearly came from the perpetrator alone. Imagine how many more factors need to be taken into consideration when DNA analysts confront more complicated evidence.

THE MESS OF MIXTURES

Advances in the instrumentation and technology of forensic DNA typing have made it ever more possible to glean some data from even minuscule or highly degraded samples, but that data is often imperfect. Even the obviousness of the complexity may at times be elusive; analysts may think they are dealing with a straightforward two-person mixture, only to learn that in fact a third contributor's profile is hidden beneath. Or a single-source sample that should have easily produced a full profile, instead appears to be missing data at one locus.

When a crime scene sample returns complicated results, analysts must determine how to assign statistical weight to those results. Choosing a particular statistical approach can effect the weight or value of the evidence, and yet analysts may lack adequate training to help guide that decision. Consider the case of a simple two-person mixture. One approach in such a case is simply to apply some guiding principles that allow analysts to separate and label the results as belonging to distinct genotypic contributors. In other words, even though the results look like a cluster of peaks at a single locus, the analyst can harness his or her knowledge of the sample itself, the functioning of the lab's equipment, and the specific data on the electropherogram to guide decisions about which alleles to ascribe to which person. Once the mixture is pulled apart, or "deconvolved," each of the resulting profiles may be treated as "single source," and their match significance assessed using a modified version of the RMP.

But pulling apart mixtures in this way has come under fire as prone to bias or error in too many cases. One anecdotal survey at a 2007 mixture interpretation workshop found attendees reporting their biggest challenges as "consistency between analysts," "a lot of 'individual interpretation' in our lab," "resistance to change," and "getting management to commit to guidelines that will be followed by everyone."[12] A similar anecdotal survey in 2011 showed that a quarter of participants, when queried "If you asked 10 analysts in your laboratory to interpret a complex mixture you would get . . . " responded, "[a] large range of answers."[13] Such variations have real ramifications if carried to a courtroom. In one California case, for instance, the analyst testified that the probability of a random match was 1 in 95,000 in the general population, even after a supervisor told him that the proper number was 1 in 47. A later review by the state revealed that the analyst had an "an insufficient understanding" of how to separate out a mixture.[14]

In place of trying to label each contributor's profile in a mixture, some analysts use an approach known as *combined probability of inclusion*, or CPI, sometimes referred to as the *random man not excluded*, or RMNE method. One poll of 138 attendees at a workshop for forensic analysts in 2011 revealed that 72 percent used some variation of the CPI method.[15] The easiest way to understand this method is to imagine that a computer took every observed piece of genetic material in the sample, and then came up with every conceivable combination of DNA profiles that might result—like populating a wild-card team by filling twenty-six open spots with every imaginable combination of players, rotating through the full rosters of the fifteen best teams.[16] The resulting statistic represents the probability that a person picked at random would have any one of those possible genetic profiles.

Because this CPI method simply counts everything, many analysts believe it to be conservative—erring on the side of underestimating, rather than overestimating, the significance of the match. But that is not truly the case, for two reasons. First, throwing the analysis entirely to the numbers can lose important qualitative assessments about whether certain theories are more or less credible. The CPI approach is typically used when something about the test results makes it too difficult to distinguish clear contributors. An example would be if parts of the accused's profile are present in the test results, but other parts are missing. In a mixture with many contributors, the analyst might nonetheless cobble together evidence of the suspect's DNA profile. But closer examination of the actual results of the genetic test make it highly unlikely that this artificially stitched profile in fact belongs together. For instance, if the test results seem to indicate that half of the suspect's genetic material was strongly present, but the other half was only weakly apparent, then, absent some good explanation for the disparity, a more likely explanation is that it was not in fact the suspect's DNA in the mixture.

Second, the CPI is commonly used as a way of circumventing potentially exculpatory information about the profile of the contributors. Recall that mixtures, highly degraded samples, and samples generated from a small amount of template often produce results that are not fully complete.[17] If analysts expect that some genetic markers may be missing, or have dropped out, then they just ignore that locus. For instance, say that a profile appears to match the defendant at every locus, except one. At the last locus, the test results are ambiguous. One allele matches, but the other is missing. Should this constitute an exclusion—such that the person is ruled out as a contributor to the DNA sample, even though the rest of the genetic markers match? Or should the person be included in the pool of people who might have been the source, on the theory that some other explanation exists for the missing material? Common practice favored the latter approach of just ignoring the missing material. This practice was also viewed as conservative, because the fewer points of comparison there are, the less powerful the match would normally be.

But as one important study pointed out, the CPI approach is "conservative only if the evidence at that locus has no exclusionary potential";[18] that is, conservative only if the defendant is guilty. In this study, researchers simulated one thousand two-person DNA mixtures meant to represent crime scene evidence. They then randomly created a totally unrelated third profile, meant to simulate an innocent defendant; in other words, someone believed by the state to have contributed to the mixture, when in fact that person had not. For each of the thousand mixtures, 10,000 of these innocent persons were created. The authors calculated the CPI for those third-party profiles, using only those loci where both of the genetic markers in the third profile were represented in the mixture.

Following this practice of just ignoring missing or contradictory material, the researchers ran the numbers for their "innocent" defendants. The results were shocking. In 87 percent of the cases, "evidence was produced that had some tendency to inculpate the random third profile." In other words, even though the innocent defendant was not in fact a contributor to the DNA sample, the CPI approach made it seem as if the sample contained that person's DNA. In 30 percent of cases, the inclusion statistic fell between zero and 0.01, meaning that if this had been an actual case, the jury would have heard that the chance that an innocent person would match the mixture was less than 1 percent. In almost half the cases, the probability of a random match was given as under 5 percent. Since the researchers knew that those persons were not in fact present in the mixture, despite these strong inculpatory statistics, they observed that this approach has the power to "produce apparently strong evidence against a surprisingly large fraction of noncontributors." As a result, they further concluded that the CPI method, coupled with the practice of dropping any locus where the "suspect" does not match, "cannot be supported."

In part due to these issues, the International Society of Forensic Genetics instead recommends using a *likelihood ratio* to express the significance of a complex mixture.[19] A likelihood ratio is a comparison between two different views of the DNA match—one in which the match is explained by the defendant having genuinely contributed to the evidence sample, and another in which the match is coincidental, because in fact the DNA was left by another person. Some people find likelihood ratios vexing, but we intuitively engage in them every day. We go to lunch and think, the tuna looks a little glossy—what is the likelihood that it is glossy because it was freshly made, versus because it has been sitting out too long? Or we notice it is overcast outside and we wonder, what is the likelihood that it is about to rain, versus that a fog has rolled in? A likelihood ratio is simply the comparison of different theories regarding the same event.

The appeal of the likelihood ratio is that it best approximates what the jury actually does, which is to contrast two views of the evidence. It also accommodates the difficulties in assigning statistical weight in complex cases. As a group of international DNA forensic scientists wrote, "With any DNA profile, if drop-out or drop-in are possible (this includes any partial DNA profile), it is not possible to think only in terms of a match or non-match, the various possibilities can only be properly evaluated in probabilistic terms by means of the likelihood ratio principles."[20] The difficulty with likelihood ratios in this context, however, is that they require the analyst to do some guesswork. In a case where the crime scene sample evidence shows only one DNA profile, imagine that the defendant matched that profile. The likelihood ratio compares the chance of seeing that DNA match under the prosecution view (the defendant left it at the crime scene) to the defense view (the defendant did not leave it).

Now imagine a piece of evidence that has DNA not just from one person, but from several people. The prosecution will have a theory about how to pick apart the profiles to support conviction; here, the likelihood ratio would calculate the probability of seeing particular genetic markers (for instance, profiles of the defendant, the victim, and a codefendant), versus the probability that the mixture contains the profiles, say, of the victim and two unknown others, thus excluding the defendant and codefendant.

On the prosecution's side, the guesswork is not usually that hard. The prosecution typically has a clear theory of whose DNA should be found in the evidence—the defendant's—and maybe what other specific contributors were present. But the defense may not always have as clear a view. A *guilty* defendant may know who is in the mixture, but it is not the guilty defendant we are most worried about wrongly convicting. The innocent defendant may have no idea who is in the mixture. The defense might guess that the profiles belong to the victim and two random parties, or the victim and the codefendant and another person, or three random people, and so on. The more complex the mixture, the more complicated the array of possible explanations that do *not* include inculpating the defendant. Likelihood ratios may also be calculated using mixtures for which an analyst has ascribed a profile to specific contributors. In that case, the analyst effectively compares the probability that the mixture is a combination of those established genotypes, as opposed to any possible combination of genotypes.

The pressure to develop new ways of calculating match significance has increased as the ability to glean results from smaller and smaller amounts of DNA has improved and mixtures have grown more intricate. When only DNA from homicide cases or rape kit samples were tested, labs more comfortably used modified RMP or CPI calculations. But testing gun grips or triggers, or light switches and key fobs, can generate far more complicated DNA results. The various scenarios must account for unexpected or missing aspects of the genetic profile. Yet even as the technology has outgrown the math, analysts have kept computing the same statistics. In the words of the FBI's DNA working group's recent advisory memo, the interpretative guidelines for mixtures that embraced modified RMP, CPI, and likelihood ratio methods were written for simpler evidence, namely "with single-source samples and two-person mixtures in mind." For more complicated samples, including "mixtures of three or more contributors, low-level DNA samples, and mixtures containing biologically related individuals . . . there are nuances and limitations" that those guidelines do not address.[21]

In the end, the result is that significant variation exists among labs when interpreting complex samples. The ultimate estimate of match significance can vary dramatically, even when analysts are given the same exact profile, and even when the variation that arises from the testing process itself is eliminated. To give one stark example, in 2013 the National Institute of Standards and Technology (NIST) conducted a mixture interpretation study among crime scene labs.[22] The goal was to follow up on a 2005 study, which had found troubling amounts of variation in sample interpretation.[23] In the 2013 test, NIST enlisted 106 labs across forty-five states. The survey did not entail any actual laboratory testing, thus eliminating one possible area for variation or discrepancy. Instead, the labs were all sent the results of five fictitious cases that included challenging conditions, such as multiple-person mixtures, low template results, and possible relatives as suspects.

The results showed improvement, but still fell far short of the degree of uniformity that most persons would expect.[24] There was wide variation in both methodological approach and actual outcome.[25] In some places, the judge and jury would have been told a match probability so low that its denominator exceeded the world's population, whereas in others the probability would not have exceeded that of a midsize city. As the NIST researchers put it politely, "there is still a great deal of variation in interpretation across the United States."

MAGIC MATH: COMPUTING THE SIGNIFICANCE OF NOTHING

Current approaches for valuing complex mixtures or degraded or low template samples invite uncomfortable levels of disparity and inconsistency. But one way to alleviate these concerns involves harnessing the power of sophisticated algorithms to improve predictions that rely on subtle variations in data. The large number of calculations that a computer can instantly process also enables analysts to shift from a model of statistical assessment that focuses on alleles versus genotypes. That is, whereas traditional methods compute statistics by taking into account each present or absent trait and its associated frequencies, more sophisticated techniques consider the whole genetic profile, and calculate probabilities accordingly. A cottage industry of statistical software tools have sprung up to facilitate statistical calculations in complex cases. But although these tools seem to be moving in the right direction, they have not quite arrived yet, as a case from a court in Brooklyn nicely illustrated.

Jessica Goldthwaite was a seasoned legal aid attorney with eight years under her belt when she picked up Jaquan Collins's case. Prosecutors alleged that Collins had ridden his bike to the crime scene, where he allegedly fired nonfatal shots. Investigators uncovered a bicycle they believed connected to the incident, and analysts purportedly found a profile matching Collins on the bike's handlebars.

Upon examination, Goldthwaite realized that the DNA match came about through the use of low copy testing methods. Concerned that New York was the only public crime laboratory performing low copy testing, she filed a motion to exclude the match from the evidence on the grounds that these methods had not gained general acceptance in the scientific community. But Goldthwaite also had another concern. To compute the significance of the supposed match, the government had used a software program it developed for cases in which the DNA tests results were less than complete. Called FST, for Forensic Science Tool, this program claimed to compensate for shortcomings in the test results by using statistical calculations to explain away what was there that should not be, or what was missing that should be there. To the defense team, FST seemed like one of those optical illusions that allow viewers to see what they want to see, like the famous image of an old woman versus a young lady.[26]

FST is just one of a handful of software packages aimed at marshaling complex statistics. The others have catchy names, such as Lab Retriever, likeLTD, TrueAllele, ArmedXpert, STRmix, DNAView, LiRa, Forensim, and LRmix. All endeavor to account for the unpredictable behavior of DNA samples with low template or too many contributors. To do that, most rely on mathematical models that aim to predict when and why erratic observed results are nonetheless explainable. These models differ in their details, and as a result the predictions they make as regard the same piece of evidence may differ as well.[27]

To return to the marathon analogy used to explain the basics of DNA typing, it is kind of like devising a mathematical model that predicts which runners are likely to finish a race, and in what time. The model might include how well the runners had trained, what kind of race they had run in the past, what those earlier times were, and the conditions of the course on that day. That data might give us a good indication that certain participants are likely to finish, versus others that might be expected to drop out or be slower than usual. The statistical models for DNA analysis likewise may rely on either general studies of how certain samples behave, or on localized studies of how samples behave on the specific instrumentation in a lab. From those predictions, the software then attempts to assign meaning to actual test results that exhibit those qualities.

One major concern about such models, however, resembles the reservation one might have about predictions of the outcome of a race. In many cases, the predictive probability model may work well. But in others it may not. Even a sophisticated model cannot account for every variable that may influence the behavior of low-quality or -quantity samples. What is more, the research in this area is still far from complete. Scientists and statisticians are still refining their understanding of how complex samples behave, and how best to take account of these oddities when it comes to fixing match probabilities. As a result, different models produce different results, because they give weight to different factors.[28]

Several of these software programs have been used with little to no challenge in criminal cases.[29] Sadly, the failure of the majority of lawyers to question the reliability of novel statistical tools is likely a sign of precisely the kind of complacency that has led to the acceptance of faulty forensic methods since time immemorial. But another contributing factor may be that some of the software architects refuse to release information about their source code or the precise manner in which their statistics are computed. Some, such as LRmix, Lab Retriever, and likeLTD, operate on open-source platforms with full transparency, but many others guard their codes as proprietary secrets.

In the Collins case, New York's Office of the Chief Medical Examiner (OCME), a public forensic laboratory and not a private for-profit company, refused to open the source code of its FST software. Undeterred, Goldthwaite and her team nonetheless assembled an array of experts to convince the judge that the OCME's methods were untrustworthy. Her case was joined with another raising similar challenges, and the result was an epic hearing on the reliability of low copy testing and the FST software program.[30] The defense witness list read like a who's who in forensic DNA typing, including Bruce Budowle, the former director of the FBI laboratory and an original champion of forensic DNA evidence, and Ranajit Chakraborty, a scientist whose work helped build the foundations of CODIS,[31] and who had served on the New York DNA Subcommittee that had initially approved the OCME's low copy method and FST software.

Goldthwaite's experts related a number of concerns about the FST statistical software, in addition to the greater challenge regarding the reliability of low copy number testing. They disputed the FST's model for disregarding in the crime scene results the presence of genetic markers that did not match the suspect or the absence of markers that the suspect in fact had. Goldthwaite also mounted a number of highly technical objections, including questioning the lab's claims that it had conducted adequate experiments with a variety of known samples to ensure that the software's calculations were in fact correct.[32]

The hearing stretched over months, with the judge carefully listening to every piece of evidence. Most of the prosecutor's attacks on the defense witnesses tried to paint them as biased in some way, but those attempts seemed strained in light of their impeccable résumés and long history of work with the government. OCME personnel conceded that the program had not been subject to any external validation or peer review of any kind, and further admitted that there were no documentation or records pertaining to key parts of the internal review process that they claimed to have undertaken.

In place of scientific evidence supporting the accuracy of the program, the prosecutor instead relied heavily on the approval that FST had received from the DNA subcommittee. But Dr. Chakraborty testified that, at the time the subcommittee granted its approval, the city had provided neither the source code nor a copy of the actual program.[33] No members had actual experience operating the program, or had tested its accuracy in any way. Dr. Chakraborty and Dr. Budowle also both pointed out that the committee met only occasionally and relied heavily on the OCME's own representations of its work as opposed to conducting an independent review. Dr. Chakraborty conceded that knowing what he did now, he would change his vote.

In December 2013, as the hearing still raged on, the New York State Bar Association awarded Jessica Goldthwaite the Michele S. Maxian Award for Outstanding Public Defense Practitioner.[34] Almost a year later, in November 2014, the judge announced his ruling from the bench. He found that both low copy testing and the FST software had not yet gained general acceptance in the scientific community, and thus the test results could not be introduced at trial. The government made a last-gasp attempt to reopen the case, but even after considering those materials, the judge affirmed his initial position.[35]

Although the ruling in Collins's case derailed government efforts to introduce the FST software, it is far from the last word on the subject. In March 2015, in Schenectady, New York, John Wakefield stood accused of strangling Brett Wentworth with an amplifier cord. The major evidence against him was DNA found on the cord and on the victim's forearm and shirt collar. Wakefield, an acquaintance of Wentworth's, disputed those findings, but contended that even if his DNA was in fact present, it was likely because he had attended a party at the victim's home shortly before Wentworth's death.

To match Wakefield to the DNA samples, investigators had turned to Mark Perlin, creator of a software program called TrueAllele. Perlin had left his job as a senior scientist at Carnegie Mellon University to lead Cybergenetics, a private company he founded, which specializes in selling his DNA interpretation software. TrueAllele purports to take into account a wide range of variables that might affect the composition of a mixed DNA sample, including the overall size of the sample, the observed genetic markers, their relative quantities, and predictions about what markers might appear or disappear. By running a series of simulations, the software computes a series of probabilities and ultimately produces a likelihood ratio to express the probability that those results would be seen if the suspect had contributed DNA to the sample, versus if he or she had not.

As with the FST program, Perlin had presented his software to the New York DNA Subcommittee to gain its approval for use in New York state crime laboratories. But also as in the case of FST, his presentation did not include any information about the actual algorithms or how his software processed each of these different variables. In fact, not only did the subcommittee not know that information—no one outside of Perlin's company does. To a degree beyond even other for-profit purveyors of software of this kind, Perlin has remained steadfast in his resistance to disclose the source code or underlying information about the operation of his program.[36]

Although the DNA subcommittee had likewise approved TrueAllele years ago, the Wakefield case constituted the first time that TrueAllele results were presented in a New York court.[37] Thus, in accordance with state law, the judge held a hearing to determine whether the software had gained sufficient general acceptance to be admitted as evidence. At that hearing, Perlin admitted that no other scientists had seen his code or reviewed it directly, and he stood by his refusal to make it available, defending it as a "trade secret." In response, Wakefield's lawyer pointed out Perlin's self-interest in promoting its accuracy while at the same time insulating the program from scrutiny. On the stand, Perlin testified to receiving $4.5 million from his contracts with New York alone, and noted that he also had established or pending agreements in five other states.

Calling the software "voodoo," Wakefield's lawyer argued that the court should not admit such damning conclusions when no one could challenge the means used to arrive at them. But the judge rejected these claims. In a ruling that relied heavily on the approval given to the program by the DNA subcommittee, the judge found TrueAllele reliable, and its results admissible evidence.[38] At trial, the prosecution suggested that Wakefield killed Wentworth in the course of a robbery, and presented two inmates and a friend, all of whom claimed that Wakefield had admitted the crime to them. But the "star witness" was Perlin, who testified that his software's conclusion that it was 300 million times more probable that Wakefield had left the DNA at the scene than had an unrelated white person, and 2.25 and 5.88 billion times more probable than an unrelated Hispanic or black person, respectively. After deliberating for six hours, the jury convicted Wakefield.[39]

By coincidence, just as the initial hearing got under way in the Wakefield case, the news broke of a major scandal at the New York State Police crime lab. The issue? The state police lab had planned to start routinely using TrueAllele for all of its casework, and so analysts had to pass a proficiency test before they were allowed to operate it. Failure meant demotion. But when the results came in, the answers looked peculiarly similar. Managers suspected widespread cheating. At the close of the ensuing investigation, state police moved to terminate fifteen of the unit's thirty-six members.[40]

In a review of different software models, one set of researchers cautioned that "computer software is only as reliable as the analyst that is using it. There is the risk that, with complicated automated program[s], analysts will not understand the limitation and the program[ ] will be inadvertently used in situations where it is not appropriate to do so."[41] Had the cheating not been caught, it seems that half of the New York state police lab was well on their way to fulfilling that prediction. As it turned out, one of the analysts accused of cheating had been scheduled to testify in another case in the state days after the scandal broke, but a supervisor went to court to present the test results in the analyst's place. The jury in that case never heard why; defense lawyers were prohibited from asking questions about the cheating scandal.[42] In the words of DNA expert Dr. Dan E. Krane, "What's happening . . . with TrueAllele is they're not in their comfort zone. . . . It's sort of like taking someone who's had high school algebra and giving them a college-level, advanced differential equations quiz."[43] An international group of researchers echoed the sentiment in a research paper on statistical methods, noting that "the adoption of probabilistic models has been inhibited by the complexity of concepts that are largely outside the experience of case-working forensic scientists, coupled with lack of suitable training opportunities."[44] This state of affairs should alarm anyone who has used a computer and knows how buggy software can be; if those responsible for running the tests and explaining the results do not in fact understand what they are doing, the legal system's faith in their conclusions is misplaced.

Even if the software is operated by a trained expert, the source code still should be open and proven able to withstand challenge from disinterested, and experienced, reviewers. That is the only way to ensure that the results produced by a program that, on its face, seems to outperform other software packages in making use of the available information is doing so in a way that does not falsely inculpate suspects. This is especially true in light of the difficulty of replicating casework conditions when conducting tests of software programs; tests that use artificial sample conditions may return seemingly justified results, even though a test more closely approximating a real case would not. Finally, although consistency across analysts is important, and thus may favor models that rely less on input from an actual person, it should not come at the expense of ignoring the qualitative value that a well-trained analyst may provide nor at the expense of having the analyst know and understand the calculations done in a case.

Probabilistic software unquestionably represents an advance in DNA science. The lesson from these stories about the FST and TrueAllele programs should not be that efforts to develop such programs should be abandoned or never admissible in court. Instead, these illustrations should sound a caution about heading blindly down a dangerous path. Specifically, we should be wary of vesting all faith in the accuracy of DNA interpretation in a single individual, or company, with both a strong financial and personal stake in its own success and a refusal to open its code to scrutiny even under a protective court order. As a group of internationally renowned forensic scientists have written, "We do not advocate a 'black-box' approach. . . . Open-source is strongly encouraged since this solution offers unrestricted peer review and best assurance that methods are fit for purpose."[45]

Fortunately, abandoning closed, for-profit software programs does not mean abandoning this method of interpretation altogether. In fact, many options have the benefit of not only being more transparent but also free. Rather than spend taxpayer dollars on secret formulas that cannot be fully checked out, laboratories can explore open-source models more freely available. For instance, a recent study by the European network of forensic scientists tested a different, open-source platform known as LRmix.[46] Critically, the report acknowledged that LRmix is not a "black box solution"—meaning that there is a "strong interaction" between the analyst and software. Analysts must make choices about which alleles to credit and theories to test, which in turn requires a sophisticated understanding of both the science behind DNA testing and the principles underpinning the software.

After a training session in the use of the software, analysts at eighteen labs were asked to review two case files. Variations and glitches arose. One lab reported problems with the software with regard to one locus that appear traceable to the software's need to be run on more powerful computers. Two labs reported the statistical result in an inaccurate way. Most commonly, the labs seemed to struggle with the correct formulation of the various hypotheses that might be put forward by the defense. But the overall results were nonetheless somewhat promising.

One of the two cases involved a dismemberment in a Spanish village, where the accused was the victim's husband, a butcher.[47] In the actual case, when confronted with the evidence, the husband ultimately confessed to killing his seven-month-pregnant wife during a fight and dismembering her body to hide his crime. For the exercise, however, labs were asked to consider the results from the test of a knife, given that the accused had admitted he had recently cut himself. The critical question for the prosecution, then, was whether the victim's DNA was also on the knife. The defense, in contrast, might or might not concede the presence of the defendant's DNA, and would likely attribute any extraneous material to persons other than the victim. A majority of labs contrasted the prosecutor's theory that the knife had DNA from the suspect and victim with only one potential defense hypothesis: that it may have come from the suspect and an unknown person. But only three considered the possibility of two unknown contributors, and only one considered a prosecution theory that the knife contained the DNA of the victim and an unknown person, not the defendant. Two labs tested *defense* hypotheses that assumed the victim's DNA was on the knife, even though that position inculpated the defendant. As the study noted, "an important part of any training course is to provide guidelines and examples of how to formulate the propositions."

The wide variety in hypotheses points to one possible concern with these programs, which is their "exploratory nature." On the one hand, that may help uncover otherwise occult yet plausible explanations for complicated DNA mixtures. On the other hand, it may encourage parties on both sides to seek convoluted explanations to confirm their own pet theories. Keep in mind that this was a simple trial run of the use of LR-mix: neither file posed particularly challenging forensic questions; each involved a two-person mixture, where a major contributor was known.

Regardless, the results of the overall test were promising. The ultimate statistics in both cases were within one order of magnitude of one another, as opposed to the ten orders of magnitude spread seen in American studies. More significantly, the findings suggest that the use of probabilistic software may aid in reducing the wide amount of variation in match statistic reporting, and enable broader explanation of competing theories to explain the presence of genetic material. But these cases also underscore the need to insist upon robust training, full transparency, documentation of validation, and proficiency testing of end users when it comes to implementing new probabilistic software.

In sum, probabilistic software has great potential for the future, but there are still no established ways of testing the accuracy of these programs.[48] As one assessment of the wide variety of programs concluded, "The true answer in DNA interpretation is somewhat elusive and plausibly does not exist at all." Instead, the most that may be aimed for is making "the best use of all the available information in a logically robust manner."[49] As scientists and statisticians continue to refine and test various approaches, more will be learned about these programs' advantages and shortcomings. Without this kind of testing, scientific breakthroughs cannot occur, and this field is one that surely should be subjected to continued scrutiny and experimentation. But if we have learned one thing about the progress of science, it is that it thrives when tested among experts in an open exchange of knowledge, not when the only experiments are those conducted in court, using the lives and futures of human beings.

CHAPTER 7

Dangers of the Database:
Cold Hits and Coincidental Matches

IN 2001, STATES had just begun to make major inroads in collecting DNA from known offenders and storing the profiles in DNA databases. Kathryn Troyer worked as an analyst in the DNA unit of Arizona's state crime laboratory. At work one day, she received notice of something interesting.[1] Two seemingly unrelated individuals—one white and one black—shared the same two markers at nine of the thirteen places in the standard DNA profile. Indeed, they also shared one marker at the remaining four places—of twenty-six possible genetic differences, they had twenty-two in common. Yet that nine-locus genetic profile should have been exceedingly rare. According to the standard means of computing the random match probability, if you plucked a non-Hispanic white person at random from the population, there would be only a 1 in 754 million chance of finding that profile. For African Americans, the number was 1 in 561 billion, and for Southwest Hispanics, 1 in 113 trillion.[2] And yet here, in a database of just 65,493 people, it was appearing twice—and in people of different races.

Importantly, at that time, one of the most popular testing kits for forensic DNA analysts came in two parts—a nine-locus kit and a six-locus kit.[3] Because the kits were expensive and conducting DNA analysis took up a lot of lab time, many analysts did not bother typing a full thirteen-locus profile in every case. Instead, they routinely did only half the tests, reporting nine-locus matches that quickly turned into defendants' convictions. Analysts also routinely wrote in their reports, and testified under oath, that nine- and ten-locus matches were highly unusual and rarely seen.[4] For instance, Harvard professor Frederick Bieber, an early champion of aggressive programs of forensic DNA typing, testified in one criminal case that he had only seen a nine-locus match between two people once, and that was in a case of brothers.[5]

Intrigued by the prospect that such matches were in fact not uncommon, Troyer and two of her colleagues wrote up a quick summary of their findings and submitted the results to a major international conference on forensic DNA typing.[6] Her observations came to the attention of Bicka Barlow, a public defender in San Francisco. Barlow, a passionate attorney who held a master's degree in genetics along with her law degree, took immediate interest. As it happened, she was in the midst of defending a California man, John Puckett, accused of a rape and murder from thirty years earlier.

In 1972, nurse Diana Sylvester was found naked near her Christmas tree. She had been sexually assaulted and fatally stabbed. Police had collected forensic evidence, but DNA typing was still decades away. The case sat open until, over thirty years later, investigators dusted off the badly degraded DNA samples and tested them, running the results through the state database. A partial match linked then seventy-year-old, wheelchair-bound John Puckett to the only testable evidence in the case—sperm found on the body that showed reliable results at just five and a half loci, and possible results at another one and a half places. On the basis of this match, prosecutors charged Puckett with murder.[7]

Barlow promptly contacted Troyer for more information, but Todd Griffith, the head of the lab, intervened and denied her request. Shut out, Barlow sought a subpoena from an Arizona court to compel the lab to disclose its findings. Barlow called Troyer to testify at a hearing to decide whether to grant the request. Troyer testified that she had found not just one matching nine-locus pair, but ninety such paired matches. When the lab offered no explanation for why 1 in 1 trillion events were happening regularly in the Arizona database, the judge granted the subpoena. The order also included a directive to the lab to conduct a full search of the known offender database and report back all matching pairs.

Ultimately, that report showed that there were actually quite a large number of these pairwise matches. The Arizona database had only 65,493 people in it, each identified by the two markers at thirteen places that constituted his or her supposed DNA profile. Yet 122 sets of people shared the same genetic markers at 9 places of the 13, twenty pairs matched at 10 places, one pair matched at 11 places, and one pair matched at 12 places.[8] Only the 11- and 12-locus matches were confirmed siblings. It is akin to assuming that you have a fairly unique identifier—such as twenty-six digits that represent birthday, bank account, and social security numbers all combined together—only to learn that a significant number of people share most of those numbers, and in the same order, as you.

As news of these unexpected pairings swept the nation, lawyers in other cities pressed for similar searches. After all, if there were 122 pair-wise nine-locus matches in a roughly 65,000-person sized database, how many such matches might be found in the 11 million–person national database? A back-of-the-envelope calculation suggested the figure could be as high as 20,000. But rather than embrace the inquiry, the FBI effectively instituted a crackdown. Officials called Troyer's results "misleading" and "meaningless," and moved to suppress her findings.[9] The FBI also used its power as the guardian of the national database to bully states into refusing to conduct similar studies in their own databases. FBI leaders reprimanded the Arizona lab, claiming that disclosing the results violated its agreement with the FBI. They further threatened to cut off access to the national database to any lab that independently conducted their own such studies, although there was evidence that the threat was intended to scare judges more than lab officials.[10]

Why were Troyer's findings so explosive? The answer turns half on an understanding of math, and half on an understanding of law. And as is so often the case with forensic evidence, the gap between those two worlds proved critical.

THE COLD HIT CASE

At the time of Troyer's findings, state and national DNA databases had started to blossom. In the early days of DNA testing, most people thought of it as a tool to confirm the identity of a person that police had identified as a suspect in a crime. But it was on the brink of becoming something much more significant. The idea of "big data"—the use of vast networks of computers to churn unprecedented amounts of information—was on the cusp of taking off. For instance, although law enforcement agencies had amassed an incredible trove of fingerprint data, it was not until 1999—approximately the same time that DNA databases were born—that computerized searching became commonplace.[11]

With the advent of computerized networks of biological information, a new kind of case came to the fore. Specifically, the "cold hit" case was born. The FBI built the architecture for its large national repository of DNA profiles, and then put it to work. At first once a week—now twice a week—CODIS software automatically searches the database for associations between all the profiles contained therein.[12] Matches are called cold hits, because they are associations prompted by genetic identity, rather than on conventional investigative leads or information. Suppose a burglary occurs at a home. Crime scene analysts recover some blood by a broken window, which they expect belongs to the burglar. They type the sample, yielding a thirteen-locus DNA profile. Analysts can enter that profile into the forensic index. There, the profile will be searched against other crime scene evidence, as well as the convicted and arrested offender indices. If there is a match, the submitting laboratories will be notified. They can in turn exchange pertinent identifying information, such as the identity of a known offender whose profile matched that from the blood from the broken window. These kind of hits are known as *offender hits*.

Matches may also be made between crime scene samples, otherwise known as *forensic, scene-to-scene,* or *case-to-case* hits. So, suppose that the burglary occurs, but there is no match in the database to a known offender. The profile thus sits in the forensic database. Later, another burglary occurs across the same state. The crime lab recovers evidence, obtains a DNA profile, and uploads that profile to the forensic database. Although there may still not be a match to a known offender, the database will return a match to the earlier burglary. Now investigators know these two incidents are related, and may be part of a broader pattern of criminality by the same person.

Some cold hit cases become "hot" immediately upon investigation. Suppose that the burglar in our example took a valuable painting from the home of the victim. If police use a DNA database to identify a suspect and go to the home of that person, it certainly helps to confirm the individual's guilt if the missing painting is hanging in the suspect's living room. Similarly, scene-to-scene matches might help investigators narrow down a list of suspects by considering unique connections between people or places that inculpate a particular individual. In other words, a match in the DNA database can always be placed in context with the rest of the evidence, such as corroborating witness identifications or recovery of missing items. Even a criminal record of behavior similar to that alleged, while not always admissible in court, might assuage some concern that the DNA match is purely coincidental.

But some cold hit cases stay cold. Despite investigative efforts, little to no additional evidence may link a suspect to the crime. Or perhaps the mere fact of a match does not conclusively prove that the suspect committed the crime. A DNA match between the suspect and an intimate swabbing from a rape kit may appear fairly clear cut, as there are few innocent explanations for the presence of the suspect's DNA. But in other cases the evidence may be more ambiguous, such as a DNA match to a sample taken from a half-smoked cigarette at the scene, which might have been left by the perpetrator or by an innocent bystander.

Prosecutors proceed in both kinds of cases, not just those in which DNA is part of a constellation of evidence against the defendant. They have proved willing to press for conviction based on the DNA match alone, even in the absence of confirmatory evidence. Or they have defined "confirmatory" evidence in anemic terms—such the suspect's being the right age or gender. Even a prior record may be misleading; after all, virtually every person in the DNA database will have a prior record of some kind. In short, DNA databases raise the stakes of DNA testing. They may change what would otherwise be *confirmatory* evidence into the *sole* inculpatory evidence in a case. They create what are in effect one witness cases—and one *genetic* witness at that.[13]

In such cases, findings like Troyer's—and the uncertainty they engender and which started a national debate among mathematicians, lawyers, and forensic scientists—become indisputably important. The heart of the explanation for Troyer's matches lies in a mathematical parable known as the birthday problem. The lesson goes something like this: How many people must there be in a group before there is just over a 50 percent chance that two people in that group will have the same birthday? For example, the probability that a person's birthday is March 18 is 1 in 365, as there are 365 days in the year (excluding the complication of a leap-year birthday). Yet that is different from asking whether, in a group of people, any two people share any one of those 365 possible birthdays. Rather than keep one side of the equation "fixed" (March 18), this inquiry opens up both sides of the equation to chance—any single birthday as held by any two persons. Crunching the numbers, it turns out that it takes only twenty-three people before it is more likely than not that two share the same birthday.

This difference between asking "Does anyone in the database match this evidence?" versus "Does anyone in the database match anyone else?" explains why some forensic experts dismissed the Arizona findings as both expected and inconsequential. A sophisticated understanding of match statistics would have led anyone to expect some number of shared nine-locus pairs in the database. But a sophisticated appreciation of criminal trial practice explains why Troyer's findings took criminal justice actors by surprise. Police, prosecutors, testifying lab analysts, and even some defense attorneys found it hard to believe, even infuriating, that nine-locus matches were likely to be common in a large databases. Cases routinely proceeded on the basis of only a nine-locus database match, even without other clearly condemning evidence, because such matches were treated by lawyers and courts alike as conclusive proof of guilt.

Troyer's findings also rekindled the debate about the accuracy of DNA statistics, and led to a public call to allow qualified researchers access to the DNA database to test the validity of the assumptions of independence underlying match statistics. Over forty scientists and academics signed onto a letter published in *Science* magazine, calling for a range of "real-world tests of propositions that previously have been addressed only by simulation."[14] Granting such access was entirely in keeping with both law and practice: the law creating the national database specifically includes a provision for access if "personally identifiable information is removed, for a population statistics database, for identification research and protocol development purposes, or for quality control purposes." And in fact the FBI has granted that access to researchers aligned with its interests.[15] But given possible adverse findings, the FBI shut down all outside inquiries.

Instead, the FBI claimed that the database was not representative of the general national population—it contained too many close relatives at one extreme, and wildly divergent population groups at the other extreme. As leading scientists at the FBI wrote, "[o]bserved departures from expectations will occur using these databases."[16] Accordingly, they asserted that "9-, 10-, 11- and 12-locus (out of 13 loci) matching profiles have been observed, are expected, and do not call into question the reliability of statistical practices." No effort was made to explain the scope or degree of such expected departures, nor square their existence with the practice of generating match statistics that presume greater randomness.

Intriguingly, one population geneticist tried to reverse-engineer the Arizona findings, using the statistical practices that would be employed in the ordinary criminal case to see whether they squared with the large number of matches found in Arizona. Using models that assume the presence of siblings and different subpopulation groups, he found that "even for the best models, the probability of the Arizona observations is only 9%–12%"—that is, a very narrow set of conditions must hold for what was seen in Arizona to comport with how match statistics are routinely computed.[17] Without knowing if Arizona's matches were typical, researchers cannot be sure whether "modification of the underlying probability models may be required."

Instead of viewing the Arizona matches as an opportunity to refine and improve on the criminal justice system's use of DNA evidence, the government chose instead to try to bury any data at odds with its interest. Indeed, that is what happened next in John Puckett's specific case. The prosecutor proposed to tell the jury the random match probability, which was calculated as 1 in 1.1 million.[18] Partly in light of the Arizona findings, Barlow pressed the court to allow her to present to the jury an alternative match statistic computed in her case to be 1 in 3. That statistic, commonly referred to as the database match probability, or DMP, aims to discount the impact of the match by factoring in the effect of a search in the database. In other words, it tries to account statistically for the difference between a truly random match, and a match made among a finite pool of candidates. Barlow did not invent the DMP; rather, it was put forward as the proper method by a blue-ribbon panel of experts in what is considered the single most authoritative report on DNA evidence in criminal cases.[19]

The government contends that the database match statistic is misleading, because it artificially deflates the match statistic based on the size of the database searched, and does not account for the many ways in which a coincidental cold hit may be undermined—such as a match's failing to square with the suspect in terms of sex, age, or geography. But it is possible to take such information into account. And besides, it is unclear whether narrowing those demographics could unfairly incriminate swaths of innocent individuals. Most crime is committed by men, within a certain defined age range, and close to home. If sex, age, and geography are the way in which we differentiate a true match from a false one, those characteristics may in many cases provide little safeguard against wrongful accusation.

Amazingly, these two approaches were not the only ways of representing the statistical significance of Puckett's match.[20] Another method, sometimes called the Balding-Donnelly approach, after its major proponents, treated a search in a database as especially informative, because a single match also constituted an exclusion of all the other persons in the database.[21] For instance, if a search in the 11 million–person national database returns a match to only one individual, it signifies that attempts to match everyone else in the database failed. The net result can be a statistic even more inculpatory than would be obtained by using either the database match or random match methods.

Finally, still another approach—and probably the one most helpful to the jury—would have asked, "Of all the men who lived in the metropolitan area at the time of the killing, and who were the right age to have committed the offense, how many would likely match the crime scene evidence?"[22] This approach, nicknamed the n*p statistic by one of its proponents, helps "place[ ] the match probability p in perspective."[23] In Puckett's case, the result of such calculation was that at least two other people living in the area at that time matched the evidence.[24]

Each of these statistics generates very different interpretations of the significance of the match. Yet all are legitimate in one way or another, and there remains a lack of consensus as to which one deserves priority within the criminal justice system. A group of twenty-five renowned statisticians signed a joint letter stating they could all agree that the fact that a match was made through a database carried statistical meaning, even while acknowledging that they could not agree on a single method to express the significance of that match. Defense lawyers have argued that this disagreement among experts, and the vastly different picture painted by varying approaches, require courts to reject database match cases altogether. Alternatively, they have sought additional confirming testing, or at the very least, presentation of conflicting statistics.

Yet courts have rejected their entreaties, for understandable reasons. Throwing out database cases too quickly disregards the value of cases that are made through a database match. At the same time, ignoring the conflict paints an unfair picture of uniformity, and risks overstating the meaning of the match. Although presenting a bunch of different statistics may leave jurors in the awkward position of having to resolve among themselves a debate that even experienced statisticians cannot decide, it may be the best solution to an otherwise intractable problem.

As databases grow, and cold-hit searches continue, these questions become increasingly important. The determination by the FBI to move from a thirteen-locus CODIS standard to a twenty-plus-locus CODIS standard is animated in part by recognition that adventitious hits may occur already. [25] After all, large US databases continue to expand. A 2014 report by the European Network of Forensic Science Institutes (ENFSI) spelled it out in plain language: "[a]s DNA-databases become larger, the chance of finding adventitious matches also increases, especially with partial and mixed profiles and DNA-profiles of relatives, which have higher random match probabilities."[26] The report gives the example of a DNA profile that has a random match probability of 1 in 1 million. The mean result of searching such a profile in a 3 million–person database is "three matches and none of them may be the actual originator of the crime stain DNA-profile." ENFSI, which since its inception has paid careful attention to the adventitious or coincidental match problem, recommends that "every DNA-database manager . . . determine the chance of finding adventitious matches in his/her database."

To facilitate that process, ENFSI even provides a table of the likelihood of a coincidental match in a particular size database, given a particular profile's random match probability, though with the caveat that the calculation is complicated by the fact that far more than one crime scene profile is searched against the database each year. That is, the estimate must take into account not just the result of a single search of a profile against a large database, but a large number of searches against a large number of profiles in the database. For instance, as depicted in Table 7.1, ENFSI provides an estimate of the expected number of coincidental hits when roughly 70,000 crime scene profiles of differing random match probability values are compared to a database with 4 million known persons (roughly a third the size of the national database).[27]

In light of these findings, ENFSI's recommendation is twofold. First, acknowledging the risk of adventitious matches whenever DNA-database matches are found, it counsels:

TABLE 7.1   Expected number of adventitious matches when searching a DNA database of a given size with a DNA profile with a given random match probability.

DNA database size	RMP crime-related stain	Number of searches	Expected number of adventitious matches
4.000.000	1 : 10.000.000.000	50.000	20
	1 : 1.000.000.000	10.000	40
	1 : 100.000.000	5000	200
	1 : 10.000.000	3000	1200
	1 : 1.000.000	2000	8000
Total		70.000	

Source: Reprinted with permission from ENFSI DNA Working Group, *DNA-Database Management: Review and Recommendations* (April 2014), 31, Table 6.

DNA-databases contain large numbers of DNA-profiles of known persons and of biological traces related to unsolved crimes. When the number of DNA-profiles in a DNA-database increases, so does the chance of getting an adventitious match with a person who is not the actual donor of the trace. This is especially true for partial-DNA profiles and mixed-DNA profiles because the chance that they would match with a randomly chosen person is greater than the chance that a full single DNA-profile would match a randomly-chosen person. If there are doubts if the matching person is the donor of the trace, for instance because there is no other tactical or technical evidence which links the person to the crime, the possibility to do additional DNA-testing can be considered. This point of attention particularly applies to matches which are found as a result of . . . large scale . . . DNA-profile comparisons.[28]

Second, ENFSI recommends that managers of DNA databases keep a record of the number of adventitious matches, along with the "conditions under which they were found (size of the database, number of searches, etc.) for future analysis." ENFSI further advises "a warning should be included . . . when reporting a DNA database match." In contrast, here in the United States neither SWGDAM nor the NDIS operational manual—the FBI's DNA guidance documents—discuss the problem, much less possibility, of adventitious hits with any depth. The FBI's response to the issue continues to mirror its response to the revelation of the Arizona matches—to truncate any questioning.

In fact, the only "bad" cold hits that come to light are those in which law enforcement seriously blunders. There are no public statistics on how many database hits generate an investigation that stalls before the suspect is notified or arrested. Instead, what comes to public attention are cases in which the suspects are fortunate enough to have ironclad alibis. The first example of such a mistake occurred in 2000 in the United Kingdom. Using a six-locus match, police arrested a forty-nine-year-old man by the name of Raymond Easton for a burglary that occurred two hundred miles away. One account placed the rarity of that profile as 1 in 37 million.[29] Trouble was, Easton was severely disabled by late-stage Parkinson's disease, and thus was physically incapable of committing the crime. Additional testing eventually exonerated him.[30]

A similar case occurred in the United States, when a woman in Chicago was arrested and charged with a burglary based on DNA evidence found at the scene. Although the precise details have not been released, it seems that lab technicians communicated the match as a "hit" to police investigators, when in fact it was only a partial match. The error came to light only after the woman offered an indisputable alibi: she had been incarcerated on the day of the offense.[31]

Finally, another burglary prosecution, this one in Ohio, perhaps most directly illustrated the dangers of allowing misunderstood DNA evidence to overshadow what is known about a case. The owner of the home wrestled with an invader—described as short, stout, and balding—and managed to grab a few hairs from his head. A six-locus profile with a random match probability of 1.6 million was entered into the DNA database, where it sat for years until a newly loaded offender profile returned a match to Stephen Myers. Myers, a tall, slender man who would have been fifteen at the time of the burglary and had no connection to the city, was indicted for the offense. Investigators waved away the physical discrepancy by noting that appearances change. Fortunately, the prosecutors assigned to the case began to have second thoughts and ordered further testing. Those results proved that Myers was not the burglar, and he was released from jail—after seven months' awaiting trial.[32] In other cases, false matches have been revealed by the "perpetrator's" failing to match the right demographic characteristics, which hardly provides strong reassurance that there are adequate safeguards against the rush to convict based on a cold hit.[33]

As for John Puckett, Bicka Barlow took his case to trial. Ultimately, it is hard to know whether Puckett was guilty of the offenses or not. On the one hand, no other evidence directly connected him to the crime. None of the many fingerprints found at the scene matched him. At the time of the incident, the sole eyewitness's description had caused police to focus on a different man, but none of the original police investigators was able to testify, given the passage of time. That man had escaped from a mental institution just before the murder, and was suspected in two different sex offenses within a close radius of the victim's apartment. A drop of blood in the man's van had matched the victim, but when Barlow requested that it be tested, it was missing from the evidence file. That man had died several years after the killing, so he could not be confronted.

On the other hand, Puckett was the right age, gender, and race, and had been in the area at that time—all conditions that diminish the probability of coincidental match. He mostly matched the description given by the sole eyewitness, who unfortunately had never been shown Puckett's picture and had died before trial. The jury also heard from three women whom Puckett had threatened with a weapon and sexually assaulted around the same time—the convictions that had landed him in the database. Was Puckett rightly snared by genetic technologies that did not even exist at the time of his offense? Or had police found a coincidental database match, seen a record that fit, and just assumed it must be him?

Thanks to the judge's order, the jury heard only part of the story recounted here. The court excluded all evidence of the alternative suspect. Jurors were informed of the government's probability statistic—that there was a 1 in 1.1 million chance that a person picked at random would match the crime scene DNA. They even heard another government expert claim that the right way to calculate the statistic would have asked, "How many individuals do I have to examine before finding one whose DNA . . . would produce the profile seen" in the crime scene evidence?[34] By that metric, the jury was again told, the relevant number was "about 1 in 1.7 million."[35]

But although the jury was told the random match probability, it never heard that Puckett had been picked as a result of a nonrandom trawl through a police database. The court excluded this evidence even after the jury sent a note during deliberations, asking just how Puckett came to be identified.[36] Thus the jurors were not equipped to contextualize the random match probability information in the context of a database search. Without that information, the jurors would likely not understand that a profile considered "rare"—had other evidence pointed to the defendant—becomes less improbable when the defendant is found through a trawl in a large DNA database. In short, if a profile's probability is 1 in 1 million, then the government should expect a match if it looks for that profile in a 1 million–person database. The nature of statistics tells us that the profile ought to appear, whether that person committed the crime or not.

The jurors also never heard about the Arizona matches, or how they brought to life the fact that sharing alleles at nine loci is not uncommon. They did not learn that, even using the government's own probability statistic, around forty other people in California matched that crime scene evidence; or that, according to the database match statistic endorsed by the bible of forensic DNA, the National Research Council report, the probability of a match in the database searched by the government was 1 in 3. They never learned that it was likely that two other people in the area also matched the same evidence. In the end, the jury convicted and Puckett was sentenced to life without parole.

Since Puckett's case, every major court that has considered the question of how to treat match probabilities in a cold hit case has rejected the idea that cases should stall until the scholarly community determines the right approach.[37] However, most courts have also not taken the opposite tack—the one absurdly enforced by Puckett's trial court—that only the random match probability should be introduced. Instead, courts have tended to treat the scientific validity of the statistic as a factual question for juries to resolve—allowing both sides to present whichever statistics they deem most favorable.

But a handful of misguided courts continue to unjustly cabin the presentation of match statistics. One court even went so far as to declare that "the means by which a particular person comes to be suspected of a crime . . . is irrelevant to . . . that person's guilt or innocence."[38] Because the suspect is tested again to make the match, the court reasoned, that second test erases the effect of the database search. But in the words of one scholar, the court's theory is "patently fallacious."[39] The "argument that later searches replicate the match from the trawl is not responsive to the concern that an initial trawl dilutes the probative value of the matching DNA."[40] In other words, if you look in a database to find a redhead and do in fact find one, it means little to confirm that the redhead found does, in fact, have red hair. What matters is that you combed a database to find that characteristic. It's the difference between asking whether you'll pick a redhead if you open a yearbook and point randomly or can find one in an entire graduating class.

The problem of database match statistics also points to something more fundamentally wrong in the way in which forensic evidence is used by the criminal justice system—that enthusiasm for technological solutions to the enduring question of "whodunit?" often outstrips the actual capacity of the technology. As unsatisfying as it feels, there may be cases in which the absence of other evidence inculpating the defendant counsels against giving undue credence to questionable evidence of a DNA match. But rather than admit that not all questions can be answered, the criminal justice system tends to embrace flawed techniques and gloss over genuine concerns about their responsible implementation.

Unfortunately for John Puckett, there will be no further testing in his case. There will not even be vindication of his attorney's position, which later prevailed in the California courts, because Puckett died while his case was pending appeal. Besides, of all the evidentiary samples that were taken, only one matched to him, and the test that was done consumed the entirety of the sample. Puckett's case exemplifies why simply retesting the evidence, or testing more loci to achieve greater certainty about identity, is often not feasible. Old evidence makes for bad verification material.

The problem with cold hits is not likely to disappear. In fact, there is reason to believe that there will only be more, not fewer, such cases going forward. The federal government has encouraged police departments to reopen old unsolved cases and check for possible DNA evidence, and Congress has allocated funds in support.[41] Advocates for sexual assault victims have pressed investigators to look through their troves of untested rape kits in search of possible evidence. These efforts should be applauded, but they should also proceed with caution. New technologies have vastly improved technicians' ability to wrest typeable results from old and degraded samples, but those results are also often more contestable than the profile gleaned from a high-quality, well-preserved stain.

Nonetheless, matches will be made. In many cases, no other meaningful evidence will develop, and a jury or judge will be asked to decide whether a probabilistic statement of guilt—which may be more or less convincing, depending on how it is presented—alone is enough for a conviction.

CHAPTER 8

Confusion in the Box: DNA on Trial

MOST OF US are not good with statistics. We fear flying even though we are far more likely to die driving. We pour hard-earned dollars into slot machines and lotteries, but fail to save for retirement. We plaster "baby on board" stickers on the back of our cars, even though there is some (granted, shabby) evidence that it actually increases the risk of an accident.[1] So, what happens when we, as jurors, are asked to decide a defendant's fate on the basis of numbers?

To be fair, it turns out that most of us are not much better with other kinds of evidence, either. We trust we can separate honest witnesses from liars, when in fact we cannot. Intuition tells us that no one would admit to a crime they did not commit, when in fact false confessions occur all too often. But perhaps these feelings do not matter that much. After all, the vast majority of cases never even make it before a jury. Defendants plead guilty at a rate of 80 to 90 percent in most jurisdictions.

DNA cases throw into acute relief the question of the criminal justice system's capacity to handle complex statistical information. Simply put, DNA is different. Viewed by most legal actors and lay persons as irrefutable evidence of identity—which in many cases means guilt—DNA proof towers over other forms of evidence, and at times even stands alone, as in a true cold hit case. Yet subtle differences in how such evidence is conveyed can make all the difference in the world. In the case of John Puckett, convicted of murdering a nurse at Christmas on the basis of a partial DNA match, the issue was which of several legitimate DNA statistics should be presented to the jury: the one that placed the statistical significance of the match at 1 in 1.1 million, or the one that put the figure at 1 in 3.

But even when there is complete agreement about the precise statistic to use, its presentation can be deceptive. Any scientist will tell you that an appreciation of the error rate is critical to an accurate assessment of a statistical finding, yet most DNA evidence is presented either without error rates altogether or with unsupported claims of total accuracy. As a result, even well-meaning jurors have no way to assess the true strength of the evidence.

Moreover, lawyers, judges, and lay people have repeatedly failed to accurately convey the significance of a match. Even testifying experts have at times confused matters. As one commentator has noted, "DNA analysts . . . are not necessarily skilled in probability and statistics," and "[t]he failure of forensic analysts to apply appropriate statistical procedures is all too common."[2]

NOBODY'S PERFECT: THE IMPORTANCE OF ERROR RATES

Suppose you went to the doctor complaining of a headache, and after running some tests you were told that you had a deadly and untreatable cancer. Based on the evidence, there is only a 1 in 50-million chance that you will survive the year. The future looks bleak. You make plans for the end, but happily that day never seems to come. Over a year after your last appointment, you go back to the doctor, elated. You are convinced you are a medical miracle.

The doctor, however, seems unimpressed, even amused: "Oh, didn't I tell you. I am only right about that diagnosis fifty percent of the time. The other half of the time it turns out it was just a headache." You probably would let loose some choice words at that doctor, not the least of which might be *malpractice*. Even an error rate as low as 5 percent would likely have been important to you in planning for your future upon hearing such shocking news. Yet the doctor just replies, "I was sure I was right; besides, it didn't seem that important."

Or, what if upon hearing your diagnosis, you asked the doctor, "Is there any chance you might be mistaken?" and the doctor replied, "Not a chance. I have never made a single mistake. I have crafted my practice such that mistake is impossible." That kind of unrealistic arrogance might have sent you rapidly in the direction of a second opinion.

In the equally serious context of presenting statistics in a criminal case—where life in prison or even the death penalty itself is on the table—courts have tolerated both kinds of these bad doctors. They have both refused to demand evidence of an error rate, and they have accepted government assertions that DNA testing methods,[3] and the manner of execution,[4] have a "zero error rate."

But, of course, no scientific method is error-free. And no human being applying that method can consistently do so error-free, either. Error is an inherent part of any scientific endeavor; the goal is to seek it out and minimize it. Yet courts have largely turned a blind eye. And in doing so, they have perpetuated the myth that DNA evidence is "virtually infallible," when in reality it can be quite flawed.[5] As a result, jurors never hear a match probability statistic that incorporates the probability of error. They rarely if ever hear statistical evidence about the rate at which a perfectly executed DNA test might nonetheless fail or the rate at which mistakes are made in DNA testing in practice.

The first kind of error is known as methodological error, and represents the likelihood that the method used to do the DNA test will fail—whether to the benefit or detriment of a suspect. By illustration, imagine a lab has a set of protocols to guide how the various technical steps in DNA testing should be completed, or how to interpret the results of a DNA test. Those procedures should have been vetted through a series of experiments using the actual equipment in the lab and reference samples that mirror a range of conditions so that the "right" answer is known. For easy samples, such as a clinical-quality sample from a mouth swab of a suspect, the methodology's accuracy rate should be quite high. But for more difficult samples, such as degraded sample or mixtures, the accuracy rate will likely dip. In other words, even when a test is executed in perfect conformance with the lab's protocols, it will occasionally produce an erroneous result.

The second kind of error measures a different way in which testing might produce an erroneous result—namely, because mistakes are made. Of course, maximal care should be taken to avoid inadvertent error in the context of laboratory testing, as in other high-stakes contexts, such as hospitals or construction work. But it is unrealistic to expect a zero error rate, and any lab that purports to have one is either lying or not checking hard enough. Getting a lab to roughly estimate its actual error rate should be as easy as conducting a review of its error logs, assuming those logs are well kept and the lab has instituted strong norms for reporting. If so, then a survey of those logs would reveal the kinds of error that might lead to either false positives or false negatives. But gauging more subtle kinds of "error" might require measurements beyond just how often analysts have faltered in handling, testing, or interpreting evidence. For instance, it might be worthwhile to gauge how often analysts depart from the laboratory's established protocols, even if those departures are authorized and permissible in any particular case.

To capture the rate of error, lab-, unit-, or analyst-specific data would prove the most useful, but even industry-wide data might provide jurors with greater context in which to assess DNA evidence. Is it not helpful to know the general rate of accidents from texting while driving, even if a particular number might vary according to the characteristics of the driver or the vehicle? As leading forensic scientist Peter Gill has argued, "[i]t will usually be impossible to identify when or how [a specific error] happened, and this is why a *generalized* error rate is needed to counterbalance the imponderable uncertainties that are inherent to any prosecution case."[6]

Unfortunately, labs make virtually no error rate data available, either to the general public or to the lawyers in a specific case, and the courts have countenanced their recalcitrance. Indeed, courts tend to dismiss these questions in one of two ways. They either consider them irrelevant to the question whether the DNA test result should be admitted in evidence but allow questions related to error at trial,[7] or else preclude inquiry into general error rates altogether. In legal shorthand, at best the court deems error rates relevant to the *weight* of the evidence, not its admissibility. So long as the error is not so pervasive that it undermines any trust in the testing, the evidence should be admitted and it is up to the lawyers to argue over its reliability in that particular case.[8] The trouble is that, without access to the data required to calculate error rates, and without a court's forcing labs to quantify that rate before bringing evidence to court, lawyers are left to little more than guesswork and speculation.

In choosing to largely ignore error rates, courts unfortunately have followed the lead of one of two blue-ribbon commissions that took opposing positions on this issue. In 1992, the National Academy of Sciences convened a panel of experts in an attempt to quell legal disputes about the reliability of forensic DNA typing, but after a groundswell of resistance rose against that group's findings, a second group was commissioned in 1996 to issue a new report. Whereas the first report recommended that error rates be presented alongside match statistics, the second report rejected the idea. That later report, which most courts have followed, concluded:

> The question to be decided is not the general error rate for a laboratory or laboratories over time, but rather whether the laboratory doing DNA testing in this particular case made a critical error. The risk of error in any particular case depends on many variables (such as number of samples, redundancy in testing and analyst proficiency), and there is no simple equation to translate these variables into the probability that a reported match is spurious.[9]

The second blue-ribbon panel also argued that applying industry-wide statistical error rates ran the risk of "punishing" good labs for the mistakes of the "bad."[10] Lacking a "simple equation," the report simply threw up its hands, effectively rejecting the need to include error rates at all.

To be fair, there is some logic to this approach. It would make little sense to admit only demonstrably perfect evidence, precisely because no analyst or test can be flawless. Acknowledging that mistakes occur need not automatically imply wholesale exclusion of DNA evidence. For this reason, requiring that the match probability always be discounted by an error rate feels somewhat arbitrary. The kind and cause of common errors reveals as much about the risk of wrongful attribution than does the naked fact of error alone.

But the other extreme—simply ignoring or minimizing the importance of error rates—is equally untenable. Nondisclosure of error rates inculcates the myth that DNA testing is infallible, and enables labs to shirk from their duty to attend to the problem of error. While it is unlikely that DNA labs exhibit an error rate as high as the 50 percent example at the start of this chapter, our inability to pinpoint any specific number should raise concerns. As a leading scholar critical of the current hands-off approach to error rates has cautioned, "before deciding that an error rate of, say, 1 percent is acceptable or even 'good,' consider the error rate that would be tolerated in a commercial airliner (where an 'error' is defined as a potentially fatal mistake). Even seemingly low rates of error may be intolerable when the cost of the error is sufficiently high."[11]

By not requiring the proponent of DNA evidence to also demonstrate a suitably low error rate, courts in effect excuse the government from having to quantify error at all. Progress would be made even if courts demanded only industry-wide figures, notwithstanding the desirability of more targeted information about a particular lab's or analyst's performance. If nothing else, an industry-wide default would give "good" labs a vested interest in documenting their more favorable rates of error and in aspiring to rise above average. Even "bad" labs that stand to benefit from application of a more forgiving industry-wide rate could be called to account by attorneys who could at least point out that those labs have failed to record or disclose the lower rates seen in more professional laboratories.

Appellate courts like to point out that defendants *are* often given an opportunity to present evidence on the industry-wide, laboratory, or analyst error rates, but that they choose not do so.[12] The problem is, absent a court mandate, it is nearly impossible for an outsider to obtain this information. There are estimates and anecdotes, but not much more. For instance, a defense expert in one case testified to a "broad estimated" rate of human error, including mistakes and departures from policy. That expert placed the figure at "1 in 200, but admitted that it could be somewhere in between 1 in 20 and 1 in 20,000."[13]

In theory, the rare attorney that takes a case to trial might pursue open-ended questions with an analyst, such as, "Have you ever made a mistake in your work?" or "Did you mess up in this case in any way?" or "How many mistakes has your lab documented this month?"[14] But few attorneys will risk asking an opposing witness a question that could be answered in such a self-serving manner. If the witness denies having made any mistakes, or knowledge thereof—the likeliest course, whether true or not—the attorney has no way of showing that answer is untrue. So long as the data kept by laboratories tends to be shrouded in secrets, only crude approximations of error are possible. Lacking precise error rate data, most lawyers either ignore the issue or gloss over it, preferring no evidence to unconvincing evidence.

The legal system's disregard for the question of error does not just handicap jurors and opposing counsel; it can blindside the prosecution as well. In 2003, the Nassau County crime lab that conducted non-DNA forensic testing on Long Island, New York, underwent a series of investigations that ultimately led to a suspension of its accreditation and the issuance of a "scathing" report detailing the lab's incompetence. The trouble began after a supervisor noticed problems in the drug unit's testing; a preliminary investigation revealed that roughly 10 percent of results were seriously flawed, resulting in the reopening and overturning of a number of criminal cases.

The district attorney for Nassau County, however, learned of the concerns long after they initially surfaced, and only indirectly and informally when a member of the state forensic commission mentioned it.[15] Neither the lab personnel nor the police department that hosted the lab had bothered to alert the district attorney of the investigation. The Nassau County case illustrates just how insulated a lab's problems can remain, unless the lab discloses its failures voluntarily.

Without accountability to legal actors, laboratories have little external incentive to document and record their errors or to undertake meaningful corrective action. And even if they did, there are few outside checks on their own decisions of self-governance. And yet the sidelining of error rates is how we end up with pervasive scandals in the crime laboratory system. Papering over cracks only causes them to disappear from immediate view, and simply makes it all the more spectacular when the foundation finally gives out.

FALLACIES

In 2009, the Supreme Court agreed to hear the appeal of *McDaniel v. Brown*.[16] The case had not attracted much attention, and even the Supreme Court eventually canceled the oral argument, electing instead to issue a written order reversing the court below on a complex procedural point. The facts of the case were unsavory—the violent sexual assault of a nine-year-old girl. Moreover, although the victim, who knew both the defendant Troy Brown and his brother, had initially identified the brother as her assailant, circumstantial evidence pointed to the defendant's guilt. It was not the kind of case that tugs at one's sense of injustice.

Key to what began as a largely circumstantial case was its DNA evidence. A sample from the victim's underwear yielded a profile at five loci, using an older version of a DNA test. That profile in turn matched the defendant's. The government's DNA expert in the case was not a hack—she was an experienced analyst who had a master's degree in cell biology and had worked at the crime lab for over five years. Nonetheless, in what seems to be an innocent error compounded by pressure from the prosecutor on the stand, she fundamentally misrepresented the strength of the DNA match. And then her error was exacerbated by the prosecutor, whose rhetorical flourishes dramatically misrepresented the actual evidence and overstated his case.

In *McDaniel*, it was undisputed that there was a 1 in 3 million chance that a person picked at random would have the genetic profile seen in the crime scene evidence, and shared by the defendant Brown. In a population of 300 million, that suggests roughly one hundred unrelated people also had this same profile. Those are powerful statistics for a jury—particularly when other evidence is taken into consideration—but even still the prosecutor did not stop there.

Instead, the analyst was pressed to illustrate this statistic in a number of ways—all of which proved misleading. Specifically, the prosecutor asked her for "another way to show that statistic," namely, "what is the [percentage] likelihood that the DNA found" was from the defendant?[17] The analyst responded: "It would be 99.99[9]967 percent,"[18] and then wrote out an equation that showed that number subtracted from 100 percent as follows:

100.000000
−99.999967
.000033

The prosecutor then asked whether it would be "fair to say" that "the likelihood that it is *not* Troy Brown would be .000033?" and that "just another way of looking at it" would be to say that "the chances that the likelihood that . . . it's not the same . . . would be .000033?"[19] The analyst agreed that the two expressions were equivalent, adding, "[t]hat's the way the math comes out."[20] Underscoring the point for the jury, the judge said: "Let's make sure. It's the same thing—it's the same math just expressed differently. Is that correct?" The witness responded: "Yes. Exactly, Your Honor."[21]

In closing, the prosecutor then took the mistake one step further. He argued not just that there was a 99 percent chance that the DNA matched, but that it meant there was a 99 percent chance that the defendant was guilty. He told the jury that even though people do not understand the mechanics of flying, they still fly because those mechanics are reliable. So, too, he said, were these DNA numbers reliable. He closed by arguing,

> Now, the DNA. When you use the DNA, by itself, it's sufficient to prove beyond a shadow of a doubt that he committed this crime . . . sometimes people use the phrase, I'm 99 percent sure about that. Well, in this case the evidence shows—how sure can you be? 99.999967 percent sure.[22]

The jurors clearly found these arguments convincing, because they convicted Troy Brown. But as a statistical matter, they were wrong. And misrepresentations of this kind occur all too often in the presentation of genetic evidence.

The confusion arises in part because the statistic that most lawyers, judges, and jurors typically want to know when they hear about a DNA match is not the one that is presented in court. That is, they usually want to know, "Does the DNA match mean this defendant is guilty?" But DNA alone does not always answer the question of the defendant's guilt, for several reasons. Most obviously, a case will often turn on more than whether the accused matches the evidence. For instance, maybe there was a match, but other evidence will show that the defendant acted in self-defense. Or maybe the defendant matches the evidence but there is an innocent explanation, or the match is the product of unintentional transfer, contamination, or lab error.

But even when the DNA seems to match, and there is no other explanation for its presence, the inculpatory power of that match is only as strong as the statistics that accompany it. Suppose an asthma inhaler was found at a crime scene. Imagine that 1 in 10 adults suffer from asthma and carry an inhaler.[23] If the fact that the suspect carried an inhaler were the sole evidence linking the defendant to the crime, we should think twice before issuing a guilty verdict. After all, the match probability suggests that, if we randomly stopped adults on the street, 1 in 10 would have an inhaler. In other words, there is a 10 percent chance that a person totally unrelated to the crime is also carrying an inhaler.

But as happened in *McDaniel*, it is very easy for people to confuse that rarity statistic of 1 in 10 for something else. Here are some things that the match probability statistic does *not* mean, even though people often assume it does:

- There is a 10 percent chance that the defendant is not guilty.
- There is a 90 percent chance that the defendant is guilty.
- There is a 10 percent chance that the inhaler at the scene is not the defendant's.
- There is a 90 percent chance that the inhaler at the scene is the defendant's.
- There is a 10 percent chance that the inhaler belongs to someone *other* than the defendant.

These examples all suffer from a common mistaken premise, which is to conflate the DNA random match probability with the probability that the defendant is guilty or is the source of the evidence at the scene. All the match probability can relate is whether the defendant belongs within a group—however large or small—of people who may possibly have left the crime scene evidence. It says only:

- What is the likelihood that a randomly selected person would have the DNA profile seen in the crime scene evidence?

To answer the ultimate questions—Was this defendant's DNA at the scene? Is the defendant guilty?—requires reference to other evidence in the case.

Thus the first mistake, in *McDaniel*, was to wrongly assert the meaning of the match probability statistic. The match probability did *not* indicate a 99-plus percent chance that the defendant was the source of the DNA evidence, nor did it suggest a 0.000033 percent chance that he was not. It simply informed the jury of the *rarity* of the profile that was seen in both the crime scene evidence and the defendant. This is akin to observing that both the perpetrator and the defendant have a rose-shaped tattoo on the left forearm and asking how commonly that trait would be seen in the general population.

This misleading evidence was even more problematic in light of the expert's second mistake. Recall that the victim in the case initially identified the defendant's brother as the assailant. We know that related people are far more likely to share genetic information than are unrelated people, so a profile that is uncommon in the population at large is more likely to be found among close relatives. That raises the questions: What was the brother's DNA profile? Might it also have matched? What about three of the defendant's other brothers, two of whom lived in the area?

The five typed loci showed a random match probability of 1 in 3 million. But given the evidence in the case, which included that the victim initially identified Brown's brother as the assailant, another important match probability was a *familial* match probability. When asked the probability that a brother of the defendant shared the same genetic characteristics, the analyst responded: "In this case that turns out to be one in 6500. Meaning those two adults would have to mate and produce offspring 6500 times to come up with that pattern again."[24]

The prosecutor asked whether it would be "fair, then, to say that the likelihood of the parents having one child, and then the very next child having the same genetic code would be .02 percent?" and the analyst responded "yes."[25] Adjusting her figures, she wrote:

$$
\begin{array}{r}
100.00 \\
-99.982 \\
\hline
.02
\end{array}
$$

On cross-examination, the defense lawyer asked whether the numbers would change if there were two brothers, but the analyst answered no.[26] But, of course, the probabilities change dramatically if one considers relatedness.

In the end, the analyst's 1 in 6,500 figure appears plucked from thin air—later experts in the case were unable to surmise how she came to that conclusion. In fact, another expert calculated the probability that any one of Brown's four brothers would share the same five-locus profile, and came up with the figure of 1 in 263. And the probability that at least one of the four brothers shared the profile was as low as 1 in 66. But the jurors never heard these figures. Nor did the jurors hear that none of these statistics support what the analyst purported to show—which is whether the defendant was or was not the source.

Despite warnings in the *Federal Judicial Manual*,[27] the 1996 National Research Council report on DNA,[28] and judicial opinions in the United States and abroad,[29] these kinds of mistakes remain common. In fact, they are so common that they have acquired a host of nicknames. The most popular is the "prosecutor's fallacy," so named by leading DNA scholar Bill Thompson and his coauthor, Edward Schumann.[30] The reverse mistake—assuming that the evidence is necessarily exculpatory because of the percentage of nonmatching persons—is sometimes called the "defense lawyer's fallacy." Both arise in part because of analysts' confusion regarding the precise meaning of the statistics they are reciting, and because of nuances that even a well-schooled statistician might overlook. Such errors are further compounded by the lack of a common, standardized language with which to convey the significance of various degrees of match. Indeed, a landmark 2009 report by the National Academy of Sciences on the state of forensic evidence in the criminal courts identified this lack of standardization as one of the chief problems plaguing the field.[31]

And it is not just lawyers or trial courts who fall prey to mistakes of this kind. Professor Andrea Roth reviewed appellate court cases in which the question presented was whether a DNA match, without much more in the way of evidence, was enough to support a conviction. Alarmingly, that survey revealed that nearly every court succumbed to the prosecutor's fallacy. In the opinions, the courts equated the random match probability with a source or guilt probability.[32] Courts routinely describe the significance of a DNA match incorrectly, calling it the "probability of the sample belonging to anyone other than appellant," or "the odds . . . that another person was the source of that DNA."[33] Even more troubling, all of the courts affirmed the convictions, meaning that they found that these bare statistics supported conviction even though they fundamentally misunderstood what the bare statistics meant.

For instance, in one Tennessee case, the DNA was the main evidence connecting the defendant to the rape. The court upheld the conviction, reasoning that a random match probability of 1 in 5,128,000,000 in the African American population sufficed to prove guilt. But Professor Roth noted that, assuming an African American population of 5 million, the *source* probability would be more like 1 in 1,000.[34] While that statistic might be impressive enough to support a conviction to some, that figure was never even considered by the court.

Given how badly an experienced analyst botched a rather straightforward presentation of a match probability and a relatedness statistic in *McDaniel*, consider how many problems might arise in a more complicated factual situation. An analyst who is presenting probabilities for a complex mixture, or for a poor-quality low-copy sample, may fumble even more seriously. The marketing of software programs designed to produce such statistics may make matters worse. Many analysts may have no idea how the program reached the very number they are entrusted to recite in court, as evidenced by the rampant cheating among analysts at the New York state police lab on a test gauging their ability to operate such software. The end result is that the analysts who take the stand to present what is likely to be the most damning evidence against the defendant, may be incapable of describing how that damning statistical figure was reached.

JUSTICE IS NOT A MACHINE

Law's clumsy handling of statistical evidence is hardly new, and gestures toward the pervasive discomfort that many lawyers feel when asked to traffic in sophisticated numbers. Mathematician and Stanford professor Keith Devlin tells the story of a lecture he gave to "experienced and numerically sophisticated scientists, technologists, engineers, and others." He used the example of a DNA match probability of 1 in 15 quadrillion (1/15,000,000,000,000,000)—a typical figure for a strong DNA case. Upon hearing the number, the class burst out laughing, since "such a figure is total nonsense." In his words, "[n]othing in life ever comes remotely close to such a degree of accuracy. In most professions where numerical precision is important, including laboratory science, 1 in 10,000 is often difficult to achieve."[35] Yet these are the kinds of numbers routinely proffered without commentary in criminal courts.

Devlin's particular complaint related to the problem of database matches. But it points toward the greater issue of pretending that DNA match statistics alone are all that are needed to prove innocence or guilt. In a case with an astronomically low match probability figure, some would argue that the possibility of another matching person has been eliminated—that the rarity is so great it signals uniqueness, and thus the DNA matches none but the suspect.[36] These are known as "source attribution" statements, because they assert that the suspect is therefore the source of the tested DNA. For instance, the FBI and some other labs allow analysts to declare a person the "source" of the DNA material where the match probability is sufficiently remote, such as 1 in 300 billion.[37]

But moving from the quantitative assessment to qualitative assertions opens the door to controversy over where precisely the line should be drawn. When is a match statistic so overwhelmingly large that jurors should be told it is inconceivable that another person might have left the crime scene stain?[38] Labs set different thresholds. Sloppy labs may even fail to police analysts' adherence to their own thresholds. In the end, source attribution statements of this kind are lazy shortcuts—attempts to avoid the hard work of explaining the actual significance of a match, which every analyst should be capable of doing.

Moreover, even if experts were allowed to make such qualitative statements such as, "Defendant is the source of the crime scene stain," such statements must be reconciled with other evidence. We can imagine a farcical scene in which the testimony goes something like:

EXPERT: I can state with scientific certainty that it was the defendant's blood that was found at the scene.

ATTORNEY: Now, that is assuming no contamination?

EXPERT: Right.

ATTORNEY: Or problems with the testing process?

EXPERT: Correct.

ATTORNEY: Or misinterpretation of the profiles.

EXPERT: Precisely.

ATTORNEY: And no twins?

EXPERT: Presumably.

ATTORNEY: Or matching relatives?

EXPERT: Uh-huh.

ATTORNEY: Or coincidentally matching people in the same insular community?

EXPERT: Yes.

ATTORNEY: So what you are saying is that, assuming that you are right that it is the defendant's blood at the scene, it is the defendant's blood at the scene?

EXPERT: Exactly.

The silliness of this dialogue exposes a deeper rift between the world of law and the world of science than we would like to admit. There are many serious obstacles for DNA match statistics—not least of which include validating the accuracy of different approaches, reaching consensus on which of those approaches should be used when, ensuring that their significance is accurately conveyed in court, and checking that jurors accurately internalize that information when it is presented to them. Even if all of those concerns were resolved, one overarching issue would remain: justice is not reducible to an equation. As one statistician persuasively asserted, "it is usually not appropriate for the forensic scientist to pre-empt the jurors' assessment of the non-scientific evidence."[39] All of these conflicts are in a sense a proxy for this greater problem, which is that there will always be some resistance to judging people on the basis of statistics alone, even if those statistics are right.

In the 1970s, a series of articles by high-profile law professors explored the proper role of probabilities in the quest for justice. One famous hypothetical involved the "prison yard scenario."[40] A witness observes a guard trip and fall in a prison yard that holds twenty-five inmates. As the guard is on the ground unconscious, the prisoners huddle in conversation. One breaks away and goes to hide; the remaining twenty-four descend upon the guard and kill him. The witness is unable to identify any of the inmates—neither the twenty-four that participated in the killing nor the one that did not. Is it fair to convict any one inmate for the killing, given a 96 percent chance of guilt? Most people recoil from the prospect, and refuse to convict a possibly innocent person based on a naked statistic, even though the same evidence presented qualitatively—say, a witness who said he was 96 percent sure that this inmate participated—would satisfy them.

In a recent case from California, an appellate court confronted a version of this dilemma when it overturned the conviction of a man named Pedro Arevalo. Arevalo was accused of a burglary of a nail salon. A careful search for evidence turned up a rock out of place at the scene, which investigators assumed was used to shatter the glass found by the door that allowed the burglar to gain entry. When Arevalo's DNA matched that from the rock, prosecutors brought charges and a jury convicted. But the court overturned the conviction. The judges found that there was insufficient evidence that Arevalo's DNA was left on the rock at a time proximate to the burglary, or that the rock was used to break into the salon. In other words, the court felt uncomfortable resting conviction on a series of raw statistics—not the overt ones about the DNA evidence, but the implied ones, such as the probability that an unexplained rock found in a recently burglarized nail salon could be disconnected to the case.

Recall the Puckett case. In a book discussing math in the court system, a mother-daughter pair of mathematicians named Leila Schneps and Coralie Colmez analyzed the broadly disparate statistics of 1 in 1.1 million offered by the prosecution and 1 in 3 suggested by the defense.

Their conclusion? "Both of [the numbers] make sense, but neither of them actually gives an estimation of the probability that Puckett is innocent of the crime; they are measuring something different."[41] Indeed, the 1 in 1.1 million figure—the random match probability—suggested that in a population of 310 million (such the United States), around three hundred people would have also matched the evidence, or that there was a 299 in 300 chance that Puckett was not the source. In contrast, although the 1 in 3 figure sounds powerfully exculpatory, it was not quite right, either. It did show the likelihood that searching in a 338,000-person database would turn up a coincidental match, but it did not account for the fact that this match would also fit the description of the assailant in other ways (age, sex, and the like). It also did not answer how likely it would be that a person outside the database would match both the DNA and those characteristics, too.

The real question that everyone wanted the DNA to answer, Schneps and Colmez pointed out, was, what were Puckett's chances of being innocent? Was the match a red herring or a mistake? The response to those questions requires a lot more calculation than captured by either the prosecution or the defense numbers. Schneps and Colmez started with the random match probability, and tacked on estimated probabilities for race, proximity to California, male, inclined to commit a sex crime, and over age sixty-five. They then calculated the likelihood that two persons fitting all these descriptors existed—if only one existed, Puckett could be presumed guilty. Their cobbled-together figures led to there being a 1 in 70 chance that a second person matched all these descriptors, including the DNA.[42]

But, of course, as noble as the effort may have been, that number is not quite right, either. A shrewd prosecutor would have tried to winnow the characteristics down even more. Did the number capture those persons who would have had the physical capacity to undertake the attack? What about the factoring out the percentage of sexual abusers not interested in adult women? At the other end, the defense would nitpick the race figures that relied on national numbers rather than state or local data, or whether the sex offenders number dramatically underestimated the actual rate of offending, and so on.

Moreover, when liberty is at stake, it is sensible for jurors to give even outlandish probabilities serious consideration. After all, rare events do occur. As any player of poker knows, the probability of dealing oneself a royal flush, in a random deal of cards, is only 0.000154 percent, or 1 in 650,000—and yet when that hand is dealt it does not mean there is a 99.9 percent chance that someone is cheating. A player at that poker game would likely determine whether to trust a purported royal flush based in part on the statistical probability, but also on whether the other player was a friend or a known cardsharp. Similarly, DNA is at its best when it bolsters other evidence, as opposed to being presented as the only real evidence of guilt.

None of this is to say that jurors always get it right. They may trust a witness who should not be trusted, based on intuitions that are faulty or founded in bias. Conversely, and probably more often, they bow to impressive numbers, lodging their faith in the science of DNA analysis. In fact, jurors may repose such trust in DNA experts that they may credit impressive statistics in the face of contrary evidence, or despite serious questions of evidentiary integrity. Whether jurors follow or rebuke DNA evidence, it is still their sense of it as fact, rather than an assessment of statistical probability, that triumphs.

This resistance to quantitation of evidence also partially explains the long-standing hostility in the American criminal justice system to what is known as Bayesian analysis. Bayes's theorem[43] is a way of assessing the strength of the DNA match while also taking the other evidence into account. It effectively asks, what is the probability that this person was guilty based on the non-DNA evidence, and then magnifies or diminishes that probability according to what would be expected if the prosecution was right, versus the defense. The non-DNA probability is called the *prior probability*, which in a typical case is then divided by the *random match probability*, or the probability that the DNA match occurred by chance.

Criminal courts have largely rejected the Bayesian approach, to the consternation of many scholarly advocates of the method.[44] The major hang-up, by many estimations, is in calculating the prior probability. It is easy to see why allowing the prosecutor or defense lawyer to fix a prior probability based on an impression of the strength of the non-DNA evidence would usurp the jury's role, and therefore violate the constitutional guarantee to judgment by a jury of one's peers. But the alternative—providing a sliding scale of probabilities that jurors could pick from based on their own sensibilities—has also met resistance. The process of weighing evidence in a case is seen as too holistic and intuitive to try to break it down into discrete bits—DNA here, non-DNA there—or assign specific probabilities. Indeed, courts have even struggled to instruct juries on how to think of the "reasonable doubt," running into trouble whether trying to describe it numerically or in ordinary language.[45]

That suggests that the reluctance comes from some place deeper than reservations about juror usurpation. It suggests an ineluctable conflict between quantitative and qualitative evidence—between Spock and Kirk, reason and intuition. It is the same conflict laid bare by Schneps and Colmez's ambitious calculation. And the same hurdle researchers encountered when testing the prison yard hypothetical.

The mathematician may see a world reducible to probabilities that, while fallible and imperfect, nonetheless well approximate what is true. But others believe there are some qualities that cold, hard numbers can never fully capture. A juror who trusts a witness's assertion of 96 percent confidence may know intellectually that the witness can be wrong, or that this trust may be misplaced, but the decision *to trust* provides shelter from those worries. In contrast, a juror told that there is one prisoner who is definitely innocent, and yet asked to ignore that the defendant on whom they pass judgment might be that one, finds little such comforts. The sterility of numbers strips away the reassurance found in human connection. We talk about the "machinery of justice" but we do not mean it literally. Intuition, gut, and instinct are the motors of the criminal justice system. However fallible they may be—and history suggests they are flawed—they are salutes to our humanity, as profoundly imperfect as that is as well. Is it any mystery why we might not readily relinquish them, even before the altar of DNA?

CHAPTER 9

Fishing for Suspects

GO FISH IS a popular children's card game. Each player draws a hand from the deck, then takes turns asking other players whether they have a particular kind of card. If a player has the card, it must be handed over to the requester. If not, the player says, "Go fish," and the requester draws a card from the deck. The goal is to amass as many full suits of cards as possible until all the cards run out. To win at Go Fish, all you need is a little bit of luck and a good memory.

DNA databases are not meant to be played like Go Fish. And yet without proper controls, that is just how they may be misused to obtain criminal evidence. Legal authorities insist that DNA databases are closely regulated, safeguarded by a litany of rules, and therefore incapable of being exploited or manipulated, at least without fear of criminal penalties. But the reality is a bit different.

To be sure, the FBI has developed national standards that limit how the national database is used and curtail its access. The most recent manual runs ninety-two pages long, and details precisely when genetic profiles may be added to the national database. These standards impose restrictions that limit uploads to profiles generated by competent analysts at qualified laboratories. They also limit access to the database to a narrow number of trained persons, and require that connected computer terminals be physically cordoned off from general use. The federal statute that created the national DNA database even warns that "access to the index is subject to cancellation if the quality control and privacy requirements . . . are not met."[1]

But, as might be expected, laboratories' actual compliance with the constellation of rules and procedures surrounding DNA databases is far from perfect. Ample evidence demonstrates that just as labs have struggled with quality-control issues concerning the testing of DNA samples, so, too, have they found it difficult to comply with the rules meant to limit and restrict the composition and use of DNA databases.

Unlike quality assurance monitoring through the accreditation process, which remains shrouded in secrecy and appears largely ineffectual, the auditing process for DNA database compliance exhibits both greater rigor and greater commitment to principles of transparency and accountability. Since 2010 the Department of Justice has standardized and published the entire audit report for DNA laboratories that participate in the national database system. Also unlike accreditation reviews, which largely constitute paper evaluations, these audits appear to have real meat to them.[2] Auditors review access and documentation policies for compliance, verifying things like whether database access is restricted to authorized users or whether documents are retained as required. Then, as part of the standard review process since 2010, national database administrators pull one hundred random files associated with DNA database uploads, and check them for full compliance with the database rules.

Considered as a whole, these audits reveal that there is a wide range of compliance. Almost half of the labs do not pass the paper review; ten labs of the twenty-two were found noncompliant due to infringements as minor as neglecting to back up data in a timely fashion to as serious as failing to confirm matches or notify investigators of hits. Several labs did not sufficiently safeguard DNA profiles from general access, or failed to maintain proper documentation to support their findings. Auditors also found instances of unreliable data that did not support an asserted profile, as well as typographical errors that resulted in incorrect entries.

Perhaps most troubling, a large proportion of labs upload DNA profiles that the rules do not authorize. On average, the twenty-two labs audited since 2010 exhibited a 6 percent error rate in uploading—that is, six in one hundred samples were put in the DNA database but should not have been there. Only one lab—in Missoula, Montana—was in full compliance. Many labs fell within the 4 to 9 percent error rate zone. But some labs showed extreme misunderstandings about the proper use of the database. The 2012 audit of the Santa Clara District Attorney's Crime

Laboratory in San Jose, California, revealed that it had loaded into the national database a whopping thirty-two DNA profiles that should not have been there—suggesting a one in three error rate (given that it has contributed almost 3,000 DNA profiles overall, by extrapolation the lab has contributed roughly a thousand DNA profiles to the national database in violation of the rules). Of those thirty-two DNA profiles, twenty were insufficiently connected to the crime for which they were created— which by inference suggests that roughly one fifth of San Jose's federal submissions may not in fact be connected to the crime scene.

From just the twenty-two audits conducted in the past five years, it would seem that mistakes of this kind are common. For instance, a number of labs have uploaded victims' DNA profiles to the national database. The 2010 audit of the Bexar County Criminal Investigation Lab in San Antonio, Texas, revealed eleven erroneously entered profiles, of which nine were the known profiles of crime victims, or one in ten of its samples.[3] Given that this lab has contributed roughly 1,800 samples to the forensic database, and almost 1 in 10 of its samples belonged to victims, it is possible to conjecture that roughly 180 victim profiles from that county may wrongly be in the DNA database.

The audits from before 2010 paint an even spottier compliance picture. Again, auditors typically selected one hundred files to assess compliance. In these spot checks, of sixty-nine labs, roughly a third had uploaded victim profiles to the database, including two labs whose rate exceeded 1 in 10.[4] Labs also routinely uploaded profiles from evidence not clearly connected to the crime scene, or associated with persons other than the perpetrator of the crime (including one sample from the victim's husband, which had been provided as an elimination sample). There were also instances of errors in entering information, including inaccurate profiles.

Of course, these audits provide only a snapshot of how well those using the DNA database hew to the law in uploading profiles and conducting searches. Over 190 laboratories across the United States participate in the national database system, yet only twenty-two labs have been audited in the past five years.[5] Extrapolating the observed data to the forensic database in total, the picture is somewhat disturbing. As noted, on average, 6 percent of the sampled entries were erroneous. Thus, of the current 600,000-odd forensic profiles in the national system, it might be estimated that roughly 36,000 should not be there.

But although audits help ensure the integrity of the national database, they nonetheless fall short of serving as a total safeguard against database abuse, in several ways. First, they review only those profiles uploaded to the national database, not the many more kept in state or local databases. Second, they only monitor compliance with the rules about which profiles belong in the database, not whether searches conducted within the database also follow the rules.

The problem of unauthorized searches came to light in a case in San Francisco. At the center of the misconduct was a laboratory supervisor named Cherisse Boland. Boland, a longtime veteran of the lab, was no stranger to controversy. In late 2009, the San Francisco district attorney's office prosecuted a 2007 murder in which it was alleged that two men chased another man on their bikes, then dropped the bikes and cornered the victim, killing him.[6] The bikes were recovered at the scene, and Boland performed DNA testing on samples from the handlebars. In her testimony before the grand jury and at trial, Boland testified that DNA from each bicycle matched each defendant.

At trial, however, one of the defendants was represented by Bicka Barlow—the same attorney who had represented John Puckett in the cold hit case that raised the question of how to represent the meaning of the match. Barlow looked beyond Boland's written report and studied the underlying data, and bolstered by defense expert Dr. Edward Blake, noticed something funny. Although a small amount of DNA found on the handles was consistent with the defendants' profiles, each handle had a much greater amount of DNA from another, unknown person. On cross-examination, Barlow drew the jury's attention to this unknown person, and peppered Boland with questions about why she had obscured those findings in her report. She also asked why Boland had not uploaded the profile of that person to the state or national database, to see whether it matched to a potential suspect. In response, Boland simply claimed that the underlying data were part of the document package she had conveyed to the prosecutor, and that she did not seek a match to any third party because she felt that person was not involved in the crime.[7]

Both defendants were acquitted, but the experience led the district attorney's office to ask Rockne Harmon, a former prosecutor best known for his DNA work on the O. J. Simpson prosecution team, for help. A staunch champion of DNA testing, Harmon had long antagonized defense lawyers with his brash demeanor and unwavering confidence in

DNA testing. Three years earlier the district attorney had asked him to consult on implementing a cold-case DNA program for the office, and he was in the midst of that process when he heard about the acquittal, and proposed looking into the case. At the time, few of his adversaries would have guessed he would turn out to be an ally to the greater cause of laboratory integrity.

In fact, Harmon's findings included a memo that excoriated the DNA lab.[8] He specifically singled out the work of Cherisse Boland in connection with the murder case, noting that Boland had substituted her personal judgment about what evidence was relevant for that of the investigators and prosecutors in the case. In a later conversation, he drew an analogy:

> Just imagine there's a rape case, and this is a vaginal swab and the cops have a suspect, and you do the typing and you get a full profile. And . . . [the cops] asked me if it was him. They report back and say it's not him, or I didn't get his profile. Well, the fact that somebody else is there screams out at you, and it can't be ignored. So her attempt to rationalize what I say is bad scientific practice, to me that makes it even worse. It was deliberate. She said, They only asked me if those two guys were in there, and not whether there was a major profile in there.[9]

Harmon submitted his findings to the district attorney in March 2010, ironically just two months before the police chief would shutter the drug-testing section of the police lab as a result of admissions by a different longtime analyst that she had been stealing cocaine for personal use. Harmon's memo also arrived just five months before auditors arrived to conduct the accrediting review of the laboratory. But when the review took place, no one at the lab shared his memo or acknowledged that grave concerns about the lab's integrity had been raised, even though Harmon had specifically asked for it to be brought to their attention, and some junior officials had prodded the leadership to disclose it.[10] The lab was accredited; had it failed that inspection, it would have lost access to the national database and its work in criminal cases would have come under intense scrutiny.

Shortly after the lab won renewed accreditation, in January 2011, a journalist at *SF Weekly* learned of the memo's existence and began raising questions about whether it had been unjustly buried. When asked, public officials denied its existence, but eventually a judge held a hearing and heard testimony from Harmon.[11] At the hearing, Harmon singled out Boland as having not just acted incompetently but disingenuously when testifying in the homicide case,[12] affirming that her behavior was "the closest thing you can get to out-and-out lying, prevaricating." Harmon added that he suspected that lab officials had tried to suppress the memo and cover up any reports of their wrongdoing, calling it "a deliberate attempt to subvert the inspection review process by the police department."[13]

Nonetheless, Boland stayed on at the lab. And the legacy of Boland's dubious practices are still playing out in criminal cases. At the turn of the new year in 2015, the case of Marco Hernandez was winding its way through the courts. Hernandez stood accused of molesting his young stepdaughter in 2011. The victim named Hernandez directly, and he partially confessed when confronted with some evidence in the case. In the course of the investigation, the victim's mother had also provided a pair of underwear for forensic analysis.

Testing fell to Mignon Dunbar, an analyst then under Boland's supervision. Dunbar's exam revealed sperm deep in the seam of the underwear. The defense expert speculated that it might be the result of laundry transfer, but the prosecution theorized that the stain was evidence of the abuse. The sample was of such low quality that testing yielded an array of data indicating that the sample was a mixture of at least two, and possibly more, contributors. Oddly, another male profile had turned up in a different test, but Dunbar disregarded those findings. A sample was ordered from Hernandez, and ultimately his DNA profile was judged consistent with that of a lesser contributor.

So far, the entire process was fairly ordinary. But then something less typical occurred. Dunbar sought permission to upload the crime scene profile to the state DNA database.[14] Such a step might be viewed as unorthodox, since typically crime scene samples are uploaded to the database when investigators are seeking a suspect; in Hernandez's case, they already had their man. Nevertheless, it is possible to enter a crime scene profile into the database that is associated with a "solved" case—that is, a case such as Hernandez's where the lab has already associated the crime scene evidence with a known person.

The reason for uploading a sample from a solved crime, as Dunbar later explained on the witness stand, "is to provide investigative information to other laboratories or other law enforcement agencies."[15] It serves, in other words, as a backdoor way of putting more known profiles into the database. Because the forensic sample will be marked as "solved," labs that upload other crime scene profiles found to match that sample can simply consult the original "solved" profile lab to obtain identifying information about the perpetrator. In this way, labs can effectively evade restrictions on when known profiles may be uploaded, or must be expunged. This practice, while technically compliant with the database entry rules, certainly seems to violate their spirit when done as an indirect way to enter a known person's profile into the database.

But in Hernandez's case, it was not just that Dunbar asked and Boland approved the uploading of a solved forensic sample. It was how Dunbar did it. When a forensic sample is uploaded into the database, the presumption is that the markers entered reflect the profiles found in the crime scene evidence. Where there is reason to doubt that those markers are reliable—for instance, if the profile has too little information to be useful or the quality of the results suggest that the markers do not reflect the actual genetic profile of the material—analysts cannot make an entry. To do so violates the basic precept of "garbage in, garbage out"—a particularly dangerous exercise when it comes to DNA databases, because "garbage in" may actually lead to a coincidental or accidental match that another lab may fail to recognize as garbage.

In Hernandez's case, however, the quality of the test results made definitive interpretation impossible. Dunbar and Boland concluded that the test results supported at least two alternative readings. Yet rather than resign themselves to such uncertainty, they decided to use the DNA database as a way of picking between the alternatives. At trial, Dunbar conceded that there are rules regarding what may be uploaded to the crime scene database, including that the sample "can't be a completely messy, indistinguishable mixture. It has to be—there has to be some—I actually try to resolve out a profile."[16] Yet she nonetheless uploaded both profiles into the state database in a game of genetic Go Fish. One version of the evidence returned five candidate matches; the other resulted in twenty-eight.[17] Dunbar later testified that she compared all the matches and concluded that the one to Hernandez best fit the evidence; another supervisor concluded that a second candidate was equally plausible. At trial, lab personnel claimed they could not reproduce those comparisons, or even attest to who had originally made the comparisons, because the lab notes had been destroyed, in violation of lab policy.[18]

Apart from the unorthodoxy of using the database as a kind of interpretive tool—querying alternative interpretations of the crime scene evidence to see what sticks, as opposed to conducting an analysis of the evidence to discern a genetic profile and then seek a match—the defense argued that Dunbar's actions also raised serious disclosure concerns. In the materials provided to the defense about the DNA testing, the uncertainty and ambiguity she had encountered in testing the evidence was largely glossed over.[19] Specifically, Dunbar's DNA report did not directly state that she was torn between two interpretations of the evidence. The report simply said that a profile in the evidence fit Hernandez, along with a second contributor to the sample that was neither the victim nor Hernandez, rather than indicate that the findings were inconclusive, or that another reading of the evidence would exclude Hernandez.[20] And finally, the materials disclosed by the lab made no mention of the two searches in the database, including the first search that had turned up five possible matches, none of whom were Hernandez. That information came to light only because a shrewd defense lawyer noticed that a document disclosed on the eve of trial referenced the "second" interpretation, which led her to aggressively seek more information about any "first" interpretation that might have been generated.[21]

In short, Dunbar, with Boland's approval, tested a crime scene sample but could not determine precisely what DNA profiles were present in that sample. Yet rather than write a report that declared the results "inconclusive," or "uninterpretable," as required by the lab's protocols, she instead went fishing in the state database to see whether any of a number of possible interpretations might work. Her first guess turned up nothing, but her second guess proved more fruitful, since Hernandez was in fact one of twenty-eight possible matches. But, of course, DNA databases are not meant to be interpretative tools, and under no circumstances is "throw it against the database and see what sticks" a proper way to interpret difficult samples. What is more, hiding and obscuring those actions—so that the report papers over the analyst's own uncertainty in the findings, and makes it seem as though there was never any ambiguity—displays precisely the kind of results-oriented, rather than science- or truth-oriented, mind-set that has long corrupted the field of forensic testing.

Hernandez was eventually convicted at trial. But Dunbar and Boland's story does not end there. As the facts of the case emerged at the start of 2015, defense attorney Bicka Barlow lodged a complaint with the San Francisco chief of police. As the entity that oversees the crime lab, the police department is the one entrusted with conducting investigations into serious misconduct, as required by a federal lab funding law.[22] It subsequently came to light that both Boland and Dunbar had been suspended from the DNA unit.[23] Each had failed a statewide proficiency test meant to ensure basic competence. Dunbar had improperly analyzed a DNA sample on the test, and Boland signed off on the analysis as accurate. According to a supervisor in the unit, they were the only two analysts in the state to get the answer wrong, and their work showed "a fundamental lack of application and/or understanding of the unit procedures, . . . "[24] The attention called to their practices in the Hernandez case eventually led the chief of police, who heads the crime lab, to announce that all 1,400 cases on which they had worked would undergo review.[25] And history has repeated itself in another way. As happened in 2010, the crisis around Boland's practices has surfaced just as the DNA unit readies for its five-year accreditation review.

Although the practices that came to light in the Hernandez case raise numerous concerns, they may not be limited to one set of rogue criminalists. In a case in Missouri, for instance, the state database administrator testified that no rules prohibited an analyst from entering the DNA profile from a crime scene sample into the database even though the analyst had already matched the crime evidence to the DNA profile of a known suspect in the case.[26] Again, the reason to do so, she surmised, would be to link that crime scene profile to any other unsolved crimes in the database—the backdoor way of inputting profiles of known persons that might otherwise be ineligible for upload. Analysts in the Missouri case also admitted to testing multiple interpretations of the same data through alternative searches, as happened in San Francisco.[27] Just how pervasive or widespread these practices are, however, is hard to know.

Clear data about how exactly DNA analysts use national, state, and local DNA databases is particularly hard to access for several reasons. Chief among them is an interpretive decision that the FBI made early on that conveniently shelters the database, and the searches conducted therein, from any external scrutiny.[28] Specifically, the FBI has taken the narrowest reading of the law authorizing the construction of a database, which limits disclosure to four categories:

(A) to criminal justice agencies for law enforcement identification purposes;

(B) in judicial proceedings, if otherwise admissible pursuant to applicable statutes or rules;

(C) for criminal defense purposes, to a defendant, who shall have access to samples and analyses performed in connection with the case in which such defendant is charged; or

(D) if personally identifiable information is removed, for a population statistics database, for identification research and protocol development purposes, or for quality control purposes.[29]

On the plus side, a narrow interpretation of these rules has led the FBI to carefully guard the identifying information of persons in the database. The rules define a "match" as any association between profiles in the database, whereas a "hit" is a match that has been verified through testing.[30] Because all profiles are stored anonymously under specimen identifiers, a laboratory cannot easily skip the confirmatory steps required to transform a match into a hit and obtain the suspect's personal information. But the drawback of the FBI's approach is that it has also been used to shield others from scrutinizing how searches are conducted, and prevented objective gathering of data about the success rate of DNA match efforts.

So, for example, in some jurisdictions, the defense may receive a "match report" that lists the number of candidates whose profiles appeared to match that of the crime scene evidence. Montana, for instance, entitles a criminal defendant to "information in the DNA Identification index relating to the number of requests previously made for comparison searches relating to the defendant and the names of the requesting parties."[31] But counsel generally cannot receive the actual DNA profiles (even anonymized) of those persons, as the FBI's manual explicitly does not "authorize access to candidate matches that are not confirmed as matches and for which no personally identifiable information is released."[32] Without that information, however, the defense is stymied from challenging the analyst's conclusion that the defendant was in fact the right hit. And in many jurisdictions, in fact, the lawyer—even the prosecutor—never receives any information about the match process at all, because analysts reason that their determination that certain candidates are nonmatching renders those results irrelevant. But, of course, this approach leaves the erroneous impression that a forensic profile "hit" only to the defendant, and erases all trace of subjective decisionmaking in weeding through available matches. It also insulates the analyst from scrutiny over whether he or she made the right call about who was in fact the best fit.

As a result of these policies, outsiders get only peeks and glimpses into how common it is that a search in the database turns up multiple matching candidates to a forensic unknown sample. In the testimony in the Hernandez case, for instance, the analyst explained that, once a match is made, "the investigating officer goes and does an investigation to see if that's even a viable option. Maybe the person was in jail at the time . . . and can't have contributed to the evidence sample."[33] The offhand nature of her response suggested that coincidental matches of that nature are not uncommon, or at the very least not rare occurrences. Yet by the time those hits make it to the judicial system, the impression presented is of a 1 in 1 trillion event.

Ironically, even though some database administrators have sanctioned exploratory searches in the DNA database by analysts who have data they cannot interpret definitively, the government routinely prevents defense attorneys from conducting searches of the exact same kind. This issue has arisen most acutely in the case of imprisoned persons' seeking to overturn their convictions after DNA testing points toward their innocence. Prisoners in such cases often have accessed and tested the evidence from the case, and have shown it not to match their own DNA profiles, and yet some prosecutors have proven reluctant to support exoneration until the prisoner points to the actual perpetrator. Doing so, however, typically requires access to the database.

In fact, California database administrators—the same authorities that enabled Dunbar's alternative searches in the Hernandez case—vigorously opposed allowing a defense request to search the database for a match to alternative profiles observed in the evidence.[34] In that case, the defendant was a homeless man accused of stabbing a resident during a burglary.[35] The key evidence was an eyewitness who had been sitting in a car with her boyfriend down the street, who saw a man she later identified as the defendant enter and leave the house with a knife. The testing laboratory found a mixture of blood samples on the knife, which it said included DNA from the victim and defendant. Examining the same results, two defense experts conjectured eight different plausible profile variations.

The defense attorney sought a database search to see whether any of those profiles matched to plausible suspects, but the state refused. Among other things, the attorney general argued that the search should not be allowed because the defense experts were not designees of the state Department of Justice, and thus not authorized to conduct searches under state and federal law. The state also contended that a search was inappropriate unless the defense could first prove that there would be a match in the database; but, of course, if that were the case, there would be no need for a search. In short, the state deemed a search for alternative profiles in ambiguous evidence when sought by the defendant "nothing more than a blatant and unimaginably broad 'fishing expedition. Defendant seeks only to cast randomly about in the highly confidential and protected Convicted Offender Database in the hopes of finding someone else to blame. . . . '"[36] When conducted by the government in the Hernandez case, however, it was apparently good proof. Ultimately, the trial court denied the defense request, and the man was convicted.

But even in cases where a local or state prosecutor expresses a willingness to run a DNA profile in the national database, the search will not always occur. The FBI has been known to throw up roadblocks. As one scholar put it, "The FBI has been the primary force opposing defense-initiated DNA searches."[37] In one notorious showdown in Illinois, the prosecutor and defense joined together in obtaining a state court order to search the national database for the profile of an alternative perpetrator in the case of Juan Rivera, discussed in greater depth in Chapter 14. But FBI officials refused, and ultimately a federal court issued an order to the FBI to conduct the search, noting that the favoritism to law enforcement requests "puts a criminal defendant at the mercy of state law enforcement authorities."[38] In reaching its conclusion, the court specifically refuted one of the government's claims, namely that somehow the search would taint the integrity of the database. Observing that the defendant did not even seek to upload a permanent profile, but merely requested a one-time "keyboard search" of data that would leave no trace, the court rejected that argument.

The most recent edition of the FBI's manual for operating the national database continues to take a hard line on the issue of defense access, even though numerous courts and commentators have found that this position violates the spirit of the DNA database laws. Some courts have felt hamstrung by the lack of explicit permission to order such searches, even when the court believes a search may uncover exculpatory evidence or find a true perpetrator. To remedy that concern, a handful of states have enacted laws expressly authorizing a court to order a search of a DNA database when a defense petition meets certain standards. But, in a supreme twist of perverted logic, only three of those states grant the right pretrial.[39] The remaining states grant the express statutory power to petition for a database search only to those defendants who have *already been convicted* at trial.[40] Thus, some defendants may hold in their hand evidence that points to another perpetrator, and yet be incapable of naming that person until after they have been wrongly convicted.

In an opinion upholding the right of a defendant to seek a court order for a database search, one court noted that the purpose of the state's law was to "level the playing field" between the prosecution and defense.[41] Unfortunately, it seems the FBI would rather keep things uneven. And thus a defendant with an undisputed profile of the likely perpetrator is barred access, even as a government analyst with no more than a hunch regarding the evidentiary profile can use the database to go fishing for a suspect.

PART III

Wild Frontiers: Privacy, Equality, and the Future of DNA Testing

CHAPTER 10

"License, Registration, and Cheek Swab, Please"

IN 2009, TWO seemingly unrelated arrests occurred across the country from each other. Alonzo King's case started on the streets of Maryland. A witness identified him as the man who approached a group (which included the witness) and pulled out a shotgun, referencing a skirmish that had occurred five months earlier.[1] The group immediately fled in different directions, but the witness notified a nearby police officer, who found King in his car, along with a shotgun. King was taken into custody and charged with first- and second-degree assault, and he eventually pled no contest to the second-degree charge.[2]

Under a Maryland law passed the year before, police could collect a DNA sample from any person arrested for a crime of violence or burglary.[3] Because the first-degree assault charge qualified as a crime of violence, a DNA sample was taken from King, even though his later conviction for second-degree assault, a misdemeanor, would not have triggered DNA collection under Maryland's convicted offender law.[4] In short, King's charge of arrest allowed the state to keep King's DNA in its database, even though his charge of conviction would not.

Across the country in California, another person had a DNA sample taken at arrest.[5] Elizabeth Aida Haskell was attending a war protest in March 2009 when she noticed police attempting to arrest another protester. She intervened, and the police placed her under arrest as well. At the jail, she was ordered to provide a DNA sample but refused. When the police told her that she would be held in custody and separately charged for that refusal, she relented. She gave her sample, and was released. But her DNA sample did not go home with her. Even though she was never formally charged with any offense, California law permits the police to take a DNA sample at the time of arrest. If the arrest does not result in charges, or the charges that are brought are ultimately dismissed or lead to an acquittal, then the arrested person has the right to petition the state in writing to have the DNA records expunged. For uncharged persons, that right arguably only kicks in after the statute of limitations for the alleged crime expires, which can be several years.

With the help of attorney Michael Risher at the ACLU, Haskell filed suit against the state of California, alleging that the mandatory demand for her DNA, including the lack of automatic expungement procedures, violated her constitutional rights.[6] She was joined in the suit by another political demonstrator, a UC Berkeley student arrested during a campus protest, and a person suspected of possessing stolen property. Only one of these four was ever charged, and those charges were later dismissed. All four gave DNA samples as required by state law.

As Haskell's case started its way through the California courts, police in Maryland made an interesting discovery. Law enforcement had taken Alonzo King's sample and sent it to a private vendor, who analyzed it four months later. When uploaded to the state's DNA database,[7] King's profile matched that from an unsolved violent sexual assault in 2003. The evidence appeared fairly damning. The victim was a middle-aged woman who was raped and robbed at gunpoint during a home invasion. She was unable to give anything more than a threadbare description, because the assailant had obscured his features. But investigators recovered traces of semen that produced the DNA profile found to match King. When the victim learned a possible perpetrator had been identified, she recognized the name. She had watched Alonzo King grow up, as he was raised by his grandmother, who lived across the street. Because he was friends with her grandson, King had regularly dined with her family and had called her "grandmom."[8]

King was arrested and charged with the rape.[9] He moved the court to keep out the evidence of the DNA match, arguing that taking DNA from a person simply charged with an offense violated the Fourth Amendment. King maintained that police cannot search without either a warrant or any individualized suspicion, and yet Maryland's blanket law allowed just that. The trial court denied his motion, and King was convicted. On appeal, the Maryland Court of Appeals reversed the trial court's decision, resting its decision in part on the "presumption that warrantless, suspicionless searches are per se unreasonable."[10] The state then petitioned the United States Supreme Court for review.

So stood two cases that in some ways marked the edges of the debate about DNA database policy. On the one hand, broad DNA collection laws helped identify King as the perpetrator of a terrible sexual assault. On the other hand, broad DNA collection laws enabled government acquisition of the genetic information of those exercising their First Amendment right to protest national policies—a practice that might easily dissuade future protesters from publicly criticizing the government. Together, the two cases embodied both the rewards and perils of compulsory DNA databasing. The question they presented came to a head before the Supreme Court, which agreed to hear King's case as the judges in *Haskell* held their own case in abeyance.[11]

The Fourth Amendment to the United States Constitution, which prohibits unreasonable searches and seizures, is the most natural place to look for protection against government testing of biological samples.[12] Unfortunately, like the rest of the Constitution, it is pretty sparing in its terms. It says only that

> The right of the people to be secure in their persons, houses, papers, and effects, against unreasonable searches and seizures, shall not be violated, and no warrants shall issue, but upon probable cause, supported by oath or affirmation, and particularly describing the place to be searched, and the persons or things to be seized.

It does not specify what judges should consider a "reasonable" versus "unreasonable" search or seizure. It does not state definitively whether warrants are required for a search to be reasonable, or whether the clause about warrants simply outlines the process by which warrants should issue, whenever they do. Indeed, the text of the Fourth Amendment does not even clearly include biological evidence under its terms—does DNA fall within "persons, houses, papers, and effects"?

An enormous body of case law, both from the Supreme Court and from courts around the nation, puts some meat on the bones of this text. Those cases give some guidance in how courts ought to interpret the

Fourth Amendment. Generally speaking, courts have created three tiers of police intrusion: searches of the home typically require a warrant and probable cause; brief detentions and superficial pat-downs can be done if an officer has something less than probable cause, specifically, reasonable suspicion that the person is engaged in criminal activity; and random group searches, such as airport searches, can be done without a warrant or suspicion so long as they are for purposes other than ordinary law enforcement. Thus, for instance, a sobriety checkpoint aimed at getting drunk or high drivers off the road is okay, because it protects the safety of drivers—even if it also has the secondary effect of leading to arrests for those driving under the influence. But a checkpoint aimed solely at finding drivers who are merely transporting narcotics is not, because its only objective is crime control.

When courts began to confront the first waves of DNA collection laws, they applied these principles. Almost uniformly, they upheld the right of states to force a convicted offender to give a DNA sample. Their reasoning was fairly uniform as well. It is true, they said, that the Fourth Amendment generally forbids searches or seizures by the police without a warrant or suspicion, when done for purely law enforcement purposes. But although these mandatory collection laws violate that principle— because the DNA samples are collected on the basis of membership in a group (convicted offenders), rather than suspicion that any one person has committed a past or future offense—the courts concluded that convicted persons, by virtue of having been found guilty of a crime, give up a little bit of their right to privacy. Courts also reasoned that the state had an interest in using that DNA as a way of monitoring the behavior of convicted offenders on probation and parole, leaving to another day the question whether the state must expunge DNA records of convicted persons after the supervision ends.

As a result, today forty-eight states require that all persons convicted of *any* felony provide a DNA sample.[13] Thus, not only robbers, rapists, or murderers must hand over a biological sample. It is also folks like Wesley Snipes and *Survivor* star Richard Hatch, who were convicted for felony tax evasion; or Martha Stewart, convicted of false statements; or Robert Downey Jr., based on his drug convictions; or Kiefer Sutherland, convicted of multiple DUIs. Only Minnesota and Missouri limit eligible felonies mostly to crimes against a person, as opposed to including drug or property offenses.

Forty-two states also require that all persons convicted of certain *misdemeanors* provide a DNA sample. Thus, in Louisiana, throwing a hot dog at your teacher or at the umpire at your daughter's soccer game could result in a DNA registration offense.[14] Two states—Wisconsin and New York—go still further, with comprehensive collection laws—there, any person convicted of any misdemeanor or felony must contribute a DNA sample.[15] Over half of the states mandate DNA collection even if the person is a juvenile. In six states, juveniles found guilty of mere misdemeanor property crimes must provide a DNA sample.[16]

ARRESTEE SAMPLING

Given the prevalence of mandatory DNA collection statutes, it stands to wonder why King's and Haskell's cases created such a fuss. The answer pertains to their status as arrestees. Courts rather easily allowed the state to take the DNA of convicted offenders, on the theory that they forfeited their privacy as a result of having been judged guilty of breaking the law. But a much thinner line divides an arrestee from a law-abiding person. Arrestees in our system are presumed innocent. Whereas the state can enter and search the home of a parolee without a warrant and without any basis for suspicion, the state cannot do the same to an arrestee. In fact, even minor incursions into an arrestee's privacy, such as taking a hair sample or drawing blood to test intoxication levels, have typically required some added showing of need.

A law that allowed the state to take a DNA sample from an arrestee, without any showing of suspected wrongdoing, therefore challenged the very foundation of constitutional doctrine in this area. That is probably why, when Alonzo King's case reached the Supreme Court, Justice Samuel Alito spontaneously interjected during the lawyers' arguments, "by the way, I think this is perhaps the most important criminal procedure case that this Court has heard in decades."[17]

Before the Supreme Court, the state tried to minimize the significance of the intrusion by arguing that taking the DNA sample was just a technologically advanced version of taking a fingerprint, a practice that has long occurred at arrest. That argument won the day—a majority of the Supreme Court agreed. In an opinion finding no constitutional violation of King's rights, five justices proclaimed that "[t]he only difference between DNA analysis and fingerprint databases is the unparalleled accuracy DNA provides."[18] Just as the state could routinely take finger-prints at the time of arrest, so, too, could it take a DNA sample.

Not all the justices viewed DNA testing through such rosy glasses. Justice Antonin Scalia, joined by Justices Ruth Bader Ginsburg, Elena Kagan, and Sonia Sotomayor, opened and closed the dissenting opinion with vehemence. He wrote:

> The Fourth Amendment forbids searching a person for evidence of a crime when there is no basis for believing the person is guilty of the crime or is in possession of incriminating evidence. That prohibition is categorical and without exception; it lies at the very heart of the Fourth Amendment.
>
> . . .
>
> Today's judgment will, to be sure, have the beneficial effect of solv-ing more crimes; then again, so would the taking of DNA samples from anyone who flies on an airplane (surely the Transportation Secu-rity Administration needs to know the "identity" of the flying public), applies for a driver's license, or attends a public school. Perhaps the construction of such a genetic panopticon is wise. But I doubt that the proud men who wrote the charter of our liberties would have been so eager to open their mouths for royal inspection.

If the dissent's premonitions seem ominous, consider how we use fin-gerprints today—the very biometric technique that the *King* majority considered the apt progenitor of DNA typing. The FBI database cur-rently contains over 100 million sets of fingerprints—the size of one third of the entire US population.[19] In fiscal year 2014 alone, law enforcement processed more than 70 million ten-print submissions.[20]

Of course, those fingerprints do not just belong to criminals. Thirty-four million prints are classified as "civil," and stem from "background checks for employment, licensing, or other non-criminal justice pur-poses."[21] As most people know, fingerprint samples are currently required in a wide array of circumstances, including from professional licensees, home health and durable medical equipment providers, educators, driver's licensees, and even volunteers of certain kinds. More broadly speaking, it little strains imagination to expect a court to find that the govern-ment's interest in "identity" extends to recipients of public benefits, such as Medicare, student aid, or unemployment insurance, as well as users of forms of mass transit.

Yet under the Supreme Court's logic, there is little difference between the FBI having on file 100 million DNA samples, rather than fingerprint cards—except maybe that DNA is "superior." In fact, given the current state of Fourth Amendment doctrine, nothing appears to stop the FBI from systematically replacing its fingerprint data with DNA profiles. And they are well on their way to doing just that, both directly and indirectly. In 2014 the research arm of the Department of Justice awarded a $250,000 grant to researchers in Virginia aimed at developing reliable methods for extracting typeable DNA from archived fingerprints.[22]

If fingerprints and DNA were truly interchangeable, and DNA was nothing more than an improvement on existing fingerprint technology, then perhaps none of this would be that alarming. But, of course, that is not the case. No one would dispute that the main purpose of taking a fingerprint is to establish the person's identity. At present, officers take prints at booking, and run them against a database containing the prints of known offenders to determine quickly whether the person has given a true name. To be sure, limiting the use of DNA to do that kind of identity check of a convicted offender would be most sensible.

If so, then the state would take the sample, test it immediately, and check it against the database of known persons. In those three short steps, police could readily resolve any question regarding the person's identity, without posing that much of a threat to genetic privacy.

But that was not what the authorities did in King's or Haskell's case, and despite what the government claimed before the courts, confirming a suspect's identity is not why it was seeking permission to take DNA samples. Instead, the government takes DNA samples so that it can solve crimes. Not just crimes in the past, but all crimes—past, present, and future. Think about what happened in King's case. The government did not just use King's DNA to make sure that he was who he said he was. Instead, once the state got around to testing the sample, four months after King's arrest, it placed that DNA profile into a database where it would be checked, twice a week in perpetuity, against an unsolved crimes database. The state even kept the actual physical DNA sample, so that additional DNA tests could be conducted at any time in the future. Although there are easy ways to use DNA for the sole purpose of confirming identity, in no way was this what the government was actually doing.

Now, some might contend that crime-solving—past, present, and future—is a good thing. They might think that if you want to keep your privacy, you should not get arrested. But under that logic, police should be able to do all manner of things to someone who has once been arrested that they cannot do to everyone else. Should police forever be able to enter the home of an arrestee, to conduct searches without a warrant or any suspicion? Or stop arrestees on the street at any time, and ask them to empty the contents of their pockets or purses? Or pull over an arrestee's car on whim, and rifle through the belongings contained therein? If those steps feel too intrusive, then what about simply installing cameras at the home or workplaces of arrestees? Or insisting that they wear a monitoring device—maybe a painless implant that would be unnoticeable? The state could even promise not to look at the data it collects unless and until there is reason to believe that an arrestee might be involved in some criminal wrongdoing.

All of these actions would probably help solve crime. For that matter, there are infinite ways that we could surrender our privacy—even negligible, inconsequential parts of our privacy—in the name of past and future crime-solving. We could register our name with the police department whenever we move, so that the government knows exactly who lives where and with whom. We could allow police to run searches across our computers, seeking only evidence of contraband or illegal activity. Each of these efforts would help solve crime, but most people would find living under such conditions oppressive, not salute them as a major advance in crime-solving. If the only question to answer about a contested police practice is, "Does it solve crime?" then there is very little the government should not be allowed to do. Framing police power as cabined only by the concern for public safety neglects values equally as compelling, such as personal privacy and the right to move and think freely without concern for how it will be viewed by a government official. It also overlooks practical concerns that deserve meaningful weight, such as whether a particular approach is the most efficient or effective use of resources.

Thus *King*, which broke down the barrier between what the government can do to convicted people and what it can do to those viewed innocent in the eyes of the law, mattered a great deal—not just to King, and not just to Maryland, but to the entire nation. By last count, twenty-nine states and the federal government have enacted provisions requiring arrested persons to give a DNA sample.[23] And there are likely to be more: a 2013 federal law gave the attorney general the power to award grants of up to $10 million to states to offset the cost of implementing DNA arrestee collection regiments.[24]

As it stands, current arrestee sampling laws have one core feature in common: they require that a person accused of an offense submit a DNA sample to be typed and uploaded to a DNA database. But apart from that, the precise scope of state laws varies quite a bit. By way of example, Maryland's law was narrower than California's, and differed from the laws in the majority of the states that allow arrestee sampling, in three very important ways: the seriousness of the qualifying offense, the requirement of judicial oversight, and the ease and availability of expungement in the event the arrest turns out to be bogus.

First, Maryland's law limited DNA collection to only those arrested for serious felonies, such as murder, rape, and aggravated assault. In contrast, fourteen states permit DNA sampling for all felony arrests. That means that a person arrested for any crime with a jail penalty of over a year—such as forging a check or tagging a building with graffiti—must submit a DNA sample. But just as convicted offender laws quickly broadened from requiring samples only from the most serious felons to lower-level offenders, so, too, have arrestee laws followed that pattern. Nine states permit DNA collection from persons charged only with misdemeanors, and eight allow collection from juveniles. Alabama, Kansas, and Louisiana have the broadest laws, authorizing the collection of DNA samples from all arrestees, some misdemeanants, and juveniles.

Second, Maryland's law included a safeguard against mistaken or bogus arrests. It allowed police to analyze the DNA sample only once a judge had validated the legitimacy of the arrest by holding a hearing to verify that there was probable cause. But only roughly half of states impose that requirement. The rest allow the police officer to take and test the DNA sample without judicial oversight of any kind.

That approach vests incredible power with police officers, who already have wide discretion. For example, a bar fight might be charged any number of ways—as misdemeanor simple assault, felony aggravated assault, an aggravated assault while armed, or even assault with intent to kill. A police officer choosing among those options can rather readily adjust the precise charge to fit the DNA collection statute, especially if the officer knows that the DNA can be taken and tested before that choice ever needs to be defended in court.

The scope of police discretion in charging decisions enmeshes DNA collection in the greater debate over selectivity and racial bias in the execution of the criminal laws. Get into a fight on a gang street corner and the police may charge a felony and take your DNA; engage in fisticuffs at an upscale bar or college hangout and the charge might be a non-DNA trigger misdemeanor assault. The same story can be told for any number of common offenses—a large amount of drugs on one person might be treated as misdemeanor possession; while the same amount on someone else is considered felony trafficking. If such charge adjustments seem preposterous, consider that a retired police superintendent in the United Kingdom claimed that officers there engaged in just this kind of behavior in order to collect more DNA samples.[25] Closer to home, police in the United States have exhibited a willingness to adjust charges strategically, so as to appear more effective during performance reviews.[26]

The final major point of distinction among state arrestee collection statutes relates to the rules regarding expungement of a DNA sample in the event of a faulty arrest. To some extent, expungement offers only limited protection. If police may take and test a sample immediately, without judicial validation of the arrest, then the profile may already have been generated and searched against the database by the time expungement proceedings can even begin. Some expungement provisions also dictate only that the DNA profile be removed from the database, and do not also require the destruction of the associated biological sample.

Moreover, the right to have a sample expunged is only as meaningful as the procedures available to assert that right. In fewer than half of the states (thirteen total), expungement ought to occur automatically if a case is dismissed or the charge reduced. In the remainder of states, expungement is available only upon request. Petition processes place a heavy burden on arrestees, many of whom may not even realize that they have such a right. There is no right to the assistance of counsel in filing these petitions, and so many arrestees may have difficulty finding the time, skill, or resources to make their claim. Labs have also exacerbated these problems by turning technocratic when interpreting DNA destruction orders, such as by interpreting orders literally so that "expunge the record" means only the record, as opposed to all the associated testing materials and documentation.[27] Finally, even if a petitioner goes to the trouble to follow through on the claim, courts have disregarded instances in which the state misrepresents its actions or fails to expunge the record so long as the wrongfully retained profile later turns up a match to crime scene evidence.

But the most perverse effect of expungement laws is that, if applied correctly, they create a nonsensical regime of DNA sampling. Take *King:* Had King been convicted of the crime he was charged with, he would have had to hand over his DNA. Conversely, if King had been charged with the crime he was convicted of, he would *not* have been required to give a DNA sample. Had the charges been altogether thrown out, he would not have to give a sample, either. The effect of the arrestee laws, then, is to ensnare a very narrow category of persons: those arrested for one crime but convicted of some *lesser* offense that does not itself require DNA sampling. Very strange logic indeed, placing exceptional power in the hands of charging authorities.

In the end, it is not at all clear that the protections present in the Maryland law, but missing from the laws in California and many other states, mattered that much to the Supreme Court. The majority opinion in *King* seemed to view DNA typing as an unmitigated good—an exciting new advance in forensic science. It characterized DNA sampling as a "brief" and "minimal intrusion," and barely gave any attention to the indefinite retention of biological samples or endless searches in DNA databases. Moreover, the Court dropped hints suggesting it viewed the Maryland law's limitations as entirely gratuitous: there need be no validating of the arrest, no limits on the seriousness of the offense, and perhaps not even a need to provide expungement procedures in the event the arrest was unfounded. Just like its analogue fingerprinting, DNA testing could be performed at the police precinct, by police officers, as a routine part of the booking process. At one point, the court even seemed to indicate that street sampling might be allowable—such as requiring a DNA swabbing whenever the police ticket a speeder.

STOP AND SPIT

The Supreme Court's enthusiasm for forensic DNA typing, coupled with existing Fourth Amendment doctrine and recent technological advances, cast a gloomy pall over the future of genetic privacy. *King* expressly gives police authority to take a DNA sample from arrested persons. But why should law enforcement stop there? Existing Fourth Amendment law already allows police to briefly detain any person whom they have reason to believe is engaged in criminal activity. Police can even conduct a superficial search—a "frisk"—if they think that a person is armed and dangerous.

"Stop and frisk" policies have been the source of recent political controversy. In New York City, for instance, Mayor Bill de Blasio curtailed the practice in 2014 after a lawsuit revealed a ballooning number of such stops unjustly targeted young black men.[28] Hard numbers are not available nationwide, and those numbers change with new political administrations. But even absorbing a steep decline, the raw number of casual police encounters remains significant. According to the most recent study available, in 2011, an estimated 30.8 million people reported some form of contact initiated by police. Of those, roughly 26 million had contact through a traffic stop, and 1.4 million through a street stop.[29]

Given the majority's view of DNA sampling as "brief," "minimally intrusive," and valuable to establish "identity," what is to stop police from swabbing every individual that they have grounds to stop? That scenario becomes even more plausible given the recent emergence of Rapid DNA typing equipment.[30] No bigger than a desktop printer, these instruments allow for ninety-minute, one-touch testing by lay persons, such as police officers. They can also readily connect to law enforcement databases. According to one National Institute of Standards and Technology (NIST) study using single-source samples, these machines presently generate an accurate profile without any human intervention with a success rate of roughly 88 percent, and that is likely only to improve in the future.[31]

Federal law presently limits access to the national database—whether to upload a profile or run a search—to qualified personnel who test DNA in an accredited laboratory. But the FBI crafted exceptions that allow uploads so long as the results are reviewed by an analyst, and in May 2015 the first forensic profile derived from a crime scene sample on a rapid typing machine was uploaded to the national database.[32] The rules are likely to relax even further. IntegenX, just one of the companies that has developed a rapid machine, has counted two senior former FBI officials among its senior leadership,[33] and has by one account already spent $70,000 lobbying Congress to amend the statute to permit direct uploads from its machine.[34] When that happens, a new database entry will require no more than a cheek swab and the press of a button.

Ultimately, widespread arrestee DNA typing laws and automated DNA instruments will enable DNA testing to supplement or replace fingerprinting as a primary identifier. Just as police now transmit a digital image of a suspect's fingerprints, they will soon be able to take a DNA swab, put it in the machine, and initiate an automated testing and searching process. A real-time test and search can return immediate hits, as opposed to the current system in which searches occur twice weekly. Real-time processing could also link the DNA profile to records held by the national Criminal Justice Information Service, which oversees the FBI's all-purpose biometric identification databases.

At present, the fingerprint repository includes over 70 million criminal files for arrested and convicted persons and 34 million civil files for those in positions of trust (such as teachers, childcare providers, etc.).[35] And in 2014, the FBI fully switched over to its Next Generation Identification (NGI) database, which combines a range of biometric data into one easily accessible file, including fingerprint records, palm prints, iris scans, voice patterns, and such biographical information as name, address, immigration status, criminal history, and demographic characteristics. The NGI system also has a facial recognition system, and the FBI projected that by 2015 the database would include roughly 46 million criminal images and 4.3 million civil images.[36] Although the NGI system does not yet link directly to the national DNA database, that may soon change. In November 2014, the FBI hosted a briefing at its Criminal Justice Information Services division. The topic? "Facilitate the future effective and efficient integration of Rapid DNA Analysis into the FBI's Combined DNA Index (CODIS) and Next Generation Identification (NGI) systems from the booking environment";[37] in other words, how to integrate ninety-minute, one-touch DNA testing instruments into the NGI system.

Rapid machines prove useful to law enforcement even if they may never be connected to a national database. Roughly 85 percent of DNA matches occur within state, and most states have more relaxed rules than the FBI regarding access to state or local DNA databases. With such a machine in every squad car, police could simply collect a mouth swab, verify identity, and check for outstanding warrants or matches to unsolved crime scene evidence. "Stop and spit" could become routine even if courts refuse to recognize the right of the police to swab a suspect lawfully detained in a traffic or street stop. That's because nothing prohibits police from strongly encouraging a "voluntary" sample by suggesting that failure to comply will result in inconvenience. Individuals routinely submit to "voluntary" searches simply to avoid the hassle of arrest for trivial charges, such as broken taillights, outdated pet license tags, disorderly conduct, or jaywalking. Such strong-arming is the overt premise behind an Orange County, California, program that offers those arrested for low-level offenses the opportunity to escape charges by agreeing to "spit and acquit."[38] Tellingly, Orange County was one of only a handful of US agencies to pilot Rapid DNA testing machines; others include Tucson, Arizona, and Palm Bay, Florida.[39]

The spread of instant-typing technology seems inevitable. After its pilot program in Tucson, the Arizona Department of Public Safety decided to purchase three machines, at a cost of roughly $270,000 apiece (akin to the cost of a patrol car), for use in several other cities. Arizona has also used the machines to test not just controlled conditions samples, such as a mouth swab from a known person, but also crime scene stains. At present Arizona's protocols limit forensic testing to sizeable samples that clearly come from one person—like a large blood stain left at the scene—that then can be confirmed through laboratory testing. When linked to a database—whether the national database or a locality's own database—law enforcement may be able to return a hit at the scene.

Eventually this evidence will find its way into court, and proponents will no doubt try to argue that it need not undergo any special legal scrutiny, claiming that it simply automates already approved processes. But if these machines do not constitute new technologies, then why did IntegenX require 37 issued patents, 165 pending patent applications, and roughly 600 nonexclusive patents just to protect its creation?[40] With a failure rate of roughly 10 to 15 percent for even controlled conditions mouth samples,[41] it is clear that the technology is still a far cry from a skilled laboratory technician. Thus all samples, especially crime samples, require confirmatory retesting.

Should these machines survive legal scrutiny, it is easy to imagine a future in which the entire process of DNA testing and matching occurs with minimal intervention by a person credentialed in DNA testing and interpretation methods. In fact, given the dysfunction and thin resources of the criminal justice system, in many cases there may be no additional scrutiny within the legal process. Police will respond to the scene, swab the evidence, return a hit, locate the offender, and send the defendant off to court. Once there, the defendant will be told that there is a DNA match, and the overworked prosecutor will offer a plea deal that the overwhelmed defense lawyer will encourage the defendant to accept. And thus a ninety-minute, one-touch DNA testing instrument transforms into an instant conviction machine.

TENTATIVE CAUSE FOR HOPE

The Supreme Court's expansive embrace of DNA testing in the *King* case decided Elizabeth Aida Haskell's fate. After the Supreme Court issued its decision, the federal appellate court in California that had held Haskell's case in abeyance heard new arguments. Then, in March 2014, the court sitting en banc—as a whole court rather than as a customary panel of three judges—ruled against Haskell. After *Maryland v. King*, the court wrote, the answer to the question of the California law's constitutionality "is clearly yes."[42] As one concurring justice stated more directly, any differences in the two laws, such as which offenses trigger collection, the judicial approval of probable cause, or the expungement procedures, was "illusory" and "constitutionally irrelevant."

But not every state has taken such a cavalier view of DNA testing. In 2014, two state courts used their state constitutions to limit the reach of DNA testing, each adopting similar reasoning. The Supreme Court of Vermont knocked down Vermont's felony arrestee law,[43] rejecting the analogy to fingerprinting and holding that it would "not equate a procedure that takes a visible image of the surface of the skin of a finger with the capture of intimate bodily fluids, even if the method of doing so is speedy and painless." The Vermont justices added that "despite the occasional usefulness of DNA samples for ordinary identification . . . , the real functionality, and statutory purpose, is to solve open criminal cases or ones that may occur in the future."

Similarly, an appellate court in California found that the state's DNA law—the same one that authorized Haskell's sampling—violated the California constitution.[44] The court concluded that "fingerprinting presents no threat to privacy comparable to that posed by DNA analysis." It went on to criticize the reasoning of the Supreme Court in the *King* case, observing that "the legitimacy of the [Supreme Court's] method and the correctness of its outcome hinge entirely on the truth of a single proposition: that the primary purpose of these DNA searches is something other than simply discovering evidence of criminal wrongdoing. . . . [T]hat proposition is wrong." The California Supreme Court will review the *Haskell* case in 2015, but for now it stands. Although state judgments like these may help stem the tide toward total genetic transparency, the future remains to be seen.

CHAPTER 11

Sneak Sampling, Dragnet Searches, and Rogue Databases

A WATER BOTTLE offered during questioning.[1] The seal of an envelope licked and mailed to supposed lawyers claiming to offer a fictitious benefit from a class-action suit.[2] A cigarette discarded during a routine walk.[3] The glass left on the table after dinner with your spouse.[4] The fork used during a snack offered during a job interview.[5] Chewing gum spit out to participate in a fake "Pepsi challenge."[6] Clothing stripped from a hospital patient during emergency care.[7] All of these items carry DNA, and all of them—along with others like them—have at one point been challenged in court as a form of impermissible "surreptitious" DNA sampling. For the most part, courts have held that such sneak sampling is okay.

Legal doctrine has thus far largely shrugged off concerns about DNA methods that push the envelope of lawful investigative tactics, including surreptitious sampling, dragnets, and rogue DNA databases. *Dragnets* refers to the practice of sweeping an area—such as a neighborhood, workplace, community center, or even entire town—to collect DNA samples. *Rogue databases* are informal DNA databases kept outside the FBI's centralized architecture and beyond the reach of established laws that govern either the origin or quality of the profiles that are uploaded.

Oddly enough, a DNA sample collected from a known felon and uploaded to the FBI's national database enjoys far greater safeguards against misuse and abuse than does an innocent person's DNA when gathered by police on a hunch or a whim. Mandatory collection laws spell out exactly who may be sampled and require that testing occur under quality-assured conditions. These laws also set rules for when a profile may be added to or searched within the DNA database, and at least nominally provide for penalties should those rules be broken.

But when police collect the DNA sample off the books—through a voluntary request or outright trickery—all these protections disappear. These gaps in the law create huge loopholes in what law enforcement and judicial advocates claim is a tightly regulated system of forensic DNA collection. Beyond the horizon lies a wild frontier in which a DNA sample is as easy to gather as a bottle from a trash barrel, databases are filled and searched according only to law enforcement whim, and the law has nothing to say about any of it.

SNEAK SAMPLING AND DNA THEFT

On the campus of a state university at the turn of the millennium, a young college student goes to the health clinic. As part of the examination, she is given a pap smear to test for cellular abnormalities. Little does she know that the sample is saved, in accordance with a law that requires preservation in the event of later malpractice suits. Even less might she anticipate that, not even five years later, police will obtain the sample without her knowledge, an act she will later describe as leaving her feeling "violated."[8] It will be DNA culled from that sample that eventually sends her father to jail for life.

Investigators linked that sample to DNA found at the crime scenes of one of the worst serial killers in recent times. Nicknamed "BTK" for "bind, torture, kill," Dennis Rader left a trail of brutalized bodies, mostly women's, during an almost thirty-year window.[9] The DNA sample from his daughter's pap smear indicated that one of her close relatives might be the killer, and later tests of Rader's own DNA confirmed matches to an array of evidence.

The BTK case is extraordinary in a number of ways. It involves one of the most sensational killers in modern history. The DNA sample surreptitiously collected from the clinic was obtained pursuant to a court order, rather than absent express legal authority. In this way, it makes the most persuasive case for sneak sampling. But it is not a representative case study. Across the country, police departments employ sneak DNA sampling methods without judicial intervention of any kind, and obtain biological material intended to solve far less serious crimes than those committed by Rader.[10] As the head of one government lab said, "When you've licked a stamp on your tax return you've sent the government a DNA sample."[11] Obtaining a DNA sample is as simple as picking up a discarded tissue, swabbing a car door handle, or retrieving a used Starbucks cup.

The true scope and extent of sneak sampling practices is not known. Police departments do not publish data reciting how much DNA they have collected or tested surreptitiously. They often do not even share what happens to that DNA when it turns out to be irrelevant to the case for which it was obtained. In many cases police simply keep surreptitiously gathered samples, adding those DNA profiles to offline or rogue databases that can be searched without restriction. Thus both the data and the databases are shrouded in secrecy; usually they only garner attention when there is no other way to explain a connection that landed a defendant in court.

In the BTK case, for instance, it was only because the pap smear led to a match that we know that police had rummaged through the daughter's medical waste. If law enforcement's hunch had proven wrong, it is likely the public would never have learned that a pap smear had been accessed, tested, and typed. Indeed, we still do not know whether Rader's daughter's DNA was the only sample surreptitiously collected in connection with that case, or whether police quietly accessed one or ten or one hundred samples before alighting on hers.

Oddly enough, the law effectively encourages police to act in the sneakiest ways possible, by according the least oversight and protection to DNA samples collected on the sly. For instance, when a court order is used to access a DNA sample, a judge can attach limits on its later use. Although that would have to be done on the judge's own initiative— because no defense lawyers are present when law enforcement seeks such orders—the order could still specify that the sample be destroyed after testing, and the profile not be used for any purposes beyond the particular case. But if police simply poke through a suspect's trash or pose as a barista at the person's favorite coffee shop, then current law places no limits on future use of the sample. Police can keep those samples indefinitely, test them as they see fit, and store them in their local database for use in any later cases—and all without ever notifying any person that DNA has been sampled.

The courts that have addressed sneak sampling have almost universally endorsed it as acceptable under the Fourth Amendment. The legal underpinning of these cases is an established constitutional doctrine known as abandonment. In most instances, abandonment is a sensible accommodation of the needs of police investigations versus the privacy protected by the Fourth Amendment. It stems from our understanding that, generally speaking, the police should be free to do the same kinds of things that ordinary citizens can do without violating constitutional rights. So, the police can say hello to a passerby on the street, or knock on the front door and ask whether an occupant is willing to chat briefly, all without a warrant or even any articulable suspicion. Similarly, if an officer riding a bus overhears the conversation of another passenger talking on a cell phone or notices what a person is wearing as he or she walks by, then the Constitution does not inhibit the officer's later use of that information. These are things that ordinary people can do, too.

Abandonment simply extends these everyday principles to physical evidence. It holds that if police see a discarded paper bag crumpled on the ground in the park, they can pick it up, open it, or throw it away, just the same as you or I might do. Historically, the abandonment doctrine has covered even things that were unintentionally abandoned. For example, if a person leaves a shopping bag on the bus, police could look at the bag and open it without a warrant, even if police would have needed one were the bag still associated with a particular person. Because the bag was abandoned—even if accidentally—it becomes fair game. The most familiar example of abandonment of this kind is probably the evidence left behind at a crime scene. A robber who drops a wallet on the way out of the bank, or who leaves behind the menacing note passed to the teller, cannot complain that the police violated the Fourth Amendment when they collect those items as evidence.

The same is true of items given to another in what turns out to be misplaced trust. Again, the fundamental logic of the rule seems sound: if a thief confides in a friend that he has stolen a watch, but the friend has a crisis of conscience, why should the law stop the friend from disclosing the secret to the police? If the thief actually gives the watch to the friend, surely the law allows the friend to hand it back to its lawful owner or to the authorities. The burden of mislaid faith falls on the thief, not the friend and certainly not the thief's victim. But should this logic extend to the invisible cells that one sheds throughout the course of a day?

The abandonment doctrine recently came under scrutiny in a case captioned *Raynor v. State*.[12] The police asked Glenn Raynor to come to the station for questioning after the victim of a rape realized that Raynor might have been the perpetrator of the offense. He obliged, but would only agree to a DNA sample if the police promised to destroy it after finishing that particular investigation. When the police refused, Raynor declined to give over his DNA. As they talked, however, police noticed that Raynor repeatedly rubbed his bare arms against the chair's armrests. After he left, they swabbed the armrest in the hopes of collecting a DNA sample. The sample turned out to match, and police eventually placed him under arrest. At argument before the state's high court, Raynor's attorney concluded that the abandonment doctrine was so insurmountable that he conceded that the police had the authority to swab the chair, and argued instead that they lacked the authority to test the DNA even if they lawfully obtained the sample. The Maryland court disagreed, holding the police's actions permissible, and the Supreme Court declined to review the case.

As *Raynor* reflects, the attitude of courts toward surreptitious sampling appears to be that the precepts of abandonment and misplaced trust ought to apply down to the molecular level. Even if a person did not intend to leave a DNA trace—in the form, say, of a handful of shed cells—the fact of abandonment nonetheless leaves the police free to collect and examine it. Similarly, if police trick or cajole a suspect into handing over a DNA sample—even if the suspect is unaware that the item contains biological traces of any kind—then that sample may be tested for evidentiary purposes. Conventionally speaking, none of the police actions implicates the person's Fourth Amendment rights at all, much less violates those rights.[13]

Although it makes perfect sense to consider abandoned any material—even the trace genetic material—left behind at a crime scene by the perpetrator of a crime, there are strong arguments against applying that rule to genetic samples obtained in other ways.

To be sure, solving crime is good. But creating a nation of suspects is not. The problem with cases like *Raynor*, which dismiss any privacy value in a person's unintentionally discarded DNA, is that they will ultimately discourage behaviors that we should protect in our society. For instance, recall that the police initially asked Raynor to the station because of the victim's hunch, which turned out to be true. But suppose it had not been. When word gets out that a trip to the precinct is equivalent to giving a DNA sample, innocent suspects, witnesses to crime, and even some victims of crime may not be as willing to aid in a police investigation. In the long run, legitimate belief that agreeing to speak to the police can lead to an entry in the DNA database works against, not in favor of, public safety.

More generally, legal permissiveness around police DNA sampling practices may lead even those who have no connection to illicit activity to err on the side of caution when invited to engage in any behavior that could result in police accessing their DNA. For instance, across the nation, parents of newborns submit a blood sample under state-run programs that unequivocally benefit public health. These tests focus on detecting devastating diseases that, caught immediately, are treatable. The high levels of compliance are likely the result of the goodwill that most new parents have toward those who help bring their children into the world, and a lack of suspicion about any nefarious use to which those blood samples might be put.

But learning that little stands between the police and your child's genetic code may cause some parents to opt out, to the detriment of public health. In 2009, five parents in Texas sued officials after they learned that the state had stored their children's blood samples without consent. The *Texas Tribune* later revealed that some of the samples, which were purportedly kept for medical research purposes, had in fact been handed over to a military laboratory to help build a forensic DNA database. The case ultimately settled, and part of the agreement resulted in the destruction of over 5 million samples.[14] But the skepticism bred from unexpected uses of this kind has repercussions. In 2015, a federal law went into effect requiring that federally funded researchers acquire consent before using newborn samples.[15]

Stories like these explain the wary response to police practices such as accessing pap smears or building a "victim" DNA database. Skeptics worry that such unsavory tactics will inhibit the next crime victim or person in need of health services from coming forward. If too cavalier an approach is taken to privacy and ethical issues of this kind, then all of society will have lost. Similarly, if the courts continue to sanction DNA collection practices that leave many law-abiding citizens feeling uneasy, the consequences to society may actually be more dire than a handful of serious cases remaining unsolved.

Lastly, better legal protection is necessary for discarded DNA because it is not just police who might want to surreptitiously collect DNA. Elizabeth Joh, a law professor and advocate for the passage of a law banning nonconsensual DNA collection, imagined a group of non–law enforcement actors who might nonetheless have an interest in surreptitiously collecting another person's DNA.[16] Her list included those seeking to prove claims of paternity, such as biographical historians or suspicious parents, owners of sports teams or businesses who might want health information about their prospective employees, and fans or paparazzi trying to trap or trace a favorite celebrity.

Absent from that list, but of course high among those who might be interested in other people's DNA, are defense lawyers and those seeking to exonerate persons they believe to be wrongfully convicted. To give just one example, in one case involving a prisoner alleging wrongful conviction, a team of investigators made a list of potential alternative suspects. They first requested a voluntary DNA sample from each suspect. If that failed, however, they resorted to more creative measures, such as collecting the discarded butt of a cigar, or the remnants of a chicken-wing dinner.[17]

In 2013, artist Heather Dewey-Hagborg brought dormant and discarded DNA of this kind to life in her work *Stranger Visions*. She roamed New York City, collecting genetic material from public places.[18] Dewey-Hagborg then extracted the DNA and used commercial kits to generate a composite of the person who left the material behind—checking for face shape, eye and skin color, hair color and texture, weight, height, freckles, and the like. From those details she created sculpted images of prospective faces. Her haunting images create beautiful art, and evoke an air of mystery. But they also prickle with discomfort and creepiness. Shed a stray hair at a subway station and suddenly a stranger may know your face, your kin, or the genetic secrets you would rather leave untold.

The law has little to say about this kind of collection, whether paparazzo or artiste. First, the Fourth Amendment only applies to state action—not to private actions. That is why the police violate your constitutional rights by breaking into your home and searching your belongings, but a neighbor who does the same thing, although a burglar, has not violated the Constitution.

Second, very few laws prohibit surreptitious DNA collection. After surveying the state of the law in 2013, Professor Joh concluded that "[m]ost legislative efforts have focused on protecting Americans from genetic discrimination in the context of employment and health insurance," most prominently the Genetic Nondiscrimination Act of 2008.[19] Only ten states even plausibly punished nonconsensual DNA collection, or what she termed "DNA theft."[20] Of those, only half were criminal statutes, and they carried minor penalties.

Moreover, many of those laws offered only piecemeal protection, focusing on a specific aspect of DNA theft—such as disclosing information learned from testing—as opposed to a comprehensive penalty scheme that addressed collection, testing, retention, and disclosure. Although it is not inconceivable that a state might try to stretch conventional theft law to cover genetic thievery, such an application is unprecedented and seems likely to fail.[21]

In sum, although government officials like to tout the rigid constraints on forensic DNA collection, and courts and politicians spend ample time debating the proper scope of mandatory collection laws, one enormous legal loophole remains: the surreptitious scavenging of DNA. This lack of protection perhaps inspired artist Dewey-Hagborg's follow-up work a year later—the creation of a company that sells sprays titled Erase and Replace. Erase purports to delete 99.5 percent of the DNA left behind in public, while Replace clouds the remaining 0.5 percent with genetic noise.[22] Both are available for $230 at the New Museum in New York City.

DRAGNETS

In the fall of 2001, police in Baton Rouge, Louisiana, were in the midst of a frustrating investigation.[23] They had linked together a gruesome string of sexual assaults and murders of women living near the Louisiana State University campus, but had made no progress in finding the perpetrator. Facing criticism for the stalled investigation, police set up a task force dedicated solely to catching the killer. Even Congress got involved in the hunt, granting the state's request for extra funding for the investigation. In August 2002, with the killer still at large, Governor Mike Foster used his weekly radio show to offer advice to the state's women: "You have the right to get a gun permit. Learn to use it." One month later, police released an FBI profile of the killer: likely white, socially inept with women, and between twenty-five and thirty-five years old. Seemingly a nice guy, does not make much money, and strong enough to lift

175 pounds. Footprints found at the scene indicated that he spent time watching the women before making his move, and that he wore a size 10 or 11 Rawlings sneaker.

Baton Rouge resident Shannon Kohler was forty-four when detectives started calling and stopping by his home in November 2002. Police targeted Kohler in part because he had been convicted of burglary almost twenty years earlier—an offense for which, incidentally, he had received a full pardon in 1996. Kohler cooperated with their initial investigation. He pointed out that he wore size 14 boots, in contrast to the killer. He explained that although he had previously worked as a welder at a business that had a shop near one of the incidents, he had not worked for the company nor been at that address in eleven years. He told investigators to check his work records, which would show his whereabouts at the time of each killing.

Still, detectives pressed for a DNA sample. Kohler initially agreed, but then refused on further reflection. He thought to himself, "Our constitutional protections are supposed to protect us from this type of behavior because, without that, we basically live in a police state."[24] In fact, the task force had initiated a "DNA dragnet" in the county, dispatching police to ask for "voluntary" DNA samples from roughly one thousand men. They did not see the request as any big deal—in the words of one officer, "What would these people have to lose if indeed they weren't guilty?"[25]

The answer was *a lot*. Because although police claimed that providing a sample was totally "voluntary," refusal came with a price. First, the detectives told Kohler that if he didn't comply, they would get a court order. They added ominously that such a court order would "possibly get his name in the paper" as a suspected serial killer. Another resident reported to a journalist that police had told him, "You gonna give DNA. . . . How you want to handle that? You want the court order? Fine with me. I'll light your ass up on the . . . news, too."[26] That person yielded, but Kohler continued to resist.

So, the detectives made good on their word. First, they asked a judge for an order compelling Kohler to give up his DNA, submitting a signed and sworn statement claiming they had probable cause to believe he had raped and killed three women. They left out of their affidavit everything Kohler had told them that showed he was likely *not* the killer—the shoe size, the job change, and the pardon. Notwithstanding that the threadbare allegations in the officer's affidavit did not meet the required legal standard (as a court of appeal later held), the judge issued the order.[27] Detectives showed up at Kohler's home two days later and collected his DNA. As threatened, they also leaked the information to the press, and Kohler was identified in television, newspaper, radio, and Internet stories not only as the prime suspect in a serial rape-murder case, but also as a suspect who had refused to cooperate with the police.

The detectives never came back to bother Kohler again—not to tell him that his sample was found not to match that from the crime scene, nor that they eventually apprehended the actual killer (a man named Derrick Todd Lee, whose story is told in Chapter 13). Instead, Kohler learned that he had been cleared when a local news channel reported it and he read two lines to that effect in the *Baton Rouge Advocate*. No formal public announcement was made, nor public record entered, to declare that Kohler had been, from start to finish, erroneously implicated. No one came to tell his friends and co-workers, some of whom probably had already mentally tried and convicted him, that it was all just a big mistake.

The closing of the case gave Shannon Kohler comfort, but it did not end his ordeal. Experience had given him little reason to believe that law enforcement could be trusted with his entire genetic code, and so he asked the police to return his DNA sample and records. When they refused, he filed suit in state court seeking to have his genetic profile wiped from all databases and his biological DNA sample discarded. Bolstered by a civil liberties group, he also filed a petition in federal court, alleging a violation of his constitutional rights. Three years of litigation later, a federal circuit court of appeals found that Kohler had a legitimate claim that his rights had been violated. Not long after that, he went to trial and won a judgment in his favor from a jury that deliberated for only thirty minutes.

Kohler's win turned on a particular legal point—the fact that police obtained a bad warrant to get his DNA sample. It in no way put a halt to DNA dragnets. In addition to Florida and Louisiana, dragnets have been conducted in Massachusetts, California, Michigan, Maryland, Indiana, Illinois, New York, Nebraska, Oklahoma, Virginia, and Kansas—in some cases on more than one occasion.[28] DNA dragnets are even more popular abroad; the largest is likely a German search that netted samples from over 16,000 men. There is even a 1995 book, *The Blooding*, by Joseph Wambaugh, which describes one of the first DNA dragnets—a search in the late 1980s to find a rapist and killer in the United Kingdom that ensnared 150 men.

Although dragnets seem to have fallen out of favor in the United States, law enforcement still occasionally initiates a troll for DNA samples. In the fall of 2014, police in Gainesville, Florida, sought the perpetrator of a series of attacks against women on or near the University of Florida campus. All of the assaults occurred in the evening: a man would approach a woman from behind as she walked, and attempt to drag her into a nearby secluded spot. In one case the assailant, who was described by one victim as a tall, heavyset white male, managed to tear clothing off the victim. Luckily, none of the incidents resulted in a sexual assault or serious injury, as each woman fought back or was aided by bystanders. Police initiated a dragnet seeking DNA from those who "look like the attacker," but ultimately the trail went cold. The attacks stopped, but the case remains unsolved.[29]

One informal national survey of DNA dragnets, based on twenty identified media-reported sweeps, concluded that the method was effective in only one of those cases.[30] That case, which involved the impregnation of a nursing home resident, involved a finite number of suspects.[31] Later reports suggest more equivocal results, including from dragnets that have occurred abroad.[32] A New York case, in which officers canvassed a neighborhood looking for DNA samples from men who resembled a police sketch of a serial rapist/robber, resulted in a match after nine individuals volunteered swabs.[33] A couple of cases have been solved indirectly by dragnet when suspects who refuse to give a voluntarily sample draw added investigation resulting in their identification.[34] For instance, after a brutal killing during a home invasion in North Carolina in 2012, law enforcement asked for DNA samples from men who lived in the adjacent area.[35] A man with a history of burglary refused, and police placed him under surveillance. They then picked up a cigarette that he discarded one day as he left his car, which later turned out to match the crime scene evidence.

Learning that dragnets are largely ineffective bolsters arguments against the practice; but even if they displayed greater success, there are ample reasons why they still should not be permitted. The fundamental problem with dragnets is that they reverse the relationship that, under our Constitution, the government is supposed to have with its citizens. The state is told by our Constitution to presume its citizens are innocent. In a democracy, the people are the *boss* of the police, not the reverse. Yet dragnets assume everyone is guilty until proven innocent. It places upon individuals the burden of establishing they are not criminals, rather than giving the government the burden of proving that they are. The misguidedness of this approach is evident in the opinions of courts that have taken the extraordinary view that failure to comply with a police request for a presumably voluntary DNA sample is itself probable cause to *order* that a sample be taken—a total inversion of basic principles of liberty.

The consequences of losing such fundamental attributes of liberty can be devastating. For instance, an Ann Arbor, Michigan, man caught in a six-hundred-man dragnet targeting African Americans in 1994 alleged that he had lost his job after detectives told his co-workers they were seeking to speak with him.[36] In a 2004 dragnet in Omaha, Nebraska, some of the "volunteers" reported that police had simply shown up at their home, asking them for a sample in connection with a rape investigation as their wife and children looked on. Based on the description of the suspect, police targeted black employees of the city's utility company, and obtained warrants for any person who refused to "volunteer."[37]

In a case involving a Miami dragnet in 2003, police sought a serial rapist accused of attacking six women. The dragnet targeted 120 Hispanic males for DNA samples on the basis of the physical description of the assailant or as a result of police tips. Jorge Garcia had the misfortune to resemble the assailant's description, and voluntarily gave a sample when asked by police. Garcia's profile did not match, and ultimately the dragnet proved unsuccessful. But rather than destroy the sample and associated DNA profile, police decided to take advantage of the DNA in their possession. When Garcia's profile was loaded into the state database, it returned a match to evidentiary samples collected from the victim of a rape in 1996. Jorge Garcia suddenly found himself under arrest, charged with rape, and police publicly touted the case as a successful by-product of their dragnet. A day later, the victim came forward to clarify that she and Garcia had been in a consensual relationship at the time of her rape, thereby explaining the presence of his DNA in the crime scene sample.[38] Garcia's three days in jail, living under the dark cloud of a rape accusation, is bad enough. But imagine the consequence had the victim died, or had not been able to be found ten years after the offense, or had not remembered him? [39]

Unfortunately, the law as it stands does little to stem the tide of large-scale dragnets for DNA samples. As with the case of surreptitious sampling, the practice is supported by a legal fiction. Recall that the law recognizes the police's right to do anything that an ordinary citizen could do. Of course, in practical terms there is an enormous difference between requests made by law enforcement and those made by strangers. If a random person tells you to move along, you might ignore the request or even tell the individual to buzz off. But if a police officer says, "Move along," most people will move along. Indeed, the police rely on the coercion underpinning a request for a "voluntary" swab—otherwise they would never solve any cases, because no right-minded guilty person would ever voluntarily submit one.

Although most courts have come to recognize that probable cause to compel a DNA sample requires more than a mere refusal to give one voluntarily, the law has been slower to curtail softer forms of police coercion. The law could recognize the difference between the requests of an ordinary person and those of a person in uniform, perhaps with a weapon, backed by the authority and power of the state—but as of now it does not. Indeed, the Constitution does not even require the police to tell the individual that the request is just that—a request, as opposed to a demand. Thus, a police officer may use a tone of voice, body position, or physical presence that suggests that compliance is not optional. If the person acquiesces and hands over a sample, there will be no recourse because, under the law, it was always their choice.

ROGUE DATABASES

In July 2012, George Varriale was homeless and living in a tent behind a liquor store just off the highway. One day, he was approached by a detective investigating an alleged rape, and Varriale agreed to provide DNA swabs of his mouth and penis to exculpate him from suspicion. He even signed a standardized consent form that was presented to him, which was labeled with the case number of the rape accusation. The form said that "any evidence found to be involved in this investigation can be used in any future criminal prosecution." At the time, Varriale understood "involved in this investigation" to mean that the sample was for the purpose of clearing him of the rape, and neither the form nor the detective suggested anything otherwise.[40]

In fact, by the time the detective got around to submitting Varriale's DNA sample to the lab for testing, he had all but finished his investigation of the rape, which was eventually declined for prosecution due to the absence of evidence. But what Varriale did not know was that after the lab analyst finished comparing his DNA profile to the evidence in the rape case, she did not throw his sample away and delete his profile. Instead, she determined that it qualified for entry into the "suspect index" of the county's DNA database.

This county database is one of several that feed into the Maryland state database, which in turn feeds into the national DNA database. But not every profile that is loaded at the local level is eligible for uploading to the national level, and some states even separate out what may be loaded in their state level database versus maintained locally. At the national level, rigid rules circumscribe what can be entered—including, most pertinently, that all samples from known persons must be ones collected according to federal or state law. But at the state level, Maryland allowed the entry of samples collected other ways—such as the one provided voluntarily by Varriale.

When questioned, the analyst claimed that the lab did not upload all elimination samples—only those associated with suspects. Thus, for instance, the DNA sample from the boyfriend of a rape victim who is asked to submit an elimination sample in the event that analysts need to disentangle his genetic profile from evidence in the case would not be uploaded. But Varriale's sample, having been labeled by police as a "suspect sample," fell within a category routinely added to the database. To be clear, these are not legislated distinctions, or even ones that might be found in printed public regulations. They were simply the uploading policy adopted by the laboratory.

Maryland's regulations for its statewide database address the quality assurance, storage, and retention rules for DNA collected in four circumstances: those charged with crimes of violence, those charged with burglaries, those convicted of qualifying crimes, and those ordered by the court.[41] But they say nothing about samples voluntarily offered, such as Varriale's. Some might assume that the absence of legal rules means that law enforcement cannot collect or retain such profiles, but in fact most jurisdictions interpret the absence of legal rules to mean they can act without impediment. This perspective leads to counterintuitive results. A sample collected from an offender convicted of the most heinous crime imaginable receives greater legal protection from misuse than one volunteered by a Good Samaritan hoping to aid in an investigation. Whereas the regulations would have required automatic expungement of Varriale's DNA profile had the case been dismissed after he was arrested and actually charged with the rape, there were no expungement rules to protect him against indefinite storage and retention of his voluntary sample. The same is true for a panoply of other protections, including restrictions on what kind of additional testing or searches may be conducted.

Varriale learned the hard way that the police had retained his sample. After the county uploaded it to the local database, a match was made between his profile and that found on a Coke can at the scene of a commercial burglary from 2008. Almost a year after the fateful day that he agreed to aid in the rape investigation, Varriale found himself in court charged with two counts of second-degree burglary, theft over $1,000, and malicious destruction of property. The sole piece of evidence against him was the sample from the can.

Varriale argued to the trial court that the retention and search of the DNA sample he voluntarily provided only to help solve the rape case constituted a violation of his constitutional rights, because it exceeded the scope of the consent he had given to the use of his sample. But his challenge to the state's retention of that sample in its rogue database was rejected by the trial court, and again upon appeal. The appellate court agreed that Varriale "may not have unambiguously consented to the use of his DNA outside the rape investigation," but nonetheless found law enforcement's actions proper—that because Varriale voluntarily gave over his sample, the police were entitled to use it in any way they saw fit. The court also rejected Varriale's claim that the state database law, which required destruction of DNA samples taken during an investigation that does not result in a conviction, should apply to his sample. Again, because Varriale volunteered his sample, it fell outside the law's scope and thus offered him no protection. The court recognized, "it may seem anomalous that a volunteer like Varriale would have fewer statutory protections than someone who had been charged with or even convicted of a serious criminal offense," but observed that a bill that would have extended protections of those kinds had recently failed to pass the state legislature.[42]

Varriale's case is now pending before Maryland's highest court. But Maryland's county databases arc no outliers. Rogue databases of this kind have sprung up around the country, with documented references in at least nine states, including California, Florida, Illinois, Missouri, Maryland, New York, Arizona, Pennsylvania, and New Mexico.[43] These databases can be as simple as Excel spreadsheets or as sophisticated as networked terminals that mimic the national database, CODIS. Because they operate in the shadows, little is known about them.

Fortunately for Varriale, his lawyer is considered one of the nation's top experts on the topic.[44] Maryland public defender Stephen Mercer filed a Freedom of Information Act request to uncover information about two of Maryland's most notorious local databases, which cover the two counties with the largest fraction of criminal cases in the state. As of 2012, the Baltimore City database contained almost 10,000 specimens, including over 3,000 victim profiles. There have also been over seven hundred matches using that database, although it is unclear how many resulted in actual prosecution or conviction. The Prince George's County disclosures revealed that the police know their practices stand on shaky footing. Whereas the forensic, staff, and suspect indices all have clear statements of authority, the victim index is listed as "authority pending." In 2012, state police officials also apparently attempted to reassure the legislature by informing them that Maryland's crime labs had voluntarily agreed not to store material gathered from living victims.[45]

The limited information about rogue database practices in other jurisdictions is equally alarming. Orange County publicly touts its local database, which has purportedly racked up over 90,000 samples and earned its lab millions of dollars in support from the county.[46] New York State has more than eight local databases containing over 2,000 profiles, according to one account.[47] The New York City database came under fire in 2005 when a defendant won a protective order that prohibited the city lab from uploading to the local database the profile that he had given for the purpose of a pending case. The litigation revealed that the city maintained a "Linkage Database" that included samples not just from arrestees and suspects, but from crime scene bystanders and Good Samaritan contributors.[48] The lab admitted it had "no policy, procedure or rules for purging profiles" from the database, and that there were no restrictions on the database's permissible use. Around the same time, state labs in

New York's Onondaga and Monroe counties ceased storing suspect or victim samples. As one deputy county attorney wrote, "I find no authority that allows for a local DNA database of suspects or 'non-convicted persons.' . . . If suspects prevail in any type of civil action, the County would be liable for damages, as well as attorney fees."[49] However, the legal question was never definitely resolved, and in other jurisdictions rogue databases continue to flourish.

Rogue databases are attractive to law enforcement in part because they allow local police to circumvent the quality assurance restrictions that the FBI imposes on uploads to the national database. The FBI requires that only qualified laboratories and technicians process samples that will later be uploaded, and imposes specific rules regarding the authenticity of samples. The DNA profile itself also has to meet certain standards for completeness. Because partial profiles can turn up so many accidental matches, the standards reject crime scene profiles that yield too little information. Plus, the national rules require that samples be acquired in conformity with state law—such as rules that require removal of profiles of arrestees whose cases have been dismissed.

National rules also require that crime scene samples be shown to have a sufficient nexus to the crime. Suppose a theft occurs at a party. Police may go in and collect all the cups from the scene, and DNA-test them in search of suspects. But the FBI forbids them from uploading all of those DNA profiles to the national unsolved crimes database, because authorities cannot pinpoint any as belonging to the actual thief. It is only if a witness were to say, "The thief was drinking from that cup," that the sample could be considered proper for upload, because of its association with the alleged perpetrator. Rogue databases, however, can hold the DNA found on each cup.

Rogue databases also offer the opportunity to store genetic information beyond that contained in the customary national DNA profile. For instance, at least one state, New Mexico, maintains a rogue DNA database with results from testing parts of the Y chromosome of DNA samples. This particular test is often useful in a rape case, where it helps to isolate the male profile in a mixture that also contains DNA from a female victim. Y-STRs have also been shown to be effective at predicting surnames, particularly rare surnames, given the cultural practice of carrying the man's surname forward.[50] Rogue databases allow a jurisdiction to conduct a new kind of genetic test or novel form of database search, all without seeking permission from a court. Many DNA misuse statutes even refer specifically to improper access to the legislatively created DNA database, so their terms do not even apply to DNA databases created on the whim of the police.

In short, local rogue databases circumvent all the legal restrictions placed on DNA samples collected in the ordinary way. Law enforcement can keep samples from victims, from persons who volunteered their DNA to rule themselves out of a police investigation, or from any individual whose DNA they manage to sample—surreptitiously or otherwise. They also can upload incomplete profiles or profiles processed at unaccredited labs or using procedures that have not been validated. Profiles also need not be complete, or unambiguous—a messy crime scene mixture can be uploaded, or a result that produced only half of the profile. And the searches conducted in rogue databases need not conform to any law. Rogue databases can even elude data reporting requirements in states, such as Maryland, which require labs to track statistics regarding matches and database composition. Finally, because state rules on expungement also do not apply, once a profile finds its way into a rogue database, it rarely comes out. In Varriale's case, the analyst testified that she believed a profile would be expunged only upon "court order," and then admitted that she had never seen any such order come through.

The attractiveness of a database that operates outside the law has led genetic entrepreneurs to start offering software that links them all together, creating a sort of shadowbase, or shadow of the federal database. One of the earliest champions of this model was a North Carolina company called DNA·SI. Founded in 1998 by Bill Britt, a colorful and conservative Amway scion who used his income to launch businesses of varying success, ranging from rental cars to cassette tapes to tax services to motivational speakers, the company advertised an array of DNA testing and database services. Britt, a veteran who had served as a city manager multiple times, had himself even had a couple small brushes with the law, including during a rocky period in his marriage during which a restraining order was issued against him at the request of his wife.[51]

Britt's company was no stranger to stumbles as well. In 2006, DNA Security, Inc., as it was then known, processed the DNA samples involved in the Duke lacrosse team case, in which a woman falsely accused members of the team of sexual assault. That work led to the company's entanglement in the controversy. The prosecutor engaged in misconduct with regard to the DNA samples, including withholding the results of tests that failed to corroborate her story. An appellate court likewise found that lab officials had "obscured findings" and deliberately used "opaque language" to make the DNA results seem more inculpatory.[52] These actions contributed to the prosecutor's eventual disbarment and a lawsuit that the company eventually settled with the wrongly accused.[53] Notably, however, it did not lead to the closure of the business, nor even the loss of its accreditation.

Thus the lab, which eventually rebranded itself as DNA:SI, was able to enter into a contract in 2006 with the Palm Bay, Florida, police department to "develop a local agency databank of forensic DNA evidence for use on most crimes."[54] DNA:SI initiated and funded the program as a showcase project.[55] It envisioned three phases: training officers in sample collection, both from known persons and from low-level crime scenes for ten-day turnaround testing; refining the automation process to allow for electronic tracking of samples and receipt of results over squad car computers; and finally, an assessment phase to track the project's outcomes and affordability.[56] The goal was to circumvent CODIS, which precluded uploading of samples from persons not charged with crimes or who gave DNA for elimination purposes only.[57] Significantly, police personnel were also asked to provide samples to help identify contamination. Although most complied, 15 percent did not.

During phase one, officers gathered 832 samples from "stop-and-frisk scenarios, arrested subjects, and victims and witnesses for purposes of eliminating them . . . in the case of a mixed sample." Officials also developed profiles from over 5,000 evidence swabs.[58] In the end, they generated 323 hits, including 145 matches between a suspect and crime scene evidence, and 83 scene-to-scene matches. Of those, 41 were "blind" hits, 34 were elimination hits, 138 confirmed a known suspect, and 93 resulted in the reopening of otherwise closed unsolved cases.

At the start of 2013, Bill Britt died, and DNA:SI simply stopped functioning.[59] By the end of the year, DNA:SI had filed for bankruptcy,[60] and a new owner has still not been found. But Palm Bay had already moved on. The foundation of the local database enabled police to enter into another agreement, testing a ninety-minute, one-touch DNA typing system called RapidHIT.[61] Developed by IntegenX, these platforms allow for immediate processing of DNA samples, with local database interoperability.

The end of DNA:SI therefore in no way marked the end of shadow-basing. The home page for SmallPond, the service now used by Palm Bay,[62] advertises that "SmallPond may be for you":

if you are currently using or considering the use of CODIS for your DNA databasing needs, but are concerned about

- the long backlogs at public state and regional DNA labs with CODIS access
- the profile entry restrictions imposed by CODIS
- the lack of local criminal elements in the CODIS database
- the costs and maintenance headaches of the required hardware/network infrastructure
- the costs and time of training and certifications required[63]

In other words, SmallPond's deliberate pitch is to lull customers irritated by the quality and privacy restrictions of the national database. As of May 2013, SmallPond alone facilitated the storage and search of over 1 million DNA profiles.[64]

SmallPond has also partnered with Arizona's Department of Public Safety to integrate its databases into the Rapid DNA identification systems currently being deployed.[65] Thus police may process a DNA sample on-scene—either from a known person or from crime scene evidence—and immediately search that profile against a local database. SmallPond will also store that profile in perpetuity, so that it might be later searched or accessed. Going back to the party example, police could simply work their way through the party, requesting DNA samples from the attendees and swabbing cups, taking only ninety-odd minutes per tray of five samples to upload all that information to rogue databases in the event such information proves useful to that investigation, or any future investigation.

All of this DNA sampling is poised to explode on the scene, and all outside the restraints of law. Although the federal law that created the national database system clearly comprehended that there would be state and local level databases, that law does no more than condition national access on the state's compliance with the rules for its portion of the national index.[66] It does not prohibit a state from creating a shadow database that retains those samples, nor does it forbid local databases. And as should now be clear, in the absence of legal authority explicitly forbidding these local databases or regulating what goes in them, law enforcement has simply built their own databases and crafted their own rules of engagement. Only Alaska, and arguably Washington State, expressly preclude local DNA databases that do not comply with laws governing the state database.[67]

Across the country, states debate important issues such as whether to include misdemeanants in their database or just felons, whether to add arrestees or only convicted offenders. State legislatures craft careful statutes that precisely detail the scope and operative rules of their databases—outlining expungement rules and oversight mechanisms. New York's DNA database law alone runs more than 1,500 words.[68] And when courts or the public seem nervous about large-scale genetic repositories, police chiefs and district attorneys are quick to promise that database access is closely regulated and tightly circumscribed, and that ample penalties exist for any person who fails to follow the law. And yet as the public conversation drones on, we ignore that law enforcement can easily circumvent these hard-fought compromises through three legal loopholes that are little acknowledged, much less closed: sneak sampling, dragnets, and rogue databasing.

CHAPTER 12

Genetic Informants: Familial Searches

IN 2004, A truck driver in the United Kingdom suffered a fatal heart attack after a brick thrown off an overpass crashed through his windshield as he passed below. Investigators had no leads, but found a small quantity of blood on the brick recovered from the vehicle. Testing revealed a DNA profile, but a search of the nationwide database returned no exact matches.[1]

Flummoxed, the investigators decided to run the profile in the database again, but this time they changed the parameters. Typically, searches for a match in the DNA database seek total identity between the crime scene sample and a known person at all genetic markers. However, it is possible to run a less exacting search, looking for profiles that match only partially.

The idea behind pursuing "near misses" derives from the scientific fact that related people are more likely than unrelated people to share genetic traits. Compile a list of near miss profiles to serve as leads, and the assailant may turn out to be a relative of one person on that list. Investigate the leads and you may find the person who actually left the crime scene stain. In the trucker's case, a near match was returned. Although the lack of complete identity in the profile meant that the person in the database did not commit the crime, the similarity between that person's profile and the DNA sample on the brick suggested that the perpetrator could be a close relative of the man in the database. Investigators probed further, and found that the man had a brother. After further investigation, including the brother's confession and corroborative DNA testing, the brother was sentenced to six years in prison.

A year later, across the pond, Denver district attorney Mitchell Morrissey stared down DNA profiles in three separate unsolved rape cases. The database search for exactly matching profiles failed to return any hits.[2] But a partial hit search uncovered matches in each case. Morrissey figured that, given the names of the persons who partially matched, he would be able to comb through their family trees to find his assailants.

The only problem was that the matches originated in Oregon, Arizona, and California, and the FBI, which administers the national database, stores its information anonymously. Even though a state can access its own information, FBI rules at that time forbade states from disclosing to other states the identifying information of anyone other than the "putative perpetrator." Because Morrissey was not looking for the perpetrator, but rather sought a possible relative of a perpetrator, he could not get the names.

Morrissey asked for an exemption to the rule, so that he could learn the identity of the prospective leads. But federal DNA database head Thomas Callaghan refused, citing concerns about privacy and fairness.[3] He was worried that the searches would discredit DNA databasing efforts, and stated that he "would be more comfortable with congressional authorization to conduct familial searches" rather than making case-by-case exceptions based on political pressure.[4]

Frustrated, Morrissey wrote to the director of the FBI laboratories in 2006, complaining that the policy "protects murderers and rapists" and warning that one of his "quite assertive" victims would generate a media maelstrom.[5] Several days later, FBI director Robert Mueller called Morrissey to discuss the issue. Shortly after that, Mueller changed the national database policy to permit the release by states of identifying information in the event of a partial match.[6]

Arizona and Oregon complied with Morrissey's request, but California still resisted. After a campaign by the state's sheriffs and district attorneys' organizations, however, then California attorney general Jerry Brown agreed to release the name. Then, in April 2008, Brown announced that California would not only share such information, but also set out the first policy in the nation that explicitly authorized intentional searches for partial matches—also known as "familial" or "kinship" searches—in its DNA database.[7] Thus a national debate about familial searching was born.

Morrissey brushed off concerns about abuse, telling a reporter for *60 Minutes* that he wasn't talking about using familial searches to solve "car break-ins," but only the most serious, violent crimes. But the method still endured sharp criticism. Upon further investigation Morrissey's first three familial search leads all turned out to be dead ends. None of the family members of those leads could have left the crime scene sample. To be fair, Morrissey did eventually secure the first conviction of a suspect identified through a familial search. What was the crime? A car break-in. On two occasions in 2008, a thief in Colorado broke into different cars. Blood found at the scene showed a single perpetrator, but a routine DNA database search did not match to any known persons. Police then ran the sample using familial search software, and uncovered six candidate leads. Five were dead ends, but one looked more promising. Among other things, the lead was himself a convicted car thief. Tests of that man's brother, Luis Jaimes-Tinajero, matched the blood at the scene, and eventually he pled guilty to one count of criminal trespass. When asked about potential privacy concerns, Morrissey again shook off any complaints: "[t]he bad guy abandoned the DNA at the crime scene," and familial searches are no more than a "valuable way to generate leads."[8]

So, who has the better argument? Is familial searching a harmless investigative tool that simply harnesses the power of existing databases? Or is it a menacing encroachment on civil liberties likely to tarnish the rights and reputations of those with the misfortune of having a relative in the criminal justice system? As with most things DNA, the answer is: a little bit of both.

HOW IT WORKS

To understand what is at stake, it is at first important to have a clear idea of how familial searching works. The basic premise is that persons who are biologically related to one another are more likely than unrelated persons to have similar genetic profiles. For instance, in a standard thirteen-locus DNA profile of twenty-six alleles, a child and a parent will match at a minimum of thirteen alleles. That is because the child gets half its DNA from its mother, and half from its father.

It follows that full siblings are likely to resemble one another genetically as well. Two full siblings might share no alleles in common—the unpredictability of inheritance means there is a 25 percent chance at each locus that one sibling inherits half of each parent's alleles, while the other inherits the other half. But there is also a 25 percent chance that they share both alleles. On average, according to one estimate, full siblings have between 17 to 18 alleles in common, as compared to the 8 to 9 alleles unrelated persons are likely to share.[9] The probability of overlap turns on several factors—most pertinently on common inheritance, but also on the likelihood that the parents themselves shared a particular allele and on the commonness of their alleles in the population at large.

Given the greater likelihood that related persons share genetic markers in common, investigators can attempt to find relatives by looking for profiles that are strongly similar to the one left at a crime scene. In a typical DNA search, investigators are interested in entries from the known persons index that mirror the profile of the forensic sample. So, if a cigarette butt smoked by the perpetrator is typed at thirteen loci, or twenty-six alleles, looking for an exact match means finding a known offender who also has the same twenty-six markers.

But suppose no exact match is returned. Instead, there is a person's profile that matches at twenty-two of the twenty-six places. It is possible that this person has nothing to do with the individual who left the crime scene sample. For instance, one study of the Arizona state database revealed 122 pairwise matches at nine loci, 20 at ten, 1 at eleven, and 1 at twelve; only the final two were confirmed to be sibling matches.[10] But it is also possible that the overlap is not coincidental. The closeness between the evidentiary profile and the person in the database may not be chance, but may instead be because the match is the father, son, or sibling of the person who left DNA at the crime scene.

A near miss match of this kind can come about two different ways: inadvertently, or after an intentional search. Inadvertent partial matching occurs when investigators search the database intending to find an exact match, but happen upon matches that are closely approximate. Such matches may come about, for instance, because the analyst searches the database using a less stringent approach, because the data appear incomplete.[11] At that point, the analyst may choose either to inform law enforcement of the partial matches or to return a report that states that no exact matches were found. Which of those routes the analyst takes often depends on the policy, custom, or laws of the particular jurisdiction, as will be discussed next.

The second method, called intentional familial searching, is a deliberate search for partial match leads. In this case, the very purpose of the search is to identify possible partial match leads, and then conduct further investigation to determine whether those leads point to a relative who is in fact the perpetrator. Of course, even unrelated people can be incredibly genetically similar. For that reason, when investigators get back the list of near misses from an intentional familial search, the persons who most closely match to the crime scene evidence are not necessarily the strongest leads. Even if a relative of the perpetrator is in the database, that person might be buried in a list of entries that have more matching characteristics by chance. And of course, investigators are still likely to get a large number of leads that partially match by happenstance, even if the perpetrator does not have any relatives in the database at all.

One way to winnow the list of leads down, on the basis of the genetic information alone, is to consider not just the raw number of markers that the near miss candidates and the crime scene evidence have in common, but the rarity of those markers. Some genetic markers are quite common, whereas others are found in fewer individuals. A near miss that includes some of those rare markers, then, may be more likely to be a relative of the perpetrator than is a near miss that has more overall markers in common with the evidence but with markers that are less distinctive. Because this is a subtle task that is dependent on tedious mathematical calculations, there has been a drive to develop software, including enhancing the CODIS software itself, to perform this kind of sophisticated familial searching.[12]

Still, studies show that the larger the database, the more difficult it is to conduct an effective familial search. In one set of studies involving simulation searches of three state databases of varying sizes, the likelihood of finding a relative in the database dropped precipitously as the database grew. Whereas a parent or child in the database was listed within in the top ten candidate leads 98 percent of the time in a 19,300-person database, that likelihood fell to 72 percent of the time in a 356,000-person database, and to less than half of the time (48%) in a 1.8 million–person database.[13] The estimate for the 10 million–person national database was that only 29 percent of the time would a parent-child relative be returned in the top ten leads. The numbers were significantly lower across the board for other relatives, such as full siblings.

Another way to narrow down a list of possible leads is to conduct additional genetic tests, such as to use certain signatures from the male chromosome that descend patrilineally (Y-STR typing).[14] For instance, Colorado undertook a project to run 1,580 forensic profiles against its 87,000 known offenders database, generating roughly 137 million comparisons. Of those, thirty-two possible leads were produced: thirteen female and nineteen male. The male candidates were then further investigated using Y-STR typing, and six matched to Y-chromosome identifiers, suggesting the perpetrator was likely somewhere in their family line. Those six, along with the females, were then slated for further investigation.[15]

Although effective, adding Y-STR typing presents its own complications. First, most databases do not currently include Y-STR data, and so physical samples must be retrieved and retested. Second, if there are a number of candidate leads, then multiple samples may require such re-testing, which adds both time and expense to the investigative process. And lastly, reliance on Y-STR typing limits the utility of familial search methods to identifying potential leads in the male population only; a perpetrator who has only a female relative in the database may still go undetected.

Once investigators have a manageable list of near miss leads, they can always seek out nongenetic information, such as the age, geographic origin, or other demographic characteristics of the lead that might support inculpatory inferences about that person's relatives. Again, however, this step can be time-consuming and labor-intensive, especially because the DNA database stores profiles anonymously and divorced from biographical data. Thus, accessing demographic data entails more than just a quick scan down the list.

For all of these reasons, the effectiveness of a familial search depends entirely on the specific parameters of that search. And there are trade-offs. Narrow search parameters increase the likelihood that a lead found via such a search is, in fact, a relative of the perpetrator.[16] But narrow parameters also increase the likelihood of missing out on that relative altogether because the criteria were too strict. Conversely, more generous parameters raise the probability that any relative in the database will be captured by the search, but this person may be buried among a long list of other entries that turn out to be false.[17] In short, if the search standard is too strict, it may miss an entry that is related to the source; but if it is too loose, it will sweep in a larger number of false leads that make it more difficult to find the true link.

The difficulty of striking the right balance has lead skeptics to question whether familial searching is worth the effort. Remember, too, that finding a lead is just the first step in the process. After a convincing lead is identified, investigators must then rummage through that person's family tree to determine whether any of that lead's relatives were the actual perpetrator of the offense. They may simply approach the database lead and ask for more information about the person's family structure. Or they may use public databases and information to determine possible suspects. They might even surreptitiously collect DNA samples from the lead's family members in the hopes that one turns out to match the crime scene evidence.

In perhaps the most high profile familial search case yet, police did a combination of all of these things. In the mid-1980s, a serial killer surfaced in the Los Angeles area. DNA ultimately linked him to at least ten rape-murders, but he managed to evade capture. Police nicknamed him the "Grim Sleeper," because of an apparent period of dormancy between strikes.

In 2008, California had become the first state in the nation to explicitly authorize intentional familial searches. Today, it remains one of only a handful of states with a clear, detailed, and public policy on when and how to conduct familial searches. Under the California policy, familial searches were limited to the most serious cases, and only when the investigative trail had gone cold. The parameters for a match dictated that at least fifteen of twenty-six alleles must match; if so, another round of testing (Y-STR) was required to further isolate true leads. The Grim Sleeper was one of the first cases that California authorities subjected to familial testing. But back in 2008, nothing turned up.

When the search was run again two years later, however, it generated a hit to the man who had been arrested on a weapons charge for which state law required him to submit a DNA sample. Given his age and the dates of the serial killer's attacks, investigators focused immediately on the man's older relatives, specifically his father. Posing as a busboy at a restaurant where the family dined, a police officer collected discarded pizza crusts and cutlery to test for the father's forensic DNA profile. When it returned a match to the Grim Sleeper evidence, the father was arrested.

The apprehension of the alleged Grim Sleeper is probably the flashiest use of familial testing, but it is hard to know precisely how representative it is. The jurisdictions that engage in the practice do not hold press conferences about their failures, nor do they publicly acknowledge how many familial search investigations they have conducted. Some do not formally announce that they have conducted familial searches at all. Still, it is possible to piece together a hazy picture of how often the technique is currently employed.

WHO IS DOING IT?

Perhaps surprisingly, the first forensic use of DNA typing was in a familial context. Officials used genetic typing in an immigration case in the United Kingdom to "test of the truthfulness of a claim to family connectedness."[18] In 1983, Christiana Sarbah, a mother who had emigrated from Ghana to the United Kingdom with three of her children, sought the admission of her son Andrew, who had stayed behind. It was undisputed that the three children were the offspring of the mother, but authorities questioned whether Christiana was in fact Andrew's mother, as opposed to aunt. The immigration court found the photographic and testimonial evidence adduced by the family insufficient, but then someone at the legal aid center advocating for the family read a newspaper article about a scientist who had developed a new kind of DNA "fingerprinting" technology.

The scientist, Alec Jeffreys, accepted the case, seeing it as a good opportunity to test his discovery. He sampled DNA from Christiana, Andrew, and her three children. From those probes he pieced together the likely profile of Andrew's father, and also showed that it was far more likely that Christiana was the mother than aunt. British authorities accepted the proof, allowing Andrew to stay in the country, and announcing that such evidence would be accepted in future immigration cases.

But though Christiana Sarbah's case resolved in the 1980s, it was not until 2002, as DNA database began to take off, that the first formal familial database search occurred. The case again came from Britain, where police pursued the perpetrator of a series of rapes in the 1970s.[19] The search proceeded in an atypical fashion: Investigators had compiled a list of potential suspects based on various conventional investigative methods, and familial search principles were used to narrow the list. One of those identified was a man by the name of Joseph Kappen.[20] Further investigation revealed that Kappen had since died, but a familial search of the UK national database revealed that his son had certain genetic characteristics in common with the crime scene samples. Although the lack of an exact match (as well as the son's age) ruled him out as the perpetrator, it did suggest the viability of a possible familial connection. Based on this information, investigators received permission to exhume Joseph Kappen's body, and subsequent testing revealed a match.[21]

Word of the early successes with familial search methods quickly spread, and a handful of vocal advocates, including District Attorney Morrissey, began promoting its adoption in the United States. But uncertainty about the legality and public reception of the method hindered widespread adoption. Although the FBI quickly changed its policy to allow sharing of familial search information,[22] questions remained as to whether it constituted a potential Fourth Amendment violation. Moreover, each state had its own set of rules and customs surrounding partial matches, most of which was informal and led to confusion.

The most common position was silence; many states neither expressly allowed nor forbid familial searches. In the absence of express legislative rules, localities or even individual laboratories simply formulated their own approaches.[23] Some laboratories assumed that the lack of a law forbidding the practice meant that it was allowed. Others treated the absence of legal authorization as a sign that it was prohibited. And still others followed a "don't ask, *do* tell" approach—intentional queries in the database for a familial match were not allowed, but if an analyst happened to come across a very close partial match while searching for an exact match, that near miss could be reported. The legal uncertainty was not just silly; it led to serious consequences. In 2007, the administrator of the Massachusetts state DNA database was fired in part for reporting four near matches, a practice that state officials claimed was prohibited even though the law was not entirely clear at the time.[24]

At present, the picture of familial searching in the states is somewhat clearer, although still incomplete. The National Institute of Justice recently funded a survey of nationwide practices,[25] but results are not yet available. The most comprehensive survey was conducted in 2009.[26] Based on that assessment, as well as some high-profile developments since then, a fuzzy image emerges.

The federal government still does not itself conduct familial searches,[27] although some members of Congress have indicated a desire to expressly authorize them.[28] In 2013, an FBI working group on familial searching released a set of policy recommendations regarding the practice, which ultimately concluded against an embrace of federal familial searching at that time.[29] The primary concern was that the enormous size of the national database would render such searches ineffective, although the group recommended reconsidering the issue once additional loci were added to the standard thirteen-locus profile. California,[30] Colorado,[31] Texas,[32] Virginia,[33] and Wyoming[34] currently explicitly engage in familial searching, using special software designed to help winnow matches more effectively.[35] At the other end of the spectrum, both Maryland[36] and the District of Columbia[37] explicitly ban familial searches.

The remainder of states, lacking clear legal rules forbidding familial searches, vary in their actual practices.[38] In one 2009 study, fifteen states expressly permitted the reporting of partial matches found inadvertently;[39] six prohibited familial searching, but were unclear about whether partial matches may be reported;[40] and eleven seemed to prohibit both reporting of inadvertent partial matches and intentional familial searching.[41] The only common thread is that these policies on familial searches—whether for or against the practice—are not enacted as a matter of law or even announced formally by political leaders; instead, they trace to a laboratory manual or internal policy applied without the benefit of a written manual.

It is hard to say whether familial searching will take off, or whether its current levels of state endorsement will remain constant. As with many questions of DNA policy, the answer probably depends on two factors. First, whether the technique gains in effectiveness, which likely it will. And second, whether the public will resist its implementation, no matter how effective it becomes.

SUSPECTS.COM

In June 1996, nineteen-year-old Angie Raye Dodge was found dead in her apartment in Idaho Falls, Idaho, by colleagues concerned that she had not shown up for work.[42] She had been sexually assaulted and stabbed to death, and police believed she knew her killers. So, when a year later a friend of hers, Benjamin Hobbs, was arrested for attacking a woman in Nevada, police wondered whether he might have been one of the culprits in Dodge's killing. They resumed a series of interrogations of one of Hobbs's local friends named Christopher Tapp. Tapp initially denied any involvement, but after repeated interrogations, including a promise of immunity that was later revoked, Tapp finally broke down and confessed that Hobbs had killed Dodge, as a result of a personal grievance.

But DNA evidence at the scene—including semen, hair, and skin cell samples—matched only one person—and neither Tapp nor Hobbs. Police surmised that the two must have committed the crime with a third party. Over the course of a long interrogation, they repeatedly pressed Tapp for a third name. He stammered, "The name—nothing comes to my head. . . . It wasn't Jer—it wasn't Russ. I mean—I'm gonna say Jeff." Eventually Tapp said, "Mike was his first name." But he never provided any additional information. Tapp was convicted and sentenced to twenty-five years to life, but Hobbs continued to deny involvement. Police never pursued Hobbs's prosecution further, possibly because he had already begun serving a twenty-five-year sentence in the Nevada case.

In an unusual turn of events, Angie Dodge's mother began to have doubts about Tapp's guilt. Although she had initially wanted him to receive the death penalty, a decade later she became a firm believer in Tapp's innocence. Her obsession with the case over time had led her to pore over every piece of evidence, including twenty hours of recorded interrogations. Her investigation led her to believe that Tapp had given a false confession. She also believed Angie's murder had been committed by one person—*not* Tapp—acting alone. She even sought the help of Idaho's Innocence Project, which agreed to take the case only to lose its federal funding in 2013, causing it to scale back. The national Innocence Project agreed to help with Tapp's case, but so far the courts have denied all of his claims for relief.

In sum, even though Tapp had been convicted, neither the police nor Dodge's family was fully satisfied that Angie Dodge's case was closed; each side still sought a third person. Despite the massive growth in the national DNA database, crime scene samples from Angie's murders have never matched to a known offender. In 2014, with national attention drawn to the case by several media outlets, the investigation took on new urgency, and the county gave the chief prosecutor $25,000 to fund an outside review of the investigation.[43] Perhaps that was why, in April 2014, investigators sent two semen samples from the case to Sorenson Forensics Lab. Sorenson Forensics is a private laboratory that performs contract DNA testing in criminal case work. Its parent company, Sorenson Genomics, provides DNA testing for a wide array of purposes, including medical testing and academic research. One of its divisions, Relative Genetics, also offered DNA testing and database matching services for recreational purposes. The Sorenson Molecular Genealogy Foundation was a relic of the company's early days as a nonprofit aimed at genetic research; through volunteers, it had compiled a database of more than 39,000 males to create "an excellent tool for surname research," as well as a 76,000 person database of markers that descend from the mother's family line. Both were searchable online.

But Sorenson eventually transformed into a commercial entity, and by the 2000s, Sorenson and Ancestry.com, a popular for-profit online portal where ordinary people can access and explore genealogical data, became partners.[44] Ancestry.com maintains a treasure trove of documentary genealogical data, including the complete census collection, ship passenger lists, and other historical papers. Thus it was a perfect marriage: at the time, Ancestry.com counted over 14 million users of its site, many of whom built elaborate family trees from personal knowledge and investigation, while Sorenson had a trove of genetic data from the DNA testing services it engaged in to aid in genetic connections of the same kind. Some of the people in Sorenson's database had even enrolled for free, because the company had initially offered free genetic testing in exchange for a chart listing four generations of pedigree.

By combining forces, Ancestry.com could offer a service that allowed users to swab their own cheeks and then log online to see genetic connections, as well as integrate genetic data into their known family history. In May 2012, Ancestry.com outright purchased all of Sorenson's genealogical data, including the Sorenson DNA database.[45] It currently boasts a web database of more than 700,000 people, along with millions of detailed family trees.[46] Thus, Ancestry.com became a powerful site for more than just finding a great-grandfather; it became a place where adoptees or donor-conceived individuals could find birth families,[47] or a man abandoned as an infant could find blood relatives.[48]

In the case of Angie Dodge, a clever detective thought that Sorenson might be able to help him crack the case of the missing perpetrator through somewhat unusual means: a familial search. By having Sorenson Forensics test portions of the male and female chromosomes, and then comparing those results to the Ancestry.com database, he hoped he could find a clue to the identity of the unidentified perpetrator.

Just over two months after submitting the samples, the detective received the genetic markers. Inputting the markers into the Y-chromosome database for males, he received forty-one results—partial matches that might indicate some degree of relatedness between the perpetrator and the person who had given the DNA sample in the database. The third result looked particularly compelling, and was the closest of all those returned: thirty-four of thirty-five markers matched. The detective consulted genetic experts, all of whom agreed that this person was likely a relative of the actual perpetrator.

When the detective tried to uncover the name of that person, however, the results came back as "protected," meaning that Sorenson had obscured the identity, consistent with its policy regarding living donors. When contacted, Ancestry.com informed the detective that it would comply with a subpoena to release the name, and so the detective obtained a search warrant for all biographical and genetic information for that individual.

Ancestry.com released the information, and the donor was identified as Michael Perrell Usry Sr. He would have been forty-four at the time of Dodge's murder, and had listed his residence as Clinton, Mississippi. Using Ancestry.com's genealogical trees, the detective pieced together five generations of the Usry family. He isolated three men who would have been the right age to have committed the homicide; one of those men had ties to the Idaho Falls area: Michael Usry's only son, Michael Jr.

Michael Jr. would have been just two years younger than Angie Dodge on the night of her murder. The detective also recalled that, long ago, Christopher Tapp had named "Mike" as a possible third person involved in the killing, and he fit the basic description that Tapp had supplied. Using Facebook, the detective discovered that two of Michael Jr.'s sisters attended college about twenty-five miles from the scene of the killing, just a few years after the homicide. He also saw that Michael Jr. listed friends in a family that split its time between Clinton and a town in Idaho just thirteen miles from Idaho Falls. Chillingly, a Google search revealed that Michael Usry Jr. has worked in connection with short horror films called "gratuitously violent" by one reporter.[49] One, titled *Murderabilia*, even depicted the murder of a young girl, with the killer leaving a token behind. Michael Jr. had no criminal record according to the FBI files, which also showed a possible address in New Orleans, Louisiana.

Having conducted a careful and thorough investigation, the detective sought a search warrant from the Louisiana courts, compelling Michael Usry Jr. to give a DNA sample. One day in early December, police officers called Usry, claiming to be investigating a hit and run and asking to photograph his car. He agreed to the meeting, and was surprised to find himself whisked to an interrogation room with a one-way mirror. When it came time to give the swab, Usry complied, in disbelief that he might be accused of a homicide.

He later described living for a month in a cloud of uncertainty, "wondering if these guys were going to use a battering ram to bust open the door and shoot my dog after he started barking at them."[50] Eventually, he received an e-mail clearing him, explaining that his DNA was not a match. But most experts speculate, and Usry himself wonders, whether some unknown person in his family tree might have perpetrated the killings. Idaho Falls police have ruled out all the known branches, but are continuing to investigate the case. It may yet turn out that Usry learns a family secret—an unspoken adoption or illegitimate child—in the most unpleasant manner imaginable.

The familial search in the Angie Dodge case differed from the typical search in a number of critical ways. First, the police conducted the final confirmatory stages of the investigation openly, with the suspect's full awareness. In many familial search cases, law enforcement simply avoids the legal process by collecting a surreptitious sample—for example, staking out a suspect until he throws away a cup or wrapper that can be retrieved for testing. Instead, in this case, the authorities obtained a court order and executed it in a way that notified Usry of their suspicions.

This approach has the benefit of minimizing the degree to which police silently stalk citizens, sweeping up their genetic information. It also has the salutary effect of ensuring greater transparency in how familial searches are conducted. In addition to the suspect's learning about the search, the request for an order creates a legal record, and a judge can exercise judgment about the propriety of seeking a sample. But overt methods have the drawback of entangling a suspect in a web of uncertainty and serious accusation that can take a while—in Usry's case, an entire month—to unspool. Usry seems to have taken the events in stride, but imagine hearing that your spouse or new boyfriend or child's teacher or dentist was under suspicion for a brutal murder. No matter how confident you felt in the person's innocence, there would be no way to fully banish the "what ifs."

Second, the police relied on a public DNA database, rather than the national law enforcement DNA database, to conduct the search. What is more, the profile in the database was not the product of government compulsion, as are those in the national database. As it happened, Michael Sr. had given a DNA sample in connection with a church project that aimed to support the Sorenson Molecular Genealogy Foundation. He had no idea that his DNA sample would be readily traceable back to him directly, much less sold to a for-profit company, much less lead to the eventual accusation of his son for murder. But to the extent that Michael Jr. paid the price for his father's decision to give his DNA, at least that decision was the result of Michael Sr.'s own free will. In the ordinary familial search case, the father's sample would have been taken by compulsion. It is thus ordinarily the judgments of the state, not one's own relative, that open the entire family to potential suspicion.

Legally speaking, the detective in this story did everything by the book. In fact, he went above and beyond the book, taking every step to build a solid case before approaching Michael Jr. for a sample, and even choosing to use legal process when sneakier and less arduous routes were available. But just because this familial search complied with the law does not mean that there is not something creepy about it. And that creepy feeling gets to the core of why familial searches are wrong.

Even some of the biggest champions of familial searches know there is something a little bit unjust and arbitrary about them. That is why even District Attorney Morrissey has stated that he would not support familial searches in victim databases,[51] and states such as California take pains to clarify that they are only using their convicted offender database for familial searches.[52] But if the paramount goal is to catch the elusive offender, then why discriminate among the databases used? Why not also conduct familial searches in victim databases,[53] or missing persons databases, or the one for military members,[54] or that of elimination samples belonging to police officers and lab technicians?

Do the relatives of convicted offenders somehow deserve less legal protection than the relatives of arrestees, or the relatives of victims, or the relatives of soldiers or police officers or lab technicians? Under the logic used to support familial searches, a lead is just that—a lead. A conduit to the person who really matters—the unknown criminal offender. What difference does it make if the criminal is related to another criminal, a crime victim, or a cop, so long as we find the killer? In the BTK serial killer case, police used his daughter's pap smear to verify her father's identity.[55] If familial searches are such a valuable tool, that clearly outweighs concerns about fairness or privacy, then why artificially restrict that tool's efficacy by looking only in offender databases?

Consider an investigation that unfolded in Lake Charles, Louisiana, in 1999.[56] A victim reported a rape to police, and law enforcement collected the evidence, including a rape kit. Unbeknownst to the victim, the DNA sample she gave to help find her rapist was also uploaded to a local rogue DNA database shared by nine counties. There were no laws authorizing the creation of this database, nor laws regulating how it could be used, who could upload data, or what quality control should be in place for those processing samples. But then, as one DNA supervisor from a lab in the consortium observed, "There's nothing in state law that precludes us from doing it," either.[57]

Six years later, investigators revisited her profile, and realized that she was likely a close relative of an unknown man who had left his DNA trail across a string of rapes. Upon further investigation, they determined that the perpetrator of those rapes was the victim's brother, who was ultimately convicted of those offenses and given a thirty-five-year sentence. Informed of their work, the victim expressed dismay, telling a newspaper reporter, "I feel betrayed. They did everything behind my back."[58] The defense lawyer ruminated that "such cases might make victims think twice before reporting an attack."[59]

If it seems wrong to use a victim's DNA profile to find one of her relatives who might have committed a criminal offense, it should feel equally wrong to use the DNA of a convicted offender the same way. At the core, the problem with familial search methods is that they discriminate among people *not* in the database. They represent a willingness to say that if you have the bad luck of being a law-abiding person in a family of crooks, you will never escape those roots. You are subject to investigation, monitoring, and suspicion. But if you are an incorrigible criminal who happens to be related to upstanding citizens, fear not. You will have to overtly attract law enforcement attention, because otherwise the police won't be looking for you. Familial searches offer a backdoor way to fill DNA databases with the profiles of people who have done nothing to forfeit their genetic privacy, and yet by virtue of their blood relationships, the state treats them as if they had.

In fact, familial searches are in some ways *more* pernicious than simply requiring that all relatives of convicted persons submit a DNA sample. Because if those relatives actually had their DNA on file, they would be more likely to avoid the harrowing experience of falling under suspicion. If Michael Usry Jr.'s own DNA sample had been in the database, and not just that of his father, investigators would have immediately ruled him out because it would have failed to match the crime scene stain. The perversity of familial match policies is that they implicate relatives in DNA searches through inference, conjecture, and guesswork—all less reliable than the straightforward profiles maintained for convicted persons. As a result, it is innocent relatives who are the likeliest subjects of suspicion and covert investigation. It is their tossed-out mail or cigarettes that is most likely to be secretly swabbed for DNA.

This is also why advocates of familial searching who point to the high number of incarcerated persons with a relative in the system have it exactly backward.[60] For instance, some people cite a statistic that asserts that 46 percent of people in jail have had at least one relative also in jail.[61] Set aside that this number is misleading.[62] Read in the reverse, it tells us that more than half of persons in jail do *not* have a relation who has been to jail. And that is what we want to know—not whether convicted people are related to other convicted people, but whether convicted people are related to other persons who commit crime, but go undetected.

Even if the family tree is criminal to its roots, that just means that the DNA database will work fine as it is, without resort to familial searches. The leads turned up in familial searches are to people who are by definition *not* in the DNA database. Thus, if a family has two members with criminal records, and two without, the two *with* the records are *already in the DNA database.* We don't need familial searching to find them—they are there. And if they are not there, it is either because the law says they are not required to be, or because the state has done a bad job executing its own collection laws.

The latter was true of one of the most celebrated familial search cases of all time—the Grim Sleeper. As it turns out, police didn't need a familial search and elaborate ruse to catch him. The man they ultimately identified had been convicted of a felony that required collection of his

DNA in 2004—by law, his profile should have been in the database for convicted offenders. The only reason it was not was—whether due to backlogs, oversight, or some other issue—it was never collected.[63] In other words, that case could have been solved by greater attention to clearing backlogs or completing the testing already ordered under the law; no newfangled, privacy-threatening search methods required.

Ultimately, familial searches represent an end-run around an important debate that is taking place all across America. In every state, there is a vibrant and at times heated conversation about who should have to contribute to a DNA database to begin with. Some people say they are happy to have their DNA on file, and believe everyone should just give a sample at birth. Other people vehemently resist this kind of government genetic banking, and think we should shut all databases down. In between are the folks who wrangle with the right scope for DNA databases—should they include just serious felons? All convicted offenders? Arrestees, too?

In choosing among these options, there are logical trade-offs. Only a universal database would ensure that every case with DNA evidence could be solved. And in the name of crime-solving, we could embrace universal sampling. Just as we could easily bring down crime rates if we allowed the government to read e-mails whenever it wanted, or listen in to any phone calls that it wished, or enter and search a person's home at will. The government would not even have to be disruptive about it—you wouldn't even have to *know* that they came, or read, or listened—unless it turns out that you were doing something you were not supposed to be. This idea isn't so farfetched; there are places in the world like that.

But no state has chosen to embrace a universal database. Our society, and our Constitution, has chosen greater distance between the police and the people. As hard as it may at times be to swallow, it accepts some unsolved crime as the cost of rejecting totalitarian control. Unsolved crime is the price that we pay for continued freedom, and privacy from relentless government surveillance.

The problem with familial searches is that they preempt this conversation. They are an "implicit database expansion,"[64] in the words of the authors of one article in the American Society for Law and Medical Ethics, but without the public debate. Familial search policies effectively impose universal DNA surveillance for some people, while allowing others to benefit from more restrictive mandatory collection laws. By what logic can we turn all of those related to a convicted offender into potential suspects, while ignoring all of those who have no such relations by sheer dint of luck?

Finally, it is important to note that the skewed racial composition of our DNA databases means that this de facto genetic surveillance will not be spread evenly throughout the population. As even advocates of familial searching have acknowledged, "[f]amilial searching potentially amplifies . . . existing disparities" in the criminal justice system.[65] Professors David Kaye and Michael Smith have observed, "on any given day, a black American is five times more likely to be in jail than is a white," and is "four times more likely to be under some form of correctional supervision, six-and-a-half times more likely to be incarcerated somewhere, and eight times more likely to be in prison than his white counterpart."[66] Data similarly shows that the rate of incarceration for Hispanic males, while less than that of black males, is nonetheless almost three times that of whites.[67] While some of that disparity is attributable to different rates of criminal offending, much of it is due to patterns of enforcement, prosecution, and sentencing.[68]

If DNA databases contain arrested and convicted persons, and people of color are more likely to be arrested and convicted, it follows that familial searches will more profoundly impact communities of color. In this regard, it is misleading for advocates of familial search methods repeatedly to suggest that a familial search is just like using a witness's memory of a partial license plate to search a DMV database for possible matches. Because of course, that analogy is inaccurate: when investigators search the DMV database, they are looking at a repository of all possible suspects. The DMV database has *all* the state's license plates in it. But when officers do a familial search, they are only looking at one part of the suspect pool, namely the people they have previously arrested or convicted, and any relatives they might have who are *not* already in the DNA database.

To be sure, quantifying the *exact* impact on those groups is inherently imprecise and difficult.[69] Most commonly cited is an estimate that relied on some standard assumptions about family structure, combined with data about the ethnic and racial makeup of the databases. That figure suggested that "more than four times as much of the African-American population as the U.S. Caucasian population would be 'under genetic surveillance.'"[70] In absolute figures, according to estimates by Stanford professor Hank T. Greely, that means roughly a third of the African American population is subject to this "genetic surveillance," as compared with about 7.5 percent of the European American population.[71] A police department would likely draw criticism if it announced a policy that, for every cold case, it would start with the assumption that all minority males did it, since statistically their rate of offending is disproportionately highest. An equivalent policy, cast under a genetic cloak, should escape no greater opprobrium.

ARE THEY LEGAL?

Given the inequities, it stands to wonder whether familial searches are even constitutional. The answer turns out to be incredibly complex. No court has yet ruled on the legality of familial searching, although it implicates important constitutional questions. Although a challenge to familial search methods might raise a number of claims with varying likelihood of success,[72] two particular rights protected in the Constitution seem most applicable to the practice.

The first is the Equal Protection Clause, which prohibits the state from intentional discrimination. At first glance, the most enticing approach would be to complain that familial search practices disparately impact certain racial minorities. But under current doctrine, that claim is least likely to prevail. Equal Protection requires proof of intentional discrimination, which would be hard to establish. Disparate impact alone—the fact that certain groups are more affected than others—does not provide grounds for relief.[73]

Rather, the stronger Equal Protection argument is one based upon general arbitrariness. That is, a formal practice and policy to focus suspicion on relatives of convicted persons arbitrarily singles out those persons.[74] Again, however, this claim will likely fail. Under current doctrine, courts only invalidate arbitrary line-drawing if it is completely irrational,[75] assuming the lines are not concertedly drawn on a suspect basis such as race or gender.[76]

Instead, the Fourth Amendment presents the most logical grounds on which to lodge a claim. The critical part of the familial search is the moment that the investigator checks the database for near misses, rather than exact matches, to the crime scene sample. But this, too, is saddled by two major doctrinal hurdles. First, typically the only people allowed to complain about a Fourth Amendment violation are those whose rights are directly affected. Suppose a thief steals an iPod and runs into a subway station. When he sees the police approaching, he slips the iPod into the knapsack of the person standing next to him. Unlawfully, the police grab the knapsack and search it, finding not only the iPod but drugs possessed by the knapsack owner. Although the knapsack owner could challenge the unlawful search, the thief cannot. The thief has no rights in the knapsack; just because something that incriminates him was found there does not give him the ability—or standing, to use the legal term—to challenge the police action.

Similarly, courts could find that the only individuals whose rights are affected by a database search are those of the people in the database, not their relatives. It is they who have the grounds to complain—not family members who may come under suspicion after the databased person is identified as a potential lead from a search. Yet constitutional challenges to the collection, databasing, and search of DNA from convicted offenders have almost uniformly been rejected.[77] In the end, their complaint is attenuated from the actual harm, since it is the relative who falls under suspicion. Under this reasoning, the same authority that gives the state the ability to collect and database the DNA also allows that state to search it, or make inferences from it, as the state sees fit.

One possible way around this conundrum would be to recognize a right held by the relatives to keep their own genetic profiles, or even inferences about their profiles, private—regardless of whether a blood relation has lost that right. In other words, even though one person in the family (say, a convicted offender) no longer can keep his or her own DNA private, the government cannot exploit that information to make conjectures about the genetic code of the remaining members of the family. As a legal matter, a right of this kind might be analogized to the right to privacy held independently by each person within a shared common space. In *Georgia v. Randolph*,[78] for instance, the Supreme Court recognized that if two people are present together in space they share—such as a husband and wife at the door of their apartment when the police come knocking—the police cannot enter their shared space so long as one person objects. This is true even if the other consents. We might likewise argue that just because a convicted offender may be forced to give over genetic information, that loss of privacy cannot diminish the privacy of the offender's relative who may share parts of that genetic code.[79]

Even if standing is no problem, the relatives may have a shaky legal claim for a second reason. Namely, courts typically vest little legal significance in the act of creating or searching a database. So long as the database contains information the police lawfully possess—as DNA databases do—they generally may make use of that information however they please. The Fourth Amendment has long focused more on how police *acquire* information,[80] and left the *use* of that acquired information completely to police discretion.[81] Courts have also tended to either ignore or minimize the legal significance of storing and later searching that stored information.[82]

But there are some suggestions that these old rules, developed mostly for physical evidence like smoking guns, could adapt to the more sensitive needs of twenty-first-century evidence. For instance, in a variety of drug testing cases, the Supreme Court has agreed that testing a biological sample is a constitutional issue independent of the legality of the sample's collection.[83] Lower courts have also suggested that novel uses of lawfully collected DNA samples would require additional court scrutiny.[84] And recall, too, that in the arrestee collection case before the Supreme Court, the assistant solicitor general agreed that the courts would have to reconsider the legality of performing additional testing of lawfully obtained DNA samples.[85]

Besides, the contrary position would be inadequate and indefensible. It is inadequate because there are so many different steps in DNA analysis that choosing the moment of collection as the only constitutionally significant act would lose the forest for the trees, and give carte blanche to potentially worrisome forms of testing or databasing. If law enforcement chooses to engage in far more invasive forms of testing, such as checking for behavioral or medical predispositions should such information become available, then it is likely that rulings that applied this cramped reasoning would have to reverse course.

Treating collection as the only legally significant act is indefensible because current doctrine authorizes a wide array of police practices that might seem appropriate when ordinary physical evidence is at stake, but that take on a more sinister dimension when biological evidence is in question. A 2009 case from a federal appellate court, *United States v. Davis*, helps illustrate why. In that case, a man was rushed to the hospital after a shooting.[86] As medical technicians worked to save his life, they discarded his bloody clothing under the hospital gurney. Unnoticed by anyone, after police spoke to the victim, they collected the clothing that had been tossed under the bed, and preserved it as evidence.

That clothing was never tested, but a year later police in another county suspected the victim of having committed an unrelated offense. They contacted the original officers, who recalled that the bloody clothes were still in the evidence locker. Police working on the new case recovered the clothes, and had them tested for the victim's genetic profile. Although it turned out not to match the offense of which he was suspected, they nonetheless entered the profile in their local database. A short time later, the victim's database profile matched that of another unsolved crime, and the victim was ultimately convicted for that offense.

In *Davis*, the court found that police had the right to confiscate the clothing, according to well-established doctrine that allows law enforcement to seize evidence that is in plain view. But the court went on to announce "that the extraction of DNA and the creation of a DNA profile result in a sufficiently separate invasion of privacy that such acts must be considered a separate search under the Fourth Amendment even when there is no issue concerning the collection of the DNA sample." Given the convoluted sequence with which the seizure, testing, and search unfolded in *Davis*, it would have been absurd to suggest that the only important constitutional question was whether the police lawfully collected the clothing in the first place. It would be akin to saying that so long as the police lawfully obtain a person's house keys at some point, there is no constitutional issue if they then make a copy and thereafter enter the home any moment of their choosing. The Constitution, the court held, did not "give a law enforcement agency carte blanche to perform DNA extraction and analysis derived from clothing lawfully obtained from the victim of a crime in relation to the investigation of other crimes."

SHOULD WE DO IT?

Privacy advocates have decried familial searching, arguing that it uses the misdeeds of one person as an excuse to pry into the genetic code of all their relatives. Defenders of civil rights have also worried about the discriminatory effect. Given the racially skewed nature of criminal enforcement in our country, they have feared that searches like this create a de facto database of all black and brown-skinned people. Civil libertarians have viewed these kinds of searches as yet another instance of the state's widening net of surveillance, including its use of information collected for one reason in a manner for which it was never intended.

In contrast, the champions of familial search methods point to the need to close cases and protect people from dangerous offenders. They claim that searches can be conducted in a way that is minimally invasive to privacy, and argue that the discriminatory effects are inadvertent.

So, which side is right? There are two ways to answer that question. The first is to weigh the costs of the search against its benefits. If the benefits exceed the costs, searches should be undertaken. If not, they should stop. But the second way to answer is to concede that, even if familial searches reap tremendous benefits, and even if they are fairly cost-free, they simply are incompatible with larger goals and principles of our criminal justice system.

The benefits of familial searches almost go without saying. They can solve cold cases. And solving cases brings closure to victims, enables the return of property, reduces the likelihood of later crime by the same offender, and facilitates the just punishment of a wrongdoer. Those benefits are real, and they are important.

How often would such benefits accrue? While it is clear that the method cannot solve every cold case, it is equally unclear what fraction it likely will help solve. The FBI has concluded that "[m]oderate stringency CODIS matches, in general, have very low efficiency in locating true relatives in offender databases."[87] When California was in the process of deciding whether to allow partial matches, a top legal adviser in the state's DNA unit cautioned that at least the FBI's version of partial match searching was likely to result in many "dead-end leads."[88] Simulated models likewise demonstrate that it is quite difficult to strike a functional balance between setting partial match thresholds low enough to ensnare likely family members, yet high enough to ensure that a manageable number of leads are returned.[89] Anecdotal evidence in the United States suggests a roughly 10 percent success rate, as measured by an arrest or conviction as a result of a familial search.[90] Denver district attorney Mitchell Morrissey maintains an online list of successful identification of suspects using the technique—culled from around the world—and it is currently only up to just over fifty.[91] On the other hand, a survey of two hundred cases submitted for investigation in the United Kingdom from 2004 to May 2011 revealed that forty were successful, which suggests a higher proportion of successful cases.[92]

Notwithstanding these benefits, the costs are real, too, if less salient. The failure rate of familial searches ought not to just reflect an inability to find a lead in the database. It must also incorporate false leads—leads that generate investigations of innocent persons. Familial search practices will result in suspicion being cast on innocent persons. They will lead to DNA samples' being taken unnecessarily, and investigations of innocent persons suspected, purely as a matter of blood relation. And as discussed earlier in this chapter, that suspicion not only falls arbitrarily, it can fall in a racially discriminatory fashion.

Familial searches may also deepen wounds in families already torn apart by crime and victimization. They could result in pressure on victims not to report crimes to police, for fear of implicating their own relatives in other offenses. Or they could exacerbate a family's current victimization. Imagine a family terrorized by the domestic violence of its patriarch. The presence of that person's DNA in a database exposes the family members to further harm, by increasing the likelihood that the law-abiding members of the family will fall under erroneous police suspicion.

Finally, familial searches may unearth secrets that were never meant to be told—least of all to police officers. In our society, families are largely social, not biological, constructs.[93] Yet when investigators follow up on genetic familial searches by asking "Do you have any children?" or "Who is your father?" they ask biological, not social, questions. Answering those questions honestly may call for the disclosure of the most intimate of information: abandoned parental bonds, adoptee relationships, children conceived with the assistance of reproductive technologies, or even family secrets about paternal identity.[94] Should a mother wishing to spare her son from suspicion confide in law enforcement that the lead in the database, presumed to be the child's father, is in fact not? Might she be convicted of lying to a law enforcement officer if she claims to have no other children, when in fact she gave a child away to relatives to raise? Or if police test a family member's sample, looking for a suspect, only to find that the purported relative is not a blood relation, what should they do with that information? What procedures are in place for dealing with incidental findings that cut to the very core of personal identity?

In sum, familial searches embody all of the pernicious instincts that our criminal justice system has long sought to stamp out: guilt by association, racial discrimination, presumption of criminal propensity, and even biological determinism. No matter how effective they may be, they pose too much of a threat to the fair and equitable administration of justice to embrace. They send a message that the relatives of convicted offenders deserve less protection from unwarranted suspicion than the relatives of everyone else, even if casting that suspicion more broadly would be equally likely (if not more likely) to solve crime. And they stand as proof of a sorry truth: many of those who tout the crime-solving benefits of this arbitrary and discriminatory practice nevertheless seek to limit its application to only some DNA databases, or wholly reject the fairer and more efficacious alternative of a universal DNA database.

CHAPTER 13

Beyond Junk: Screening for Physical and Behavioral Traits

IN THE 1800s, an Italian scientist named Cesare Lombroso theorized that criminals could be identified by features such as eye shape, forehead slope, or eyebrow hair.[1] Since then, and probably even before, science and criminal justice have been constant, if contentious, bedfellows. For as long as there have been criminals, there have been efforts to identify, classify, and restrain them with the aid of scientific principles.[2] Unfortunately, most of those efforts have been deeply misguided, including those that have focused explicitly on genetics.

For instance, the last time prominent American statesmen and scientists joined to promote "the marriage of the biological sciences, including medical genetics, with the then new discipline of biostatistics," the field of eugenics was born.[3] Eugenicists of the early 1900s sought to improve society by encouraging procreation among those they deemed genetically superior, while banning reproduction by those deemed inferior. Eugenic fever swept through the states, and a wave of laws were passed that barred reproduction by—in the words of one statute: "Criminals, Rapists, Idiots, Feeble-Minded, Imbeciles, Lunatics, Drunkards, Drug Fiends, Epileptics, Syphilitics, Moral And Sexual Perverts, And Diseased And Degenerate Persons."[4]

In 1927, the Supreme Court of the United States confronted one of these forcible sterilization laws. The petitioner, eighteen-year-old Carrie Buck, and her mother, were described in proceedings as follows:

Carrie Buck, mental defectiveness evidenced by failure of mental development . . . ; and social and economic inadequacy; has record during life of immorality, prostitution and untruthfulness; has never been self-sustaining. . . . Emma Buck, . . . Mental defectiveness evidenced by failure of mental development . . . ; and of social and economic inadequacy. Has record during life of immorality, prostitution, and untruthfulness; has never been self-sustaining; was maritally unworthy; having been divorced from her husband on account of infidelity. . . . These people belong to the shiftless, ignorant, and worthless class of antisocial whites of the South. . . . Generally feeblemindedness is caused by the inheritance of degenerate qualities; but sometimes it may be caused by environmental factors which are not hereditary. In the case given, the evidence points strongly toward the feeblemindedness and moral delinquency of Carrie Buck being due, primarily, to inheritance and not environment.[5]

In a dark moment in legal history, the Supreme Court upheld the law in a case called *Buck v. Bell.* Then justice Oliver Wendell Holmes infamously reasoned in the majority opinion that "It is better for all the world, if instead of waiting to execute degenerate offspring for crime, or to let them starve for their imbecility, society can prevent those who are manifestly unfit from continuing their kind. The principle that sustains compulsory vaccination is broad enough to cover cutting the Fallopian tubes. . . . Three generations of imbeciles are enough."[6] Amazingly, *Buck v. Bell* has never been expressly overruled; it was simply undercut in practice fifteen years later by *Skinner v. Oklahoma,* which held that a state cannot mandate sterilization for certain offenses and not others.[7] Given popular reluctance to penalize, say, embezzlement, with a vasectomy, the practice has more or less abated.[8]

But interest in biological connections to crime continued. Americans have flirted with phrenology (the "science" of measuring mental qualities by head shape);[9] polygenesis (the "science" that claims biologically distinct races descended from different species),[10] and mesomorphy (the "science" asserting certain body shapes are more criminally inclined).[11] Eugenics flourished until its aggressive and catastrophic implementation by the Nazi regime led to its being widely discredited. Today, even the whiff of an ideological or political agenda emanating from biological basis causes elites to turn a skeptical eye.[12]

Still, one does not have to look far into the past to find continued efforts to solve the problem of criminality with genetics.[13] In the early 1960s, scientists realized that some men appeared to have an extra Y chromosome, so that they were genetically XYY instead of the customary XY.[14] Not even a decade later, as crime rates slowly began to rise and a culture war unfolded in the United States, scientists attempted to link that genetic profile to criminality. They surveyed "criminal males in Pennsylvania" and found that one in eleven had an abnormal number of chromosomes, and five of those were XYY males.[15] Their conclusion? "[G]ross chromosomal errors contribute, in small but consistent numbers, to the pool of antisocial, aggressive males who are mentally ill and who become institutionalized for criminal behavior. Our data show, furthermore, that these men are to be found in general prisons as well as in mental hospitals for the 'hard to handle.'"[16]

The mainstream media, including a newspaper as august as the *New York Times*, flamed the fire of the association. Articles reported that "studies have shown that such an abnormality is 60 times as prevalent in men convicted of violent crimes as in the general population,"[17] and that "geneticists have found that boys born with XYY chromosomes (XY is normal) seem to have an uncommon chance of becoming tall, stupid, pimply-faced criminals" and that they had "a tendency toward acne; . . . unusual sexual tastes, often including homosexuality, and a record of criminal or antisocial behavior."[18] It was proposed that XYY carriers be issued special identity cards, or required to take tranquilizers, or at the very least that the world "keep an eye on" the estimated 5 million XYY carriers.[19] Finally, in 1976, after a series of poorly designed or incomplete efforts to study the connection,[20] a definitive study from Denmark revealed no link between aggression and the XYY profile. The myth of the tall, pimply XYY criminal was debunked.

This tempestuous relationship between biology and criminology likely explains why, when the state and federal government argued to the Supreme Court that compulsory collection of arrestee DNA should be constitutional, government lawyers repeatedly underscored that tests of forensic samples only look to meaningless, nonsensitive information. Differentiating the cheek swab from the intrusive act of hunting through a person's papers or personal belongings, the state's attorney argued that "there's a very real distinction between the police generally rummaging in your home . . . [and] looking only at 26 numbers that tell us nothing more about that individual."[21] The federal attorney reiterated that the limitation against searching a home without a warrant exists because "going into the home will expose a substantial number of highly private things to the view of the state," whereas "taking a DNA sample is not of that character. It is far more like taking a fingerprint."[22] When the chief justice pressed him on that point, noting that the government retains the entire genetic sample, not just the twenty-six-number profile, the attorney replied that current law prohibited looking for "anything except identification information."[23] Of course, he did not clarify what exactly qualifies as "identification information."

The government's reassurances were bolstered by the term that a scientist once gave these noncoding regions: "junk DNA."[24] The name alone makes the point—since when does anyone find anything good in junk? This language has worked its persuasive magic in the legal community. The "it's only junk DNA" refrain has frequently been repeated by lower courts as they uphold DNA collection statutes. Given that the legal test balances between the competing interests, calling it "junk" puts a thumb on the scale in favor of crime-solving, and against the suspect's privacy interest.

Yet law's "junk" may still be scientific treasure. Scientists are far from completely understanding of the workings of the human genome, and debates rage over even simple questions, such as how to define a "functional" region.[25] At present, the places on the genome used for forensic identification have no clear purpose. The sole exception is the THO1 locus, which appears to have some regulatory function, as yet unknown; "at some point [it] might be shown to affect individual health."[26] But it would be inaccurate to suggest that law enforcement's interest in DNA more generally does not go beyond "junk" identifiers.

Consider, for example, that the research arm of the Department of Justice, the National Institute of Justice (NIJ), has funded studies to isolate genetic polymorphisms keyed to sex, age, ethnicity, skin tone, hair color, hair texture, hair distribution, eye color, face shape, body shape and size, and other physical characteristics.[27] Just one year after the Supreme Court's decision in *King*, headlines announced, "Genetic Mugshot Recreates Faces from Nothing but DNA."[28] The NIJ has also funded "biosocial criminology" research, such as an examination of the link between genetic traits and antisocial behavior.[29] And it recently underwrote a study of parts of the DNA strand that might "link relatives as distant as third cousins with high confidence."[30] If money talks, the government—including the law enforcement arm of the government—is telling us that it is very interested in genetic tests that go far beyond the "string of numbers."

And, of course, researchers disconnected from criminal justice continue to probe the genome for insights into traits that might later be appropriated by criminal justice actors. Scientists continue to investigate a wide spectrum of genetic characteristics, ranging from innocuous attributes (such as ear wax type or voice pitch), to slightly sensitive traits (such as albinism, dwarfism, sickle-cell anemia, or the propensity for smoking, left-handedness, or stuttering), all the way to the most inflammatory type of genetic dispositions (such as propensities for violence, serious disease, sexual orientation, or deviance).[31]

There are two ways to think about the government's interest in such research. One is to believe in the government's benevolence. It is to keep faith that the government will never delve into truly sensitive information, or if so, will use it only judiciously and with circumspection. It is perhaps to believe that the government is not and will never test any of the millions of known offender samples that it has taken and retained, and adds to every day. In this view, most genetic information pried from a crime scene sample will be comparable to what you would get from a good eyewitness— such as hair and eye color, height, age, ethnicity, face shape. More sensitive information, such as familial associations or even behavioral or medical conditions, will be mined only in the most serious cases, if at all.

But the alternative perspective is more cynical. It may stem from distrust of government, but even a well-intentioned government program can have unanticipated consequences. For instance, in the early 1900s in the Netherlands, the central government had established a national registry that aimed to facilitate the provision of social services.[32] Registration included religious affiliation, so as to help the government ensure burials consonant with that individual's traditions. However, when the Nazis occupied the Netherlands, those lists took on a sinister character. One scholar notes that "[t]hese registration systems and the related identity cards played an important role in the apprehension of Dutch Jews and Gypsies prior to their eventual deportation to the death camps. Dutch Jews had the highest death rate (73 percent) of Jews residing in any occupied western European country—far higher than the death rate among the Jewish population of Belgium (40 percent) and France (25 percent)." That same scholar compiled a list of ten separate instances of misuse of population data, including two from the United States (persecution of Native Americans and the internment of Japanese Americans during World War II).[33] In short, the numerous instances of abuse of government registries, even in just the past one hundred years, provide ample reason to suspect even seemingly harmless requests.

The collection and retention of tens of millions of DNA samples from known persons, at the same time as the government actively funds research into unearthing genetic origins for mental disease, deviance, or behavioral propensities, should therefore give even the most trusting of citizens pause. That those 10 million samples belong to those least able to exert influence over the political process—many of whom, in fact, are formally disenfranchised as a result of their convictions—should be more troubling still.

TESTING CRIME SCENE SAMPLES TO FIND A PERPETRATOR

Current tests of DNA evidence for heritable characteristics, beyond the standard DNA profile, have focused on analyzing unknown forensic samples for physical traits in totally cold cases. Such tests produce a "genetic mugshot" composed from examination of the coding regions of the DNA strand, as opposed to the noncoding regions used in typical DNA testing. These parts of DNA can paint a visual picture of the offender, giving clues to that person's physical appearance. This method is sometimes called FDP, for "forensic DNA phenotyping," because rather than study the genes themselves (or genotype), the analyst is interested in how those genes are expressed (or phenotype). It is also known as molecular photofitting, because it draws inference about a person's appearance from the DNA molecule.

Tests available today come in two varieties. The less precise kind simply predicts a person's characteristics based on generalized ancestry information. But the more sophisticated form of FDP looks at a wider number of places on the genome and reaches more precise conclusions about specific traits. Using this method, researchers purport to draw a "genetic mugshot" of the individual.[34]

These mugshots might then be used to help locate a perpetrator through live witnesses or, eventually, through facial recognition software that combs through enormous databases. The Department of State currently has a database of 244 million facial images, and roughly forty states run facial recognition software in their driver's license photo databases.

And, of course, there are innumerable public repositories of photos; over 350 million photos are uploaded daily to Facebook alone, which stores more than 250 billion photos in total.[35]

Forensic DNA mugshots are still emerging as a field, but one researcher claims that they have already resulted in at least six arrests.[36] The most prominent example involved the 2002 Louisiana hunt for a serial killer linked to at least seven murders. Law enforcement had very little by way of leads; one of the few possible witnesses identified the perpetrator as a white male in a white van. DNA linked the homicides to one another, but the perpetrator did not have a DNA profile in any law enforcement database and so could not be identified.[37] Desperate, law enforcement enlisted the help of forensic psychologists and other "profilers," and engaged in a seven-hundred-man dragnet, but found no leads.

As the investigation stalled, police turned to a new company, DNA Print, based in Sarasota, Florida. That company marketed a service called DNA Witness, which tested biological samples for ancestry, thereby allowing crude conjectures about skin tone. After testing the samples, the company reported that the perpetrator's ancestry was 85 percent sub-Saharan African and 15 percent Native American. Based on its associative studies of ancestry and pigment, the company projected that the "skin shade of the subject was most likely of average to darker than average tone relative to that of the African-American group."[38]

This phenotypic information proved useful. It prompted police to refocus their entire investigation. As a result, they made an association between the serial killer's profile and another unsolved killing that they had failed to connect because the perpetrator in that case was identified as black. They then compiled a new short list of suspects, which included a troubled man named Derrick Todd Lee, who had earlier been brought to police attention but ultimately ignored when he did not match the description (including skin tone) offered by the sole witness. A sample from Lee was collected, which turned out to match. Lee fled the jurisdiction, but police used cell phone records to find and apprehend him in another state. In October 2004, he was sentenced to death for one of the murders.

The success in the Lee case did not open the floodgates of phenotypic DNA testing. As it turns out, determining phenotypes from genotypes is more difficult than middle school biology perhaps suggested. You might remember the neat Punnett squares of Mendelian inheritance that schoolchildren routinely draw. Those could lead you to believe you inherit one eye color gene from your mother and one from your father, and if you get different genes, then the dominant one will determine your actual eye color. In fact, however, the actual biological mechanisms dictating even traits as simple as hair or eye color prove profoundly complex.[39] No single gene codes eye color as "blue" or "brown"; instead, an assortment of regions all seem to play a role, and yet even those do not simply dictate a particular color when considered together. More complex genetic traits may also be the product of epigenetic forces that are presently little understood; think of the fact that identical twins, who share identical DNA, nonetheless are not carbon copies of each other.[40] They may have subtle differences in their features, and pronounced differences in their tastes, mannerisms, sensitivities, and medical histories.

In addition, superficial assessments of physical traits suggests little variability—eyes are brown, blue, green, or hazel. But in actuality much wider diversity exists. Are those blue eyes, cobalt, cornflower, or cerulean? Is that ash blond or dirty blond or light brown hair? Is that skin tone chocolate, mocha, or caramel? DNA tests are useful only inasmuch as they can discern these subtle variations. Otherwise, they cannot provide enough nuance to describe a possible perpetrator with useful precision. And care must be taken during the test development and validation stage to be sure there are objective measures of accuracy. If the subjects themselves have different ideas of "chestnut" and "honey brown" hair, they will differently classify the same trait.

Given this complexity, it is perhaps unsurprising that the scientific community is itself divided about the predictive power of this research. On the one hand are the staunch advocates for forensic phenotyping, who foresee a fruitful future in criminal justice (and a lucrative one, it should be added, as law enforcement pays for these services). On the other hand are the skeptics, who claim that the current assertions at best overreach, and at worst actively mislead.

The leading champions of FDP are an international cadre of scientists known as the VisiGen Consortium, or the International Visible Traits Genetics Consortium, which is led by Dr. Manfred Kayser of the Netherlands and Dr. Tim Spector of the United Kingdom. Within the United States, the leading advocate is Dr. Mark Shriver, a member of the anthropology department at Pennsylvanvia State University. In October 2012, VisiGen announced the results of a study validating the Identitas (VI) Forensic Chip, the first commercially available tool that can simultaneously analyze genetic information from an array of sites on the genome and produce information related to biogeographic ancestry, eye and hair color, relatedness, and sex. Using 3,196 DNA samples of varying quality intended to emulate some forensic conditions, scientists found that 95 percent of samples produced results that were highly accurate for sex and first- to third-degree relatedness, averaged 94 percent accuracy for ancestry, 70 to 85 percent accuracy for eye color, and 48 to 85 percent accuracy for hair color.[41]

The Identitas Chip builds upon other systems already in use that purport to predict eye color with 90 percent–plus accuracy for varying hues of blue and brown eyes and hair color (including red, black, brown, and blond) with 80 to 95 percent accuracy.[42] A new multiplex that can test both hair and eye color simultaneously from even low-quality, degraded biological samples, showed similarly high rates of success in accurately predicting eye color, and variable success for hair color. When combined with bioancestry, that system (known as HIrisPlex) could ostensibly predict with upward of 86 percent accuracy whether a brown-eyed, black-haired individual is of European versus non-European descent.

Oddly enough, age is a genetically predictable characteristic; studies have also recently demonstrated the capacity to predict age with accuracy within five years.[43] Research into predictions of facial appearance—such as the size and shape of the nose, lips, eyes, bone structure, and face shape—continues to develop.[44] Future work is intent on uncovering genetic indicators of probable adult body height, male baldness, freckling, and hair morphology.[45]

Skeptics acknowledge that "[t]he idea that we can reconstruct a human face from a DNA sample has great appeal: DNA from a crime scene could be used to create a facial image of a suspect; the faces of prehistoric peoples could be reconstructed from their remains; the face of a child could be predicted in utero from amniocentesis."[46] But, they warn, "We should not be fooled, however, into thinking that we are anywhere close to understanding developmental genetics at the level where prediction of complex morphological traits is feasible."

For instance, a large study of facial shape recently "revealed few causative loci."[47] The study was a "genome-wide association study," or GWAS. These GWAS studies try to reverse-engineer genetic causality by making comparisons between a huge dataset of full genome and the known characteristics about the persons each genome came from. This particular study looked at roughly 10,000 people—looking for correlations between 3-D MRIs of their actual head shape along with their full genetic profiles. Although it found five genes that might influence face shape, none of those genes exerted particularly strong influence. In other words, they seemed to have some effect on face shape, but not so much that knowing the genes would tell you what shape to expect.

An anecdotal test of DNA mugshot services likewise suggested the technology has a ways to go. In a test case, a reporter for the *New York Times* sent the DNA profiles of two colleagues to a company and received the rendered facial images. The reporter then sent the images to other colleagues and friends of the two volunteers, to see whether they would recognize them, explicitly cautioning that both age and weight might vary from the depiction. None identified a middle-aged reporter, whose youthful image failed to trigger recall in some and elicited erroneous guesses from roughly fifty others. Roughly ten people guessed the other reporter's identity, who was younger and half-Asian.[48]

Consistent with these findings, the results from actual criminal investigations involving forensic DNA phenotyping have largely failed to match the success of the Derrick Todd Lee case. Some of that may be because a genetic mugshot has limited utility. When a crime occurs, and a DNA sample believed to belong to the perpetrator is recovered from the scene, the easiest and best way to identify an offender will always be to type the noncoding loci and then match that to a known person, either a suspect identified through other evidence, or one found through a DNA search. Those standard identifiers provide fairly conclusive evidence of identity, assuming the samples have been correctly collected, analyzed, and interpreted.

Testing an evidentiary sample for physical traits only comes in handy when there is no information about the perpetrator and no match in the database. But that is the case in only a small fraction of crimes. The vast majority of crimes are between people who know each other, or where genetic traces are helpful mainly to associate a known person with an object or place.[49] DNA testing in those cases can be critical to develop evidence supporting the guilt of a known perpetrator (for instance, to test an intimate swab to corroborate the victim's account that her acquaintance sexually assaulted her), but the noncoding, "junk" test suffices; there is nothing to gain from creating a genetic mugshot.

For these reasons, perhaps, DNA Print did not succeed as a business. It closed in 2009, suggesting that if the market is an indicator, law enforcement did not find its services particularly beneficial. It should be noted, however, that DNA Print offered one flagship service—ancestry and skin tone information. It also made those predictions with more primitive technology than is currently available.

DNA Print's failures have thus not stopped advocates of phenotyping from barreling ahead. In 2014, Toronto police announced a partnership with Identitas to create police sketches from cold cases.[50] Several conventional DNA testing companies also have begun to offer limited profiling services. And in February 2015, a Reston, Virginia, company called Parabon NanoLabs launched Snapshot, a genetic mugshot service that purports to identify a person with as little as 50 picograms of DNA. Its service offers "a report and detailed composite profile that includes face morphology; eye, skin, and hair color; and genomic ancestry."[51] In its public debut, Snapshot announced its first "mugshot": an image released in the hopes of finding a homicide suspect in South Carolina, who left DNA at the scene.[52] Then on Earth Day in 2015, Parabon announced a campaign in Hong Kong aimed at reducing the high rate of littering. The partnership takes trash collected from the street, creates mugshots from genetic information found on it, and then plasters those images on billboards across the city.[53]

But, like those who blazed the trail before them, the fire that burns hottest often dies quickest. The South Carolina case remains unsolved, despite widespread publicity of the image. Some social media commenters viewed the littering campaign in Hong Kong with horror. And members of the scientific community have questioned Parabon's decision not to publish or subject to peer scrutiny any of the science behind its work.[54] As some skeptics further caution:

> Overselling and overpromising in science is dangerous because it creates unreasonable expectations both at the public and policymaker levels. Ultimately, this runs the risk of diverting valuable scientific resources away from the important task of understanding how variation in genes plays through developmental process to produce the amazing diversity of organismal form.

In other words, if too much is promised too soon, policymakers and funders may prematurely give up on the science when it fails to deliver. Whether that is a good or bad thing, of course, depends on one's perspective.

Even if law enforcement fails to find use for the current technology, genetic phenotyping may yet find another audience. Embedded in Parabon's business model is perhaps another consumer base, beyond the police. Intriguingly, its FAQ includes an inquiry that states: "I'm unhappy with how law enforcement is handling my case. Can I send you a DNA sample of someone I suspect committed a crime, and have you analyze it?" The official company reply explains that the service is limited to law enforcement and government agencies, but tantalizingly includes the qualifier "at the present time." Perhaps the doors may be opening again.

TESTING KNOWN PERSON SAMPLES

Whereas testing of unknown crime scene samples is likely to focus on developing the "mugshot" from nonsensitive genetic traits, such as hair or eye color, analysis of known offender samples cuts right to the core of the ethical and privacy concerns that DNA testing raises. When a DNA sample is linked to a known person, there is no reason to test for that individual's physical traits. Even if law enforcement desires to associate the person with the crime, the most effective way to do so is through matching the noncoding genetic identifiers of the standard DNA profile, as opposed to discerning vague physical traits that are shared by a large number of people.

But more sensitive genetic information could be viewed as greatly useful to other criminal justice determinations. For instance, a genetic basis for certain behavioral or cognitive traits—such as mental illness, chemical dependency, sexual deviance, violence, sociopathy, and other asocial tendencies—could prove extremely useful to criminal justice actors. When a person is arrested, immediate decisions must be made about granting bail or detaining the person pretrial. At sentencing, a judge wants to know how likely it is that a person will reoffend, and whether the individual will be able to refrain from harmful conduct. A propensity to injurious behaviors, such as violence or pedophilia, or a severe mental illness, would also be useful in judging whether to commit a person—such as a sexual predator—to detention even in the absence of a criminal offense. Defense lawyers might want to access such evidence for mitigating purposes—for instance, to show that an individual had a predisposition to mental disease or drug addiction that should minimize his or her personal responsibility for bad behavior.

While efforts to find a genetic basis for traits as complex as sexual deviance, chemical dependency, or propensity for violence may send chills up the spine, they are unquestionably under way. Although some such research has been funded by federal law enforcement, most of this research is conducted by industry, academic, and medical scientists who do not depend on criminal justice dollars. Most experts would say that such findings, if they occur at all, are likely far off in the future. They would also caution that, even if genetics exerts a causal influence on deviant behavior, these regulatory systems are likely so complex, and so subject to environmental influences, as to be of limited utility for criminal justice decision making.

But what scientists consider the clear limits of the science often gets lost in the translation to criminal justice. The criminal courtroom is a magnet for fanciful theories, unsupported hypotheses, and general "junk" science. As a 2009 National Academy of Sciences report by a blue-ribbon panel of experts attests, some of the most familiar forensic techniques have absolutely no basis in science, and yet they are commonly offered as proof in courthouses around the country. Based on this history, what reason is there to believe that criminal justice actors won't latch onto the first indication of a "violence" gene or "pedophilia" gene?

If such a conclusion sounds outlandish, consider the 2011 report of the JASON advisory group to the Department of Defense (DoD), which contemplated the relevance of advances in genetics to various questions of national security. The report explains that "[m]any phenotypes of relevance to the DoD are likely to have a strong genetic component," such as "short- and long-term medical readiness, physical and mental performance, and response to drugs" as well as "phenotypic responses to battlefield stress, including post-traumatic stress disorder" or tolerance for physically harsh conditions.[55] The group recommended that the DoD "take a leading role in the personal genomics era, and become full partners with industry and academia in creating useful information from genotype and phenotype data."[56] Given the "enormous reach-back potential" and comprehensiveness of the military's collection of Veteran's Administration health records, the report speculated that the DoD could conduct research on the 3.2 million–plus genetic samples that it collects from military personnel aimed at identifying some of those "phenotypes of relevance." If military advisers view phenotypic testing for sensitive traits as a fertile area for research, development, and subsequent decision-making that could potentially benefit both its soldiers and society at large, it is hard to imagine that criminal justice officials would disagree.

In fact, the criminal justice system already relies on crude and largely subjective risk assessment instruments with minimal scientific basis. These predictive tools take the form of surveys that intend to determine a person's likelihood of recidivism. They typically measure both static factors such as "raised in a single-parent household," as well as dynamic ones such as "highest level of education" or "current employment." Some sex offender programs even rely on penile plethysmography, a dubious method of measuring arousal so as to judge deviance.

Every day, determinations about detention and release are made on the basis of subjective interviews conducted by bail officials, intuitive guesses based on criminal records, and biased attestations by the friends and families of victims and offenders. The criminal justice system relies on these imprecise tools because there are no better ones. There is no way to know for certain whether someone will reoffend or relapse, so we administer hundred-page tests as a way to provide some grounds for prediction and afford some sense of security. Who is to say that adding even a primitive genetic component to the mix—a check in the "genetic predisposition to deviance" box—is so far-fetched or outlandish?

WHAT THE LAW HAS TO SAY ABOUT IT

When the specter of trawling for genetic information beyond "junk" is raised, government officials tend to protest, claiming that the law clearly forbids this kind of testing. But that is not the case. There are three primary sources of legal regulation of DNA testing: the Constitution, federal law, and state law. None is as restrictive as is often claimed. To make matters messier, the protections available under current law may change according to which kind of samples are being tested, which kind of tests are being done, and why.

Under current doctrine, trait-testing samples collected by compulsion from known persons—such as the convicted offender and arrestee samples that populate the enormous national database—present the clearest case for constitutional prohibition. As discussed earlier, samples that were handed over voluntarily, were recovered from a crime scene, or that the government obtained through surreptitious methods, may receive no constitutional protection at all. Just as the law offers little recourse to a person who complains that another individual took his or her discarded trash and repurposed it, so, too, does conventional doctrine afford little protection for DNA samples that were effectively thrown or given away.

Of course, the idea that there would be *no* regulation of voluntary and abandoned samples seems farcical, even if technically legally correct. Endorsing this kind of loophole, and allowing police to circumvent Fourth Amendment protection by taking advantage of the ease with which DNA is "abandoned," would reduce the rule of law to a mockery and ridicule the special character of genetic data. Indeed, at the Supreme Court argument about sampling DNA from arrested persons, the justices pressed the government about whether it could test for other, more sensitive genetic information using the sample in its possession. In response, the government attorney agreed that it was "probably correct, that the individual will retain a reasonable expectation of privacy in the genomic material that does not reveal identity," and "additional Fourth Amendment scrutiny would be required before the government could make use of the rest of the genome."[57] In other words, the government admitted that even though the Constitution allowed testing of the noncoding loci used to establish identity, it might not allow more intrusive tests to take place. But it is also significant because this tentative concession was just about samples collected *by compulsion*. Neither the court nor the government lawyer said anything about whether that same principle would extend to samples the police had acquired all on their own.

Suppose, however, that the court did believe that any testing of noncoding loci—anything not "junk"—deserved constitutional review. That still does not mean the courts would find those tests impermissible. DNA tests have always identified the sex of the DNA donor, and have been used to make inferences about probable ancestry, but courts rarely stumble over this kind of information as they label as innocuous the "junk" testing. Nor have courts moved to stop the use of the "junk" identifiers to find relatives of persons in the database, which might be viewed as a form of invasion of genetic privacy. It is easy to imagine courts' endorsing a sliding scale, in which a DNA sample is first examined for noncoding identifiers, then tested for coding but superficial traits, such as sex, hair or eye color, ancestry, likely skin tone, or age, or even nonsensitive medical information, for instance, cleft palate, albinism, or a propensity to stuttering.[58]

From there, is it so difficult to conceive that the court might endorse even more intrusive forms of genetic testing, should they become available. In the arrestee sampling case, the court described the state's interest in identifying individuals in its custody as compelling, and explicitly included information about a "record of violence or mental disorder," and "character and mental condition" within the scope of important identifiers.[59] If the "pedophile" gene were found, or the "violence gene" established, this reasoning would seem to support law enforcement efforts to mine genetic information for that "identification purpose." After all, law enforcement needs to know "just whom they are dealing with." Statements such as these made in *King* leave open the possibility that DNA samples might be tested not just for superficial traits, but for more sensitive characteristics, such as propensities toward violence, mental illness, or addiction.

If these ideas seem fanciful, consider three additional propositions. First, if genetic testing becomes capable of revealing individual predispositions, such as violence or pedophilia, surely at some point a *defendant* will wish to use the results of such tests, to argue for mercy or bolster a claim of innocence. For instance, a defendant who pleads guilty to a heinous crime might wish to show a genetic predisposition to violent behavior, say, perhaps to earn a slightly less severe sentence (assuming that the effects of such predisposition fade with age). Or a defendant accused of an act of child sexual abuse might wish to prove the absence of a genetic inclination of that kind, to bolster a claim of innocence or to show a capacity for rehabilitation. If such evidence is admitted, and courts become accustomed to hearing it, they will naturally develop less resistance to allowing the government to marshal such information in support of its own claims.

Second, if it seems far-fetched that our system would tolerate incarcerating people based on inferred predispositions, recall that we currently do a low-tech version of just that. As previously noted, we presently use "risk assessment" tools of questionable reliability to make determinations from bail to sentencing and beyond, including long-term civil commitment of people labeled sexual predators.[60] It is hard to imagine that those soft science tools would somehow be deemed permissible, but harder genetic science not. At the very least, it seems entirely plausible that a genetic assessment would simply become folded into the profile—so that the offender's report includes both performance on a clinical or actuarial test as well as any genetic predispositions that may be of concern.

Keep in mind that, as of now, the state and federal governments have over 10 million DNA samples in their possession, and that those samples have already been accessed as new forms of testing develop, and without court permission. For instance, states have pulled old samples to conduct Y-STR testing to determine familial relatedness—without informing anyone as it was happening, much less seeking judicial permission. Samples have also been released to researchers to conduct studies,[61] as permitted by law. And, of course, crime scene stains have already been used to create "genetic mugshots," with little fanfare. Because law enforcement does not announce when it has authorized access to a sample set for study, or undertaken its own new tests, it is difficult for anyone to mount a challenge against them. Similarly, in the absence of a formally announced, public program to conduct phenotyping, it seems plausible that such efforts could be well under way before anyone even noticed, much less brought it before a court to rule on its legality.

As it stands, very few laws on the books expressly prohibit testing of this kind. No state forbids all phenotypic testing. Instead, the vast majority of states pattern their DNA collection and database laws after the federal statute.[62] That law has a loophole that leaves room for testing of even the most sensitive traits, because it does not spell out the particular kind of testing allowed, or even declare that testing should be limited to certain parts of the genome.

Contrary to frequent assertions by officials, nothing in the federal law precludes testing for sensitive traits, or testing of coding—as opposed to "junk" loci. Instead, the law simply requires that testing be for "identification purposes only," or for "research and protocol development purposes."[63] But that language is easily interpreted to include testing for more than just noncoding data. After all, hair color or skin tone is "identifying." So is a propensity to sexual deviance. And, as noted, the Federal Bureau of Investigation has already interpreted the federal statute as allowing testing for sex, as well as use of genetic profiles to draw inferences about ancestry and family relatedness.[64]

Only a handful of states depart from this statutory model. But even those that incorporate language explicitly intended to curtail some forms of phenotypic testing—such as New Mexico,[65] Rhode Island,[66]

Wyoming,[67] Indiana,[68] Michigan,[69] Vermont,[70] South Dakota,[71] Washington,[72] Utah,[73] and Florida[74]—apply those limits only to samples collected or stored in a database under the authority of the statute; that is, collected as a part of a compulsory DNA sampling program. The laws no longer apply when any *other* form of collection is at issue. Suppose a crime occurs at your workplace, and police ask all employees to give a sample to help narrow down possible perpetrators. If you volunteer your DNA, these laws do not protect you. Similarly, DNA samples recovered from a crime scene or obtained through surreptitious methods are not covered, because they are considered abandoned and without legal protections. Thus, even states that impose some restrictions on this kind of testing did not draft laws that effectuate a true and total ban.

Finally, one state, Texas, has enacted a law that explicitly *authorizes* phenotyping. In the statute approving the creation of a DNA database, Texas lawmakers provided that "information contained in the DNA database may not be collected, analyzed, or stored to obtain information about human physical traits or predisposition to disease *unless the purpose for obtaining the information is related to a purpose described in this section.*"[75] What purposes does the law specify? Permissible reasons include: "investigation of an offense, the exclusion or identification of suspects or offenders, and the prosecution and defense of the case."[76] In other words, pretty much anything under the sun. Under this law, for example, the police can test a DNA sample for "physical traits or predisposition to disease" even if all it will do is help them locate a witness or identify potential suspects, as both of those clearly aid in "prosecution or defense."[77]

WHY SHOULD WE WORRY ABOUT PHENOTYPIC TESTING?

The expansion from "just junk" to real genes should give every person pause, if not raise outright alarm. History is littered with failed efforts to weave together biological science and criminal justice, often because the latter tends to rush ahead of the former. All too often, criminal justice actors have embraced the latest fad in science, at the expense of accuracy, justice, and individual liberty. And the same seems likely to be true when it comes to phenotypic testing, for one technical reason and another philosophical one.

The technical problem with phenotypic testing stems from the fact of free will. Genes can only take an investigator so far, because many genetic dispositions of interest are subject to human manipulation. Genetics may say my hair is brown, but with ten dollars I can make my hair blue. Genetics may say that I am ninety-three, but ninety-three can look as sprightly as Betty White. More seriously, genetics may say I am prone to pedophilia or violence, but I may never wrestle with those impulses. Or I may experience them, but my moral and cognitive self may suppress and stifle them. Phenotypic traits are of use to the criminal justice system only inasmuch as they represent some essential biology that is unalterable. Once free will intervenes, they become less valuable.

The flip side of the same coin is that to the extent that we treat such traits—rightly or wrongly—as *not* subject to personal manipulation, we may undermine the goals of the criminal justice system more broadly. Right now, most of the phenotypic traits that could provide real value to the criminal justice system—such as propensities to addiction, asocial behavior, or mental disease—are the ones that are least understood. The expression of such traits may be most influenced by factors beyond mere genetics, such as a person's environment or upbringing.

Embracing phenotypic testing, therefore, negates individual free will. It privileges biology over choice. And that both demoralizes a population with unsavory predispositions and denies its members their humanity. It might even push individuals to view their life path as so ordained by genetics, rather than their own decisions, as to encourage them down a path of asocial behavior that otherwise would not have appealed to them. This is particularly true given that predictions for such characteristics as violence or sexual predisposition might be harder to prove "untrue" even if they do not match up to a suspect's history of behavior. The consequence is to swap individual agency for genetic predetermination.

Crediting genetics in this way also runs up against a fundamental precept of American criminal justice, which is that we punish people for what they *do*, not who they are or what they believe. The criminal law typically requires, as any first-year law student can recite, an *actus reus*, or guilty act, before punishment. It leaves condemnation for impure thoughts to religious institutions. But bending that rule to penalize not thoughts but *genes* fosters an injustice that runs two ways. Designating a person as genetically "violent" or "deviant" unfairly labels those souls who might never act on those inclinations; at the same time, it supplies a ready excuse to those who would. One part of the criminal population will be clamoring, "Let me out, I am not my genes!" while the other part cries, "Let me out, my genes made me do it!" The criminal justice system cannot have it both ways. It cannot condemn individuals based on genetic traits that they have no power to change, while also punishing the actions of others under the fiction that they exercised their free will.

Concerns of this kind are what animate a concept of the "right not to know"[78] in medical ethics. This right protects an individual in the medical context from exposure to information that the individual, for whatever reason, has decided not to learn. With ignorance comes control, or at least the illusion thereof. Perhaps one sibling wants to know whether she is a carrier of the breast cancer gene, because it will affect her health decisions. But another sibling prefers to remain uninformed, because she worries it will infuse her life with fear. Under conventional ethics, doctors honor those choices.

This is not to romanticize the way in which important predictive assessments are made. Under current practice, courts use primitive psychological assessments and other crude tools to decide such important questions as whether a person is likely to reoffend or possesses some fundamental cognitive deficit exculpating them from liability or mitigating the severity of punishment. Many risk assessment instruments in use today have some quantitative component, which reduces the individual to a numerical risk based on that person's character and history. None of these methods can see the future, and inevitably errors will be made. But probabilities built from psycho-social and behavioral history, versus those based on pure biological assessment, at least leave room for individual choice and redemption. And besides, the current use of bad information to make important decisions should not justify resort to different sorts of equally problematic predictive tools.

A second concern with phenotypic testing mirrors the same scourge that plagues all aspects of the criminal justice system: discrimination. There is a risk that phenotypic testing will simply cloak the dysfunctions of our current criminal justice system in a mantle of science, and thereby mask the very inequities that such testing helps to perpetuate. How can that be? How does a laboratory test discriminate? Unlike the flawed or biased identifications made by humans, the results of a DNA test would seem mercifully free from racial or ethnic prejudice. But that is not necessarily the case.

First, the science itself may render certain demographic traits visible and others invisible—such as a test that can detect brown, kinky hair but not smooth, blond hair. Although a lab test result may objectively report what it finds, the tests themselves may be less objective than they seem. If certain characteristics are more readily discerned than others, biological tests may identify only persons with those characteristics. For instance, DNA tests for eye color have struggled with predicting green eyes, as have hair color tests struggled with accuracy for black and blond hair colors. In contrast, blue and brown eyes, and red and brown hair colors, are more readily predicted accurately.

To be sure, the tests that are currently available are more a function of the capacity of the science—we know how to find blue eyes because they are genetically distinct, not because law enforcement was desperate to develop a test for blue-eyed perpetrators. If phenotypic genetic testing is fully embraced, research might logically take aim at subpopulations currently strongly associated with criminal justice issues. We can easily imagine tests that, by dint or design, prove especially effective at identifying suspects belonging to particular populations.

That in turn runs the risk of replicating and inscribing racial and ethnic biases in the criminal justice system, rather than alleviating them. Genetic eyes that only see in certain colors may dress discrimination up as science. For example, one report of genetic sex typing showed a high rate of the male chromosome dropout among males of South Asian ancestry when compared to Europeans. Although there is a technical scientific basis for the dropout, related to the chemical primers used to splice the relevant section of the genome, repeated public misidentification of male perpetrators as female, or even reports of unknown sex due to uncertainty in the genetic tests, might be used as fuel for xenophobic or racist ideas. Similarly, studies suggest that dark skin tone is a common ancestral trait, a thesis consistent with the notion of a single origin of humans from Africa. Yet such findings could be misconstrued to feed racist and white supremacist claims that lighter skin tones signal "evolution."

Tests could similarly cherry-pick for characteristics that are strongly associated with racial or ethnic identities—consider the racial and ethnic significance of developing genetic tests for carriers of sickle-cell anemia or Tay-Sachs genes, which are strongly associated with African Americans and Ashkenazi Jews, respectively. In the United States, much attention was devoted to discerning regional variations for different populations of Hispanics.[79] Forensic scientists in the United Kingdom received sharp criticism when they announced that British Afro-Caribbean persons exhibit high rates of genetic variation, making it easier to differentiate members of that population.[80] Tests that succeed at identifying only members of one certain subpopulation will direct disproportionate law enforcement attention that way, while insulating other "genetically invisible" groups from the same attention.

By way of illustration, consider one commonly cited case from the United Kingdom.[81] In 2004, investigators sought a burglar and rapist who had committed over eighty offenses, mostly against elderly women, over a twenty-year span. DNA evidence linked the cases to a single perpetrator, but no match was found in police databases. DNA Witness was hired to examine the evidence, and concluded that the suspect's ancestry was 82 percent sub-Saharan African, 6 percent European, and 12 percent Native American. Closer scrutiny discerned that one parent was dominantly sub-Saharan African, while the other had greater admixture. Moreover, because Native American admixture is uncommon in Europeans, investigators concluded that this parent must have been a recent immigrant.

The researchers then turned to UK immigration data, which revealed that the Caribbean immigrants to the UK from countries with high proportions of Native American influences came from Guyana, Trinidad, Belize, Dominica, and St. Vincent. But some of those countries also tended to have strong European influence, however, of which the suspect profile showed very little. Piecing together all of this information, investigators surmised that the suspect was most likely the child of an Afro-Caribbean from the Windward Islands area, rather than Jamaica.

Because of the particular legacies of slavery and colonialism, and due to known migratory patterns and in-depth studies of the ancestry of those populations, law enforcement was able to pinpoint the likely genetic ancestry of the offender. Based on that information, moreover, police initiated a dragnet—which turned out to be unsuccessful, incidentally, and so the case remains unsolved. But what if the genetics research only allows that level of granularity with respect to subgroups with colonial histories? What if European descent is not as finely parsed, due to either lack of research interest or scientific hurdles? If there is less capacity to determine that a suspect is likely the child of a North Country Briton and a southeastern American,[82] then those communities will remain sheltered from aggressive policing—such as DNA dragnets—and may more readily elude capture altogether.

Or suppose two crime scene samples at the scene of a violent robbery failed to match any suspects in the DNA database, and thus each was tested for physical traits. Assume that current tests were particularly good at detecting dark skin and hair tones and facial shapes in men, and less sophisticated with light skin tones and hair tones, or with female samples. One sample might produce a "genetic mugshot" of a dark-skinned, dark-haired man with certain facial features, while the other sample returned no results, or made only loose estimates of European descent. To what consequence?

Law enforcement aggressively pursues suspects who might match the mugshot, perhaps even finding other minor illicit behavior (possession of illegal drugs or weapons, say), as they stop and frisk possible perpetrators. Perhaps a dragnet is conducted, and a "voluntary" sweep for DNA samples is done of persons fitting the description. In the South Carolina murder that used the Snapshot service, police reported that they interviewed over two hundred people in connection with the case, including 150 who submitted their DNA.[83] Presumably all of those "look-alikes" were young, African American men, cast under suspicion because of their physical appearance. That case remains unsolved, but even if efforts are successful and the perpetrator apprehended, every aspect of investigation and enforcement traces back to that first moment when one sample type produces information for police to act upon, but the other did not. Both the effects of aggressive investigation and public perception about what kinds of people behave criminally directly flow from a determination made in a laboratory as to what genetic features or characteristics to study. Attention on the visible groups may wrongly lead the public to believe that science explains criminality, when in fact the disparity is the product of social demographics, scientific knowledge, or choice.

This example points at base to the concerns that arise when crime and criminality is framed in biological terms: it opens a conversation that history suggests rarely ends productively. As scientists know, race has no genetic expression. There is no "white" genome or "black" genome. Those categories are socially constructed—they were made up by humans. That is why some "white" Italian Americans have darker skin tones than "black" African Americans—because the essence of "racial" or ethnic identity has more to do with geographic patterns of ancestry than it does with the way a person appears.

Of course, geographic ancestry does exert an influence on a person's genetic makeup. And when social structure is layered on top—especially in societies with highly segregated populations—certain genetic traits can be more or less prevalent within those groups. In layman's terms, Irish Americans appear somewhat genetically similar because the Irish have a long history of marrying and having children with other Irish people. But the more that groups mix, the less pronounced those differences become. In countries such as the United States, the legacy of slavery and rising rates of interracial partnership combine to increasingly blur the genetic picture of any individual person, even as a gross matter of ancestry.

Ordinary DNA testing in the United States relies on these loose social categories when it reports the significance of a match. But statements such as "1 in 1 quadrillion among African Americans, and 1 in 8 quadrillion among southeastern Hispanics" can foster the mistaken impression that there is a clear biological basis for race.[84] Reporting conjectures about skin tone, facial morphology, or group identity drawn from genetic testing may further elide the distinction between race as a social category and as a genetic classification. Widespread phenotypic testing that produces results in terms that ring familiar racial bells—kinky hair, brown skin, wide nose, etc.—may lead unthinking minds to wonder whether other genetic variations are observable among the races. Put simply, the public may come to think that if genes can tell us that a Native American committed this crime, then they might also suggest a possible biological explanation for Native American crime.[85] Of course, such generalizations can occur even in the absence of genetic tests. But introducing biology lends credibility to bias.

Apart from the lack of scientific basis, too much attention to biology distracts from more important conversations about environmental, socio-cultural, or political influences on crime. For instance, informed of a high rate of arrest of young urban minority males for marijuana use, people might start asking after a biological explanation, rather than inquire whether law enforcement is targeting elite college dorms as aggressively as they are poor neighborhoods. This is true even when a biological association is founded in legitimate science.[86] Fruitful conversations about meaningful distinctions among different groups ought to include, rather than begin and end with, biology.

To be sure, the potential for abuse from phenotypic testing is high. We human beings have failed quite miserably when we have tried to use biology as a means of addressing social problems, whether with regard to the sterilization programs of the first half of the twentieth-century, the eugenics theories of the midcentury, or the immigration debates that

rage today. But before dismissing out of hand even nonsensitive phenotypic testing, it is worth imagining that an entirely different set of consequences from phenotypic testing could, in theory, unfold.

It is quite possible that phenotypic testing would in fact undermine
and uproot, rather than affirm, racist and unfounded ideas. As described
earlier in this chapter, phenotyping helped redirect a Dutch investigation
that initially focused on a disfavored immigrant group, and it helped
solve the Derrick Todd Lee case, which had erroneously zeroed in on
(and conducted DNA dragnets among) persons of the wrong race. Or
consider a case in the Netherlands that involved the killing of a young
Dutch girl. Suspicions focused on a nearby hostel popular with Middle
Eastern and North African asylum seekers, which became the target of local rage. But hysteria subsided when testing revealed the killer was likely
of Western European descent.

In its most glorious form, phenotyping might help bridge the divide
of culture rather than deepen it. Consider a 2003 case from Mammoth
Lakes, California, which unfolded like a murder mystery story. A hiker
in the area came across a shallow grave with human remains. The forensic
team that came to the scene found what appeared to be women's clothing
nearby, and the medical examination concluded that the victim was a
thirty- to forty-year-old female, likely Southeast Asian, of slight stature,
who had died six to nine months earlier. That description jogged the
memory of a park employee, who recalled that several months before the
discovery, a small Asian woman had visited the area with her large, heavy
set white husband, and shared with the park official that he treated her
badly and she was afraid. Following this lead, police circulated a sketch
of the husband, and for a year investigated the case as a domestic killing.

With no new leads, investigators turned to a genetic ancestry company
to have the remains tested for their geographical origin. With the help of
several academic anthropologists, investigators located possible evidence
of a stabbing, and also revealed that the victim's genotype fit a Native
American from southern Mexico or Guatemala. From another round
of DNA testing, it was determined that the victim perfectly matched a
Zapotec sample group from Oaxaca, Mexico, and was possibly related to
a donor in the sample. That led to the precise village, but the woman told
investigators that she was unrelated to the victim.[87] After generating a genetic mugshot that indeed strongly resembled the descriptions offered by
witnesses, investigators finally located a woman in Oaxaca who claimed

to recognize the image. She identified herself as that person's stepmother, gave the missing woman's name, and attested that she had not seen her in seven years.[88]

As the case shows, the "genetic eyewitness" knows both more and less than the human eyewitness. Biological samples are arguably less susceptible (although not immune) to superficial biases,[89] and in a time in which the evidence offered by human eyewitnesses has come under great scrutiny, there is obvious benefit in being able to glean such information with high levels of probabilistic accuracy.

Moreover, if DNA phenotyping comes into common use, eventually law enforcement will get it wrong. They will announce a blue-eyed suspect and the actual perpetrator will turn up brown-eyed, or seek an individual of strong African ancestry and apprehend a person with porcelain skin. Even sex, arguably among the easiest traits to discern given the determinant role played by the Y chromosome, can for complicated reasons at times be inaccurately reported. Disjunctive moments of that kind may result in increased public awareness that race and other supposed "natural" categories are far more constructed and indeterminate than otherwise believed. If so, then society might begin to loosen its death grip on those identifiers as biologically ordained features of social ordering. Consider this the Sally Hemmings effect—a bigot can no longer deny that at core we are all the same, when only the narrowest biological basis divides a black family and white family that share Thomas Jefferson as an ancestor.

But even if we accept DNA testing for superficial or nonsensitive traits, such as hair and eye color, height, skin tone, and face shape, can we successfully draw a line that prohibits testing for more sensitive, and less determinate, characteristics? As it stands, there is a strong legal and cultural barrier between testing of "coding" and "junk" loci. If that line is breached, will another rise to take its place at a better point of demarcation? Does opening the door to *some* testing of expressed traits imperil privacy by compromising the clarity of an unambiguous line between "junk" and "gene" DNA testing?

An iron-clad rule that forbids all phenotypic testing and permits analysis of only noncoding loci avoids the difficulty of charting a principled course through the perilous waters delineating various kinds of genetic information. There is much to be said for the certainty and simplicity of a clear line. But the fact that we do *currently* engage in some testing for expressive information—such as family associations or sex—suggests that the proverbial ship may have sailed. Surely the ascertainment of natural hair color through genetics is less sensitive than is sex at birth or biological parentage.

It is also clear that phenotypic tests for highly sensitive traits will eventually be developed regardless of whether law enforcement specifically goes looking for them. A wide array of interests (academic, medical, corporate, etc.) would benefit from advances in genetic understandings of the mechanisms of addiction, mental illness, violence, sexual deviance, and other behavioral traits. And once even rudimentary inroads are made, both law enforcement and criminal defendants will seek to harness some of the power of genomics for themselves. With 10 million–plus biological samples from known criminal offenders sitting in storage across the nation, it seems irresponsible to ignore the issue and assume that temptation will never come. Much better to stare the demons in the eye, and use law to mold them into angels.

CHAPTER 14

DNA at the Fringes:
Twins, Chimerism, and Synthetic DNA

PLENTY OF THINGS can go wrong with DNA testing in a run-of-the-mill case. Problems with interpreting the sample, determining the right match probabilities, and ensuring the integrity of the collection and testing process exemplify the everyday, ordinary kinds of issues that may arise. But, of course, sometimes the extraordinary occurs.

Forensic DNA testing is to some extent a field of frontiers. Researchers continue to probe how our DNA works, filling the pages of science journals with their new discoveries. Technologists constantly refine the instruments used to conduct DNA testing, enhancing speed and sensitivity. Forensic DNA testing takes advantage of some of these advances as they occur, but it does not have frictionless adaptability. For instance, the government has built an enormous DNA database around a specific kind of DNA test, and sunken costs in that structure prevents laboratories from instantly converting to the latest in testing instrumentation.

But cutting-edge science still crops up in the criminal justice system, typically inspired by the exigencies of an individual case. Three such examples livening up the otherwise predictable environs of the American criminal court include issues related to twins, chimeras, and synthetic or planted DNA.

TWINS

As every fifth grader learns, identical twins share the same DNA profile. That lone fact says so much about how little we know about how DNA works. To be sure, identical twins resemble each other—so much so that they often can only be distinguished by their loved ones. But they are not otherwise identical in every way. They may have different tastes in clothes, music, or food. They may have different aptitudes scholastically, athletically, or artistically. They may have different preferences for temperature or proclivities to illness. In short, they may be genetically identical, but they are very much distinct.

When one of those differences is that one twin is prone to criminal activity, the other twin may provide the perfect cover. DNA left at the crime scene will match both of them, so how is a prosecutor to prove who the actual perpetrator is? That scenario has arisen repeatedly, to various effects. In one case in 2009 in the United Kingdom, police investigated the theft of roughly $15,000 worth of watches during a shopping mall burglary.[1] Police found blood on a shard of broken glass at the scene, and tested it for a DNA profile. The results yielded a match, only there were two candidates—twins James and John Parr.

Police arrested both men, and each denied the offense. In a newspaper report, one brother expressed frustration at the arrest, noting that it jeopardized his job security. He added that he could show his innocence, as he had been watching his young daughter at home at the time of the crime. His twin, meanwhile, simply denied having committed the offense, without providing an alibi. In this case, it is easy to assume that the brother with the thin denial is the likely culprit. In other cases, one sibling might have a long criminal record, while the other is an upstanding member of the community. But even if conventional wisdom supplies a likely answer, a prosecutor tethered to a high burden of proof may still be at a loss. Without a way of establishing beyond a reasonable doubt which brother was responsible, police in the UK burglary could not charge either man, and the offense went unsolved.

The problem of twin matches is uncommon, but it has arisen not just abroad but in the United States as well. Often, one twin will have a conclusive defense—as was the situation in a 2002 Tennessee case, where one of the pair was incarcerated at the time of the offense.² But if both remain suspects, and no one talks, the investigation may totally stall. That was what happened in a Boston case, but there the district attorney and the police took a gamble on a cutting-edge technique designed to solve this very problem. In the fall of 2004, two young women were pistol-whipped and raped in separate incidents within two weeks of each other.³ One of the women managed to hide a used condom, and turned it in to police when she reported her attack. DNA tests of that item, along with other evidence, showed two suspects.

The DNA matched a man named Dwayne McNair, whom police suspected, but it also matched his twin brother. Without more to differentiate the two, they could not be charged. But then police found and arrested the second participant in the crimes, Anwar Thomas. Prosecutors secured a plea deal with Thomas, who admitted the rapes and fingered McNair as his accomplice. McNair was arrested, and held for nearly two years while prosecutors worked out the details of the case. Then, in April 2014, just before trial, prosecutors asked for an extension so that they could conduct a recently developed technique that promised to distinguish twins from each other. Frustrated that the request arose so late in the case, and after delays had resulted in the defendant's being held for so long without a trial, the judge ordered McNair's release.

Eurofins Scientific, a global DNA testing group, had announced its twin test in December 2013.⁴ Rather than looking at the long stretches of repeat sequences used by conventional DNA typing, the test looked for single-letter variations, known as single-nucleotide polymorphisms (SNPs). These SNPs (pronounced "snips") are known places where one might see unexpected mutations in the A-T-C-G letter sequence. In theory, twins should have identical sequences, because they have inherited the same combination of letters from their parents. But any mutations in the genome that occurred after the embryo split would belong to that twin alone.

Scientists with Eurofins thus studied a set of male twins, along with a child fathered by one of them. They sequenced each man's genome, and looked for these hidden mutations—single places where the sequence differed—between the brothers. They then compared those changes to the sequence observed in the child. The child had the father's mutated sequence, which differed from that of his uncle. Thus, scientists concluded that the mutations had occurred *after* the twinning event, and were inherited by the man's offspring. By these means they could distinguish between the two twins who were otherwise genetically identical.

Prosecutors asked for Eurofins' assistance, and five months and $120,000 later, McNair found himself back in jail. The company's tests purportedly identified McNair as the source of the DNA sample, and he was again charged in the rapes.[5] But that is unlikely to be the end of the story. Assuming McNair does not accept a plea deal, the next step will be for a court to determine whether the test was sufficiently reliable to introduce as evidence in court. Prosecutors may face an uphill battle. Not only does it use a method—next-generation sequencing—that has not regularly been employed in criminal cases, but it also relies on mutation theories that were tested largely through examination of a single set of twins.

What is, and should be, enthusiastically embraced by the scientific community ought never to be rushed to court, especially since it may set precedent for future cases, where the evidence apart from the DNA is not so strong. Under the law, a judge should demand clear proof of scientific soundness before allowing such evidence to serve as a basis for conviction, as opposed to investigation.

Assuming the theory behind the technique pans out, it could provide a solution to the problem of twin DNA. Researchers have estimated that roughly ten to forty single mutations of this kind are likely in each generation. Nonetheless, some limits remain. For instance, the moment in which the "twinning" event occurs is not always the same—sometimes the embryo splits as early as five days after fertilization, but it is possible that the split occurs much later. For the method to work, researchers have concluded, twins must have been created within a particular window of five to nine days postfertilization.

Even if McNair's case never makes it to trial, it seems likely that twin tests will surface again one day soon. McNair's case was not even Boston's first struggle with twin DNA. Almost a decade earlier, a prosecutor charged Darrin Fernandez with rape based on a DNA test that showed a match that fit either him or his twin, Damien.[6] There was evidence that the defendant alone had a tattoo spotted by the victim, but the defendant claimed that he got that tattoo after the assault occurred. After two deadlocked trials, the prosecution won conviction on a third attempt. In the future, it may not take quite so long.

CHIMERAS

In 2003, twenty-six-year-old Lydia Fairchild applied for public assistance in the state of Washington. She had two children already, and a third child on the way.[7] Washington law required that Fairchild submit a DNA sample for the entire family to prove relatedness and to pursue paternal support if appropriate. Those tests confirmed her partner's paternity, but revealed something unthinkable to her: she was not the children's biological mother. Lab reports had excluded her as a possible genetic mother.

Officials called her into the office and badgered her with questions. As she continued to insist she had borne all her kids, they accused her of fraud and threatened to have the children removed by child services. Panicked, Fairchild went home and rummaged for photos and birth certificates as proof, even enlisting the support of the doctor who had delivered the children. She requested retests, but they, too, confirmed that she was not the mother. When her third child was born, a court officer was present to witness the birth and an immediate DNA test. When those results, too, showed that Fairchild was not the mother, she was suspected of being some kind of unconventional surrogate.

Fairchild sought legal assistance but attorneys turned her down, viewing the DNA tests as conclusive proof. Finally, attorney Alan Tindell agreed to take the case. He believed Fairchild's story, and so he tried to get to the bottom of the mystery. He found his answer in the *New England Journal of Medicine*.[8] There, doctors told the story of Karen Keegan, a Boston woman in need of a kidney transplant. Her entire family had undergone tests to find a match; the testing revealed that her two sons were not her own. Treating it as a "medical mystery," doctors probed further. They took samples from different parts of Keegan's body, and even dredged up some old tissue from her thyroid that had been removed in the past. That old thyroid solved the case—it contained DNA that was different from the other parts they had sampled, and that matched her sons'. The study also referenced two other known cases of the kind. Tindell asked for similar testing of Fairchild, which likewise ultimately revealed that she was in fact her children's mother.

In the decade since the Fairchild and Keegan discoveries, scientists have learned more about their conditions. The notion that a person's DNA might not be stable, or rather that more than one genetic profile might be present in an individual, is loosely labeled "chimerism."

In Greek mythology, Chimaera was the hybrid offspring of two monsters, one of whom was Echidna, herself half-woman, half-snake.[9] But the more we learn, the more it appears we all have a little monster within. Still, this powerful imagery has even fueled a British play about motherhood, microbiology, and genetic puzzles.[10]

Chimeras can come about in several ways, summarized by one commentator as "transfusion, transplantation, or inheritance."[11] Put simply, chimeras can result from a person's receiving a blood transfusion or organ transplant, from the passage of DNA between a mother and fetus while the child is in utero, and from the spontaneous dissolution of what had been two zygotes into a single embryo, as it turned out happened in the Fairchild case.

One common source of chimerism may be blood transplants and transfusions. It should come as no surprise that injecting blood from one individual into another, or transplanting one person's organs into the body of another, will result in the donor's genetic profile showing up in a DNA test. Although red blood cells do not contain DNA, transfusions that contain white blood cells or platelets may readily transfer DNA. Although such transfers in general are temporary, more lasting traces may be seen.

In the case of bone marrow, transplants may result in wholesale replacing of a recipient's DNA with the donor's DNA, particularly older, aggressive forms that destroy the recipient's DNA entirely. For instance, in a sexual assault investigation in Alaska in 2005, police typed a semen sample and found a match in their DNA database.[12] The suspect, however, had an alibi—he was incarcerated at the time of the offense. Upon further investigation, police learned that the incarcerated man had a brother who had donated bone marrow to him years earlier. Because the recipient's skin cells had not yet been contaminated by the donor's DNA, a simple confirmatory cheek swab removed all suspicion from the accused.

A second source of chimerism, known as microchimerism, is actually quite common, and stems from the free passage of fluids between a pregnant woman and her fetus. Researchers now believe that these cells may actually aid in maternal health. A recent study of 272 Danish women showed that in nearly two-thirds of them, the male Y chromosome was present in their blood.[13] Amazingly, a 2005 study tested 120 women who had *never* given birth to sons, and found traces of male DNA in 21 percent of them.[14] Scientists believe these traces are the result of fetal cells that "migrate all over a mother's body, becoming part of the heart, the brain, and blood."[15] Although the highest percentage of microchimerism was found in women who had induced abortions, a significant number of women who had only had daughters or had no children at all also showed signs of male DNA. Any woman who has recently become pregnant may have learned of this phenomenon firsthand. Invasive genetic tests, such as amniocentesis and chorionic villus sampling (CVS), have now largely been supplanted by a simple blood draw at ten weeks, which can test for major genomic defects in the fetal cells floating within maternal blood.[16]

The final form of chimerism—the one that led to the confusion in the Fairchild and Keegan cases—is known as tetragametic chimerism. *Tetra*, meaning "four," refers to the creation of two zygotes from four cells (two eggs and two sperm), rather than one zygote from two cells (one egg and one sperm) as is typically the case.[17] This condition is characterized by the idea of the "vanishing twin": instead of producing twins, those two zygotes fuse into one. In Keegan's case, for instance, researchers determined that her blood cells contained one DNA line, whereas her other tissues (such as mucous membranes, skin, and hair) were a mixture of two different cell lines.[18] This form of chimerism can arise in both women and men, as the "collapsed twin" can occur in either gender.

The precise scope and extent of chimerism is still a topic of considerable research. Some forms are fairly readily ascertainable—such as those acquired through transfusions or transplants—even if the precise extent of the chimeric effects is still unknown. Inherited forms of chimerism are much harder to gauge. In addition, chimerism is most easily measured when the sex of one line differs from that of the other. That is why researchers focus largely on finding evidence of Y chromosomes in females—because the Y chromosome is distinctly male, and thus easily stands out against the woman's own double-X chromosomes. In contrast, traces of a foreign Y profile in a male, or a foreign X profile in a female, may be less readily uncovered.

Estimates of inherited chimerism range wildly, from as many as 1 in 2,400 persons in the population, to 10 percent, to as much as 50 to 70 percent.[19] One 2014 report in the *American Journal of Medical Genetics* stated that "chimerism in humans is not as rare as previously thought, although it has been studied only recently."[20] Some scientists predict that chimerism rates are even likely to rise as a result of assisted reproduction techniques that implant multiple embryos, without all those embryos' resulting in live births.[21] In such cases, the shadow profiles of those vanished embryos may show up as genetic traces in their siblings' blood.

It is also hard to project precisely how chimerism could play out in a criminal investigation. For the most part, many forms of chimerism may leave only a bare trace of the foreign cells in the body, so that ordinary sampling is unlikely to pick them up. On the one hand, if a suspect leaves a chimeric profile at the crime scene (say, a blood sample from a person who received a transfusion), it may appear that two persons committed the crime instead of one. If a suspect is known, and the chimeric condition endures, tests may show that this suspect has the unusual combined pattern and result in a pretty powerful match. But if a suspect is unknown, DNA analysts may attempt to pull apart two profiles to find two different "contributors," and it is not hard to imagine that a search in an enormous national database might then lead to an accidental match. Or what appears to be a triallelic pattern, or low-level contamination or "noise," may in fact mask chimerism.

Similarly, highly sensitive testing methods, such as low copy number testing, may result in a DNA profile emerging from the chimeric cells of an individual. Again, this could result in the exclusion of a known suspect who seems to have a different DNA profile when tested. But that profile, too, may turn up an accidental match when run through a database trawl. Recall that the likelihood that two people share the same DNA profile is much higher than the probability that a DNA sample will match a person who has been picked at random.

Law enforcement should stay alert to the possibility that a match could result from fortuity of this kind, unusual as such scenarios are, especially since just how uncommon they are remains a matter of some dispute. Some have warned that chimerism may "undermine the very basis of the forensic DNA system."[22] Others conclude that "considering the nature and type of chimerism and the implications of each type for forensic identity testing, it should be clear that the fears about chimerism are exaggerated."[23] At this point, it seems only time will tell.

SYNTHETIC AND PLANTED DNA

In August 1992, just north of Chicago, eleven-year-old Holly Staker was raped and murdered as she babysat two children, one five and the other two years old, in her neighbor's home.[24] Police conducted an exhaustive investigation, but over the course of two months they found few leads. Headlines broadcast their desperation—"Cops Turn to Roadblock in Hunt for Sitter's Killer"[25]—and organizers of a sexual assault awareness march that drew 350 people invoked her name.[26] On October 31, police announced they had their suspect: nineteen-year-old Juan Rivera, who had a history of mental health issues. It was alleged that, in a "chance occurrence," Rivera had bumped into the girl on her way to her babysitting job, and then followed her inside to attack her.[27]

When police took Rivera into custody, they questioned him relentlessly for more than four days. Although he initially denied any involvement, they eventually wore him down, and he narrated a confession so incompatible with the known facts of the case that the prosecutor ordered the police to resume the questioning to elicit a more plausible confession. At one point, Rivera became so distraught that police observed him banging his head against the wall and pulling out his own hair. When approached by the press, Rivera's mother said, "He didn't do it. He doesn't kill. He's nice, . . . He robbed and all that stuff, but he is no murderer. I have a feeling, as a mother, he did not kill." His family also stood behind him, and warned that by arresting the wrong man, police left the real killer at large.[28]

In the media reports surrounding the case, a number of a creepy details emerged. The mother of the children Staker was babysitting announced that "police had recently jarred" a memory she held from the evening of the slaying: Rivera had come over to her as police combed the scene, and asked, "What's happening?"[29] She claimed to recognize him as a regular at a local bar. Because Rivera had been under electronic monitoring at the time for a theft offense, and it showed he was home that evening, authorities concluded that the monitoring system must have failed or malfunctioned.[30] The Staker family even sued the county for its faulty system.[31]

Although Rivera's confession had been the centerpiece of the case, in March 1993 authorities made a shocking announcement. Blood found on a shoe supposedly belonging to Rivera matched a DNA profile belonging to Holly Staker.[32] An inmate claimed that Rivera had traded his shoes for the inmate's television, but he maintained that the shoes had no stains.[33] Rivera's public defender, Henry Lazzaro, fought back vigorously, maintaining his client's innocence and insisting on additional testing, but the court refused to order a DNA sample from the inmate as well.

Even before trial, the case was hard fought. The prosecution was so aggressive that at one point authorities filed contempt charges against Rivera's lawyer, whom they alleged had tried to shield Rivera's girlfriend from the grand jury.[34] Lazzaro, in turn, accused the state of selectively leaking falsehoods to bolster its case in the press.[35] Shortly thereafter, Lazzaro resigned from his job at the public defender; reports speculated a falling-out based in part on his defense of Rivera, whose case he kept as he moved to private practice.[36]

On the eve of trial, the prosecution hit some bumps. First, a sperm sample recovered from Staker's body failed to turn up at the California lab where the defense had requested it be sent for testing. When finally located by the prosecution and tested, it failed to match. Prosecutors simply concluded that the victim must have been sexually active, and that Rivera did not ejaculate. They even put Holly's twin sister, Heather, on the witness stand to address concerns about that DNA, having her testify that the sisters had been abused earlier in their life and that they were sexually active (she later refuted the latter claim).[37] Then the mother of the children—a key witness—suddenly recanted, admitting that police had prompted her to identify Rivera.[38] One of the children testified that he did not recognize Rivera. In a surprise move, the prosecution did not offer the shoe evidence; instead, it put forward one of Rivera's cellmates, who claimed that Rivera had confessed the killing.[39]

Jurors convicted Rivera, but spared him the death penalty. An appellate court overturned the conviction due to errors at trial, but he was convicted again at a second trial. The judge in that trial then overturned that conviction, citing new DNA tests. By that time, DNA testing had recovered yet another profile from specks of blood on the doorjamb where the attacker had broken in. The third trial, which began in 2009, also led to conviction. After twenty years and three trials, however, an appellate court reversed the conviction due to lack of evidence, thereby foreclosing any retrial. In 2012, Rivera finally walked free.[40]

Rivera's saga is, unfortunately, all too familiar for many exonerees. In fact, there were at least four other similar cases from the same district attorney's office. But it differs in one critical respect, which may become the most explosive allegation of all. Rivera's attorneys now allege that police planted the supposed blood evidence on the shoe.

In support of their claim, lawyers cite several damning facts. First, the shoes supposedly worn by Rivera were not available for purchase anywhere in the United States at the time of the killing.[41] Second, more sensitive DNA tests uncovered something suspicious. In addition to Staker's blood on the shoe, tests found traces of semen—the same semen found in Staker's body, but that did not match Rivera. The prosecution simply ignored that evidence. But a court granted Rivera's request to order a search of that profile in the national DNA database.[42]

Prosecutor and law enforcement officials deny any misconduct in Rivera's case, although they settled his civil suit by offering $20 million. But this riveting story points to another unlikely, but possible, danger with regard to DNA testing. Some may claim that planting evidence, to the extent that it is a problem at all, is a problem that has no special connection to forensic DNA. After all, anyone inclined to set another person up can plant a weapon or item of clothing as readily—if not more readily—than biological evidence. There is truth to that assertion, but at the same time, the special strength of DNA evidence makes its discovery a particularly conclusive form of proof. That may especially be the case when trace amounts of DNA are found, because the suggestion is that the suspect might have left them behind unwittingly.

In some ways, the most remarkable aspect of Rivera's story is his defense team's unshakeable faith in his innocence. When the case stood only on a shaky confession, it would be easy to question Rivera's guilt. But as the prosecutor produced live witnesses and biological proof, Rivera's lawyers still refused to roll over. Rather than assume that the DNA tests established guilt, they continued to mount what appeared to be an unwinnable challenge. And as more discriminating tests developed, they continued to pursue the state-of-the-art testing to prove Rivera's claims.

The ease with which DNA can be collected surreptitiously and transferred, particularly in an era in which very little source material may yield a profile, should give everyone pause. The occasional corrupt cop may be worthy of fear, but the true threat may come from a nefarious offender trying to cover his or her tracks, or from a victim intent on lobbing a false charge. As forensic DNA becomes more commonplace, stories of this kind are likely to surface with greater frequency.

For instance, an Australian jury heard evidence in a recent murder case that the defendant had planned to "frame dead people for the murders by planting their DNA at the crime scene or on a murder weapon."[43] The defendant supposedly had a contact at a local funeral parlor that could supply DNA from persons of the right age and sex, some of whom might even have seemingly inculpatory criminal histories. In another case, prosecutors alleged that the defendant had contaminated his own mouth with foreign DNA in the hopes of covering his own DNA profile, thereby excluding himself as a suspect in a fatal shooting (while, it seems, possibly inculpating another person).[44]

In fact, persons intent on using DNA to either exculpate themselves or inculpate another can manufacture false DNA, using skills and tools no more sophisticated than those available to a college biology major. In 2009, a team of Israeli scientists announced that they had fabricated DNA in two ways: by building it from a single sample, and by creating an entirely new profile from snippets of other material.[45] That artificial DNA can then be mingled with red blood cells (which lack DNA) to generate fake blood stains, or else applied directly to a surface to imitate saliva- or touch-based samples. Although the Israeli scientists also stated that they had developed an authentication method to distinguish true from fabricated samples, that test is not in general use by investigators.

Indeed, a researcher in western Australia found that simply filling a spray bottle with a solution containing bits of DNA not only could confound investigators, but could mistakenly lead them to believe they were looking at fragments of crime scene evidence.[46] In fact, these bits of DNA appeared to dominate over the actual samples in the room. As described by Professor William Thompson, a leading authority in forensic DNA typing, "when amplicons from person A were spritzed with the atomizer over a bloodstain from person B, and a sample from the bloodstain was typed using standard STR procedures, the result sometimes appeared to be a mixture of DNA from person A and person B, but sometimes it appeared to consist entirely of DNA from person A."

Although an ordinary criminal is unlikely to engage in such an elaborate ruse, it does not strain credulity to imagine that more sophisticated criminal organizations might view such efforts as worthwhile. Is it so hard to imagine that a sophisticated drug cartel, perhaps even one with chemists on payroll to manufacture its narcotics, might also swipe a discarded cigarette or cup from the competition? With just that little bit of biological evidence, leadership could fabricate DNA samples that might then be used both to cover the tracks of the group's own crimes as well as to eliminate the competition. After all, who would believe the protestations of a known felon who claims innocence, when his DNA profile turns up as matching evidence left behind at a homicide or robbery?

The prosecutor in a Maryland case argued that just that kind of trickery had occurred. When a bandana and orange juice bottle recovered in connection with a drug rip-off–style robbery were tested, and the profiles run against the DNA database, they returned hits to individuals that the prosecution believed were not connected to the crime. The defense pointed out that one of those persons was a "known gang member who had recently pled guilty to a nearly identical type of robbery."[47] The defense requested that the prosecution compare all of the crime scene evidence for more matches to that individual, arguing that the presence of his DNA on more items associated with the offense would further exculpate the defendant. Even though Maryland had a law that specifically authorized defense access to the database, the trial court denied the request.[48]

At trial, the defendants sought to introduce simple testimony about the other matches, but the prosecutor moved to foreclose it. The government declared that if such evidence were allowed, it would seek to introduce proof that one of the matching persons was a member of a gang, as were the defendants, and that gangs were "known to use kits designed to contaminate DNA evidence at crime scenes."[49] Specifically, the state referred to "'robbery kits,' a practice in which gang members purposefully deposit items containing the DNA of others at crime scenes." Arguing that such evidence would be distracting, the state sought to exclude all reference to DNA matches on the two items.

The trial court granted the motion in part, and two later courts affirmed the convictions and decision to exclude the evidence. The court claimed that the defense had failed to seek confirmatory testing of the two items, as required by the statute, even though the defense had sought additional testing from the lab and the courts throughout the entirety of the case, and those petitions had consistently been denied. In the end, the jury in the case heard only that a bandana and juice bottle found at the scene had not matched the defendants, not that it had matched other known gang members, including one with a recent history of having committed the same kind of offense.

Although the Maryland case involved the defense's crediting the other DNA as legitimate, and the prosecution's attempt to undermine that claim, an equally probable scenario involves a defendant's argument that his or her own DNA was planted. In that case, the defense might claim that the "robbery kit" was used to falsely inculpate him or her, while the prosecution will no doubt claim that it was wielded strategically to cover one's tracks. An underground market might even develop with the precise purpose of selling DNA masks. Professor Thompson has recounted how Nobel Prize–winner Kary Mullis once joked about founding a business called DN-Anonymous that would peddle DNA spritzers that could be used to cover one's tracks.[50] Artist Heather Dewey-Hagborg has already brought that vision to life.[51]

CHAPTER 15

Race and the Universal DNA Database

IT IS IMPOSSIBLE to talk about the criminal justice system in twenty-first-century America without also addressing the issue of race. It is now well known that our penal system is the most punitive regime in the world. In the stark terms of a 2014 report on mass incarceration issued by a blue-ribbon panel convened by the National Academy of Sciences:

> The U.S. penal population of 2.2 million adults is the largest in the world. In 2012, close to 25% of the world's prisoners were held in American prisons, although the United States accounts for about 5 percent of the world's population. The U.S. rate of incarceration, with nearly 1 of every 100 adults in prison or jail, is 5 to 10 times higher than rates in Western Europe and other democracies.[1]

The brunt of our harsh criminal justice policies has not fallen equally among all members of our society. As the report details, "Those who are incarcerated in U.S. prisons come largely from the most disadvantaged segments of the population. They comprise mainly minority men under age 40, poorly educated, and often carrying additional deficits of drug and alcohol addiction, mental and physical illness, and a lack of work preparation or experience."

Although all of these demographic categories are important, it is the racial disparity that stands out. "More than half the prison population is black or Hispanic. In 2010, blacks were incarcerated at six times and Hispanics at three times the rate for non-Hispanic whites." A table

TABLE 15.1 The racial and ethnic makeup of the incarcerated population versus the national population.

Race/ethnicity	% of US population	% of US incarcerated population	National incarceration rate (per 100,000)
White (non-Hispanic)	64%	39%	450 per 100,000
Hispanic	16%	19%	831 per 100,000
Black	13%	40%	2,306 per 100,000

Source: Reprinted with permission of Prison Policy Initiative.

prepared by the Prison Policy Initiative presents this disparate incarceration rate starkly (see Table 15.1). [2]

The reasons for America's high rates of incarceration, and its racial disparity in incarceration, are complex and too numerous to address here. For purposes of this discussion, it is important to note that our prisons are not filled with hardened criminals. Over half of state prisoners serving sentences a year or longer are nonviolent offenders.[3] Drug offenders constitute 50.6 percent of the federal prison population and almost a quarter of the state prison population.[4] Aggressive drug enforcement has played a major role in exacerbating racial disparity in the criminal justice system. Again, in the words of the report:

> The best single proximate explanation of the rise in incarceration is not rising crime rates, but the policy choices made by legislators to greatly increase the use of imprisonment as a response to crime. Mandatory prison sentences, intensified enforcement of drug laws, and long sentences contributed not only to overall high rates of incarceration, but also especially to extraordinary rates of incarceration in black and Latino communities. Intensified enforcement of drug laws subjected blacks, more than whites, to new mandatory minimum sentences—despite lower levels of drug use and no higher demonstrated levels of trafficking among the black than the white population.[5]

In sum, although some of the racial disparities in the criminal justice system relate to different rates at which groups commit offenses, a significant fraction is due to disparate patterns of enforcement and case processing. As one study concluded, "[a] large residual racial disparity in imprisonment thus appears due to the differential treatment of African Americans by police and the courts."[6]

In some respects, DNA technologies have served to leaven some of the inequality within the system. It is already evident that DNA testing has helped rectify the injustice wrought by erroneous eyewitness identification. Studies show that eyewitnesses are particularly prone to mistakes in a situation involving cross-racial identification, which may be why exoneration cases have disproportionately fallen across cross-racial lines. For instance, even though only 5 percent of all rapes involve a black perpetrator and white victim, more than half of misidentifications involved a white victim wrongly accusing a black man.[7] In this light, DNA testing might help unseat racism in the criminal justice system—be it conscious or unconscious—by exculpating the wrongly accused.

It is also the case that DNA testing most often plays a role in solving violent crimes, such as rape, murder, robbery, and serious assault. And studies have consistently shown that minorities are disproportionately likely to be victims of violent offenses.[8] If that is the case, then DNA testing would likewise be expected to disproportionately benefit those communities, whose cases would then have a greater likelihood of being closed. More indirectly, it might be argued that successfully removing violent offenders from the community is likely to have a greater impact on preventing further crime in poor, minority neighborhoods than in wealthy and largely white enclaves, where victimization rates are already quite low.

In sum, the benefits of DNA testing to minority communities are real, and should not be understated. But the racial disparities in the criminal justice system are real, too, and cannot be ignored. These twin realities have the potential to turn DNA testing into a double-edged sword for communities of color. On the one hand, forensic DNA can solve and prevent the crimes that terrorize poor neighborhoods; on the other, it can serve as yet another tool of heavy-handed policing and surveillance, meted out disproportionately against certain groups.

There is already ample evidence that the burdens of DNA testing programs have fallen disproportionately on minority communities. Foremost, there is the imposition of compulsory DNA collection laws. If those laws were limited to only the most serious, violent convicted offenders, as they were in their inception, then it would be harder to argue that they invite racial discrimination. Police tend to exercise less discretion when it comes to making arrests for violent crime. They have less power to choose to notice some homicides while ignoring others, even if they may allocate more resources to victims they deem more "deserving."

But DNA collection laws sweep in far more than just serious convicted offenders. They apply both to low-level, nonviolent convicted offenders, and also to mere arrestees. Given the dramatic racial disparities in the policing and arrest rates of low-level offenses, compulsory collection laws can easily become a burden that arbitrarily falls on persons of color. Research has shown that the decision to arrest, the kind of charge to pursue, the offer extended in a plea bargain, and the ultimate sentence of conviction are all moments when whites fare more favorably than do other racial groups. If compulsory DNA collection laws apply broadly, then these disparities will be reflected in the makeup of DNA databases.

For instance, DNA databases will be racially disparate if police routinely sweep poor, minority neighborhoods for drug possession but leave affluent neighborhoods and college towns unbothered.[9] DNA databases will be racially disparate if police break up a fight at a college bar by telling both parties to walk it off, but make arrests when the same fight happens among high school dropouts. DNA databases will be racially disparate if the arrests are all the same, but the college students are offered community service and a chance to wipe the record clean, whereas the dropouts have no choice but to tender a guilty plea. DNA databases will be racially disparate if everyone pleads guilty, but the sentence handed down against the college students is probation, whereas the dropouts go to jail. Using the outcomes of the criminal justice system as the basis upon which to make decisions about who must contribute a DNA sample will simply replicate the dysfunctions of that system in the composition of the DNA databases.

Because the federal government does not collect the racial identifiers of those in the national database, there is no definitive assessment of its precise racial makeup. Compulsory DNA programs are tied to arrest and conviction rates, and every state has a criminal population that overrepresents blacks and/or Hispanics, while underrepresenting whites.[10] Thus, it is safe to assume that the national DNA database itself is racially skewed. Not only does that mean that blacks and Hispanics disproportionately endure genetic surveillance, but it also specially exposes those groups to any errors or abuses in the operation of the database. In consequence, the risks of erroneous matches, mistaken interpretations, or wrongful accusations are borne unduly by black and Hispanic persons.

In fact, as raised throughout this book, there are innumerable ways in which forensic DNA testing imposes special risks and burdens on black and Hispanic people. The language of statistical matches may mislead casual observers into believing that race is a biological category. Familial search methods result in a far greater proportion of minority communities falling under de facto "genetic surveillance." Tests for physical or behavioral traits can end up cloaking social or cultural influences in the language of biology. Dragnets may be more commonly undertaken in communities of color. To debate forensic DNA policy and not to discuss race is not only misleading, but irresponsible.

UNIVERSAL DATABASES

In light of the possibility that DNA databases may perpetuate grave racial injustice, whether real or perceived, several commentators have proposed a universal DNA database. Professor David Kaye, who is most strongly associated with this position, has argued that "settling for a DNA identification database restricted to convicts, or to convicts and arrestees, is sure to aggravate racial polarization in society, undermine the legitimacy of law and law enforcement, and further compromise public safety by halting far short of the deterrent and investigative capability that a population-wide database would afford."[11] In other words, the DNA database we currently have simply exacerbates racial tensions, and falls short in its crime-solving capacity. Why not solve both problems at once and adopt a universal database?

As it is, DNA samples are taken from every newborn in the hospital to check for certain genetic diseases; it might be easy to add a basic identity check and database entry at the same time. Alternatively, persons could simply be asked to submit their DNA upon reaching a certain age. In fact, given that an overwhelming amount of crime—especially violent crime—is committed by men, perhaps it makes the most sense as a matter of resources and efficiency to develop a universal *male* database. At the same time that men register for the draft, they could provide a mouth swab that would then be typed and entered into a national database.

Of course, it seems fairly clear that compulsory universal DNA sampling, whatever the precise details, could never withstand legal challenge even if it passed political muster. On the political side, given the tension over legislation proposing a national identity card,[12] which boiled so high that the plan had to be withdrawn, any politician who voted in favor of universal sampling would risk finding him- or herself out of a job. On the legal side, it seems clear that the Constitution would prohibit such an approach. The *King* case, which dealt with arrestee DNA sampling, leaned heavily on the fact that the police had probable cause to suspect a person of criminal wrongdoing. Other cases have strongly intimated that the police may not even demand a single person's name without first having some individualized need.[13] A law requiring every person to contribute a DNA sample to a national database, for the purpose of solving crime, seems to strike against the heart of the values protected by the Fourth Amendment—even if that heart is all that is left.

But supposing that politics and law posed no obstacle, is it right to assume a universal database could alleviate racial tensions while also solving more crime? As to the latter point, it clearly is the case that a universal database would solve more crime. For starters, in theory it should reduce to zero the number of unsolved crime scene samples held in the database, because every upload would result in a match. A universal database might also have a powerful deterrent effect, because it would dissuade prospective criminals from breaking the law, for fear of getting caught. At the same time, however, those criminals might simply adapt by doing as much as possible to mask or cover their DNA trail.

In the end, the actual efficacy of the database would have to turn on the rate at which crime scenes produced DNA evidence. If no changes were made in the number of times technicians were dispatched to the scene, or the rate at which they could recover evidence, the efficacy of the database would improve, but we would still fall far short of solving all crime. In fact, given the shockingly low rates of crime scene evidence collection today, it would be fair to expect that a universal DNA database would have no impact on the investigation of over 95 percent of crimes.

What about the pitch for greater racial harmony? Would a universal database alleviate concerns about inequity and injustice? Certainly a number of problems immediately disappear. The discretion that pervades policing and prosecution no longer could exert influence over the composition of the database, because every person would be included. Concern about abuse or misuse of the database might become less founded, because everyone—and especially those in power—would have an interest in ensuring its integrity.

But to truly assess the racial impact of a universal database, one must recall that the database has two dimensions. A universal database addresses the entry of *known* persons, but it does nothing to affect what crime scene samples are uploaded. It in no way affects law enforcement's broad discretion to select how and where to police. It does not change the neighborhoods that police target or the crimes they pursue. It does not dictate which crime scenes have a technician respond to comb for evidence. It does not affect the cases that prosecutors bring versus the ones they drop. In short, it only affects one small piece of the equation—the ability to find the criminal. It does nothing to influence whom we are calling a criminal to begin with.

That would not matter if our criminal justice system largely targeted violent crime. But an enormous volume of what we deem criminal is taken up by lower-level offenses. And even with aggressive enforcement of such crimes as marijuana possession, disorderly conduct, or driving while intoxicated, plenty of offenders still go unpunished. The difference, moreover, often turns on race. Nationwide data shows highly racially disproportionate enforcement especially of low-level offenses, such as marijuana possession. Indeed, skewed traffic enforcement has acquired a cultural shorthand: "driving while black."[14]

These disparities in policing will remain unaffected by universal databases. Testing the empty glassine bags found in a poor neighborhood, as opposed to on Wall Street, may result in the identification of a lot of drug users via a universal database, but it will do nothing to change inequities in drug policing. Or suppose police choose to crack down on teen drinking. They might decide to collect the cups they see while breaking up a party at a fancy estate, or in a crammed public housing apartment. In either case, a universal database will help them identify who was drinking underage. But if the police always pick the public housing apartment, and rarely the mansion, the universal database will have done little to defuse racial tension. Indeed, it may exacerbate those tensions, because it will simply enhance law enforcement's capacity to target particular communities. A universal database just leaves the impression that the playing field is level, while not actually addressing the advantages consistently given to one team.

PART IV

Building a Better DNA Policy

CHAPTER 16

The Road to Reform: Efficiency, Accountability, Accuracy, Privacy, and Equality

DNA TESTING REPRESENTS an incontrovertible step forward in crime-solving and a boon to the pursuit of justice. But in its rush to embrace the latest technological advance, our criminal justice system has often allowed mythology or romance to outstrip reality. A legacy of faulty forensic science plagues us today, as DNA-based exonerations have exposed the lack of a scientific basis to familiar methods like hair or bite mark analysis. Unlike those techniques, forensic DNA testing stands on a solid scientific footing. But it is a mistake to think that this underlying scientific legitimacy will, on its own its own, ensure the integrity of DNA evidence.

In a training session for government analysts, Boston University professor Dr. Robin Cotton posited the question, "Why are we so reluctant to embrace the complexities of our system?"[1] Her response indicated the scope of resistance in addressing the problem. First, she observed that "[t]he courts do not appear to embrace complexity; lawyers and judges want us to make the complicated into the simple." Second, she noted that "lab directors would prefer something simple," because complexity impairs productivity. Last, she stated that some of the leaders of the scientific establishment paint too rosy a picture of forensic DNA typing. For instance, she called out the National Academy of Sciences, which has aggressively sought to expose flaws in other forms of forensic analysis, for simply giving "DNA a pat on the back for being scientific," even though practices in the United States are "not generally keeping pace with the literature on the topic or practice in Europe, New Zealand, and Australia."

Although Dr. Cotton's attention focused solely on the scientific aspects of DNA testing, the same could be said for the procedural and evidentiary rules surrounding the use of DNA proof. Improving the use of DNA evidence requires direct confrontation with the forces within the criminal justice system that allow scientific findings to be pushed too far, paper over signs of systemic malfunction, or too readily disregard nebulous but indispensable values like personal liberty. To fairly and accurately harness the power of forensic DNA testing, we must attend to issues surrounding efficiency, accountability, accuracy, privacy, and equality. Serious change entails trading hollow superlatives for broad systemic reform, but in exchange we can expect improvements not just in the quality of DNA evidence, but in the delivery of criminal justice services more broadly. At the very least, efforts to undertake reform of this kind might prompt a new conversation about forensic DNA typing—one informed by its limits, and mindful of its potential for excess.

EFFICIENCY

Thanks to television shows, most people think that the first thing that happens when a crime occurs is that a cadre of trained investigators in Hazmat suits descends upon the scene to collect evidence. These (probably very attractive) technicians expertly comb the area, picking up even the faintest traces left behind by the perpetrator. They then return to their state-of-the-art laboratories, where a small army of assistants sits at the ready to immediately analyze the evidence using the latest dazzling instruments of forensic interpretation.

The reality could not be more starkly opposite. America's forensic laboratory system is wholly decentralized, with dramatic variation in quality. Many of the nation's 411-odd crime labs are understaffed, underfunded, and overtaxed. A 2005 study of public crime laboratories concluded that only 21 percent had sufficient employees to complete their workload. Although there have been some improvements since that time, most DNA labs still find themselves woefully underresourced. Many facilities are outdated, some so physically cramped that analysts must take special care to avoid contaminating samples. For instance, Cincinnati's lab suffers from critical space deficiencies and an electrical system so old that wires overload, wreaking havoc with complicated DNA instrumentation. A 2012 report recommended that the lab double its size, but some politicians have stonewalled efforts to make improvements.[2]

The last major census of crime labs nationwide, completed in 2009, showed that 90 percent of requests for forensic testing of any kind had been waiting for so long they qualified as "backlogged."[3] Even though DNA testing constituted only a third of all new requests, it made up three quarters of the backlog, which was equally split between samples from known offenders and crime scenes. An enormous portion of that backlog came from the FBI's laboratory, as a direct result of compulsory DNA collection laws. Roughly three quarters of all new requests for DNA testing in 2009 were to process the DNA sample of a convicted offender or arrestee. Meanwhile, law enforcement officials in Oklahoma were apparently so overwhelmed by how to implement a new misdemeanor conviction collection law that they simply failed to do so altogether.[4]

Compulsory collection laws are hardly the sole cause of laboratory congestion. One compilation of DNA casework backlogs alone—not including backlogs in known offender sample processing—shows an upward trend from 2005 to 2010 that now hovers in the hundred thousands.[5] And as DNA testing has helped police and prosecutors earn convictions, those successes have led to greater demands for DNA services, further slowing processing rates. In the words of a 2012 review of progress made since a 2010 study, "Backlogs continue to exist at high levels because the demand for DNA casework continues to outpace increased capacity."[6]

Any discussion of the laboratory's need to balance resources between testing crime scene evidence and known individual samples ought not to overlook one important precursor question: whether crime scene evidence was ever collected at all. Whereas DNA testing of known persons has skyrocketed over the past decade, collection and processing of crime scene evidence has stayed essentially flat. In recent years—the same years that have witnessed an explosion in arrestee DNA testing—the rate of forensic sample collection has actually *fallen*. In other words, as legislators continuously push for more aggressive compulsory DNA sample laws, they have all but ignored enhancing the collection and testing of the samples that those offenders are supposed to match to—the ones from actual crime scenes.

FIGURE 16.1   Total forensic samples versus new samples added annually, 2002–2014.

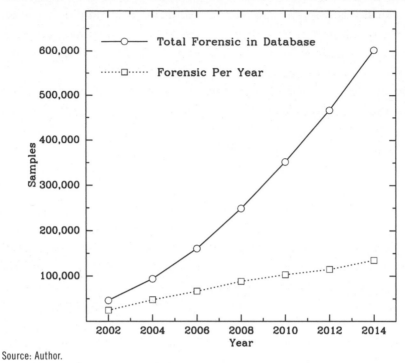

Source: Author.

The real crisis in forensic DNA is not the inadequacy of the 10 million–plus person database of known offenders, but that there are only 619,280 crime scene samples in the database.[7] There are typically over a million violent crimes per year,[8] yet less than half a million crime scene samples have been loaded into the database over its fifteen years of existence.[9] In other words, of the roughly 20 million violent crimes that occurred between 2000 and 2013, only 3 percent of those crime scenes produced samples that made it to the DNA database. When you add burglary, theft, and vehicle theft, this percentage drops to 0.4 percent. Even looking at only unsolved crimes during that period, using estimates based on clearance rates, only 0.5 percent of evidence from those cases was loaded to the DNA database.[10]

This lack of interest is so profound that we do not even have comprehensive data on the state of crime scene collection in the United States, though snapshots taken by existing studies paint a dim picture. In a 2010 report, a research team led by Joseph Peterson randomly examined over 4,000 crime scenes across five offense types: aggravated assault, burglary, homicide, rape, and robbery.[11] The researchers surveyed five jurisdictions intended to represent city-, county-, and state-level law enforcement practices. What they learned was shocking.

First, in an overwhelming number of cases, no physical evidence was collected from the crime scene, even though these were serious offenses. Physical evidence was collected in only 20 percent of burglaries, 25 percent of robberies, and 30 percent of aggravated assaults. Even one third of rape cases generated no physical evidence.[12] A 2007 survey of unsolved crimes reflected similar rates. Forensic evidence was collected in 88 percent of homicides, 73 percent of rapes, and only 29 percent of property crimes.[13]

Without a more in-depth study, it is impossible to know precisely where the breakdown occurs. It may be that the facts of many cases do not lend themselves to the collection of physical evidence—although that just seems facially implausible. For instance, a burglary crime included physical evidence in roughly 1 in 10 investigations, yet that offense is highly amenable to recovery of physical evidence.

A more likely explanation is that less care is devoted to collecting physical evidence from offenses other than homicide or rape. Trained crime scene investigators (CSIs) may not routinely respond to the scene in nonhomicide cases, and police officers often lack sufficient training and support for more detailed evidence collection. Although there is no definitive national survey of crime scene investigation practices, one unambiguous and defining feature that emerges from studies of local practices is the lack of standardization. There are over 16,000 independent state and local law enforcement agencies across the United States, ranging from sheriff's offices to the city or town police to fifty state police departments.[14] But the size, sophistication, and resources of each of those departments varies greatly. Many police departments are actually quite small, and do not have resources to hire dedicated CSIs. For instance, over half of all local police departments have fewer than ten full-time officers; at the other end of the spectrum, 5 percent of all local police departments employ 61 percent of all local police officers. In the absence of specialist CSIs, evidence collection becomes the duty of the responding police officer or assigned detective, or is left to nonpolice personnel, such as a coroner or medical examiner, or hospital personnel.[15]

When responsibility for crime scene collection falls entirely on the responding officers, both the quantity and quality of evidence may suffer. The officers called to an incident may be juggling multiple tasks. They may need to calm victims or secure suspects, identify witnesses and collect their information, while perhaps dealing with other emergency responders or agitated or curious community members. They also may be under pressure to wrap up a particular scene so that they can respond to another call or return equipment at the end of a shift.

In addition, even well-intentioned officers may simply lack the skills to recognize and preserve viable sources of evidence, particularly if the department or academy does not prioritize training in evidence collection. Expecting responding police officers to be able to do the kind of sensitive assessment necessary to milk the scene for all possible information, among their other obligations, may simply be demanding too much.

But the problem does not stop with a failure to collect physical evidence. Collected evidence all too often just sits on the shelf, neither sent to the lab for testing nor tested even if it forwarded there. In the Peterson study, only one third of the evidence collected in rape cases and roughly 11 to 13 percent of the evidence garnered from burglaries, robberies, or assaults was submitted for testing by a lab. What is worse, an even smaller fraction of those submissions were ever tested. Examination rates for submitted evidence hovered around 18 percent for rape cases and 9 to 10 percent for the other offenses.

The 2007 study of crime scene processing looked into why law enforcement did not submit already collected forensic evidence for testing, and found that nearly half responded that "a suspect had not yet been identified."[16] Nearly 20 percent said they were unsure whether the evidence would be useful. These responses led researchers to conclude that "some law enforcement agencies are still not fully aware that forensic evidence can be used as an investigative tool and not just used during the prosecution phase." One survey estimates that about 40 percent of unsolved rape and homicide cases have unanalyzed forensic evidence that likely contains testable DNA. Moreover, "23% of unsolved property cases contain [. . .] forensic evidence that was not being submitted for analysis"—meaning roughly 5 million property crimes could have evidence that if tested would help close the case.[17]

In sum, even among the most serious and violent offenses, evidence collection and testing rates are abominably low. Homicide is the only offense for which evidence is routinely collected (81 percent), submitted for testing (89 percent), and actually tested (81 percent). For other serious crimes, the rates fall precipitously.

Sadly, collecting and testing rates remain low even though we know that expanded collection and testing pays dividends. For instance, at present physical evidence is collected from roughly 20 percent of burglaries, submitted for testing in only 13 percent, and actually examined in only 9 percent of cases. Yet one field experiment that sought to demonstrate the positive impact of training and evidence collection with respect to burglary and auto theft in five communities showed that with proper evidence collection in such cases, the arrest and prosecution rate doubled.[18] That experiment took place in 2008. Since then, enhancements in crime scene evidence collection techniques and processing methods would likely increase success rates even higher. A 2010 study showed a 72 percent hit rate in the DNA database when evidence collected from burglaries was subjected to a streamlined testing process.[19]

What is more, we know that the benefits of improving the collection and testing of crime scene evidence accrue *even when undertaken at the expense of further expanding compulsory collection laws*. Obviously, no DNA database search can work without a companion known persons database. But it is also true that, in our world of limited resources, indiscriminately amassing known profiles defies logic. In fact, study after study has shown that improving the collecting of DNA from crime scenes, not from known offenders, would make the real difference in solving cases.

For instance, one study by the RAND Corporation concluded that "database matches are more strongly related to the number of crime-scene samples than to the number of offender profiles in the database."[20] A superficial glance at national database statistics seems to support this view. The number of hits per year seems to more closely track the addition of forensic, crime-scene samples than known individual samples. (See Figure 16.2.)

The RAND study therefore concluded that "[f]ocusing on uploading proven offenders and crime-scene profiles has a greater impact on database matches . . . than uploading suspected offenders at the point of arrest. That is, the marginal value of adding more suspects or arrestees to the database is lower than the value of adding more crime scenes, under existing legislation."[21]

FIGURE 16.2 Investigations aided *per year* in relation to known and forensic samples loaded per year, 2002–2014.

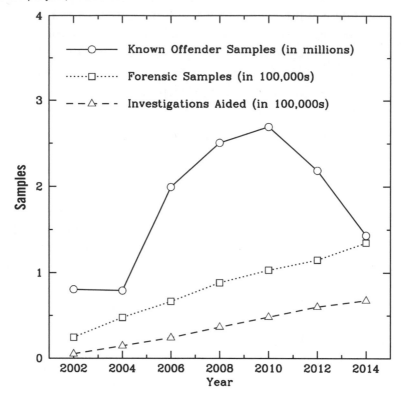

Source: Author.

Similarly, a 2014 report on the United Kingdom's DNA database reached the same conclusion. A series of court rulings required that the government curtail its broad collection practices;[22] as a result, the influx of new profiles slowed and officials expunged over 1.7 million DNA profiles from innocent persons and children.[23] Yet, when assessing performance statistics at year's end, the report concluded that "[t]he reduction in profiles . . . has not led to any reduction in the number of matches the database produces."[24] The match rate had actually increased slightly, from 61.4 to 61.9 percent. Interestingly, crime scene sample uploads also ticked up slightly, after a five-year decline.

Data released during litigation over the California database similarly show that an influx in crime scene samples has a powerful impact on the database hit rate. In that case, the government argued that arrestee sampling had "doubled the crime-solving efficacy of California's database program" from 2008 to 2011. But it failed to acknowledge that crime scene sampling had doubled during that time as well. In fact, during a two-and-a-half-year period in which the laboratories temporarily stopped processing arrestee samples as a result of a court case that ruled them unconstitutional, the number of crime scene samples exploded. Tellingly, throughout that period of crime scene ascendancy, and despite the abrupt drop in known samples, the number of database matches remained level.[25]

Finally, in a 2013 study of European databases, researchers analyzed the forensic DNA practices of twenty-two countries.[26] They classified countries as having either "expansive" or "restrictive" compulsory DNA sampling policies, based on criteria such as the crimes that require that an offender be sampled and the policies regarding retention of profiles. They then assessed each country's person-to-stain matches, an imperfect measure that disfavors larger databases but still captures some idea of database efficiency. The study concluded that "a DNA database's performance in terms of person-stain matches is not linked to its size in terms of individuals included." A 2012 study comparing the British and Dutch experience proved the same point. As of May 2011, the British database contained over 5.3 million known profiles, or roughly 10 percent of the population, as compared to the Dutch database of just over 100,000 known profiles, or less than 1 percent of the population.[27] In contrast, by proportion, the Dutch database contains roughly four times as many crime scene samples as the British database. The result? The match rate of the Dutch database (.23) essentially equals that of the British database (.26).

In sum, study after study shows that we are missing opportunities to solve cases by choosing to expand our known person databases in place of shoring up our collection and testing of evidence from crime scenes. To be sure, no one would dispute that enlarging the offender database increases the likelihood of a DNA match. In a world of limitless resources, there would be no trade-off between processing known samples and collecting and testing crime scene evidence. After all, even adding petty misdemeanants or mere arrestees will result in some crimes' being solved—perhaps even violent crimes. But the DNA databases do not operate in a world of infinite resources, not to mention the political and privacy effects of unfettered collection policies. In the real world, broad and indiscriminate testing of known persons does not come without a cost. The state of Vermont learned this principle recently when legislators were forced to shelve plans to expand its DNA collection to all misdemeanants. The lab protested that it was already buckling under the weight of a 2,500-sample backlog,[28] and the extra load of DNA testing would only further slow the lab's processing times.

The resources spent—both financial and political—on DNA sampling programs ought to reflect a level-headed assessment of their proper place in the pantheon of criminal justice tools, not the whims of law enforcement officials infatuated with new technologies (or, worse, in the grips of private industry interests). After all, even if we sank all of our efforts into improving crime scene evidence collection and speeding the testing of forensics samples, it would still be the case that DNA testing enables only a small fraction of crimes to be solved. No matter how advanced the technology becomes, not every crime scene will produce a useable sample, and not every sample will be useful in proving the guilt of the defendant. In crafting DNA policy, it is essential to keep the limitations of the technology in perspective.

If a balance must be struck, these studies suggest that it should be struck in favor of more crime-scene collection and testing, rather than expansion of compulsory sampling laws. Instead, many jurisdictions are moving in precisely the wrong direction. Arrestee sampling in particular simply creates administrative headaches and wastes resources. Arrestees who are convicted already will, in most states, be required to submit DNA samples upon conviction. Those whose cases are dismissed, as a significant fraction are, are either entitled to or automatically have their DNA profile removed from databases. Thus, arrestee sampling gathers in its nets only two kinds of individuals: those convicted of a charge that does not qualify for database inclusion, and those whose charges at arrest were dismissed but failed to seek expungement. Even a cursory glance at so-called preventable crime studies done by advocates of arrestee sampling bears this out: many offenders supposedly caught by arrestee sampling in fact had a history of prior convictions.[29]

To be sure, forensic analysis of crime scene evidence requires far greater investments in personnel and infrastructure than does that of known person samples. Expanding evidence collection efforts would require localities to hire, train, and equip more technicians. Testing challenging forensic samples is both more time and labor intensive than testing clinical-quality known individual samples. To truly make a difference, funds would have to be allocated to expand and renovate laboratory space, hire and train new crime scene investigators and analysts, and buy new equipment. Although federal funds are available to help meet some of these needs,[30] some states have laws that prevent the use of temporary grants of this kind to fund personnel or other enduring expenses. Other labs are simply reluctant to take on the responsibility without a guaranteed income stream. As a result, labs may be more inclined to spend money on purchasing one-touch DNA processing systems that mainly handle known offender samples, rather than on hiring new analysts or instrumentation to better address crime scene samples. But what is the point of expanding our known person databases, if not to solve crime? And how much crime will get solved if all the resources are allocated toward gathering more known person samples, rather than collecting and testing crime scene evidence?

Moreover, the savings gained by reorienting our use of DNA evidence would accrue in benefits as measured both in real dollars and in emotional capital. Those dividends are already paying out with respect to a national effort to test long-ignored evidence in rape cases. Officials in Ohio, New York City, Detroit, Memphis, and Houston, among other cities, have all engaged in high-profile pushes to test old rape kits.[31] And the results have been breathtaking. As one journalist reported, "[i]n virtually every city where a concerted effort has been undertaken to reduce the backlog, offenders have been identified and indicted."[32]

For example, in 2009 with the help of federal funds, the county prosecutor in Detroit, Kym Worthy, began testing 11,000 rape kits found languishing in a police storage facility. As of May 2015, analysis of 2,000 kits has led to 1,266 hits in the database to investigate, the identification of 288 alleged serial rapists, and 15 convictions along with 6 pending trials.[33] In Houston, a $6 million initiative cleared a backlog of 6,600 rape kits, resulting in 2,305 DNA profiles that, when uploaded into databases, led to 850 database matches and 29 prosecutions thus far, already resulting in 6 convictions.[34] From those matches, it became apparent that six suspects had gone on to commit other sexual assaults.[35] Testing in Memphis revealed that the same man who raped a sixteen-year-old girl, leaving DNA evidence that went untested for nearly a decade, had subsequently raped six more women.[36]

A 2012 Ohio initiative to test a backlog of more than 9,000 rape kits has resulted in analysis of over 5,600 kits, leading to 2,000 matches in the DNA database.[37] An estimate by the county prosecutor for Cleveland placed the cost of not pursuing cases earlier at a minimum of $183 million, which included such things as the medical care for future victims.[38] Given that testing across all jurisdictions has revealed that a significant fraction of suspects identified through DNA testing—in some cases over half—are linked to more than one case,[39] speedier apprehension of such persons could clearly have prevented more crime.

As a result of efforts like these, the tide may slightly be turning. These successes spawned a national movement focused on testing rape kits, including advocacy projects like EndTheBacklog. California, Colorado, Illinois, Michigan, Ohio, Texas, and Wisconsin have all passed laws mandating that police send nearly all rape kits for DNA testing.[40] In March 2015, Vice President Joe Biden announced a $41 million initiative to help localities clear the estimated 400,000 backlogged sexual assault kits.[41]

Even still, more resources are needed. The federal funds cover just the cost of testing each kit, assuming an expense of roughly $450 apiece. These funds are not targeted at a sustained buildup of infrastructure necessary to continuously process large volumes of cases. Yet that support is essential. Houston's backlog effort required the lab to double its employees, as well as increase its space and supplies.[42] Detroit's backlog of rape kits was so profound that the city launched a public fund-raiser for the $10 million needed to process and prosecute the cases generated from those 11,000 untested rape kits.[43]

And, of course, sexual assaults are not the only crimes that merit greater attention. Pilot projects aimed at using DNA evidence to prosecute property crimes—such as using task forces to swab the airbags of wrecked stolen cars or tools left at burglary scenes—have likewise met with resounding success.[44] For instance, lab directors in Minnesota undertook a major effort to make a dent in intractably low rates for solving property crimes by using DNA evidence. They found that DNA recovered from property scenes turned up a match "more than 70 percent of the time" in the national DNA database. Other law enforcement officials show signs of recognizing the potential to solve property cases with DNA; one study reported that in 2011, 38 percent of DNA casework requests related to property offenses; in 2013, that figure was 58 percent.[45]

Improving DNA collection methods, by timely dispatching trained personnel to recover evidence from crime scenes, also may offset some of the tendency to push DNA testing too far. If recovered material suffers in quantity or quality because of the manner in which it was collected, analysts may be tempted to push the science beyond its fair point. As numerous experts warn, even though sophisticated probabilistic methods allow interpretation of seriously compromised results, that does not mean such estimates should always be attempted. They still recommend a "rigid assessment of the overall quality of a given DNA profile and its suitability for further analysis based on criteria described in the laboratory's quality management guidelines."[46] In other words, just because more DNA is collected does not mean all of it will be interpretable. But optimizing evidence recovery may improve the odds both that a sample yields sufficient DNA for reliable testing, as well as that losing "one" in a sea of many does not feel like as great a loss.

Finally, efforts to collect more crime scene evidence must also be coupled with clear and exacting policies on the preservation and retention of that evidence. One survey of law enforcement retention policies found wide variation in both the practices and policies of evidence retention, not to mention the training that officers received in proper handling and storage.[47] For instance, less than half of respondents had a policy in place that preserved biological evidence after a defendant was found guilty: one third had no such policy, and 16 percent were unsure of their agency's policies. This lack of guidance means that evidence could be destroyed even while a case was still on appeal.

Evidence preservation and retention is critical—even after a conviction is final—for several reasons. For starters, DNA is an evolving technology. Just as samples that in the past could not yield results today may be used to exculpate or inculpate an offender, it is easy to anticipate that in the future still more sensitive tests will become available. Forensic samples should therefore be preserved, with full integrity, in the event that a need develops to reopen a case.

Former Virginia crime lab scientist Mary Jane Burton can attest to the value of preserving samples. Although it was contrary to the lab's policy, she acquired the habit of taping evidence to her case files. As a result, more than five men have been cleared by exculpatory DNA test methods that did not become available until years after her work. In addition, offenders who had eluded arrest were brought to justice.[48] Some advocates for the wrongfully convicted have observed that, perversely, the high rates of exoneration in some jurisdictions correspond to their commitment to justice, rather than the reverse. That is because localities with strong evidence preservation and postconviction access policies are simply more likely to find wrongfully convicted persons than are jurisdictions without them.

Evidence preservation and retention remains important even if DNA testing methods never change. As has been shown, nearly every major crime laboratory in the country has endured a scandal of some kind, many of which led to retesting of what had been closed cases. But when evidence is destroyed, or preserved in substandard conditions, the errors made by officials cannot as easily be rectified.

The Innocence Project, a national nonprofit devoted to exoneration of wrongfully convicted persons, maintains a searchable website that includes every state's evidence preservation policies.[49] The National Institute of Standards and Technology also commissioned a blue-ribbon panel of experts to produce a report on best practices for evidence handlers, which includes preservation practices.[50] Several states have taken the lead and enacted laws requiring the preservation of any evidence that might contain biological samples throughout not just the pendency of the case, but the entirety of the defendant's sentence.[51] But many laws still have shortcomings, such as defining in unduly restrictive terms the scope of covered crimes, requiring a defendant to make a preservation request rather than impose the duty automatically, or failing to impose the requirements retroactively so as to protect evidence still in custody but previously collected. Some officials complain that broad and lengthy preservation requirements impose too great a burden when departments are strapped for resources. But as a nation, we have managed to find a way to preserve over 10 million biological samples from known offenders—despite requests to destroy them in the name of privacy. Finding the storage capacity to preserve the physical evidence used to convict people of serious crimes should not be an insurmountable hurdle.

Finally, improving the efficiency of forensic DNA usage requires better information about how our DNA databases are working. As it stands, assessments of that kind all too often turn on hunches and speculation, or anecdotal information about the solving of a single gruesome crime or one dramatic episode of error. The recent litigation over arrestee DNA databases provides a good illustration of the need for actual data. A significant question in the case was how to value the DNA typing of arrestees as weighed against the cost to liberty and privacy. No clear, scientific studies answer that question. Instead, each side hurled anecdotes at each other, and in the end the Supreme Court simply assumed that more arrestee sampling would greatly serve the interests of law enforcement. In contrast to American practice, the United Kingdom's National DNA Database Strategy Board issues annual reports that contain a wealth of information about the nation's collection, retention, and use of genetic information, and as a result researchers in Great Britain have been able to conduct much more thorough examinations of database efficacy.

To engage in a truly informed debate about DNA collection and testing laws, we must collect and make available for research data about how those practices actually function. Yet at present, the only national statistics collected on forensic DNA are the basic numbers recorded by the FBI: the number of known profiles in the national database, the cumulative number of crime scene samples loaded, and the number of times that an investigation has been aided as a result of a hit in the database. This last figure, the "investigations aided" metric, is the most vexing number of all. Simply indicating that number of times that a DNA match "added value to the investigative process,"[52] this figure is barely useful; for instance, it includes the many cases in which "investigators have already identified a key suspect and . . . expect a database match."[53]

A robust data collection program would include far more information, and far more sensitive inquiries. Some questions that we might want answered include the following:

- What is the composition of the database by sex, race, ethnicity, geography, and age?
- What is the most serious charge for each known arrested or convicted person?
- What is the most serious offense alleged for each crime scene profile?
- How many searches result in a match of some kind?
- What is the average number of matches returned per search?
- How many searches are conducted at each level of stringency?
- What is the match rate upon first search after loading a new known profile?
- What is the match rate upon first search after loading a new crime scene profile?

- How many crime scene samples are marked solved versus unsolved?
- How many requests for expungement have been received?
- How many expungement requests were granted versus denied?
- How many profiles have actually been expunged?
- What is the average length of time from request to expungement?
- What are the legal bases for those expungements?

About each DNA database match:

- The most serious offense alleged in connection with the match
- This match identified
    - A possible perpetrator of the offense
    - The victim of the offense
    - A witness to the offense
    - A person connected to the incident, but not a victim, witness, or perpetrator
    - A person unconnected to the offense
- The known person's basis for inclusion in the database (e.g., felon, misdemeanant, arrestee, elimination sample, etc.)
- For matches to a possible perpetrator, that individual was (without the DNA evidence)
    - Totally unknown
    - Suspected, but without probable cause
    - Suspected, with probable cause
    - Known
- With regard to the person found to be a match, the match allowed law enforcement to
    - Make an arrest of that person, or seek an arrest warrant
    - Conduct further investigation, which led to an arrest/warrant for a different person
    - Conduct further investigation, which eliminated suspects but identified no alleged perpetrator
    - Close the case, without any arrests
    - Do little more than eliminate the matching person, and the case remains unsolved
    - Do nothing in relation to the match
- Did the DNA match ultimately lead to prosecution?
- What was the outcome of that prosecution?

- How critical was the DNA evidence to proving the case or obtaining a plea offer?
- Were there any challenges to the admissibility of the DNA evidence, and if so, on what grounds?
- What were the outcomes of any challenges?
- If DNA evidence was admitted in evidence at trial, did the defense challenge the DNA evidence in any way, or concede that it matched the defendant?

To be fair, the decentralization of crime labs, police, and prosecutors in the United States makes collection of DNA statistics difficult. Most jurisdictions do not have interoperable tracking systems even among their own arms of law enforcement, much less with outsiders. Although better collaborative tools might be desirable for other reasons, the decentralization of the national database remains, as it was intended to be, a good thing. One of the few reassuring aspects to our DNA databasing system is that information is diffused throughout the states, making it more difficult to hack or tamper with the system. That structure was chosen wisely, and should remain in place.

But although decentralization poses a challenge to piecing together a national picture of the use of DNA, it need not be an obstacle. Policing and prosecution are also decentralized, but federal authorities manage to compile incredibly nuanced data about arrests, sentences, and case dispositions, not to mention a wealth of information about other criminal justice topics. All of this raw data is made broadly available to academic and industry researchers seeking answers to interesting questions.

One means of improving DNA metrics might be to include within the CODIS software features intended to better track DNA searches and their outcomes, just as there already is a system in place to alert labs when a hit occurs between two samples. According to recent studies, 80 percent of crime labs have an electronic system for managing their laboratory workloads.[54] Most large prosecutor offices and court clerks have systems—including electronic—for tracking case files. As criminal justice systems move toward better electronic tracking of evidence, test results, and cases, a priority may be made of finding ways to integrate those interfaces. We already chart a defendant's motions, court appearances, warrants, and the payment of fines; we might also seek to trace the role DNA played in the case.

In 2009, California launched a pilot program titled CHOP, for "Cold Hit Outcome Project," that attempted to track outcomes in cold hit cases.[55] Other local agencies have developed programs of the same kind, and California also aims to fully implement a statewide tracking program.[56] As of 2015, New York was in the midst of a multiyear process to devise a statewide system accessible to police, laboratory officials, and prosecutors. Although these efforts are laudable, they remain idiosyncratic. The federal government has sunk only the smallest fraction of money into encouraging states to undertake evaluation and tracking programs, as compared to its enormous expenditures to expand the architecture for collecting and storing more and more DNA from known persons.[57] But these priorities are exactly backward; ideally we would have started with a modest collection program and measured its strengths and weaknesses, and used that as a platform from which to assess how best to spend additional dollars.

ACCOUNTABILITY

Nearly every major forensic laboratory across the United States, including the Federal Bureau of Investigation lab and the lab for the US Army, has at some point endured a significant scandal. A shocking number of cases involve outright fraud—the falsification of data or intentional cover-up of mistakes. But most alarming, these instances of exposure most often reveal not a single case gone wrong, or one egregious mistake, but rather pervasive and entrenched incompetence, mismanagement, or faulty if not fraudulent training and testing practices. These scandals tell us something incredibly important about our DNA forensic laboratory system: systemic accountability is either wholly lacking or in crisis.

The first step toward safeguarding the integrity of DNA evidence in the criminal justice system is to implement a meaningful system of structural oversight. Labs would be subjected to rigorous standards of quality control, akin to those applicable to labs engaged in medical testing. There would be random, unannounced inspections to ensure those standards were met, and inspectors would write detailed reports, perhaps assigning a score reflecting the lab's competency. Compliance reports would all be posted publicly, perhaps on a readily accessible website. At all times, the lab would have on hand a supervisor certified in quality assurance who would watch over line workers and ensure proper procedures are followed. Failure to meet these standards would lead to swift repercussions. Authorities would occasionally shut down labs that show problems in need of systemic remediation—no matter how popular or how much their services are in demand. Although burdensome, such a system would not only create powerful incentives for these audited labs to perform to the highest of standards, and ensure transparency to the consumers of their services, but also serve to minimize and deter misconduct from occurring in the first place.

If this sounds unrealistic and implausible, too costly or too cumbersome, make no mistake—it is far from impossible. The regime described is one that New York City employs to safeguard the integrity of its 24,000 restaurants. Programs with similar degrees of strict oversight are likewise in place for other critical services, such as health-care providers or child-care centers. Many of those entities must undergo routine unannounced spot checks, when their files are combed for missing material or workers observed for noncompliance. Fees and fines and even a temporary shut-down of the entire business may follow if violations are found, and all of the inspection reports are posted publicly for consumers to see.

Right now, forensic laboratories undergo nowhere near this level of regulation. They are instead mostly islands of self-governance. As geneticist Eric Lander famously once lamented, "clinical laboratories must meet higher standards to be allowed to diagnose strep throat than forensic labs must meet to put a defendant on death row."[58] Laboratory accreditation requirements are one of the mechanisms intended to minimize these kinds of problems, and yet in their current iteration, they have utterly failed to do so. Truly effective structural oversight would prevent and minimize error and guide remedial action when problems arise, as well as implement procedures for identifying and addressing the root causes of any observed errors. Without a meaningful system of broader oversight, it is all too easy to move from crisis to crisis, never taking the time to see larger patterns at work that might point toward strategies for prevention.

Much of this work must be done internally by laboratories themselves. That means that organizations with excellent accountability practices must model and share their protocols with those still struggling. But self-monitoring is not enough. It is equally important to have a functioning system of external audits.

The most important changes for DNA laboratories would be to introduce random spot-check audits, regular blind proficiency testing, and total transparency in testing and auditing results. Given the highly decentralized nature of the forensic laboratory system, no single law or regulation can achieve these goals. But targeted incentives might be able to coax local and state compliance. In this respect, the government wields two powerful inducements: access to the federal database system, as well as to the myriad funds doled out for laboratory improvements.

First, for many DNA labs, access to the national database and its software architecture serves a critical purpose. Because the federal government sets the standards that labs must meet to enjoy such access, it wields an incredible stick—or offers a juicy carrot—to nudge laboratory compliance in a particular direction. Interestingly, when it comes to auditing compliance with its database upload rules, the FBI flexes its muscle. The FBI audits participating labs by taking a sampling of one hundred files and reviewing them to determine whether uploads to the national database complied with CODIS rules as to the nature and quality of samples. When questions arise, it conducts further investigation. And not uncommonly, the FBI uncovers samples that should not have been put in the database and either requests or orders their removal. Review of those documents show that the auditors take the process seriously.

These detailed audits ensure that the rules about database access and sample storage are actually followed despite the lack of a centralized screening mechanism. But the audits serve another worthwhile purpose. Although not an explicit goal of the process, they educate laboratory technicians about the nuances in the upload policies, and likely also deter laboratories from trying to stretch the rules or slip by some profiles. In addition to risking losing access as a sanction from the federal government, a lab caught bending the rules may also suffer embarrassment or come under scrutiny because these audit reports are publicly available online.

Unfortunately, the FBI's approach to quality assurance when it comes to actual evidence handling and testing is not as rigorous. It does require mandatory accreditation and asserted compliance with certain procedural and qualification requirements. But the FBI takes no independent steps to ensure these requirements are actually honored. Like many oversight boards, it instead largely defers to the accreditation process. Yet that accreditation process is inadequate and faulty, and has failed to catch nearly all of the systemic shortcomings that have led to the litany of DNA lab scandals in the past ten years. Without an accreditation system that immerses itself in the actual functioning of the lab, the accreditation and paper-based requirements imposed by the FBI are ineffectual—both provide detailed standards for procedures, but neither checks to see if they are working.

Instead, the FBI could use the leverage of CODIS access either to undertake the kind of random spot-checking it conducts with regard to DNA database integrity, or it could change its own standards to accept only truly rigorous programs of accreditation. For instance, if accreditation only counted if the accrediting agency had to conduct random spot checks or reopen a selection of cases for total reanalysis, then existing accreditors would likely shore up their services. That might even have the salutary effect of spilling over to labs with no federal connection.

The move toward greater accountability can only succeed, however, if it occurs in tandem with a move toward greater transparency. Although the FBI's audits of CODIS compliance are publicly available and readily accessible, virtually no other information about laboratory quality is. A person who gets in a bar fight must hand over his or her genetic code for perpetuity, but labs routinely shroud audit reports and error logs in secrecy, and a technician fired for incompetence or even deliberate fraud may go on to find employment in another lab.

Despite our enormous national database of over 10 million samples, we have no public repositories for accreditation reports or documented malfeasance. There is no centralized place to learn whether a lab has engaged in significant error, what kind of investigation took place, what it uncovered, and what corrective actions have been taken to prevent it from happening again. As a result, it is impossible to get data on national trends, a perspective on the actual rate of error, or learn from experiences with successful corrective reforms.

At most, outsiders may consult the list on the accreditors' websites of laboratories on probation or who have withdrawn their accreditation requests, but those lists often remain suspiciously empty. Even when a lab incurs a sanction, that sanction is not always reflected on the website, and no website contains a history of the laboratory's accreditation status or documented sanctions.[59] The lack of transparency trickles down to the individual employee level: a lab has no obvious source to consult to ensure that the employee it seeks to hire was not previously terminated for gross incompetence or outright fraud.

That is not to suggest that no records of such information exist. Both the FBI and the ASCLD/LAB accrediting standards require labs to track their errors internally and undertake corrective measures. Increasingly, labs must undertake "root cause analysis" of significant errors, which ideally includes a detailed accounting of what happened and the measures taken to ensure it will not occur again. But rarely does any of this data see the light of day. Neither accreditors nor the FBI has any shown interest in publicizing the mistakes made by crime labs.

Federal officials took one important step toward exposing flaws in crime labs when they enacted the Paul Coverdell National Forensic Sciences Improvement Act.[60] That act conditioned the grant of public funds on the existence of an independent authority within the state to investigate allegations of serious negligence or misconduct. Outside review of this kind is essential, because it provides an objective look into the practices of the crime lab and circumvents self-serving yet ultimately hollow assertions that identified problems have been fixed.

Unfortunately, despite the passage of that act, the entity responsible for implementing the oversight requirement—the Department of Justice—did little to enforce it. In fact, an inspector general report found that many recipients either lacked independent auditors or named auditors that "had not even been previously informed that their entities had been named to conduct independent external investigations."[61] Moreover, many of the labs that did name auditors simply chose the police department—an entity typically ill-equipped to conduct a searching review and ill-disposed to do so, given its naturally aligned interests.

Curtailing the widespread and shocking incidence of error and malfeasance in forensic labs requires a commitment to truly independent review, record-keeping and documentation of material laboratory errors, and transparency and openness regarding the audit and inspection process. Making records of this kind more available would place forensic laboratory services on par with other providers of critical services. Careful and thorough corrective action instills public confidence in a well-run system. Imagine if, after an airplane disaster, transportation authorities simply refused to investigate and the airline could decline to release any information about what happened. Or they did investigate, but rather than publicly announce their findings, they simply promised consumers that any problems had been addressed. An airline that took that approach to safety would quickly go out of business, but public crime labs that have experienced problems have managed to stay in business for years.

That is in part because the very people who might be auditing them—the government—are the chief beneficiaries of corrupt services.

The final piece of a complete picture of accountability, beyond meaningful audits and transparent records, involves two important shifts in forensic science culture that have already begun. The first is marked by the formation of the National Commission on Forensic Science, inspired by the landmark 2009 National Academy of Sciences report advocating the creation of a federal agency for forensic science. Cochaired by the Department of Justice and the National Institute of Standards and Technology (NIST), the commission has already undertaken a broad agenda for reform that holds tremendous potential to better the future of forensic science. Although its work has not been entirely smooth sailing, as detailed in the next section, it has nonetheless already drafted proposals relating to a host of essential topics on the reform agenda.[62] What is more, the commission follows public process requirements: meetings are open and broadcast over the Internet, and the body accepts and makes public any comments on its work product.

The specific engagement of NIST in the formation of the National Commission on Forensic Science (NIFS), and the increasingly central role it plays in forensic DNA, marks the second major advance in recent years. The entry of NIST into the forensic DNA research community has dramatically improved the quality of conversations around best practices in the field. In a number of key areas, including mixture interpretation and statistical representation of evidence, NIST scientists have both undertaken critical research as well as offered invaluable training modules designed to enhance understanding of difficult areas.

But even more valuable than these specific undertakings is the culture of science that NIST has brought to the field. Rather than hide data or—even worse—shrink from knowledge altogether, NIST actively seeks out new information and publishes its work with full transparency. NIST scientists maintain a website with rich amounts of information, including webinars and slideshow presentations, which is freely and openly available to interested parties, whether lab employees seeking to improve the quality of their work or lawyers hoping to learn more about best practices.

Finally, NIST seems thus far to have largely avoided the conflicts of interest that have otherwise characterized the Department of Justice (DOJ) and FBI's role in the development of DNA policy in the United States. The DOJ, in particular, has been repeatedly reprimanded for its failure to administer DNA-related programs in an even-handed and fair way. For example, a report by the Office of the Inspector General concerning DOJ's grant award process contained sharp criticisms of the National Institute of Justice (NIJ), the awarding body. The report specifically singled out fifteen grants involving lobbying conflicts; half concerned companies with interests in DNA typing.[63] One example included numerous grants to a lobbying firm known as Smith Alling Lane, which since 2000 has lobbied Congress on behalf of a number of major players in the forensic DNA industry. Under a July 2002 grant from NIJ, for instance, Smith Alling Lane was tasked with conducting a study to investigate various aspects of DNA processing in the United States, including an assessment of backlogs and crime lab capacity. As the report noted, "The study was designed to provide data to NIJ and Congress to help guide future policies and legislation related to DNA testing," and yet it was conducted by an entity whose "clients could significantly benefit from additional funding"—especially for their particular kinds of tests.

In this respect, NIST has helped move American forensic science—which has languished in the adversarial culture of our criminal courts—more toward the European model, in which forensic scientists tend to view themselves more as scientists than as law enforcement officers. NIST's primary shortcoming, as its title suggests, is that its role is to survey existing practices and delineate universal standards, not to ask whether certain practices are advisable at all. Thus, for instance, NIST might address the most effective parameters for conducting a familial search in a DNA database, but it would not engage the deeper legal, moral, or ethical issues of such a search. Similarly, NIST might set out the parameters for low-quantity testing, but not opine that such testing is inadvisable due to its inherent difficulty. But perhaps it is in part because it deliberately steps back from those deeper policy debates that NIST is able to effectively navigate among the various purveyors and consumers of forensic services.

ACCURACY

In January 2015, Judge Jed Rakoff, a member of the National Commission on Forensic Science, resigned in protest. In his departure letter, Rakoff explained that the deputy attorney general of the US Department of Justice had informed him that the DOJ deemed the topic of discovery—the rules that govern what information the prosecutor must disclose to the defense in advance of trial—outside the commission's scope and therefore off the agenda.[64] He accused the DOJ of putting "strategic advantage over a search for truth." In the mild media storm that followed, the DOJ quickly backtracked and Rakoff resumed his seat. But even though the DOJ agreed to consider discovery reform as a topic, officials made no promises about endorsing new standards.

It remains to be seen what comes of the proposals, but this particular showdown was emblematic of a pervasive problem. Just as DNA laboratories have little structural accountability for the quality of their work across the range of cases, so, too, is there little direct accountability for the accuracy of their work in a particular case. Time and again cases have arisen involving an analyst who has misinterpreted, misstated, or even outright falsified the DNA evidence in a criminal case.[65] And yet these errors have gone undetected not only by laboratory quality-control programs, but also by the legal actors—the prosecutors, defense attorneys, judges, and juries—who are charged with scrutinizing such data. Although the main consumer of forensic DNA testing is the legal system, it has largely failed to stem the tide of faulty forensic science, much less unmask instances of fraud, malfeasance, or gross negligence when they occur.

The success of DNA testing programs hinges primarily on the skills and abilities of the people who execute them. But the adversarial process can still serve as a second-line defense. To understand why the adversarial process has thus far failed to expose bad forensic science, one must appreciate two realities of our current system: (1) the nature of criminal adjudication, and (2) the lack of meaningful repercussions for those who choose to walk along a blighted evidentiary path.

First, in contrast to the rosy picture painted by procedural rights to counsel and a jury trial, criminal adjudication in the United States is defined by crushing caseloads, indigent defendants, and astronomically high plea rates. These conditions combine to make it highly unlikely that a laboratory's output endures any kind of meaningful scrutiny. Most lawyers—prosecutor and defense alike—have very little time to devote to learning the complexities of the scientific evidence presented in a case. Some lawyers and judges could not understand these complexities if they tried—there is a reason that few lawyers majored in biology or math in college. In place of mastering the nuances of scientific testing, prosecutors often just trust the representatives of the laboratory, whom they may view as an adjunct of law enforcement.

Some law enforcement officials may even have a reason to bury their head in the sand. Apart from the professional benefits of a high conviction rate, police, prosecutors, and laboratory officials in some jurisdictions have a financial interest in masking error and churning out conviction-ready findings. A 2013 study in the journal *Criminal Justice Ethics* found that at least twelve states allocate funds to labs based on the number of convictions that arise from their work.[66] For instance, Kansas law states that convicted defendants must "pay a separate court cost of $400 for every individual offense if forensic science or laboratory services or forensic computer examination services are provided in connection with the investigation."[67] A website maintained by a lobbying group for forensic DNA industry interests has a section about "Public Safety Fees for DNA Programs."[68] It lists eight states that levy a charge on criminal defendants specifically to help finance DNA laboratory services.[69]

Laws such as this send a clear message to the laboratory that conviction pays. The more that city officials value the lab's work, because it helps secure convictions, the more funds the lab may perhaps obtain for improved facilities or added personnel. Refusing prosecutor entreaties, or routinely helping the defense, earns the lab little favor and may even cost it critical capital with the city's major political players. A few labs have embarked on even more aggressive efforts to raise revenue. New York's OCME, for instance, intensively marketed its services for low copy number testing and a statistical tool that quantified the significance of a match. As a result, not only did the lab have a reputational interest in promoting its work in criminal cases, it also had a strong financial interest in foreclosing any challenges to its methods.

Defense lawyers, for their part, are also poorly situated to serve as true checks on the quality of forensic evidence. Generally speaking, the quality of counsel available for the indigent, even for routine representation, is abysmal.[70] Some lawyers may not even know the name of their client, much less take time to learn complicated evidence in a case. But even if a defense lawyer aims to mount a full investigation into the scientific evidence in a case, the total lack of transparency when it comes to laboratory testing and reliability hinders his or her ability to perform quality control. It is not as though a single criminal defense attorney can audit the files of a random assortment of criminalists.

Lawyers who seek to learn as much as possible about the lab or a particular analyst's performance history often find themselves blocked, as few jurisdictions authorize the scope of public disclosure necessary to uncover improprieties or irregularities. ASCLD/LAB exacerbates this problem with its own lack of transparency in its auditing process, including the failure to communicate or require labs to be more forthcoming about flaws in their operations. Active investigations can proceed without any notice being provided to the prosecutor, much less defense counsel. Most laboratory deficiencies have been long-standing by the time that those outside the lab are notified. Follow-up reports, detailing the extent of corrective action, can be equally hard to find. For instance, one recent news story criticized the lack of information or status reports available with respect to the 230 cases under review after the 2010 North Carolina meltdown.[71]

The rules governing disclosure of the evidence specifically related to the case are likewise thin and paltry—as Judge Rakoff bemoaned in his resignation letter. Shockingly, litigants in civil cases fighting over money generally have more rights to learn about and test the scientific evidence against them than do those in criminal court facing a loss of liberty or even life. In the federal system, which is copied by many states, criminal defendants receive only truncated summaries of the evidence tested and its results, along with a basic résumé of the analyst. There is often no requirement that the analyst's proficiency test scores or history of corrective actions be disclosed, or even any obligation to hand over the laboratory's audit history. In contrast, civil litigants are entitled to complete statements about any proposed testimony, access to exhibits, and extensive histories of the witness's qualifications and prior testimony. Expert witnesses also typically must answer questions from the opposing party pretrial under oath.[72]

Criminal defendants who wish to independently probe a supposed DNA match have limited capacity to do so. Defendants have no constitutional right to have evidence collected, preserved, disclosed, or tested; there is only a right to stop the government from destroying evidence in bad faith.[73] In many cases, independent testing may not be possible.

But even when testable evidence exists, defense lawyers may not be able to access it. Although many jurisdictions extend a right to examine evidence as a matter of rule, those rights are often less than absolute. Many states lack an all-purpose provision to inspect *all* the evidence collected in the case, and to conduct independent analysis on demand. Rather, the right to inspect and test is limited to the evidence the government chooses to introduce at trial. Indigent defendants also must rely on the state to supply the funds for expert assistance and retesting, and many laws impose nearly insurmountable barriers to obtaining such funding. Defendants often must justify their request for help by pointing to something facially flawed in the state's analysis. But without experts to back that up, most defense lawyers will be unable to convince a judge that the evidence may in fact merit reexamination. Finally, independent analysis, even if authorized, may prove of limited utility. After all, defendants in most states have virtually no access to DNA databases in order to search for matches to profiles obtained through their independent analysis.

In the absence of a ready means of checking the reliability of a DNA match, many lawyers will choose not to investigate the forensic evidence further, particularly when so many other responsibilities beckon. Even well-intentioned defense lawyers may find it preferable to work around DNA evidence rather than to expend the resources necessary to challenge it, given that DNA matches are often viewed by lay people as conclusive proof. And considering that over 90 percent of defendants accept plea offers rather than take their case to trial, the very cases in which a challenge may seem especially appropriate are likely to be those in which the prosecutor offers a plea deal too sweet to refuse.

Finally, for the few defendants that actually take their case to trial, the constitutional rules requiring that the defendant be able to confront the evidence offer little protection when it comes to scientific test results. In a series of convoluted cases, the Supreme Court has interpreted the Confrontation Clause of the Sixth Amendment in a manner that allows the analyst who actually performed the test to evade taking the stand.

For instance, in *Bullcoming v. New Mexico*, the government could not offer testimony by the analyst who tested the blood results in a drunk driving case, because that person was on unpaid administrative leave.[74] Instead, a co-worker took the stand, but that person was never asked the reason for the original analyst's leave, and it is not even clear whether that person would have been able or permitted to answer even if asked. By the time the case wended its way to the Supreme Court, the record in the proceedings still did not answer what would seem to be a central question:

did the leave relate to misconduct or incompetence? In *Bullcoming* the court found error in the failure of the analyst to testify, which seemed to signal a new era of accountability. But the court reversed course shortly thereafter, holding that the analyst who conducts the tests does not necessarily have to take the stand to present his or her findings.[75] The lack of opportunity for meaningful adversarial testing at trial helps explain how so many laboratory malfunctions are able to go so long without detection. Even with open access, many of the errors may be hard to catch. But without it, there is no hope.

Of course, when errors do come to light, the judicial system has only one crude remedial tool: dismissal of cases. But both courts and prosecutors are reluctant to let possibly guilty people go free just to send a message to a wayward testing laboratory. Many judges will go out of their way to find reasons to refuse to reopen cases even when there is overwhelming evidence of forensic fraud. In many of these cases other evidence points to the defendant's guilt, so reopening transmits a sense of impunity. These reservations may be especially pronounced when the problems are written off as one bad apple in an otherwise good batch, or as the result of unintentional error rather than overt malfeasance. Yet, if lab misconduct resulted in lost cases, strong institutional forces would align to address the structural problems that allow such errors to occur. And, more troubling, allowing systemic dysfunction to go unchecked can itself enable and mask the extent of the malfeasance.

For instance, in 2005 the US Army Criminal Investigation Laboratory, which tests evidence for military cases, weathered its own DNA laboratory scandal. A forensic examiner employed at the lab, Phillip Mills, had made scores of errors across a range of cases. In the words of one court, "Mills had cross-contaminated and/or switched samples within and between several cases, made a false data entry and altered documentary evidence, falsely stated the results of an examination which he had not performed, and misrepresented work he had performed."[76] Mills had also "found DNA where it didn't exist, and failed to find it where it did. His mistakes may have let the guilty go free while the innocent . . . were convicted."[77] Two years after his errors came to light, lab employees found a box he had left in an insecure storage area, which contained evidence samples from thirty-six cases dating back twenty years.[78] Mills also inflated his credentials; for instance, in one 1999 case, he testified that he received his degree from "Catholic University" when in fact he attended

Pontifical Catholic University in Puerto Rico, not the well-known, and more prestigious, Catholic University in Washington, DC.[79]

Ultimately, inspectors identified 465 cases that Mills handled during his ten-year tenure at the lab. Retesting of cases that had sufficient evidence yielded disagreement with his findings a quarter of the time.[80] But unfortunately, retesting only works when there is evidence left to test. In over 80 percent of Mills's cases, his testing had exhausted the sample or investigators had destroyed it pursuant to policies then in place.[81] As such, the true scope of Mills's abuses will never be known. Mills resigned after being told he would be fired, and has since avoided any public attention.[82] As it turns out, Mills represented only the tip of the iceberg; a handwriting examiner at the lab was arrested and convicted for embezzling funds to support his gambling addiction, and a firearms examiner was caught falsifying statements and destroying evidence to cover up his trail of fabricated test results.[83] In addition, a supervisor helped cover up Mills's misconduct, by failing to hand over to investigators evidence, including specimen slides, that had been misplaced.[84]

Yet defendants who sat in prison as a result of Mills's work did not all receive timely notice of his misdeeds. Tellingly, a 2013 Department of Defense Inspector General report investigating Mills's actions found that "no law, rule, or regulation specifically required the Services to notify individuals about possibly compromised evidence in their cases."[85] Although military officials did undertake some courtesy notifications, "each Service developed separate standards and processes for identifying individuals to notify and for completing notifications."[86] Indeed, some notices took years, and not everyone received any notice at all.[87] For example, in one of Mills's cases, he claimed to have found DNA on a condom that matched all three men accused in a rape case.[88] Notwithstanding this evidence, all three had been acquitted of rape at the trial, but each was nonetheless convicted of lesser offenses related to their conduct during the investigation. At least one accused ultimately resigned his military commission. When Mills's cases were reopened, retesting proved that the condoms in fact did not have the men's DNA on it after all, but the men were not notified of that finding until years later.[89]

The Inspector General recommended adopting more systematic notification procedures, and some rules of that kind did go into effect in January 2015. On its own initiative, the lab also switched its accreditation from ASCLD/LAB to Forensic Quality Services International (FQS-I), which some observers believe to be more rigorous.[90] ASCLD/LAB had accredited the lab during the period in which the misconduct occurred; when they were notified of the issues, they simply asked the lab to submit documentation attesting to an internal investigation before recertifying the lab for five years.[91]

Even those defendants who received notice of possible flaws in the forensic evidence used to support a conviction against them often found little relief in the courts. Judges refused to reopen cases or allow retrials and permit juries to hear of the scope of these abuses and potentially discount the evidence accordingly.[92] They ignored findings by one investigation that the lab "was lax in supervising Mills, slow to reexamine his work, and slipshod about informing defendants." And they disregarded claims that the lab simply turned a blind eye, in the sense that "[o]fficials appeared intent on containing the scandal that threatened to discredit the military's most important forensics facility, which handles more than 3,000 criminal cases a year."[93]

Unfortunately, the typical judicial response to the discovery of laboratory malfeasance all too often looks just like it did in the army lab cases—denial and dismissal. But instead of ignoring and enabling laboratory failures, the courtroom might become a site of second-line defense against faulty forensics. To improve detection of case-specific mistakes, every jurisdiction should pass laws adding to the defendant's existing discovery entitlements, which should include: (1) the right to obtain broad disclosures, commensurate with those available for civil litigants, about all scientific evidence in the case, not just that which the government intends to use at trial; (2) the absolute right to access and independently test any seized evidence, rather than one conditioned on any preliminary showing; (3) the right to compel that the government search its DNA database for any profile reasonably found in the evidence by a qualified expert; (4) the right to pretrial notification of any instances of severe misconduct that taint the reputation of the lab; (5) the right to obtain and introduce error rate data; and (6) a panoply of postconviction rights, including the right to notification of later-discovered serious misconduct and access to materially exculpatory evidence, including authority to test it using more sophisticated DNA methods. Localities can also shore up the adversarial process by providing attorneys with the resources needed to effectively challenge DNA evidence. Each of these recommendations is addressed below.

First, the time has come to broaden the defendant's procedural and pretrial disclosure, otherwise known as discovery, rights. The Constitution grants no general right to discovery, plus many courts and prosecutors do not believe that exculpatory evidence must be turned over prior to a defendant's tender of a guilty plea.[94] As a result, the prosecutor can convince a defendant to plead guilty without ever disclosing that it had potentially—or even actually—exculpatory evidence in its possession. Ideally, states would engage in timely testing of biological samples prior to offering any plea, but a sensible compromise would simply accord notice to the defense of the existence of potential biological material, along with a reasonable opportunity to test in confidence prior to the expiration of a plea offer. In any event, prosecutors should not be permitted to condition plea deals on an agreement not to conduct biological testing; such offers can only favor the guilty, who have nothing to lose, and harm the innocent, who might be coerced by sheer uncertainty about future findings.

The injustice perpetrated by restrictive disclosure rules, along with wasteful back-end legal wrangling, is exemplified by the case of Joseph Buffey in West Virginia.[95] In 2001, Buffey was charged with the robbery and rape of an elderly widow, whose son happened also to be a local police officer, along with some unrelated commercial burglaries. Although he maintained his innocence of the offense involving the widow, he accepted the prosecutor's plea offer, fearing a life sentence if he lost at trial. What Buffey did not know was that police had recovered sperm from the rape kit conducted on the woman. He also did not know that the results of those tests excluded him, because the prosecutor failed to disclose that in advance of his plea.[96]

In fact, more sensitive testing performed by the Innocence Project ten years later proved Buffey's innocence, and matched a man with a criminal history that included breaking into a home and assaulting a woman. But Buffey remains in jail as of 2015, serving a seventy-year sentence as he fights in both state and federal court to overcome procedural obstacles that prevent him from even arguing the cause for his release. That is because in West Virginia, as in most jurisdictions, the law does not require that the prosecutor even *inform* the defendant that a rape kit exists prior to a plea, much less give the defendant access to it for testing. What is more, the prosecutor has no duty to test the kit in a timely way, or even at all. It is only if the defendant turns down the plea and goes to trial that the discovery rules kick in.

Remarkably, had Buffey chosen to go to trial, his rights to access the evidence would be only marginally broader. West Virginia's rules of discovery largely mirror those in the federal system, which require only that a defendant be allowed to "inspect and copy" physical evidence or scientific test results that "are material to the preparation of the defense or are intended for use by the state as evidence in chief at trial."[97] But some prosecutors might argue that even if a test of the kit finds that the DNA does not match, it need not be disclosed. In this way of thinking, so long as the *prosecutor* has a plausible explanation for the lack of a match, it arguably is not "exculpatory evidence." In this view, it is just *irrelevant* evidence—even though the defendant and a jury might not see it that way at all. The problem with expecting the prosecution to serve as the gatekeeper for what counts as material evidence to the defense is that it invites the prosecutor to take a narrow view of "materiality" and refuse to disclose all but the kind of test results that would cause the prosecutor personally to conclude the defendant was innocent. In addition, the state's rule regarding disclosure of expert witness testimony requires only that a "written summary" be handed over, and nothing more.

The justifications for rules of threadbare disclosure typically rest on a combination of prosecutorial expedience and a presumption about the ambiguity of evidence. The reasoning goes something like, if we required prosecutors to turn over all the evidence the minute it was obtained, we would upset the whole purpose of the plea process—which is to give defendants a discount for admitting guilt, rather than taxing government resources. In addition, it is thought that defendants might use such disclosures to obstruct justice, either by tampering with witnesses or manipulating the evidence.

But none of these rationales makes sense when the physical evidence contains biological matter. Defendants cannot readily manipulate or destroy such evidence, as it will be handled only by lab professionals. At the same time, lack of disclosure makes it particularly hard for defense lawyers to attack perceived problems with the evidence, or even to seek outside input on the quality of the testing. It also inhibits the ability of the defendant to make an informed choice about whether to accept the government's plea offer.

In cases in which the government has already undertaken testing, whether before or after a plea has been offered, disclosure should include every component of the testing file, not just summary documents, and not just that information the prosecutor deemed "material" or intends to use at trial. For instance, it should include all bench notes, electropherogram results, a digital file containing the raw, uninterpreted data, and any corrective actions or reviews undertaken in the course of testing. Use of a standardized "profile interpretation worksheet," like the one proposed by NIST scientist John Butler, would further improve transparency and assist lawyers and judges in understanding the interpretive decisions in a case.[98] Finally, disclosures in cases involving a database search should also include the full match report, which includes the search strings entered into the database, and all matches generated as a result—not just the hits the analyst deemed probative.

All reports should be drafted in plain language that details all testing undertaken and its results. Training of analysts should include instruction on standardized terminology that reports results in a way that is both clear and understandable to jurors. Forensic analysts should receive additional training in how to testify, and supervisors should take a more active role in auditing performance in court, not just at the lab bench. It is also hoped that the National Commission on Forensic Science will help improve the quality of testimony in this regard, as it is currently working on recommendations along these lines.

In addition, prosecutors should stop serving as the intermediary between the lab and the defense. Analysts should instead be encouraged to send their files directly to both sides, and to express willingness to address defense questions or undertake testing of items or contemplation of theories as directed by the defense. Removing the direct hand of prosecutors from the equation would also help ensure that prosecutors do not knowingly or inadvertently attempt to influence the analyst's conclusions, or tilt or obscure findings that might be adverse to their winning the case.

Discovery should also include a complete account of the analyst's personal qualifications, including his or her résumé, history as an expert, publication record, recent proficiency test scores, and information regarding any significant corrective actions involving the analyst over the past three years. Finally, the protocols and standard operating procedures in place at the time of testing, along with the accreditation audit report covering that period, should be made available. And, of course, if an analyst or laboratory is under investigation at the time of testing, such information also ought to be disclosed.

Some of this material is no doubt cumbersome and bulky to regularly reproduce. That is why it might instead be easily posted, such as on an open web page, which would also ensure ease of access to concerned parties. More sensitive materials, such as the individual analyst's history, could be made available through a password-protected site accessible only to litigants. New York City took a step in this direction in the wake of its lab scandal. The city council now requires that lab protocols, validation studies, and accreditation certificates, among other things, be posted on its laboratory's website.[99]

In addition, as analysts increasingly turn toward software platforms to assign statistical meaning to matches, disclosure rules must address the particular concerns that arise from computational evidence. The point of these software programs is to perform calculations that are too difficult to do by hand. But these programs all embed different assumptions, and operate on different parameters. Thus gauging the accuracy of one gives little insight into the accuracy of another. Properly safeguarding the integrity of this evidence is likely to prove difficult, but at minimum it requires a commitment to algorithmic transparency.

Algorithmic transparency is an expression that captures the value in demanding that developers make public the source code behind their software platforms. The code is critical to understanding and assessing the reliability of the program and the statistic that it ultimately generates. Just as courts would not accept opinions from witnesses not shown to have qualifications as an expert, so, too, should courts not accept opinions from digital "experts" without probing the "qualifications" of the technology. The self-serving assertions of those who promote that technology for financial gain should no more suffice to curtail the inquiry in the digital context than it would were a witness to come in, recite a number, and then just claim, "trust me, I'm a statistician." In both cases, the opposing party deserves a chance to probe to the assertion's underlying basis.

Fortunately, many of these statistical programs are already open source. But a good number of programs remain closed, with their code guarded as proprietary. Given the availability of free, open-source software, we might hope that public crime labs would simply choose to make use of that option. But that may be too much to wish for; recall that the New York Office of the Chief Medical Examiner refused to open the source code for the program it developed. Thus, when confronted with an expert who relies on a complex statistical calculation performed by a computer program, courts should insist that the algorithms and formulas used to arrive at that calculation be open to challenge and inspection by the defense. If there are concerns about intellectual property, then such information may be disclosed under a protective order. In any case, courts should disallow statistical evidence generated by probabilistic software whose operators refuse to reveal their code.

From history, we know that such orders do not compromise the business interests of the company. A similar fight unfolded in the early days of DNA typing, when industry refused to release the primer sequences used to isolate the relevant portions of the DNA strand. Ultimately some courts stood firm and refused to accept results from test kits that would not disclose that data, and ultimately both of the major manufacturers released their data—Promega Corporation in a public scientific journal, and Applied Biosystems under protective court order.[100] As both companies remain leaders in the field today, it would seem that allowing access to their code did not in fact destroy their business.

In sum, when it comes to disclosure, the trend should be toward greater openness with regard to scientific evidence. Those states that have addressed disclosure have tended to move from more restrictive regimes to approaches that encourage greater transparency. For instance, in January 2014, the Michael Morton Act went into effect in Texas.[101] Morton spent twenty-five years in prison, having been wrongfully convicted of killing his wife. After his exoneration, a court ordered the arrest of the prosecutor in the case—then a sitting judge—for deliberately concealing evidence pointing to Morton's innocence. He ultimately pled no contest to charges of contempt, and served five days of a ten day sentence.[102] The act passed in Morton's name dramatically broadened criminal discovery in Texas, and included a provision that required documentation of all disclosures made prior to entry of a plea.[103] Many of the recommendations advanced here also find support in the standards on DNA evidence approved by the American Bar Association in 2006.[104]

But enhanced disclosure, without more, is not enough to fully shore up the adversarial process. Three additional corrective measures are required, though each likely will prove more contestable. The first involves granting a right to the defense to run searches in the DNA database. In some cases, particularly those involving complex mixtures or low amounts of template, a defense expert may determine that the test reveals a profile that not only does not match the defendant, but may point toward another perpetrator. In such an event, the government should not be able to block access to the database for exculpatory purposes. The defendant should be allowed to move the court to require the state to search the database for a profile legitimately derived from a crime scene sample. Such a search either will turn up a possible alternative suspect, in which case all parties ought to be aware of a plausible different perpetrator, or else it will come up empty-handed. In either case, there is little unwarranted threat to privacy. Although the FBI has resisted this entitlement, several states have already enacted such laws, as detailed in Chapter 9, and there are no reports that the privilege has been abused.

Second, access to and inclusion of error rates must become a standard part of the presentation of DNA match statistics. So long as the system treats error as ancillary and remote to the pursuit of truth, rather than as central to the assessment of the evidence in the case, gross error will continue to go unchecked. Although an estimated national laboratory error rate may unduly penalize outstanding labs, while unfairly boosting the status of substandard ones, that concern does not apply to the formulation and introduction of any one specific lab's error rate. To arrive at a suitable error rate estimate, a robust accrediting agency might review the corrective logs of laboratories and then rank them according to an absolute scale in a number of areas, which might include, among other things, a measure of the number of contamination events, interpretative disputes or overrides, and database entry compliance and execution. Meanwhile, the quality assurance program of the FBI already conducts audits with regard to database entry; we could simply extrapolate from those selected reviews a proxy for the overall performance of the lab in that area, or shore up the quality assurance dimension to achieve a more complete picture. A combined statistic could then be presented independently, and juries could be informed that they may choose to discount the match probability accordingly, or not.

The alternative is to assume, as some commentators seem wont to do, that laboratories effectively police themselves, and that once errors are made, a laboratory and a specific analyst "would not likely make the same error again."[105] It is a lovely sentiment, and one that understandably bestows a great deal of faith and trust in the managers and analysts that make up the hundreds of DNA testing labs in the country. But accountability systems are not designed to reward the upstanding majority. They are designed to weed out the malfeasant and complacent—even if few there be.

Finally, the systemic shortcomings in our system of indigent defense are both well known and well documented. Funding for improved defense services is advisable regardless of whether a case contains DNA proof or not. But there are some specific ways in which localities can support attorneys faced with sophisticated scientific evidence, like DNA test results, despite crushing caseloads and limited resources. Specifically, localities can fund attorney-specialists, either in the form of specific lawyers assigned to receive cases within a specific jurisdiction, or as nonpracticing resource counsel for a broad swath of attorneys.

Several major public defender officers already have developed specialist units for DNA, or all forensic science. For instance, public defense agencies in Washington, DC, Chicago, New York, and Los Angeles all have lawyers specially trained to handle cases in which the DNA proof plays a critical role. Allocating funds to create, train, and support such units helps ensure that DNA test results do not evade scrutiny simply due to lack of capacity or capability.

But many jurisdictions do not have dedicated public defense offices, or they may have only a few cases involving DNA. In those localities, training a particular cadre of lawyers makes little sense. As an alternative, states can develop state-level Forensic Resource Counsel offices, patterned on the one formed by North Carolina in 2010.[106] That office, staffed only by one full-time lawyer, maintains a number of critical resources aimed at supporting the state's public defenders. Apart from a website that contains a wealth of foundational readings on a range of forensic topics, there are also online forensic training modules, a blog that discusses breaking issues, an expert database including prior transcripts, and model motions and orders.

The office also serves as a forum for discussion of emerging issues, as well as a clearinghouse for information about particular labs. For instance, the site contains internal audit documents from some laboratories, historical and current protocols, and the CVs of personnel. The storage function is particularly important, given that many cases take a long period of time to go to trial, and thus material that is publicly available at the time of trial may not represent the policies in place at the time testing was conducted.

A statewide forensic resource counsel office could revolutionize an attorney's ability to put forward the proper claims in a case. Adding a staff scientist, who might be able to function as both an informal consultant and keep the community apprised of important scientific developments, would be a further boon. Most important, in commanding a modest but dedicated staff, offices of this kind are realistic and affordable ways to improve defense understanding and analysis of scientific evidence, especially during a period when it may be difficult to fund individual experts. They also can serve as the backbone of a national community of indigent defense attorneys seeking to remain current in a rapidly evolving field. Already there is a small cadre of committed public defenders serving as leaders to offer training, support, and counsel to one another in forensic DNA matters, but if DNA continues to assume greater prominence in criminal cases, those numbers must also increase exponentially.

All of these recommendations, if implemented, would go far to improve the accuracy of evidence in any individual case. But of equal importance is that they would create pressure on the actors in the forensic science system to enact structural changes that would help safeguard the integrity of evidence that never makes it to court at all.

PRIVACY AND EQUALITY

Many contemporary impediments to DNA testing may fade as technology develops, the laboratory system matures, and the criminal justice system acclimates to a sophisticated world of scientific evidence. But the one piece of the puzzle that seems unlikely to change—except to grow—is the potential threat DNA testing poses to basic precepts of privacy, autonomy from the state, and equality. The battlefronts are many and the list of potential incursions long. A comprehensive treatment of this issue merits a book of its own, but this chapter closes with some general thoughts on the topic.

We are at a critical moment with regard to the use of genetic tests for criminal justice purposes. The fulcrum is tipping. Until now, DNA testing plausibly concerned only police officers and convicted criminals, mostly felons. For the most part, DNA evidence played a supporting role in the machinery of justice, by bolstering the evidence against known suspects, exculpating the wrongfully accused, and occasionally closing a serious cold case.

But this period of relative restraint is about to come to an end. Ninety-minute single-touch rapid test machines have come to market, and are already being piloted for both known offender and crime scene sample testing. The Supreme Court robustly endorsed DNA testing of a person based on a police officer's mere suspicion of crime, hastening the era of stop-and-spit. The new FBI CODIS software facilitates familial search methods, and potentially will enable interconnectivity with the FBIs Next Generation Identifier database—a clearinghouse of biometric and demographic data. Private companies are lining up to run connected databases that circumvent the national database rules, or offer "mugshot" images from invisible specks of DNA. The genetic material of over 10 million persons sits in lockers across America, awaiting further exploration. In short, forensic DNA testing may soon transform from a rather narrowly tasked piece of evidence in only the most serious cases to the equivalent of a speeding ticket—a common point of interface with the criminal justice system, even for law-abiding people.

Most frightening of all is that the legal landscape that ought to guide and shape the use of DNA in the criminal justice system remains remarkably bare. What legal rules exist focus on deliberate malfeasance. Very few laws address negligent uses of DNA—the kind of sloppiness or carelessness that more commonly causes mistaken arrests or wrongful accusations. Virtually no laws regulate offline databases and creative exploitation of genetic material such as testing for physical characteristics or conducting familial searches. In the absence of anyone saying no—or even, "Proceed according to these plans"—law enforcement and private entrepreneurs have simply barreled ahead, milking the brave new world of forensic genetic testing for all that it might have to offer.

It thus falls to those concerned about personal privacy and the reach of the state to ensure the passage of laws that proactively circumscribe the use of DNA in the criminal justice system. The precise contours of such laws may be difficult to define, because the technology of tomorrow is nearly unimaginable today. But each state could start by passing one simple law that would go a long way toward stemming the tide that inadvertently erodes privacy. That law would read: "No public official may collect, test, use, or examine any DNA sample, or search or compile any database containing genetic information, for any reason related to the enforcement of the criminal laws, unless explicitly authorized by statute."

Such a law would immediately require the passage of a number of exemptions, of course. Consistent with existing law, states would carve out space for the collection and databasing of known offender samples. They would likewise allow for collection of samples from crime scenes, ideally addressing the permissible uses of certain categories of samples, such as to identify victims, certain suspects, or missing persons. But such laws could then be appropriately tailored. For instance, a provision allowing the collection of voluntary samples offered by victims of crime or those seeking to eliminate themselves as suspects might statutorily restrict the use of such samples to investigation of that specific case, and require destruction of the sample and profile once the case has closed. Rules pertaining to the collection of DNA from crime scenes might be limited to testing items for which there is a reasonable belief that the evidence will lead to the apprehension of the perpetrator. Finally, such rules should dictate the terms under which a DNA sample may be taken surreptitiously—such as requiring an officer to seek judicial approval and forbidding inclusion of a surreptitiously gathered sample in a DNA database for perpetuity.

The main advantage of a law presumptively forbidding collection and testing of DNA for criminal justice purposes is not to foreclose most use of DNA. Rather, it is to encourage debate and deliberation as we broach each new frontier in DNA technology. Right now, law enforcement acts first, and awaits a law that curbs its ingenuity later. An all-purpose provision would require restraint as regards novel or innovative uses of DNA testing, until a legislative body had deemed a cutting-edge approach permissible. In the current environment, innovations like familial searches, phenotypic testing, and local databases occur before the public has passed judgment on their desirability; in the proposed context, each would be prohibited absent a deliberate grant of authority (and, hopefully detailed regulation).

Of course, the major shortcoming of this proposal is that it still relies on the politics of the majority for protection. A jurisdiction might move swiftly to endorse the broadest forms of genetic testing for criminal justice purposes, especially since history suggests that the majority is often willing to sacrifice the privacy of a minority in the name of its own security. Nevertheless, at the very least this approach would prevent law enforcement from embracing some radical new DNA test without first ensuring some measure of popular support, and might create incentives for interest groups to demand evidence of the actual advantages of proposed new techniques. Requiring debates of this kind might even promote more open dialogue about the proper scope of police authority in a democratic state.

Of course, to the extent that majoritarian politics favor broad genetic testing, the last redoubt of genetic privacy may be our old friend, the United States Constitution. Finding the doctrinal support for curbing widespread collection and testing of genetic material may be difficult. But it is not impossible.

In this age of mass incarceration, our society treats criminal law as an all-purpose system of governance, invoking it to address domestic disputes, the problem of homelessness or addiction, or insolent children.[107] With such an uncabined view of police authority, it is no surprise that we have lost the notion that not everything should be accessible to the police. There might be things that—no matter how helpful for crime-solving— police just should not do. Even as the crime rate falls to historic lows, we continue to rely on police to defend us as though we are under siege. If there might be any possible gain to security, we reason, police should be able to engage in an investigative practice, not matter how threatening to personal privacy or disruptive to community harmony.

Under that view, the Fourth Amendment, which prohibits unreasonable searches and seizures, becomes purely about defining investigative rules, not laying down absolute bans. The values of the Constitution became negotiable—distilled to striking the right balance between competing interests, rather than safeguarding some essential zone of rights and entitlements. With enough showing of compelling need, the government can do just about anything. Constitutional law rarely blocks outright a police investigative technique, or says, "No, that is just not allowed." Instead, the judge's answer will always be, "Okay, but only if police jump through the right hoops," such as getting a warrant or offering a legal justification. That is the view that permits familial searches, so long as they are conducted in a "reasonable" way. Or that would allow DNA testing for personal traits, but only if police first show a compelling need.

But it is not too late to reclaim an idea of an inviolable zone of privacy. In the past, courts have cobbled together a trio of constitutional protections—shoring up the Fourth Amendment search and seizure provisions with the Fifth Amendment self-incrimination and due process clauses—to find that certain investigative techniques go beyond what we can support as a civilized society, even if the consequence is that some crime goes unsolved. In *Winston v. Lee*, for instance, the government forced a suspect to undergo surgery to remove a bullet that could tie him to the crime scene. In *Rochin v. California*, the government ordered a man's stomach pumped against his will, to recover evidence of drugs. In both cases, the Supreme Court held the police action unconstitutional.[108] No procedure, no warrant, and no suspicion could justify that kind of intrusive searching. The body could not be so brutally invaded, even in the name of crime-solving.

Similar reasoning might justify sharp curbs on the investigative collection, retention, testing, and databasing of genetic information. In a sense, a person's DNA represents the intersection between the physical and emotional selves. DNA is, of course, the physical embodiment of a person—it is the code that dictates everything from hair color to taste preferences. But it also is a metaphysical representation of the self. Familiar expressions such as "it's in my DNA" capture the symbolic value of DNA as a marker of identity. Our DNA connects us to the past via our families and ancestral history, and also thrusts us into the future by forecasting the traits of our children or the manner of our death. The romance of genetic testing is what propels people to send in their samples to total strangers, hoping to connect their biology to others in the world, both alive and dead, wholly unknown to them. That same drive should counsel against allowing the criminal justice system to appropriate DNA testing in ways that may be disruptive or destructive to personhood, identity, and a sense of belonging.

To put these lofty ideals into more practical terms, legal policy ought to recognize that swabbing a person or crime scene for DNA is different in kind from gathering ordinary forms of criminal evidence—even fingerprints. The reason that compiling victim databases, or surreptitiously gathering up cells from a pap smear, or testing newborn heel samples without permission all intuitively ring wrong is that the expropriation of genetic material for crime-solving purposes strikes too close to the heart of other values. It runs the risk of discouraging people from engaging in desirable behaviors likewise entwined with our genetic identities, whether forming familial bonds or seeking health care or safeguarding against fatal disease.

Fear of these kinds of unintended consequences is also why the debates about race and DNA testing strike many at such a profound level. Our criminal justice system is bound up in questions of racial justice. At one extreme, the disproportionate representation of persons of color within the justice system reflects a long history of oppression that has entrenched minorities in a cycle of poverty and discrimination from which it is nearly impossible to break. At the other extreme, these disparities map onto patent inequalities in the manner in which certain laws are investigated and enforced in our community today. To bind complicated issues of race and poverty, as played out in our unequal system of justice, to a governmental program of DNA collection, testing, and databasing, poses the gravest of dangers. And those dangers are only magnified the more that DNA practices serve to perpetuate misperceptions about the link between biology and racial categories.

Although these cautions are real, they are not intended to suggest that all use of DNA by the criminal justice system ought to grind to a halt. To be sure, some forensic use of DNA is appropriate. But if it is ultimately the Constitution that prompts a more sensitive analysis of DNA practices, then current doctrine must move away from its current moorings. Courts must relinquish the misconception that DNA is not different, and recognize that acquisition of genetic material by law enforcement acts raises weighty concerns.

There is a concept in Fourth Amendment law that a search or seizure can begin lawfully but exceed its permissible scope. For instance, police may respond to a crime scene and cordon off an area for evidence preservation, but after several days may be required to get permission to continue to keep the scene closed.[109] Although the search began with lawful permission, once it exceeds a certain duration or intensity, additional justification is required.

So, too, might it be said that police may lawfully collect and conduct rudimentary tests on crime scene samples, but more invasive practices—if allowed—invoke additional protections. So, for instance, testing of a sample for anything other than the standard identifiers might require some added justification, as would retention of the sample beyond a certain point. Certain database practices—such as compiling offline or "rogue" databases or engaging in familial searches—might also be deemed to exceed the scope circumscribing the permissible use of a collected sample.

In this respect, DNA samples might be treated akin to another form of new evidence that has lately confounded courts: smart phones. A smart phone, like a DNA sample, is a treasure trove of potentially private information. Like DNA samples, smart phones can tell you a great deal about their users, including what they look like and who their family members may be. Phones also often hold the key to other highly personal information, whether in the form of incriminating photos or access to bank accounts or e-mail data. Police may lawfully acquire a phone by arresting someone for a minor offense, but in searching the phone discover evidence of serious criminality. Like a DNA sample, the device is a tiny package of temptation—urging police to tap the resource for all it may be worth.

The Supreme Court, in deciding a case about the lawful scope of a search of a cell phone lawfully acquired during the arrest of its owner, held that police must have a warrant before searching the phone's contents.[110] Because warrants must be founded on probable cause to believe that the item harbors evidence of a crime, and must state with particularity the places to be searched, in theory this ruling strongly limits a police officer's power to exploit the contents of a cell phone without some reason to believe that evidence of a crime will be found there.

In distinguishing legal precedent that pointed the opposite direction, the court observed, "[c]ell phones differ in both a quantitative and a qualitative sense from other objects that might be kept on an arrestee's person."[111] The same could be said of a genetic sample. DNA contains information that is both quantitatively and qualitatively different in kind than that obtainable through searches of physical objects, including searches of the body. The Supreme Court, in addressing compulsory DNA sampling laws, analogized genetic samples to blood or urine tests for drugs or alcohol, breathalyzers, or fingerprints.[112] But those analogies are all misguided. Sampling for DNA is more like acquiring a cell phone than rolling ten fingerprints. It is a container that holds layers of information—some superficial and readily ascertainable, and some profoundly personal.

Although the Supreme Court failed to recognize the right analogy in the DNA case, it unintentionally stumbled upon it in the cell phone case. Specifically, the court drew an inadvertent connection between cell phones and biological evidence when it noted that "modern cell phones, . . . are now such a pervasive and insistent part of daily life that the proverbial visitor from Mars might conclude they were an important feature of human anatomy."[113] Although intended as a joke, there is something quite telling in that statement. Because right now our laws afford more protection to a physical object than they do to the biological blueprint that is the foundation of our very existence.

CONCLUSION

I spent five years in the belly of the criminal justice system, and have been its careful observer for my entire career. Like anyone who has studied the criminal justice system up close, I know all too well that the law as practiced often gravely departs from the law on the books. We promise a right to trial, but penalize defendants for exercising it. We promise assistance of counsel, but assign lawyers so overtaxed or incompetent that they often do not know their own clients' names. We promise a right of confrontation, but deny access to the information necessary to unearth the truth. The law on the books may say our forensic evidence system is working just fine, but the law in action, time and again, proves that it is not.

The goal of this book is twofold. First, it hopes to show readers that forensic DNA testing is not as infallible as popular culture makes it out to be. Instead, forensic DNA analysis involves slipups and subjective judgment calls, uncertainty and ambiguity. Second, even though DNA science is fundamentally sound, the same forces that corrupted other, older forensic methods still remain very much alive in the criminal justice system today. Without addressing those underlying dysfunctions—in the way DNA evidence is collected, analyzed, disclosed, and challenged in court—we cannot expect the story of DNA to end much differently than that of the forensic methods now undergoing intense scrutiny. Together, these two points underscore the overall message of this book, which is that DNA testing is neither savior nor cure-all; it is just another form of proof deserving of careful attention.

To put blind faith in forensic DNA is to put an enormous amount of trust in a system that, by all accounts, has failed in spectacular ways. It is to think that a criminal justice system that peddled wishful thinking as science and pushed legitimate science past its limits, has somehow changed its ways overnight. It is to believe that a set of rules and practices that produced an alarming number of false convictions—through shoddy science, misrepresentations in court, and lack of any meaningful adversarial challenge—now acts with unimpeachable integrity. And it is to assume that a laboratory system that has time and again been exposed as sustaining profound and long-standing forms of incompetence, fraud, and deceit has suddenly corrected course.

It is uncomfortable to think about science that is not accurate, about an innocent person in jail while a serious offender skirts free, about privacy that may cease to exist. But now is the time to confront these unpleasant thoughts. Confronting discomfort now may avert disaster later. The technological and legal landscape of DNA testing is at the brink of a tectonic shift. There are promising signs on the horizon, such as the entry of National Institute of Standards and Technology into the field, and the convocation of the National Commission on Forensic Science. But there are also dangers. Our only weapon against them is knowledge.

ACKNOWLEDGMENTS

In many ways, this book owes its existence to my talented, thoughtful, and dedicated agent, Ed Maxwell, who convinced me that there was a way to write it and that it ought to be written, and then supported me every step of the way. I also owe great thanks to Carl Bromley, who believed in the book from the start, and to my editor Alessandra Bastagli, who inherited that faith and embraced it wholeheartedly. Without her careful feedback, I could not have found the right way to tell the stories in these pages.

There are a handful of people who generously offered their own time and effort to support this project, and to each of them I wish to express the deepest gratitude. Simon Ford labored—even while on vacation—to create images for the text, and helped me with some of the nuances in the science. Bicka Barlow, whose impressive advocacy has created an incredible record of how DNA evidence actually works in criminal cases, proved relentlessly willing to help me locate a document, find a file, or answer a question. Yun Song kindly crunched some numbers that I could not have computed myself. And finally, the amazing (and mathematically-inclined) Andrea Roth always answered my questions, no matter how urgent or absurd.

A small army of research assistants from NYU Law aided me over several years, dredging up difficult to find documents and organizing reams of legal and scientific information. I am grateful to Nicole Geoglis, Emily Mullins, Hunter Haney, Ben Notterman, Taylor Stevens, Jess Heyman, and Sean Stefanik, and especially to Molly Lauterback and Elizabeth Daniel-Vasquez, who expertly carried the heaviest loads.

In many ways, this book represents the culmination of ten years of thinking and writing on these topics, and throughout that time I have greatly benefitted from the scholarship and support of colleagues, researchers, and practitioners working in the field. My colleagues at UC Berkeley School of Law and NYU Law School, along with many others, provided feedback and critical input on earlier versions of this work that improved and refined my ideas. And, in the course of writing, I learned tremendously from the work and presentations of others, many of whom happily answered a question or provided information whenever I asked. All opinions in the book, and any errors, are of course my own, but at the risk of overlooking someone I wish particularly to acknowledge: John Butler, Mike Coble, Robin Cotton, Jennifer Friedman, Alan Gardner, Brandon Garrett, Jessica Goldthwaite, Allan Jamieson, Elizabeth Joh, Dan Krane, David Lynch, Jennifer Lynch, Tom Main, Stephen Mercer, Jennifer Mnookin, Peter Neufeld, Michael Risher, Rori Rohlfs, Marvin Schechter, Barry Scheck, David Sklansky, Montgomery Slatkin, and Bill Thompson.

Finally, there are simply not enough words to convey what is owed to my extraordinary husband, Jeremy Tinker, who was pressed into service as sounding board, lay reader, graph creator, single-parent, order-keeper, and literary critic. Without him, nearly everything I hold dearest would not exist.

GLOSSARY

Accreditation: A credential issued to a lab after undergoing a process through which an outside auditor determines that the laboratory meets specified standards of competency. The precise details of that process—for instance, the intensity with which the auditor reviews whether the lab meets a standard, or even the particular standards themselves, can vary among different accrediting agencies. The international standard pertinent to testing and calibration laboratories is known as ISO/IEC 17025, and was first issued by the International Organization for Standardization in 1999.

Algorithmic transparency: The idea that software developers must make public the source code behind a software platform, because programming choices invisibly influence outcomes.

Allele: The variants of the DNA pattern found at a locus or gene.

Allele frequency: The rate at which a particular genetic allele is observed in the general population. For instance, it might be said that the alleles associated with red-green colorblindness have a lesser frequency in the population than do the alleles associated with normal vision.

Amplification: A process, namely PCR, by which sections of the genome are spliced off and copied so as to increase their quantity.

Chimera: A condition in which some cells of a person may carry genomic material different from that directly associated with the individual.

CODIS (Combined DNA Index System): The name given to the software that serves as the architecture for the DNA databases, whether at the national (NDIS), state (SDIS), or local (LDIS) levels. These databases contain reference samples (DNA profiles from known persons) and forensic samples (profiles from crime scene evidence, which may or may not have yet been associated with a known person). At times people also use "CODIS" as a shorthand reference to the national DNA database. Some people also distinguish between a *database*, which is a repository of genetic profile information, and a *databank*, which is a collection of physical biological samples (of blood, saliva, etc.).

Cold hit: A match made between samples in a DNA database. Typically it refers to a match between the profile of a known individual and that associated with a crime scene, but it may also be used to mean matches between identical profiles found at different crime scenes. Some people differentiate between a *match*, which indicates that there is an association between two profiles, and a *hit*, the term used after a match is verified through review or investigation.

Database match probability (DMP): A statistical probability that aims to capture the likelihood that a profile would be observed after conducting a database search, derived from dividing the random match probability by the size of the database in which the profile was searched.

DNA polymorphism: Variations in genetic characteristics, including in their sequence (the letters) or length (the size of a strand).

DNA profile: The combination of observed alleles at target locations; in forensic testing, the profile refers to the twenty-six alleles seen at thirteen loci on the genomic strand. The FBI will soon announce an increase in the number of loci used in the standard reference profile.

Dragnet: A sweep to collect DNA samples from a community or demographic group, to find a match to a sample associated with an unsolved crime.

Electropherogram (EPG): The document that shows the results of electrophoresis testing; the standard illustration of data from DNA testing.

Electrophoresis: A method used to measure the size of DNA fragments.

Error rate: The rate at which mistakes are made. Error rates might be industry-wide (all forensic DNA labs), lab-specific (one particular DNA lab), unit-specific (this unit within the lab), or analyst-specific (this analyst). Error might also be gauged as to all the tasks performed by the lab or analyst or other unit, or by specific tasks (for example, everything ranging from innocuous administrative mistakes to profound mishandling or misinterpretation of evidence).

False negative: The finding of a negative result—for instance, a DNA nonmatch—when in fact the contrary is true (the two items did match). At times called a Type II error.

False positive: The finding of a positive result—for instance, a DNA match—when in fact the contrary is true (the two items did not match). At times called a Type I error.

Familial search: A search conducted in a DNA database to find a person in the database who might be related to the individual who left a crime scene sample. Familial matches are undertaken only if a search in the database for a direct match fails. In that case, analysts can search again looking for near misses or partial matches, on the theory that such persons might be relatives of the person who left the crime scene sample. Because many unrelated people may share the same partial genetic profile, and even related people may have fewer traits in common than unrelated people, partial match searches return a list of candidates that must then be narrowed to probable relatives using other genetic and nongenetic investigative methods. Familial searches are distinguishable from inadvertent partial matches, which may occasionally arise as a by-product of a search for a direct match.

Forensic sample: A DNA sample taken from a crime scene, which may or may not be associated with a known individual.

Gene: A defined sequence of DNA nucleotides on the genetic strand.

Genome: The entire sequence of a person's DNA, as stitched together from the fragments found in the chromosomes.

Genotype: The genetic profile of a person, either in the entirety or with reference to certain specified parts of the genome.

Heterozygous: People are heterozygous at a particular locus (a place on the genomic strand) if they inherited a different allele (genetic variant) from each of their biological parents.

Homozygous: People are homozygous at a particular locus (a place on the genomic strand) if they inherited the same allele (genetic variant) from each of their biological parents.

LCN DNA testing ("low copy" or "low template"): This term can refer to a number of different things, all of which signal some aspect of DNA testing that calls into question the reliability of the observed results. One definition focuses on the quantity or quality of DNA available to test, because samples made up of very few cells or degraded cells may be more likely to succumb to problems during the testing process. Another definition focuses on whether the ordinary testing process was tweaked so that results may be elicited from samples that otherwise would not produce results.

Likelihood ratio (LR): A statistic that expresses the likelihood of observing the data under one condition versus under an alternative. Mathematically, the likelihood ratio may be expressed as 1 (to indicate "this is the person") over the random match probability, or RMP (to indicate the probability that a person picked at random would have the same DNA profile as the evidence). The likelihood ratio thus conveys that it is certain that you would observe the DNA profile of the evidence in the defendant's sample if the evidence came from the defendant ("1") versus if it was the result of chance (the RMP).

Locus (pl. loci): Any defined region on the genomic strand.

Mixture: A DNA sample that contains genetic material from more than one person. Because DNA tests simply measure all the alleles present in the sample, and do not label which alleles came from which contributors, it can be difficult to discern the genetic profiles of each contributor (in other words, which alleles go with each person).

mtDNA: DNA found in the mitochondria, outside the cell nucleus, and is inherited matrilineally. It is stored in large quantities in the cytoplasm outside the nucleus and thus can be useful when unclear DNA has been degraded or destroyed.

NDIS (National DNA Index System): The federal DNA database overseen by the FBI. At times NDIS is referred to as CODIS, which is technically the name of the database's operating software.

Next generation sequencing (NGS): A general term used to refer to a new wave of technologies that allow rapid sequencing (that is, determination of the actual nucleotides) of the genome.

NIST: The National Institute for Standards and Technology, a federal agency within the Department of Commerce that has assumed an increasingly prominent role in the forensic DNA community.

Nuclear DNA: The DNA found on the chromosomes inside the cell nucleus, and which is inherited from each biological parent in equal parts.

OSAC: The acronym for the Organization of Scientific Area Committees, a series of advisory groups launched in 2014 under the auspices of NIST, which aim to improve the use of forensic science by establishing standards and guidelines across a wide range of disciplines.

Phenotype: The observable characteristics that result from the expression of particular genetic traits. *Phenotyping* is a word used to signify testing undertaken to determine physical or expressed traits (like hair color or disease propensity), as opposed to *genotyping*, which is concerned only with an actual genetic trait regardless of its purpose or function (or lack thereof).

Proficiency test: A test administered to analysts to measure their competency as regard any number of tasks. Proficiency tests may be open (the analysts are aware they are being tested) or blind (they are not aware). They may replicate casework conditions (the test either copies or approximates an actual case file) or more approximate ideal or controlled conditions.

Prosecutor's fallacy: A phrase given to a common mistake in expressing a DNA random match statistic, which is to conflate it with the source probability or guilt probability. In other words, to wrongly assume that the statistic indicates the probability that the defendant left the DNA found on the evidence, or the probability that the defendant is guilty.

Random match probability (RMP): A statistic that conveys the probability that a person picked at random from the population would have the traits observed in the crime scene evidence. Also known as a rarity statistic, because in effect it expresses how rare a genetic profile is expected to be within a particular population of unrelated persons.

Rapid DNA (R-DNA): The nickname given DNA testing platforms that can rapidly produce results, often with minimal input from a human being. For instance, the platforms in use now are roughly the size of a large desktop printer, and can process a DNA sample with "one touch" in approximately ninety minutes.

Reference sample: A DNA sample taken from a known person, such as a convicted offender required to submit DNA to the national database, or a person sampled in connection with a particular case.

Rogue database: A collection of DNA profiles in a form—whether a formal database or other format—that is not directly regulated by law or subject to any formal quality control checks or targeted limits on its permissible use.

Short tandem repeat (STR testing): The most common form of forensic nuclear DNA testing performed today, in which analysts examine the number of times certain short, known sequences repeat at various locations on the genome.

SOPs (Standard Operating Procedures): A lab's protocols that detail everything from how testing should be conducted in each case to what rules of interpretation the lab uses to assign values to test results. SOPs also typically include procedural or administrative instructions about how work is reviewed or conflicting interpretations will be resolved. Access to the SOPs is a critical part of reviewing the results in a DNA test, because any deviations from those procedures ought to be defensible and explained.

SWGDAM (Scientific Working Group on DNA Analysis Methods): An advisory group under the auspices of the FBI, which among other things is responsible for drafting the quality assurance standards that govern the national database.

Touch DNA: A DNA sample retrieved from an item that was touched, as opposed to a sample from a bodily fluid, such as blood, semen, or saliva. Touch DNA is at times conflated with low copy DNA, because many touch samples exhibit the kinds of issues that make low copy testing problematic (low-quantity or -quality samples). But a sample from a touched object need not have these characteristics, and so these terms should be distinguished.

Validation testing: Experiments undertaken in controlled conditions that ensure that a testing procedure is reliable. Validation studies are necessary to legitimate either a new technique or methodology, as well as to implement a known methodology on specific equipment within a lab. Thus, for instance, validation studies may show both that a particular DNA testing kit reliably produces data about a particular set of loci, but also that a laboratory still must undertake internal validation studies to ensure that its particular standard operating procedures and instrumentation function reliably.

Y-STR typing: A type of DNA typing that focuses on regions of the genome found on the male Y chromosome, which is descended from a father to his sons. Because this information is passed patrilineally, it provides strong evidence of a man's relatedness to other persons, but does not effectively distinguish that man from any of his relatives as a matter of isolating his single identity.

APPENDIX:
THE MECHANICS OF DNA TESTING

Forensic DNA testing focuses on thirteen places, or loci, on the genomic strand. The entire genome is stitched together from fragments found on twenty-two matched pairs of chromosomes (one from the father, and one from the mother) along with two sex determining chromosomes (again, one from each parent). Combined together, the DNA strand comprises roughly 3.2 billion base pairs. These base pairs—made up of A (adenine), T (thymine), C (cytosine), or G (guanine)—appear in an ordered sequence that is identical in every person for over 99 percent of the genome. It is the remaining 0.1 percent of variation that distinguishes one person from another.

One way a genome may vary is for the letter sequence to be different in one person versus another. For example, one person may have an ATCT sequence, while another person's sequence at the same spot is AGCT. This is known as a *sequence polymorphism*. A second way that individuals might vary is to have the same sequence at the same spot, but to have variations in the number of times that this sequence repeats over a particular stretch on the genome. This is known as *a length polymorphism*, because it is a change in the length of a known sequence, rather than a change in the letters (or nucleotides) that make up the sequence itself.

The standard form of forensic DNA typing focuses on length polymorphisms. Specifically, it examines thirteen established places on the genome, although the FBI will soon expand that number to twenty or more. At these places, known singly as a locus (Latin for "place") or in plural as loci, certain known sequences repeat variable number of times from person to person. Figure App. 1 depicts these thirteen loci, and their position on the chromosome. Notice that the reference set also tests the sex chromosomes, or amelogenin, to determine sex.

READING AN ELECTROPHEROGRAM

Testing a DNA sample is typically done using a process known as polymerase chain reaction, or PCR, along with capillary electrophoresis. The

FIGURE APP. 1   13 CODIS core STR loci with chromosomal positions.

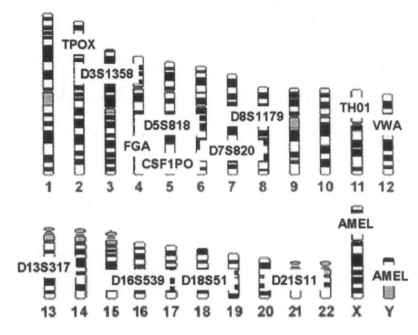

Source: Federal Bureau of Investigation.

results of these tests appear as data on an electropherogram, or EPG. Reading an EPG is simpler than it seems at first glance. The results of a genetic test are depicted in Figure App. 2 in black and white; typical EPGs use a particular color scheme.

First, notice four different lines. On each line are the results from more than one place, or locus, on the genetic strand. The specific loci are labeled in the boxes that run across the top of each line. In this illustration, the first line shows the results at four loci, the second line at five loci, the third at four loci, and the last line at three loci (the first of which is the amelogenin, or sex marker). The loci are typically referred to by the first letters or numbers, rather than by their entire designation. Thus the first locus on the first line is known as D8.

The actual DNA results are the *peaks*—the spiky bits that pop up from the baseline as you read across each of the lines. The particular alleles, or re-peats found at that locus, are labeled in the boxes beneath the peak. Some people intuitively assume that the *height* of the peaks on an EPG represents the allele—for instance, that a 10 allele would be taller than a 9 allele. But the height of the peak simply indicates how *much* genetic material of that kind was detected by the machine. The second locus (D21, for short) on the first line illustrates this point. The 30 and 34 alleles are roughly the same size.

FIGURE APP. 2   Single-source DNA electropherogram.

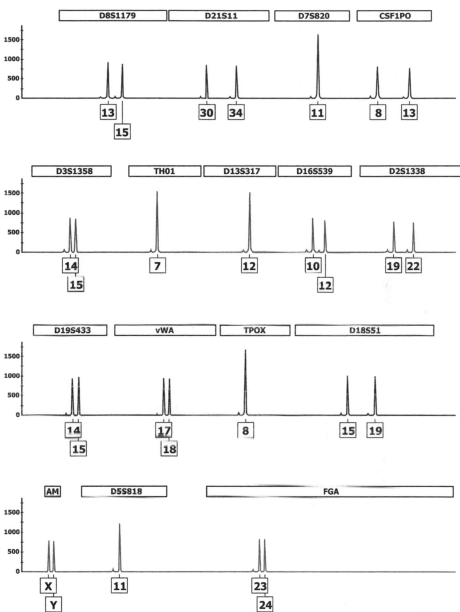

Source: Image courtesy of Dr. Simon Ford, Lexigen Science & Law, San Francisco.

Instead, the numbers to the left, on the y-axis, are actually quite important. They indicate the *relative fluorescence units* (RFU): how brightly the fragments shined as they passed through the machine, which is a function of how many were observed. In other words, the more genetic material is present at that locus, the higher the peak. The less material, the lower. Thus, the 11 allele at D7 was detected in roughly twice the quantity of each allele at the other loci on that line. Although it is not depicted here, at times there appears a second box beneath the allele; that indicates the RFU, which is the precise amount of genetic material detected for that peak.

A sample that contains genetic material from only one person typically will show only one or two peaks at each locus. Specifically, if the person inherited the same allele from both parents, there will be one peak; this is called being homozygotic. If the individual inherited different alleles from each parent, there will be two peaks representing those alleles; this is known as being heterozygotic. A small number of people, for somewhat complicated reasons, show three alleles at certain loci; this is known as a triallelic pattern. The National Institute of Science maintains a list of triallelic observations here, http://www.cstl.nist.gov/strbase/tri_tab.htm. But for the most part, a standard single-person DNA profile will have only one or two peaks at each place.

In interpreting a DNA profile, both the absolute size of the peaks *and* their size relative to one another are possibly the two most important pieces of information in an EPG, apart from the alleles themselves. The absolute RFU range value is critical to notice because it is an important clue to how reliable the test results might be overall. Peaks in the thousands represent clearly detectable amounts of DNA that suggest an accurate measure of the tested sample. But peaks that fall to the low hundreds indicate that only small amounts of DNA were observed, calling into question whether those amounts in fact reliably reflect the actual sample as opposed to contamination from stray cells, transfer, or errors or idiosyncrasies in the testing process.

An electropherogram that has nice, even peaks, all of which fall above a certain RFU threshold, generally indicates a reliable, successful test. That is why a high-quality sample measuring a heterozygotic locus will have *two peaks of similar height* at that locus, indicating that roughly the same amount of genetic material passed through for each allele. If the person is homozygotic, however, the peak should be twice as high—because the amount of genetic material at that locus doubled as a result of inheriting the same allele from both parents.

Even single-source, controlled-conditions samples can sometimes behave erratically in testing, or produce peaks that are predictably explained as artifacts of the testing process. But when a sample is known to come from a single person, it is much easier to explain away the presence of unexpected material. In contrast, a sample that has quality or quantity problems may produce results that make it much more difficult to discern "true" genetic material from a product of a glitch in the testing process, including what material disappeared or dropped out from the results entirely. In such a case, the interpretation of the profile will be less unambiguous, assuming an interpretation is possible at all.

How does the analyst make these determinations? Ideally, by applying a combination of tools, including parameters set by the manufacturer of the kit used to conduct the test and guidance from the lab's protocols, which are founded on experimental tests designed to help calibrate those general standards to the lab's particular processes and instruments. Those protocols typically address and anticipate some recurring factors that influence the interpretation of a challenging sample.

PEAK-HEIGHT THRESHOLDS AND IMBALANCES

Generally speaking, the goal is to produce a test with peak heights that meet a minimum RFU threshold, which in turn ensures that what is observed is genuine genetic material. But many samples may fail to meet that goal. A sample may be low quantity (very little DNA to test), low quality (having degraded from handling or exposure to the elements), contain inhibitors (such as dyes) that complicate the testing process, or contain a mixture of multiple persons, not all of whom contributed equally to the sample. Or, in some cases, the sample may be challenged by all of the above. When the amount of observed DNA falls below a certain level, it becomes less likely that what is there reliably indicates the presence of actual genetic material. Setting thresholds serves a critical role in determining which peaks to trust and interpret, versus which are insufficiently reliable.

At the same time, setting thresholds is a tricky business. If the threshold is set too low, many small peaks that do not represent true alleles, but that appear for other reasons, could be treated as genuine genetic material. An overeager analyst might ascribe a profile to a suspect that in fact does not fit, because some of the observed material was unreliable. Conversely, a peak height threshold that is too high may ignore valuable results, and lead to an erroneous conclusion about whether a comparison profile may or may not match.

In contemporary practice, the setting of thresholds is a topic of significant debate. But some resolve this quandary in part by setting two different thresholds. The first, measured in RFUs and typically called the *stochastic threshold*, is the level above which the analyst does not expect to see purely random results. A peak that rises above the stochastic threshold is usually considered to represent the true presence of genetic material. For instance, if the stochastic threshold is set at 200 RFU, and a single 12 allele peak rises to 300 RFU, it is safe for the analyst to assume that the person has a 12 at that locus and is homozygotic (a 12, 12), because otherwise a sister allele should have appeared. The stochastic threshold is like a green light to interpret that peak as accurate, and use it to draw inferences about associated material.

Peaks below the stochastic threshold may still be of use if they are above the *analytical threshold*, which refers to the minimum amount of DNA that should be present to even consider crediting the peak. Peaks that fall above the analytical threshold, but below the stochastic threshold, can be interpreted with a yellow light. A peak that falls below the analytical threshold cannot even be interpreted with caution; it should be wholly disregarded. Peaks falling in the yellow light zone may be reliable, although an analyst should be alert that they also may be spurious.

Because peak heights transmit important information about the amount of DNA observed in the sample, the relationship among the observed peaks can also say a great deal about the overall quality of the test results. Setting peak height ratios—the anticipated relationship between the size of two alleles at the same locus, as well as the alleles across various loci—also helps the analyst assign meaning to the peaks that appear. Again, these values should be set on the basis of lab-specific experiments, and documented in protocols followed by all analysts. Otherwise, an analyst may be unduly biased by the presentation of a particular case. For instance, an analyst who knows that a defendant is homozygotic at a locus might interpret a very large peak as evidence of that homozygosity, and dismiss any additional peaks at that locus as spurious. Even if the peak is not extremely high, the analyst might still claim that it represents a "true" allele that matches the defendant, while at the same time dismissing another peak of the same size for various reasons. The reliability of that determination should in part turn on the application of established protocols; no analyst can state without reservation that certain peaks will always, and others will never, count as "true."

An informal survey of laboratory personnel at a 2012 workshop showed an array of practices with regard to threshold-setting, but the majority of respondents indicated that the lab's stochastic threshold was over twice as high as the analytical threshold.[1] An RFU of 150 or 200 is common for matching purposes, although some labs consider 50 RFU an acceptable limit. Applying these thresholds, an analyst can then call peaks; that is, the analyst can make determinations about which DNA profiles are apparent from the electropherogram. What are some of the reasons, then, that an analyst might ignore or dismiss the peaks that appear in an EPG?

Generally speaking, there are two categories of extraneous materials— "artifacts" are known or anticipated by-products of DNA testing, whereas "stochastic effects" are random peaks that occur less predictably. *Stochastic* just means that the peak occurs as a result of a random variable. In this sense, artifacts tend to be "reproducible," meaning that subsequent runs of the same genetic material will produce the same results, whereas stochastic effects may change or disappear on retest. But in actuality, the line between artifacts and stochastic effects is not so stark, and many people simply lump them all together.

FIGURE APP. 3   Single-source electropherogram excerpt illustrating low-quantity or -quality testing conditions.

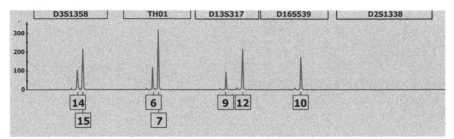

Source: Image courtesy of Dr. Simon Ford, Lexigen Science & Law, San Francisco.

ARTIFACTS AND STOCHASTIC EFFECTS

However classified, extraneous peaks manifest in numerous way that have acquired expressive names, such as stutter, drop-in, pull-up, bleed-through, spikes, and blobs. By way of illustration, consider Figure App. 3, an excerpt from the same hypothetical person that produced the DNA test results in Figure App. 2.

First look at the locus for THO1, the second locus from the left. From Figure App. 2, we know that this person is homozygotic at this locus, with a 7, 7 allele. So why, when the test quality drops, does a second peak appear at the 6 location? That 6 may represent stutter. *Stutter* refers to a well-documented phenomenon whereby a peak appears in a position just short or long of the true genetic peak's position. It is the result of a glitch in the amplification process. Instead of full copies of the "Xeroxed" fragment, occasionally a chunk or single repeat length slips, resulting in the amplification of material just short of the actual material. In high-quality samples, the anticipated size of a stutter fragment is considered fairly predictable, as the laboratory's protocols should express. Lower-quality or -quantity samples can prove challenging in part because stutter sizes become more erratic, or more closely approximate the height of a true allele, which facilitates misinterpretation.

Now look at the third locus from the left, the D13 locus. Again, from Figure App. 2, we know that the subject is also homozygotic at this locus, with a 12, 12 allele. In Figure App. 3, however, we see not just the 12 allele, but also a 9 allele. We also notice that the 9 allele is quite sizeable; it is roughly the same size as the 14 allele at the D3 locus, for instance. We know the 14 allele is true genetic material because we know this person's actual DNA profile. But if we did not know the profile (because, for instance, this was a sample from an unsolved crime scene rather than a known offender), we would have to differentiate between the true and the false 9, even though they are the same size.

If the 9 is not true genetic material, and it is not clearly stutter, then what else might it be? *Drop-in* refers to the presence of peaks that represent true genetic material, but that do not come from the sample being tested. It is often the result of weak levels of contamination, where just a small fragment of DNA manages to pop into a sample, where it is generally overwhelmed and dwarfed by the actual sample's alleles. Again, drop-in becomes most pronounced when lower-quantity or -quality DNA samples are being tested, because the original DNA template is so small that even minuscule amounts of extraneous material becomes visible.

There are several other ways in which peaks appear where they do not belong. *Bleed-through* or *pull-up* refers to the appearance of a peak in the wrong color channel, due to misreading by the detector. Generally that material will appear outside the area for the known loci, but in at least one popular European kit, the peaks from one locus could bleed through and were masked by another. Certain loci are also known troublemakers—for instance, an atypical ("off ladder") allele at the D19 locus occasional shows up in the THO1 location, as a D18 allele sometimes shows up at D16. D22 is a notoriously finicky locus: it routinely produces triallelic peaks (three alleles rather than two) and stutter in both the −1 and +1 positions. Finally, glitches in the testing process itself can cause strange peaks. *Blobs* are typically short, squat peaks that result from stray bits of dye, whereas *spikes* are tall, sharp peaks attributed to a variety of quality-control issues.

ALLELIC OR LOCUS DROPOUT

Although the presence of unexpected peaks may pose interpretive difficulties for an analyst, the absence of expected alleles typically causes the most controversy in interpretation. That is because missing peaks may be interpreted in one of two ways. Missing material may signal an exclusion. A suspect who matches the evidence at all but one allele does not, in the end, match the evidence. But when there are plausible explanations for missing material in the crime scene sample, an analyst may consider the failure to match indicative of dropout in the sample, rather than an exclusion of the suspect.

Comparing line 2 of Figure App. 2 and App. 3, you can see that at the D16 lows there's no peak for 12 allele; it simply disappeared, even though its sister allele, the 10, is present. This is known as allelic dropout. Immediately to the right, the last locus, D2, shows no alleles at all; this is known as locus dropout.

Some alleles and some loci are prone to dropout, particularly in degraded or low-template samples. That is because the DNA fragments associated with those loci run particularly long. Much like a jogger who eats a rich meal before the race, they simply are too sluggish to make it across the capillary to be detected during the testing process. Alleles or loci may also drop out due to problems in the amplification stage, when an allele simply fails to reproduce. For instance, if a suspect's DNA contains a mutation, the genetic "scissors"

FIGURE APP. 4   Low-quality mixture.

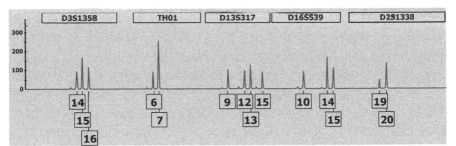

Source: Image courtesy of Dr. Simon Ford, Lexigen Science & Law, San Francisco.

that splice the relevant fragments of the genetic strand may fail to recognize their cutting point and that allele will not be measured.

Dropout is a vexing problem that, like many of these issues, particularly plagues low-quantity or low-quality samples. Studies of drop out can help set thresholds to help determine when it might be anticipated. If a lab runs tests that help it determine the likelihood of allelic dropout given the amount of material present at a sister peak, then some of these concerns may be blunted. However, even though dropout is more common in certain conditions, apart from retesting that produces a different result, it is never certain whether it has, in fact, occurred.

MIXTURES

To the extent that low-quality and -quantity template complicates analysis of single-source samples, these conditions become incredibly problematic with regard to samples containing mixtures of more than one person. The problem with mixtures is that the analyst does not know the number of contributors or their exact ratio in the sample—both critical pieces of information for interpreting a sample, particularly in challenging conditions. The different components of a mixture may have alleles that overlap or that mask one another, or that stack to create artificially high peaks, and so on.

Mixtures also often go hand in hand with low copy number testing, because multiple contributors to a mixture deplete the available genetic material for each contributor when it comes to the time of testing. A 1 nanogram sample from one person contains far more DNA per person than does the same size sample from two, three, or more individuals. And the ratio of persons within the mixture can be a concern as well; if a 1 ng sample is composed of two people who contributed equally, the results are likely to look much different than one in which one person contributed nine times the amount of the other. That raises concerns with misinterpreting a profile because of allelic or

FIGURE APP. 5   Reference sample.

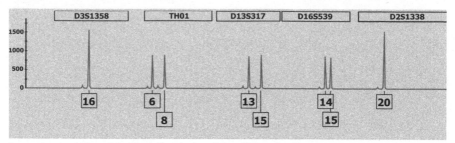

Source: Image courtesy of Dr. Simon Ford, Lexigen Science & Law, San Francisco.

locus dropout that the analyst fails to appreciate, or conversely assumes present, when in fact that is not the case.

Consider Figure App. 4, which depicts an electropherogram from a low-quality mixture sample. With no other information, we can make some conjectures—such as that there are two contributors, based on the appearance of four peaks at a locus. But we do not know the precise profiles of each contributor, and, in fact, we may have a hard time piecing together which alleles are trustworthy at all. Suppose we knew that one of our likely contributors to the sample had the profile shown in Figure App. 5.

Looking at Figure App. 4, we might find that the results are consistent with a mixture of our reference sample (App. 5) and the suspect (App. 2). But that conclusion requires some subjective judgments. We must dismiss the fact that some peaks are not as high as we would expect them to be—for instance, even though the reference is homozygotic at D3 with a 16 allele, the peak is smaller than that of the 15 allele. Yet other genetic material from that supposed person, our reference, appears at other loci in high amounts (such as the 14 allele at the D16 locus).

In addition, we must also explain some inconsistencies. For instance, the D2 locus has a small 19 and a larger 20 allele. The 20 fits our reference, but should the 19 be considered stutter from that 20 peak, or an indication that our suspect's 19 allele did in fact appear in the mixture? If so, where is the suspect's 22 allele? Did it drop out, or should the absence of a 22 indicate that the suspect did not contribute to the mixture? By way of one final example, consider the D13 locus. The reference seems clearly represented by the 13, 15 alleles, but what about the suspect? There is a 12 allele, but it is not very tall compared to the 7 allele at the adjacent locus, THO1, which we also ascribed to the suspect. What is more, there is a 9 allele that does not fit either the reference or the suspect. It may be explainable drop-in of some kind, or it may indicate that the true contributor is a 9, 13. That might also explain why the 13 allele is a bit taller than the 15 allele, even though presumably they come from the same contributor.

These illustrations just scratch the surface of the complexities inherent in DNA interpretation. Consider that these figures reproduce only one line of a four-line electropherogram, and that we knew with certainty at least one of the potential contributor's DNA profiles in this example. But they hopefully provide a rough guide as to why forensic DNA samples, particularly mixtures, can pose such challenges and engender such debate.

LOW COPY NUMBER TESTING

Low copy number testing, also known as low template or LCN testing, refers to the analysis of a DNA sample under conditions that require heightened sensitivity, and that may call into question the reliability of the test results. Sometimes this method is called "touch DNA" or "trace DNA" because many of the samples derive from small traces of biological material left behind as a result of fingerprints or other contact with an item. But "touch DNA" is not a good fit conceptually, because it is very possible to leave ample sample—well above 500 picograms (pg)—from contact alone. Thus some "touched" items might be readily amenable to ordinary testing, whereas others require the special low copy techniques discussed in this appendix.

LCN testing is an area so fraught with dissent that experts cannot agree even on how to define it. The most common approach is with reference to the amount of template—whether from a single-source sample or from any one person within a mixture. Most commercial kits prescribe 0.5 to 2 nanograms (ng) as the ideal sample size, thus low copy is anything that falls below that. A single cell containing DNA from both the mother and father contains roughly 6.6 pg of DNA; thus 500 pg (0.5 ng) translates to roughly 75 cells.

A second way to define LCN testing is to focus more on when the results of DNA tests become less predictable and reliable. Although unpredictable, or *stochastic*, results may arise in any DNA test, when the quantity of DNA falls to low levels, those stochastic effects magnify in every way. It is kind of like having an old car that gets finicky as the temperature drops. When the temperature is warm, the car will start reliably; but if a chill sets in, it will sometimes start but other times just sputter. One way to mitigate these effects is simply through experience. If the owner of the car, through trial and error, learns that 35 degrees seems to be the tipping point, then the owner has set a *stochastic threshold*—the border between reproducible results and erratic performance. The owner might even figure that the car starts 50 percent of the time if it is over 30 degrees, and only 25 percent of the time if it is 25 to 30 degrees out. A laboratory that is testing its instruments should likewise learn, through experiments, how much DNA is needed to produce reliable results.

According to this definition, then, LCN testing is anything that produces results below a certain line of predictability. This is effectively the definition used by the FBI. They define "enhanced" typing as "any DNA typing results generated from limited quantity and/or quality DNA template using conditions that have demonstrated increased stochastic effects."[2]

A final way to think about LCN testing is to look at the testing process itself. In order to increase the likelihood of producing a profile from a very low-quantity sample, analysts tweak the testing process. For instance, they may enhance the extraction and purification stages, or prolong the PCR process, adding additional cycles to the amplification stage, or lengthen the time taken to inject the sample into the capillary. Of these, increasing the number of PCR cycles is the most commonly cited way of conceiving of low copy testing. These cycles (say, 32 or 34 cycles instead of 28) generate additional copies of the material, which in turn enable more sensitive testing. However, just as running copies of copies on a Xerox machine causes the quality of the replicates to suffer, so, too, can the biological version of that process diminish the quality of the testable material.

The battle over low copy number testing—both its definition and its wisdom as a forensic method—played out in academic journals long before it played out in court. In 2011, a fight broke out in the pages of *Forensic Science International: Genetics*—a premier publication for forensic DNA researchers. On one side stood Peter Gill and John Buckleton, luminaries in forensic research laboratories in the United Kingdom and New Zealand, respectively. Peter Gill had worked directly with Alec Jeffreys, considered the father of forensic DNA typing, and had even been tapped by Russian authorities to resolve the mystery of the last tsar of Russia. Buckleton likewise had a long career as a prominent scientist in New Zealand, and had developed cutting edge techniques for forensic interpretation. On the other side stood Bruce Budowle. A former senior scientist at the FBI, Budowle played a central role in introducing DNA typing systems to the criminal justice system. Described by *Science* magazine as "the FBI's premier biological scientist,"[3] Budowle had defended the use of DNA in criminal cases throughout the "DNA Wars" that defined the early years of DNA typing. Eventually Budowle left the FBI to join the faculty at the University of North Texas.

In 2009, Budowle and two associates published a critique of low copy number methods, styled in a way that spoke directly to the legal standards required for admission of novel scientific evidence. The article, titled "Low copy number typing has yet to achieve 'general acceptance,'" asserted that the "methodology does not yield reliable results." It noted that, in the absence of mature protocols for interpretation, the custom was to leave "most of the interpretation to the discretion of the analyst."[4] Moreover, Budowle found "substantial evidence that the interpretation by practitioners often is not based on the results of validation studies and is steeped in practices of bias." In other words, even if the lab has developed guidance on how to handle the particular concerns raised by LCN typing, analysts routinely disregard that guidance in favor of their own discretion.

As the two sides duked it out in the journal pages, the debate grew heated. Publications and letters continued to flow, relating to the forensic genetic analysis of low amounts of DNA. Eventually the editors intervened, declaring a ceasefire that was unusual for a scientific debate. "With the publication of this editorial," they announced, "the journal will not accept any further letters on this issue."[5] In July 2014, the FBI's major advisory group on DNA methods, popularly known as SWGDAM (for Scientific Working Group on DNA Analysis Methods), released a guidance document on the topic. That document takes no stance on the question of whether labs should engage in the practice; it simply offers cautions as to the special problems that might arise.[6]

To give an example of the kinds of concerns imaginable, consider a study done by scientists at the National Institute for Standards and Technology, testing samples of 100 pg, 30 pg, and 10 pg. Importantly, these were not forensic casework samples, which are subject to environmental insults and other inhibitors. Instead, they were pristine samples containing the DNA of only a single person, and because the tests were controlled, it was possible to compare the output to the known genetic profile. NIST's tests revealed instances in which plausible-looking peaks that should not exist suddenly appeared—otherwise known as drop-in. In one case, up to four such peaks were evident. Moreover, at times it would have taken more than three replicate tests for the true peak to be observed—of course, it might have then been dismissed as an artifact.

The FBI "strongly encourages" labs to address the erratic behavior of LCN tests by running multiples of the same test. Many of the false peaks have a low probability of recurring in the same place in multiple tests, and so running different tests and comparing them against one another can allow the analyst to compile a "consensus" or "composite" profile. A consensus profile would consider the DNA that appeared in all the replicate tests, whereas a composite profile counts all the peaks seen in any of the replicate tests.

But although running multiple samples has some advantages, there are also trade-offs. The point of the multiple runs is to compensate for the erratic behavior of low-level DNA samples, but those effects may only be amplified by chopping an already small amount of DNA into even smaller pieces. One study tested this approach by comparing the results from testing a single low template sample, as compared to three subdivided samples from the same original size.[7] That study concluded that testing of the nonsplit samples yielded a higher percentage of accurate information than did the "consensus" replicate testing method. Although splitting the sample did help eliminate the appearance of spurious alleles, it also significantly increased the likelihood that true material also disappeared.

In sum, both the methods and the wisdom of DNA testing of low-quantity and -quality samples is still very much a topic of debate. The technology and instrumentation will continue to advance, as perhaps will probabilistic software programs that aid in interpretation. But, as some courts have already found, the method does not yet appear ready for prime time.

NOTES

INTRODUCTION

1. The Innocence Project, "DNA Exonerations Nationwide," accessed May 17, 2015, http://www
.innocenceproject.org/Content/DNA_Exonerations_Nationwide.php.

2. Federal Bureau of Investigation, press release, "FBI Laboratory Announces Discontinuation of Bullet
Lead Examinations," September 1, 2005, http://www.fbi.gov/news/pressrel/press-releases/fbi-laboratory
-announces-discontinuation-of-bullet-lead-examinations.

3. National Research Council, Committee on Scientific Assessment of Bullet Lead Elemental
Composition Comparison, *Forensic Analysis: Weighing Bullet Lead Evidence* (2004), 1.

4. David Grann, "Trial by Fire," *New Yorker*, September 7, 2009, http://www.newyorker.com/magazine
/2009/09/07/trial-by-fire.

5. Spencer S. Hsu, "Federal Review Stalled After Finding Forensic Errors by FBI Lab Unit Spanned Two
Decades," *Washington Post*, July 29, 2014, http://www.washingtonpost.com/local/crime/federal-review
-stalled-after-finding-forensic-errors-by-fbi-lab-unit-spanned-two-decades/2014/07/29/04ede880–11ee
-11e4–9285–4243a40ddc97_story.html.

6. Spencer S. Hsu, "FBI Admits Flaws in Hair Analysis over Decades," *Washington Post*, April 18, 2015,
http://www.washingtonpost.com/local/crime/fbi-overstated-forensic-hair-matches-in-nearly-all-criminal
-trials-for-decades/2015/04/18/39c8d8c6-e515–11e4-b510–962fcfabc310_story.html.

7. For a list of cases through 2009, see Innocence Project, "Wrongful Convictions Involving Unvalidated
or Improper Forensic Science That Were Later Overturned Through DNA Testing," http://www.innocence
project.org/docs/DNA_Exonerations_Forensic_Science.pdf.

8. National Research Council Committee on Identifying the Needs of the Forensic Science Community,
Strengthening Forensic Science in the United States: A Path Forward (Washington, DC: National Academies
Press, 2009), 7.

9. Michael J. Saks and Jonathan J. Koehler, "The Coming Paradigm Shift in Forensic Identification
Science," *Science* 309 (August 5, 2005): 892.

10. Peter Gill, *Misleading DNA Evidence: Reasons for Miscarriages of Justice* (Oxford, UK: Academic
Press, 2014), x.

CHAPTER 1

1. I. E. Dror and G. Hampikian, "Subjectivity and Bias in Forensic DNA Mixture Interpretation,"
Science and Justice 51, no. 4 (2011): 204.

2. John M. Butler and Bruce R. McCord, "STR Mixture Interpretation" (presentation at AAFS
Advanced Topics in STR DNA Analysis Workshop, Seattle, Washington, February 20, 2006), http://www
.cstl.nist.gov/strbase/pub_pres/AAFS2006_mixtures.pdf.

3. Eva Bianconi, "An Estimation of the Number of Cells in the Human Body," *Annals of Human Biology*
40, no. 6 (November–December 2013): 463–471.

4. We shed roughly 30,000 to 40,000 cells per minute, or 50 million cells a day (resulting in a new
skin roughly once a month). Patricia S. Daniels, Lisa Stein, and Trisha Gura, *Body: The Complete Human*
(Washington, DC: National Geographic Society, 2007), 46. Roughly 65,000 cells would cover a football
field, the amount we shed about every two minutes.

5. Each cell contains about 6 to 7 picograms (pg) of DNA; DNA testing kits typically require about 500 to 1,000 pg of template.

6. Exceptions include certain blood or hair cells.

7. NobelPrize.org, "The Nobel Prize in Physiology or Medicine, 1962," accessed on May 17, 2015, http://www.nobelprize.org/nobel_prizes/medicine/laureates/1962/. Rosalind Franklin was a fourth critical contributor to the discovery of the molecular structure of the genome. She died before the Nobel was awarded, and thus would have been ineligible, but records show that she was never nominated. NobelPrize .org, "The Discovery of the Molecular Structure of DNA—The Double Helix: A Scientific Breakthrough," accessed on May 17, 2015, http://www.nobelprize.org/educational/medicine/dna_double_helix/readmore .html.

8. National Human Genome Research Institute, "All About the Human Genome Project," accessed May 17, 2015, http://www.gcnomc.gov/10001772.

9. For a fun interactive game involving different species and human genetic overlap, see National Geographic, "Genes Are Us. And Them," accessed on May 17, 2015, http://ngm.nationalgeographic .com/2013/07/125-explore/shared-genes. Of course, scientists have come to learn that even though the genomes look the same, they have different functions in different organisms. Ibid.

10. National Institutes of Health, Biological Sciences Curriculum Study, NIH Curriculum Supplement Series, "Understanding Human Genetic Variation," (Bethesda, MD: National Institutes of Health, 2007).

11. Ibid.

12. Federal Bureau of Investigation, "Planned Process and Timeline for Implementation of Additional CODIS Core Loci," accessed on May 17, 2015, http://www.fbi.gov/about-us/lab/biometric-analysis/codis /planned-process-and-timeline-for-implementation-of-additional-codis-core-loci.

13. John M. Butler, *Fundamentals of Forensic DNA Typing* (Oxford, UK: Academic Press, 2009), 156–157. This variation is called a DNA polymorphism—"many shapes" in Latin. These variations may be *sequence* polymorphisms, which are differences in the actual ATGC letters from person to person; for example, a sequence polymorphism may be GTAATACGTACTA in Person 1 and GTAATACGTATTA in Person 2. Or they may be *length* polymorphisms, which are differences in the number of *times* a particular known sequence repeats; a length polymorphism may be ATTA ATTA ATTA ATTA (a 4-repeat allele) in Person 1 and ATTA ATTA ATTA ATTA ATTA (a 5-repeat allele) in Person 2. Forensic testing is interested in the latter kind—length polymorphisms.

14. Ibid., 23.

15. John M. Butler, *Advanced Topics in Forensic DNA Typing: Interpretation* (Oxford, UK: Academic Press, 2014), 246.

16. Butler, *Fundamentals*, 101.

17. Peter Gill, "Forensic Application of DNA Fingerprints," *Nature* 318 (1985): 577.

18. Butler, *Fundamentals*, 101.

19. The prize was awarded to Kary B. Mullis "for his invention of the polymerase chain reaction (PCR) method," along with Michael Smith for his separate contribution to DNA-based chemistry. NobelPrize.org, "The Nobel Prize in Chemistry, 1993," accessed May 17, 2015, http://www.nobelprize.org/nobel_prizes /chemistry/laureates/1993/.

20. Butler, *Fundamentals*, 126. Low copy methods, discussed in greater depth in Chapter 5, often employ more cycles to make more copies, which introduces the possibility of errors.

21. Ibid., 175. For instance, the 9.3 allele at the THO1 locus varies from the 10 allele by only one base pair.

22. Ibid., 199. Single-touch machines are discussed in Chapter 10.

23. The manufacturers of different DNA kits occasionally add other loci, to offer even greater degrees of identification power, but those thirteen loci appear in every system. The FBI is currently in the process of adopting additional loci, so that the new standard will include profiles with genetic information for twenty or more loci.

24. John M. Butler, *Advanced Topics in Forensic DNA Typing: Methodology* (Oxford, UK: Academic Press, 2012), 226.

25. The DNA Identification Act of 1994 (42 U.S.C. § 14132).

26. Federal Bureau of Investigation, "CODIS—Crime," accessed May 18, 2015, http://www.fbi.gov /about-us/lab/biometric-analysis/codis/codis_crime.

27. Federal Bureau of Investigation, "CODIS—NDIS Statistics," accessed May 17, 2015, http://www .fbi.gov/about-us/lab/biometric-analysis/codis/ndis-statistics.

28. Federal Bureau of Investigation, Uniform Crime Reports, "Persons Arrested," in *Crime in the United States, 2013,* http://www.fbi.gov/about-us/cjis/ucr/crime-in-the-u.s/2013/crime-in-the-u.s.-2013/persons -arrested/persons-arrested.

CHAPTER 2

1. As a result, there is a blooming industry in processing techniques that work notwithstanding these inhibitors.

2. Keith L. Alexander and Julie Zauzmer, "Director of D.C.'s Embattled DNA Lab Resigns After Suspension of Testing," *Washington Post*, April 30, 2015, http://www.washingtonpost.com/local/director -of-dcs-embattled-dna-lab-resigns-following-suspension-of-testing/2015/04/30/1c619320-ef80-11e4 -8666-a1d756d0218e_story.html.

3. Keith L. Alexander, "Prosecutors Criticize D.C. Crime Lab's Handling of Some DNA Evidence," *Washington Post*, March 5, 2015, http://www.washingtonpost.com/local/crime/dc-prosecutors-criticize -city-crime-labs-handling-of-some-dna-cases/2015/03/05/b5244f88-bea4-11e4-b274-e5209a3bc9a9 _story.html.

4. Ibid.

5. Associated Press, "National Board Suspends DNA Testing at DC's New Crime Lab," *Washington Post*, April 27, 2015, http://www.washingtonpost.com/local/national-board-suspends-dna-testing-at-dcs-new -crime-lab/2015/04/27/09087240-eceb-11e4-8050-839e9234b303_story.html.

6. William C. Thompson, "A Setback for Forensic Science," *Washington Post*, May 8, 2015.

7. John M. Butler, *Advanced Topics in Forensic DNA Typing: Interpretation* (Oxford, UK: Academic Press, 2014), 175.

8. David R. Paoletti et al., "Empirical Analysis of the STR Profiles Resulting from Conceptual Mixtures," *Journal of Forensic Sciences* 50, no. 6 (2005): 1351.

9. For example, using the genotypes of 959 individuals, it is possible to construct roughly 146,536,159 possible different three-person mixtures. Ibid., 1363.

10. Butler, *Interpretation*, 162. It similarly becomes difficult to separate out contributor profiles where the quantity of material from one source compared to that of a second appears in a sharply skewed ratio. Ibid., 159–162.

11. Peter Gill et al., "DNA Commission of the International Society of Forensic Genetics: Recommendations on the Evaluation of STR Typing Results That May Include Drop-out and/or Drop-in Using Probabilistic Methods," *Forensic Science International: Genetics* 6 (2012): 679–688.

12. Butler, *Interpretation*, 175–176, 309.

13. Generally speaking, scientists expect there to be roughly the same amount of DNA at each locus from a single person in the sample. So, for instance, if an analyst thinks that there might be two people in the mixture, and one set of peaks is very low while another is very high, the analyst may conclude that the low peaks belong to one person who contributed a small amount of DNA to the sample, whereas the high peaks are those of a second person who contributed more.

14. Butler, *Interpretation*, 176.

15. Barry Scheck, Peter Neufeld, and Jim Dwyer, *Actual Innocence When Justice Goes Wrong and How to Make It Right* (New York: New American Library: 2003), 167–169.

16. Ibid., 171.

CHAPTER 3

1. Georgina Meakin and Allan Jamieson, "DNA Transfer; Implications for Casework," *Forensic Science International: Genetics* 7 (2013): 434–443.

2. Roland A. H. van Oorschot and Maxwell K. Jones, "DNA Fingerprints from Fingerprints," *Nature* 387 (1997): 767. A subsequent study showed more equivocal results, but those were also conducted with typing techniques far less sensitive than the ones in use today, and applying rigid thresholds for data interpretation. A nice summary of the debate was written by Norah Rudin and Keith Inman, "The Urban Myths & Conventional Wisdom of Transfer: DNA as Trace Evidence," *CAC News*, Third Quarter (2007): 26–29.

3. A. Lowe, C. Murray, J. Whitaker, G. Tully, and P. Gill, "The Propensity of Individuals to Deposit DNA and Secondary Transfer of Low Level DNA from Individuals to Inert Surfaces," *Forensic Science International*, 129, no. 1 (2002): 25–34.

4. M. Goray and R. A. H. van Oorschot, "DNA Transfer During Social Interactions," *Forensic Science International: Genetics*, 4, no. 1 (2013): e101–e102.

5. Matthew Phipps and Susan Petricevic, "The Tendency of Individuals to Transfer DNA to Handled Items," *Forensic Science International* 168(2-3) (May 2007): 162; Eleanor Alison May Graham and Guy

Nathan Rutty, "Investigation Into 'Normal' Background DNA on Adult Necks: Implications for DNA Profiling of Manual Strangulation Victims," *Journal of Forensic Science* 53, no. 5 (2008): 1074.

6. Meakin and Jamieson, "DNA Transfer."

7. Tracey Kaplan, "Monte Sereno Murder Case Casts Doubts on DNA Evidence," *San Jose Mercury News*, June 28, 2014.

8. Sunita Schrabji, "Gangster Convicted of Murdering Millionaire Raveesh 'Ravi' Kumra," *India West*, November 12, 2014, http://www.indiawest.com/news/global_indian/gangster-convicted-of-murdering-millionaire-raveesh-ravi-kumra/article_af328f02-6a96-11e4-9d9b-ef6df1bfc32d.html.

9. O. Cook and L. Dixon, "The Prevalence of Mixed DNA Profiles in Fingernail Samples Taken from Individuals in the General Population," *Forensic Science International: Genetics* 1 (2007): 62–68.

10. E. A. Dowlman et al., "The Prevalence of Mixed DNA Profiles on Fingernail Swabs," *Science and Justice* 50 (2010): 64–71.

11. Graham and Rutty, "Investigation."

12. Nicholas J. Port et al., "How Long Does It Take a Static Speaking Individual to Contaminate the Immediate Environment?" *Forensic Science, Medicine, and Pathology* 2, no. 3 (2006): 157–163.

13. Graham and Rutty, "Investigation."

14. Ibid.; G. N. Rutty, "An Investigation into the Transference and Survivability of Human DNA Following Simulated Manual Strangulation with Consideration of the Problem of Third Party Contamination," *International Journal of Legal Medicine* 116, no. 3 (June 2002): 170.

15. David A. Warshauer et al., "An Evaluation of the Transfer of Saliva-Derived DNA," *International Journal of Legal Medicine* 126, no. 6 (2013): 851.

16. Recommendation for Dismissal, 14, People v. Strauss-Kahn, Indictment No. 02526/2011 (NY Sup. Ct. August 22, 2011), 18n20.

17. E. Kafarowski et al., "The Retention and Transfer of Spermatozoa in Clothing by Machine Washing," *Canadian Society of Forensic Science Journal* 29, no. 1 (1996): 7–11.

18. Sarah Noel, "Intrafamily Sexual Assaults on Children: Have You Considered the Possibility of DNA Transfer in the Laundry?" (presentation at International Symposium on Human Identification, Phoenix, Arizona, October 2, 2014).

19. M. Goray et al., "Secondary DNA Transfer of Biological Substances Under Varying Test Conditions," *Forensic Science International: Genetics* 4, no. 2 (2010): 62–67.

20. Meakin and Jamieson, "DNA Transfer."

21. V. J. Lehmann, R. J. Mitchell, K. N. Ballantyne, and R. A. H. van Oorschot, "Following the Transfer of DNA: How Far Can It Go?" *Forensic Science International: Genetics* 4 (2013): e53–e54.

22. Meakin and Jamieson, "DNA Transfer."

23. Mariya Goray, John R. Mitchell, and Roland A. H. van Oorschot, "Evaluation of Multiple Transfer of DNA Using Mock Case Scenarios," *Legal Medicine* 14 (2012): 40–46.

24. R. v. Steven Wayne Hillier, [2010] ACTSC 33 (April 16, 2010), available at http://www.courts.act.gov.au/supreme/judgment/view/3070.

25. Goray, et al., "Evaluation of Multiple Transfer."

26. "DNA Bungle Haunts German Police," BBC, March 28, 2009.

27. Mike Silverman, "The Strange Case of the 'Time Travel' Murder," BBC News, April 28, 2014, http://www.bbc.com/news/science-environment-26324244.

28. Graham and Rutty, "Investigation."

29. John O. Savino and Brent E. Turvey, *Rape Investigation Handbook*, 2nd ed. (Oxford, UK: Academic Press, 2011), 352–353.

30. A significant number of studies have been done by a research group associated with Roland A. H. van Oorschot of the Victoria Police Forensic Services Department in Australia.

CHAPTER 4

1. Larry Celona, "OWS Shock in Unsolved '04 Sarah Slay," *New York Post*, July 11, 2012, http://nypost.com/2012/07/11/ows-shock-in-unsolved-04-sarah-slay/.

2. Larry Celona, "Cold-Case Slay DNA Match the Result of Lab Contamination: Sources," *New York Post*, July 12, 2012, http://nypost.com/2012/07/12/cold-case-slay-dna-match-the-result-of-lab-contamination-sources/.

3. William K. Rashbaum and Joseph Goldstein, "DNA Match Tying Protest to 2004 Killing Is Doubted," *New York Times*, July 11, 2012.

4. Gary Buiso and Kimon de Greef, "Suspect in Juilliard Murder Says Victim Still Talks," *New York Post*, May 11, 2014, http://nypost.com/2014/05/11/juilliard-murder-suspect-claims-victim-talks-to-him/.

5. New York Exec. Law § 995-a (McKinney 2014).

6. Ibid., § 995-b(13).

7. Office of the Inspector General, State of New York, "Investigation into the New York City Office of Chief Medical Examiner: Department of Forensic Biology," December 2013, 14.

8. Ibid., 14.

9. Ibid., 15.

10. Ibid., 17.

11. Ibid., 18.

12. Ibid.

13. Ibid., 20.

14. Ibid., 20. Of 116 such cases, reexamination revealed that 26 in fact contained DNA. Ibid., 20.

15. Ibid., 21.

16. Joseph Goldstein and Nina Bernstein, "Ex-Technician Denies Faulty DNA Work," *New York Times*, January 11, 2013, http://www.nytimes.com/2013/01/12/nyregion/former-lab-technician-denies-faulty-dna-work-in-rape-cases.html?_r=0.

17. Office of the Inspector General, "Investigation," 22.

18. Letter from Barbara A. Butcher, Office of Chief Medical Examiner, to quality assurance manager, ASCLD/LAB, February 7, 2013.

19. Ibid.

20. Goldstein and Bernstein, "Ex-Technician Denies Faulty DNA Work."

21. The Innocence Project, "The Cases: Marlon Pendleton," accessed May 17, 2015, http://www.innocenceproject.org/Content/Marlon_Pendleton.php.

22. Brandon L. Garrett, *Convicting the Innocent: Where Criminal Prosecutions Go Wrong* (Cambridge, MA: Harvard University Press, 2011), 109–110 (describing cases of Ulysses S. Charles and Larry Peterson).

23. Ibid., 101; The Innocence Project, "The Cases: Gilbert Alejandro," accessed May 17, 2015, http://www.innocenceproject.org/cases-false-imprisonment/gilbert-alejandro.

24. Lawrence Mower and Doug McMurdo, "Las Vegas Police Reveal DNA Error Put Wrong Man in Prison," *Las Vegas Review-Journal*, July 7, 2011, http://www.reviewjournal.com/news/crime-courts/las-vegas-police-reveal-dna-error-put-wrong-man-prison.

25. "Former Inmate Gets $1.5M in DNA Mix-up Case," Fox5 KVVU-TV, July 21, 2011, http://www.fox5vegas.com/story/15124423/former-inmate-could-get-15m-for-dna-mix-up?clienttype=printable.

26. Mower and McMurdo, "Las Vegas Police."

27. For a list of the laboratories, see David Faigman et al., *Modern Scientific Evidence: The Law and Science of Expert Testimony* (Rochester, NY: Thomson West, 2014–15), § 31:15.

28. Toby Helm, "Outrage at 500,000 DNA Database Mistakes," *The Telegraph*, August 27, 2007, http://www.telegraph.co.uk/news/uknews/1561414/Outrage-at-500000-DNA-database-mistakes.html.

29. Joseph Goldstein, "F.B.I. Audit of Database That Indexes DNA Finds Errors in Profiles," *New York Times*, January 24, 2014, http://www.nytimes.com/2014/01/25/nyregion/fbi-audit-of-database-that-indexes-dna-finds-errors-in-profiles.html.

30. Ibid.

31. M. S. Enkoji, "DNA Lapse Puts Scrutiny on Lab Work," *Sacramento Bee*, September 14, 2006.

32. Robert A. Jarzen, crime laboratory director, Technical Problem Review—Analyst Casework, Ref. LFS-03-008755, memo to Jan Scully, district attorney, Office of the District Attorney of Sacramento County, August 14, 2006.

33. "'Unexplained' DNA on Bag Containing Dead M16 Spy Gareth Williams," BBC News, April 24, 2012, http://www.bbc.com/news/uk-17826633.

34. Peter Gill, *Misleading DNA Evidence: Reasons for Miscarriages of Justice* (Oxford, UK: Academic Press, 2014), 31.

35. People v. Andrew Peaks and Jaquan Collins, Nos. 7689/2010 and 8077/2010, Frye hearing (testimony of Bruce Budowle), Supreme Court, Kings County, New York, December 10, 2013.

36. People v. Leiterman, No. 265821, 2007 WL 2120514 (Mich. Ct. App. July 24, 2007) (unpublished opinion).

37. William C. Thompson, "Tarnish on the 'Gold Standard'": Understanding Recent Problems in Forensic DNA Testing," *The Champion*, January/February 2006, 14.

38. Dr. Theodore D. Kessis, "Report of Findings, People v. Gary Leiterman, No. 04-2017-FC," May 8, 2006, http://www.garyisinnocent.org/web/CaseHistory/NewDNAFindings/tabid/58/Default.aspx.

39. Ibid.

40. Texas, Maryland, and New York all require that a state body issue accreditation certifications; see, for example, 37 Tex. Admin. Code 28.141. Other states simply require that the lab seek accreditation from an authorized body; see, for example, Calif. Penal Code § 297. Some states have statutes that require labs follow a vague term, such as "national standards"; see Ind. Code Ann. § 10–13–6–14 (West 2015).

41. Kathleen Keough Griebel, "Fred Zain, the CSI Effect, and a Philosophical Idea of Justice: Using West Virginia as a Model for Change," *West Virginia Law Review* 4, no. 3 (2012): 1155, 1190. Nonetheless, many government labs have voluntarily undertaken accreditation. Although only a handful of states require accreditation, a recent government survey found that, as of 2009, 83 percent of the 411 publicly funded crime labs in the nation were accredited. Matthew R. Durose et al., *Census of Publicly Funded Forensic Crime Laboratories, 2009*, Bureau of Justice Statistics (August 2012), available at http://www.bjs.gov/index.cfm?ty=dcdetail&iid=244.

42. The California Crime Laboratory Review Task Force compiled a list of oversight entities in various states, California Crime Laboratory Review Task Force, "An Examination of Forensic Science in California," November 2009, Appendix K.

43. It started as a committee within ASCLD in 1982, and then became a separate nonprofit in 1984.

44. American Society of Crime Laboratory Directors/Laboratory Accreditation Board, http://www.ascld-lab.org/about-ascldlab/.

45. The National Registry of Exonerations, A Project of the University of Michigan Law School, Gregory Taylor, accessed May 17, 2015, http://www.law.umich.edu/special/exoneration/Pages/casedetail.aspx?caseid=3677.

46. Chris Swecker and Michael Wolf, *An Independent Review of the SBI Forensic Laboratory*, 12, http://www.ncdoj.gov/getattachment/120489be-3c0b-4515-a522-19de759e5e07/Independent-Review-of-SBI-Forensic-LAB.aspx.

47. Ibid., 4.

48. Ibid., 3.

49. Ibid., 3, 9.

50. Ibid., 19.

51. Ibid., 22–24.

52. ASCLD/LAB's accreditation system has long been subject to criticism. Initially, complaints focused on the utter lack of rigor in setting and enforcing the standards. Instead of signaling laboratory excellence, accreditation was basically a courtesy extended after the lab paid a fee. In 2009, however, ASCLD/LAB discontinued that approach and adopted the international ISO/IEC 17025 standard. Today, only forty-one labs are accredited by ASCLD/LAB under the older "Legacy" program; the vast majority are accredited according to one of the newer "International" standards. As a "Legacy" lab, the North Carolina lab did not come up for reaccreditation until 2013.

53. Problems include mistakes in the identification of fibers, destroyed blood samples, DNA contamination, failure to perform maintenance and calibration, mix-up of key physical evidence, faking of calibration dates, false credentials, faking of drug test results, failing proficiency tests, safety deficiencies, substandard ventilation, ineffective operating procedures, evidence integrity issues, delay in reporting DNA evidence, expired chemicals, "dry-labbing," supervisory failure, incorrect drug weights, theft of drugs, incorrect and/or misleading blood serology results, lack of proper certification, and use of outdated tests and destruction of laboratory records. Memorandum to members, the New York State Commission of Forensic Science, from Marvin E. Schechter, Esq., "ASCLD/LAB And Forensic Laboratory Accreditation: An Analysis," March 25, 2011, 12–14.

54. A California task force entrusted with reviewing the state's crime laboratories identified several important dimensions of crime lab competence that the standards did not cover. First, the standards do not measure how resources are allocated within the laboratory, including whether a lab operates efficiently or not. Thus, a lab that processes a high volume of samples in a short period is awarded the same accreditation as one that has a five-year backlog that effectively renders its work meaningless. Second, standards do not directly regulate how DNA testing results are communicated, another critical component of forensic testing. Although there are recommendations related to the information that must be included in a report and to the need for clarity, there are not standardized terms that every analyst must follow. Thus, two analysts may have matches that carry the same statistical significance, but they can testify in wildly different ways about the meaning of that match, and it will not affect accreditation. Third, standards do not impose requirements for independent investigations of misconduct. California Crime Laboratory Review Task Force, "An Examination of Forensic Science in California," November 2009, 81–82.

55. Lab supervisors select the review cases from the files, rather than allowing inspectors to select from the files at random. Mark Hansen, "Crime Labs Under the Microscope After a String of Shoddy, Suspect and Fraudulent Results," *ABA Journal*, September 1, 2013, http://www.abajournal.com/magazine/article/crime_labs_under_the_microscope_after_a_string_of_shoddy_suspect_and_fraudu/. That report did note that, according to the ASCLD/LAB executive director, "inspectors always ask to see additional cases." Ibid.

56. Arvizu has described the accreditation process as "essentially a paperwork audit, reviewing casefiles and records." Janine Arvizu, "Forensic Drug Lab Issues" (presentation to the Texas Criminal Defense Lawyers Association, 25th Annual Rusty Duncan Advanced Criminal Law Course, San Antonio, Texas, June 9, 2012), http://www.tcdla.com/cleanevents/docs/A060712/Arvizu,Janine_ForensicDrugLabIssues.pdf.

57. People v. Andrew Peaks and Jaquan Collins, Nos. 7689/2010 and 8077/2010, Frye hearing (testimony of Bruce Budowle), Supreme Court, Kings County, New York, December 10, 2013, 1005.

58. Ibid.

59. And once a lab has acquired initial accreditation, the ASCLD/LAB board imposes weak continued monitoring systems for the five-year period of presumptive renewal. Annual visits may be conducted if "deemed necessary by the Board," but no public data exists on how often such visits actually occur. Primarily, the board relies on the lab to submit regular documentation affirming its continued good standing. That includes a requirement that accredited labs report "substantive occurrences of non-compliance with essential criteria." Schechter memorandum, 9. But it is left to labs to determine what is sufficiently "substantive" or not.

60. Mandy Locke and Joseph Neff, "Legislators: SBI Needs a New Accrediting Agency," *News & Observer* (Raleigh, NC), September 17, 2010.

61. Swecker and Wolf, *Independent Review*, 7, 12. See also American Society of Crime Lab Directors/Laboratory Accreditation Board, position statement, "Position on Reporting of Blood Screening Tests in the 1980's and 1990's," February 18, 2011.

62. Schechter memorandum, 19–20.

63. ASCLD/LAB position statement.

64. Schechter memorandum, 13.

65. Jordan Michael Smith, "Forget CSI: A Disaster Is Happening in America's Crime Labs," *Business Insider*, April 30, 2014, http://www.businessinsider.com/forensic-csi-crime-labs-disaster-2014-4#ixzz3N4ORFkgq. In 2011, the Connecticut State lab lost accreditation, but regained it in February 2012. Jennifer Swift, "The Cleanup of the Connecticut Forensic Science Lab Continues," *Connecticut Today*, January 20, 2014. As of this writing, nine labs are listed as having voluntarily withdrawn their accreditation, which the website describes as "due to laboratory closures or other reasons" (merger, loss of personnel, etc.), http://www.ascld-lab.org/voluntary-withdrawal/, accessed May 18, 2015. But further investigation reveals that some of those labs withdrew accreditation due to corruption or malfeasance. For instance, the Houston Forensic Science Center has weathered three major scandals in the past ten years, including the most recent revelation that a former DNA technician lied, departed from protocols, and tampered with records. Brian Rogers, "Scores of Cases Affected After HPD Crime Lab Analyst Ousted," *Houston Chronicle*, June 18, 2014, http://www.houstonchronicle.com/news/houston-texas/houston/article/Scores-of-cases-affected-after-HPD-Crime-Lab-5562835.php. ASCLD/LAB, however, does not even mention the possibility that the Houston lab's voluntary withdrawal may have been undertaken by a troubled lab as a means of avoiding official censure.

66. Joseph Neff and Mandy Locke, "Forensic Groups' Ties Raise Concerns," *News & Observer (Raleigh, NC)*, October 13, 2010.

67. Swecker and Wolf, 19–20.

68. "NC Crime Lab Says Some Analysts Didn't Pass Certification Exam," WRAL.com, June 14, 2012, http://www.wral.com/news/local/story/11209765/.

69. Mandy Locke and Joseph Neff, "SBI, DAs Spar over Failed Tests," *Charlotte Observer*, June 15, 2012.

70. Michael R. Bromwich, "Final Report of the Independent Investigator for the Houston Police Department Crime Laboratory and Property Room," June 13, 2007, 214, http://www.hpdlabinvestigation.org/reports/070613report.pdf.

71. Ibid., 208. Other reports listed the probability as 1 in 15 or 1 in 16.

72. Ibid., 211.

73. Ibid., 212, 214.

74. Ibid., 55–56.

75. Ibid., 217.

76. Ibid., 54–55.

77. Ibid., 55.

78. Ibid., 121.

79. Ibid., 122.

80. Roma Khanna, "State Hires DNA Chief Despite Houston Crime Lab Probe," *Houston Chronicle*, January 30, 2008, http://www.chron.com/news/houston-texas/article/State-hires-DNA-chief-despite -Houston-crime-lab-1785193.php.

81. Brian Rogers, "Scores of Cases Affected After HPD Crime Lab Analyst Ousted," *Houston Chronicle*, June 18, 2014, http://www.houstonchronicle.com/news/houston-texas/houston/article/Scores-of-cases -affected-after-HPD-Crime-Lab-5562835.php.

82. Brian Rogers, "Ex–Crime Lab Analyst Told HPD Colleagues of Wrongdoing," *Houston Chronicle*, June 25, 2014, http://www.houstonchronicle.com/news/houston-texas/houston/article/Former-HPD -crime-lab-analyst-told-colleagues-of-5580097.php#/0.

83. Ibid.

84. ASCLD/LAB-International, *Supplemental Requirements for the Accreditation of Forensic Science Testing Laboratories, 2011 Edition* (Corresponds to ISO/IEC 17025:2005), (2010), § 5.9.3.1.

85. Matthew R. Durose, Kelly A. Walsh, and Andrea M. Burch, "Census of Publicly Funded Forensic Crime Laboratories, 2009," U.S. Department of Justice, Office of Justice Programs, Bureau of Justice Statistics, 8.

86. See, for example, Brendan J. Lyons, "Cheating Scandal Fouls State Police Test," *Albany Times Union*, January 16, 2015, http://m.timesunion.com/news/article/Cheating-scandal-fouls-State-Police -test-6021600.php.

87. Joseph L. Peterson et al., "The Feasibility of External Blind DNA Proficiency Testing. II. Experience with Actual Blind Tests," *Journal of Forensic Sciences* 48, no. 1 (January 2003): 32, 38.

88. New York, Virginia, DC, and Texas all use a general oversight model, whereas Connecticut, Arizona, New Mexico, and Oregon have employed more narrowly tasked commissions.

89. Thus, for instance, Arizona's Cold Case Task Force was convened to study best practices for cold case investigations. California's Crime Laboratory Review Task Force was charged with a number of tasks related to crime lab performance. And Minnesota's Genetic Information Work Group was created to establish policies related to the use of genetic information.

90. People v. Andrew Peaks and Jaquan Collins, Nos. 7689/2010 and 8077/2010, Frye hearing (testimony of Ranajit Chakraborty), Supreme Court, Kings County, New York, December 16, 2013, 1100–1102. He characterized the "reviews . . . not necessarily completely exhaustive." Ibid.

91. New York Executive Law § 995-a (McKinney 1994).

92. California Crime Laboratory Review Task Force, *An Examination of Forensic Science in California*, November 2009, i–ii, http://oag.ca.gov/sites/all/files/agweb/pdfs/publications/crime_labs_report.pdf.

93. Initially, the commission had two defense attorneys and one scientist from an independent lab. But the scientist later stepped down and was replaced by a public defender.

94. California Crime Laboratory Review Task Force, minutes, June 3, 2010, http://ag.ca.gov/meetings /tf/pdf/TF_Minutes_060310.pdf.

95. Editorial, "Crime Labs Should Welcome Scrutiny," *Sacramento Bee*, June 29, 2010.

96. California Crime Laboratory Review Task Force, 3–10.

97. Andy Furillo, "California Crime Lab Overseers Split," *McClatchyDC*, June 18, 2010, http://www .mcclatchydc.com/2010/06/18/96147_california-crime-lab-overseers.html?rh=1#storylink=cpy.

CHAPTER 5

1. Kristina Davis, "Were Teens Mutilated by Same Killer?" *U-T San Diego*, October 25, 2014, http:// www.utsandiego.com/news/2014/oct/25/brown-tatro-hough-nantais-dna-murder-beach-police/.

2. Mike Silverman, "The Strange Case of the 'Time Travel' Murder," BBC News, April 28, 2014, http:// www.bbc.com/news/science-environment-26324244.

3. John M. Butler, *Advanced Topics in Forensic DNA Typing: Interpretation* (Oxford, UK: Academic Press, 2014), 175. See also Peter Gill, *Misleading DNA Evidence: Reasons for Miscarriages of Justice* (Oxford, UK: Academic Press, 2014), 13. As Gill himself recently proclaimed, "Now the analysis of just a 'handful' of cells is not only possible, but also routine in most forensic laboratories."

4. Butler, *Interpretation*, 164.

5. John Buckleton and Peter Gill, "Low Copy Number," in *Forensic DNA Evidence Interpretation*, ed. Christopher M. Triggs, John S. Buckleton, and Simon J. Walsh (Boca Raton, FL: CRC Press, 2005), 275; I. Findley et al., "DNA Fingerprinting from Single Cells," *Nature* 389 (1997): 555–556.

6. Even determining precisely how to decide what constitutes LCN has proven difficult. There are three prevalent conceptions, based (1) on the size of the sample tested, (2) on the results of the testing, and (3) on the kind of test itself. The first approach is the most common. It simply asks how much DNA was present in the sample at the time it was tested. DNA kits function optimally when a precise amount of biological material is tested. For most kits on the market today, the manufacturer prescribes sample sizes in the range of 0.5 to 2 ng (500 to 2,000 pg). John M. Butler, *Fundamentals of DNA Typing:* (Oxford, UK: Academic Press, 2009), 111. A sample of 500 pg translates to roughly 75 cells. Much more DNA than that, and the test may produce false peaks or peaks so enormous that they are difficult to assess. Much less DNA than that, and the analyst starts to encounter the kinds of concerns raised in this chapter. Accordingly, one common threshold for LCN testing is the presence of less than 200 pg (roughly 30 cells) of material. Bruce Budowle, Arthur Eisenberg, and Angela van Daal, "Validity of Low Copy Number Typing and Applications to Forensic Science," *Croatian Medical Journal*, 50, no. 3 (2009): 207–217. Low copy number methods are discussed in greater depth in the Appendix.

7. People v. Andrew Peaks and Jaquan Collins, Nos. 7689/2010 and 8077/2010, Memorandum of Law in Support of Defendants' Motions to Preclude Admission of the OCME's LCN and FST Evidence at Trial, Supreme Court, Kings County, New York, April 14, 2014, 1.

8. Theresa Caragine, slides from testimony in People v. Andrew Peaks and Jaquan Collins, Nos. 7689/2010 and 8077/2010, December 12, 2012.

9. Ibid.

10. People v. Megnath, 27 Misc 3d 405 (Sup. Ct. Queens Co. 2010). Other courts have not even gotten to the stage of rejecting a hearing, because they have refused to acknowledge LCN's taking place at all. David Faigman et al., *Modern Scientific Evidence: The Law and Science of Expert Testimony* (Rochester, NY: Thomson West, 2014–2015) § 31:32 (reviewing cases). Given the definitional dispute, prosecutors can argue that a test is not low copy, simply by shifting to another classification that works. In this view, only a test that started with a template under 100 pg, required extra amplification cycles, and produced results below the stochastic threshold might arguably qualify for special attention. One particularly sketchy approach is to measure only the sum total of the forensic sample, even where it includes a mixture of more than one individual. In such cases, one (or more) person's contribution may qualify as a low copy template, even if the sum total of the DNA from all persons falls within the ordinary range. But ignoring the special problems of low copy testing in such cases, while common, is indefensible.

11. United States v. McCluskey, 954 F. Supp.2d 1280 (D. N.M. 2013).

12. In addition to the case discussed in the text: People v. Espino (CA. Sup. Cr. L A Co., 2009, NA076620) (oral decision, not generally accepted); United States v. McCluskey, 954 F. Supp.2d 1280 (D. N.M. 2013); but see United States v. Morgan, 53 F. Supp. 3d 732 (S.D.N.Y. 2014).

13. B. Budowle and A. van Daal, comment on "'A Universal Strategy to Interpret DNA Profiles That Does Not Require a Definition of Low Copy Number' by Peter Gill and John Buckleton, 2010, *Forensic Science International: Genetics* 4, 221–227," *Forensic Science International: Genetics* 5, no. 1 (2011): 15.

14. Ibid.; A. D. Kloosterman and P. Kersbergen, "Efficacy and Limits of Genotyping Low Copy Number DNA Samples by Multiplex PCR of STR Loci," International Congress Series 795 (2003): 1239.

15. People v. Jaquan Collins and Andrew Peaks, Nos. 8077–2010, 7689–2010, Affirmation in Reply to Notice of Motion for Judicial Subpoena Duces Tecum, April 25, 2013.

16. Liz Robbins, "Helping Decide Guilt or Innocence," *New York Times*, December 15, 2012.

17. Office of the Inspector General, State of New York, *Investigation into the New York City Office of Chief Medical Examiner: Department of Forensic Biology* (December 2013), 29–40.

18. The detective said something to the effect of, "I don't believe that you knew she was fourteen; I bet you thought she was older," and Brown allegedly replied, "I didn't," and later, "I had no idea." Brown also allegedly told an old friend, after the investigation began, that a girl he had photographed had later turned up dead. Kristina Davis, "Warrants Reveal Evidence in 1984 Killing," *U-T San Diego*, October 31, 2014, http://www.utsandiego.com/news/2014/oct/31/warrant-brown-hough-murder-dna-photo/2/?#article -copy.

19. "DNA Evidence Could Have Been Contaminated in Cold Case," KUSI-News (San Diego), December 18, 2014, http://www.kusi.com/story/27665318/dna-evidence-could-have-been-contaminated -in-cold-case.

20. Sarah Sapeda, "Attorney: Cross-contamination Led Police to Suspect Retired Lab Worker in 1984 Murder," ABC 10 News, December 18, 2014, http://www.10news.com/news/attorney-cross-contamination-led-police-to-suspect-retired-lab-worker-in-1984-murder.

CHAPTER 6

1. Even the same alleles held by two people might be inherited differently. Say that two people have the 10, 14 alleles at a particular locus. They still could have received those markers in different ways: for one person, ten from the mother and fourteen from the father; and for the other person, the reverse. The probability calculation must take this into account.

In addition, at each of the thirteen loci are a wide array of alleles. At the low end, some loci display as few as eight, but others have as many as twenty-seven. That degree of diversity diminishes the likelihood that any two unrelated people share the same genetic profile across all loci. It is as though there were fifteen different natural hair colors and twenty different eye shades. And just like some traits and combinations are less common than others—such as blond hair and green eyes versus brown hair and brown eyes, some of the alleles used in forensic typing are less common than others. Thus a genetic profile with some very rare alleles will be more distinguishing than a profile that has many common alleles. In the end, a conventional thirteen-locus DNA profile, with two alleles of information at each loci, can produce a rarity statistic with tremendous power.

2. Special thanks to Dr. Yun Song for aiding in this calculation.

3. Nancy Szokan, "With Earth's Population Now at 7 Billion, How Many People Have Ever Lived?" *Washington Post*, October 31, 2011, http://www.washingtonpost.com/national/health-science/with-earths-population-now-at-7-billion-how-many-people-have-ever-lived/2011/10/27/gIQA6SLtZM_story.html.

4. Genetic traits at one locus also must not be connected to or influence the genetic information at another locus. Known as linkage, this connectedness undermines the accuracy of a probability statistic that assumes the information at each locus is independent. Of all forensic loci, the two nicknamed vWA and D12 are the closest together on a single chromosome and thus most at risk for linkage disequilibrium, although studies seem to have determined no need for concern. Some studies suggest two of the loci used in the European typing system, which are also closely spaced on the same chromosome, might exert influence on one another at least as regard close relatives. John M. Butler, *Advanced Topics in Forensic DNA Typing: Interpretation* (Oxford, UK: Academic Press, 2014), 259–260.

5. Loving v. Virginia, 388 U.S. 1 (1967).

6. Butler, *Interpretation*, 302, citing B. S. Weir, "DNA Match and Profile Probabilities: Comment on Budowle et al. (2000) and Fung and Hu (2000)," *Forensic Science Communications* 31, no. 1 (2001).

7. See B. Budowle, B. Shea, S. Niezgoda, and R. Chakraborty, "CODIS STR Loci Data from 41 Sample Populations," *Journal of Forensic Sciences* 46, no. 3 (2001): 453–489.

8. Jonathan Kahn, "Race, Genes, and Justice: A Call to Reform the Presentation of Forensic DNA Evidence in Criminal Trials," *Brooklyn Law Review* 74, no. 2 (2009): 325, 348.

9. Butler, *Interpretation*, 249, DNA Box 10.3 (describing history of terms like "Caucasian," "Hispanic," and "Latino," and noting that "Hispanic" was a category adopted by the government to denote persons of Spanish-speaking descent in Europe and the Western Hemisphere).

10. Kahn, "Race, Genes, and Justice," 325, 348.

11. L. A. Foreman and I. W. Weir, "Statistical Analyses to Support Forensic Interpretation for a New Ten-Locus STR Profiling System," *International Journal of Legal Medicine* 114, no. 3 (2001): 147–155.

12. John M. Butler, "Mixture Interpretation" (presentation to NYC OCME, New York, New York, March 25, 2009).

13. John M. Butler, "What We Have Learned & Where We Need to Go" (presentation at NIJ Conference Mixture Workshop, Boston University, Boston, Massachusetts, June 20, 2012).

14. Andy Furillo, "California Crime Lab Overseers Split," *Sacramento Bee*, June 18, 2010, http://www.mcclatchydc.com/2010/06/18/96147/california-crime-lab-overseers.html#storylink=cpy.

15. John M. Butler, "Introduction to Interpretation: Statistical Approaches and Assumptions" (presentation at the International Symposium on Human Identification, Nashville, Tennessee, October 15, 2012), http://www.cstl.nist.gov/strbase/training/MixtureWebcast/2_InterpretationFundamentals-Butler.pdf.

16. This method simply takes all the genetic information present and contemplates every possible combination of alleles. For instance, if a locus shows an 11, 12, and 17, it imagines four different homozygotic individuals (with 11, 11; 12, 12; and 17, 17), as well as every other combination (11, 12; 11,

17; 12, 17; etc.). The frequency for that locus is the sum of all these possible individual frequencies, which in turn can be multiplied against the same calculation when done for every other locus. (It does not require the analyst to make any assumptions about the number of contributors or the demographic group to which they belong, but cannot work if contributors are related, because then the probability of observing similar profiles would change dramatically.)

17. Mixtures exacerbate these concerns for two reasons. First, the more people who contribute their DNA to a single stain, the less total amount of DNA per person, and the more opportunities for such distortions to occur. Second, when multiple DNA profiles are combined, the more likely it is that there will be coincidental overlap at some alleles. As a result, alleles can mask one another, or stack to form peaks that might mislead an analyst into believing that genetic material derived from one person, when in fact it came from many. For instance, what at first glance appears explainable as stutter—a predictable artifact—may on closer examination turn out to be actual genetic material from one contributor. Accordingly, many labs ignore a problematic locus or conflicting allele, so long as they can provide a logical explanation for it and calculate the match probability from the remaining available information. Suppose the crime scene sample produces alleles of 11, 17, and 21 at a locus and the suspect is an 11, 14. Analysts may simply drop that locus from their calculations. Analysts may view this approach as "conservative," because losing one piece of the profile diminishes the overall match probability, but in fact that is not the case. John Butler, *Interpretation*, 335–338.

18. James M. Curran and John Buckleton, "Inclusion Probabilities and Dropout," *Journal of Forensic Sciences* 55 (2010): 1171–1173.

19. Peter Gill et al., "DNA Commission of the International Society of Forensic Genetics: Recommendations on the Interpretation of Mixtures," *Forensic Science International* 160 (2006): 90–101.

20. Peter Gill et al., "DNA Commission of the International Society of Forensic Genetics: Recommendations on the Evaluation of STR Typing Results That May Include Drop-out and/or Drop-in Using Probabilistic Methods," *Forensic Science International: Genetics* 6 (2012): 679–688.

21. John Butler, *Interpretation*, 319 (quoting SWGDAM (2014); *Frequently Asked Questions (FAQs)*, http://swgdam.org/faq.html.

22. Michael D. Coble, "NIST Inter-Laboratory Studies for DNA Mixture Interpretation" (presentation at 66th Annual AAFS Meeting, Seattle, Washington, February 20, 2014), http://www.nist.gov/forensics/upload/coble.pdf.

23. John M. Butler and Margaret C. Kline, NIST Mixture Interpretation Interlaboratory Study 2005 (MIX05) (poster presentation at International Symposium on Human Identification, Grapevine, Texas, September 26–28, 2005).

24. Ibid.

25. For instance, 30 percent of the labs calculated the statistical match probabilities of one sample by using the CPI method, yet did not all arrive at the same number. Their statistics ranged from 1 in 3,070 to 1 in 862,000, with a median of 1 in 14,380. In contrast, 56 percent of labs used a modified RMP calculation, and 14 percent expressed that in terms of a likelihood ratio. For those labs, the statistical significance ranged from 1 in 358,000 to 1 in 412 quintillion, with a median of 1 in 2.58 quadrillion. Ibid.

26. For an interesting collection of such images, see Alexis C. Madrigal, "Things You Cannot Unsee (and What They Say About Your Brain)," *Atlantic*, May 5, 2014, http://www.theatlantic.com/technology/archive/2014/05/10-things-you-cant-unsee-and-what-that-says-about-your-brain/361335/.

27. Traditional statistical calculations followed a binary mode of interpretation—that either an observed allele counted or it didn't—based on the application of a lab's interpretive guidelines. Thus, genetic material that appeared in the results but fell below a certain threshold of reliability was ignored as though it did not exist. The logic of this approach is that it refused to credit information that had indicia of unreliability, whether to the benefit or detriment of a particular defendant. The new statistical programs, however, follow a continuous model of interpretation: these consider all the information in the test results, even those of questionable reliability. This model further subdivides into semicontinuous and fully continuous methods. Semicontinuous interpretation counts any present allele without regard to its precise characteristics; whereas fully continuous methods weigh the value of observed alleles on the basis of certain known parameters. For instance, an allele that is in a stutter position, or has a size in a particular ratio to another allele, is counted with those attributes in consideration. TrueAllele, STRmix, DNAView, and a program called DNAmixtures are examples of fully continuous models. Most others are semicontinuous; these include FST, LRmix, like-LTD, Lab Retriever, ArmedXpert, LiRa/LiRaHT, and GenoProof Mixture. Even these classifications may oversimplify; in fact, models can account for or ignore a wide array of factors. As the creators of Lab Retriever, an open-source, free software program, have highlighted, there is an enormous array of variables to potentially include when drafting the source code, such as information about peak heights, stutter

parameters, allele overlap, analytical thresholds, the number of contributors, the probability of dropout or drop-in, population substructure models, population frequencies, and the impact of close relatives. In this respect, no program is fully continuous across all variables, because all of the programs make choices about what to include versus ignore.

28. Todd W. Bille, Steven M. Weitz, Michael D. Coble, John Buckleton, and Jo-Anne Bright, "Comparison of the Performance of Different Models for the Interpretation of Low Level Mixed DNA Profiles," *Electrophoresis* 35 (2014): 3125–3133.

29. Lab Retriever was admitted after an admissibility hearing in a trial court in San Mateo, California, in 2010, and has also been used roughly a dozen times without a hearing. See Lab Retriever website, News tab, accessed May 17, 2015, http://scieg.org/News.html. TrueAllele has been admitted in California, Ohio, New York, Louisiana, Pennsylvania, and Virginia, but many of the cases were weakly contested. See the Cybergenetics website, Admissibility tab, accessed May 16, 2015, http://www.cybgen.com/Information /admissibility/page.shtml.

30. The team included Clint Hughes, Susan Friedman, Dan Ades, Karen Faraguna, and Susan Morris.

31. In his testimony, Dr. Chakraborty recounted the story of how he developed the thirteen original CODIS loci, birthing a "ten billion dollar industry" in kits and instrumentation. People v. Andrew Peaks and Jaquan Collins, Nos. 7689/2010 and 8077/2010, Frye hearing (Testimony of Ranajit Chakraborty), Supreme Court, Kings County, New York, December 16, 2013, 1082.

32. Witnesses also raised a number of more technical concerns, such as that the program's use of dropout rates did not sufficiently account for possible dependence those rates, the validation testing had troubling absences in the underlying data that were unexplained, and there were no data about tests to ensure that the FST did not erroneously identify suspects. (False positive testing checks the software to ensure that an actual contributor, versus a random unknown contributor, returns the highest likelihood ratio.) People v. Andrew Peaks and Jaquan Collins, Nos. 7689/2010 and 8077/2010, Memorandum of Law in Support of Defendants' Motions to Preclude Admission of the OCME's LCN and FST Evidence at Trial, Supreme Court, Kings County, New York, April 14, 2014. Dr. Budowle testified that he guessed that the OCME had developed its low copy method with the expectation that it could simply use CPI to assign statistical weight, but that plan had suffered when it became clear that CPI methods could not work with low copy tests. He imagined the FST was an after-the-fact attempt to devise a way of calculating statistics for those samples, but it constituted an inadequate and nonsensical solution. People v. Andrew Peaks and Jaquan Collins, Nos. 7689/2010 and 8077/2010, Frye hearing (Testimony of Bruce Budowle), Supreme Court, Kings County, New York, December 10, 2013, 925–926.

33. Chakraborty testimony, December 16, 2013, 1103–1106.

34. New York State Bar Association, http://www.nysba.org/Sections/Criminal_Justice/Awards/The _Michele_S_Maxian_Award_for_Outstanding_Public_Defense_Practitioner.html.

35. The ruling in the Collins case joined another opinion from a federal court in New Mexico that had found low copy number testing not yet sufficiently reliable for presentation in court. United States v. McCluskey, 954 F. Supp.2d 1224 (D. N.M. 2013). But some other trial courts in New York have not been as careful. In the case of *People v. Rodriguez*, the judge seemed to assume that the only issue was the use of a likelihood ratio to address concerns about dropout, rather than the way in which dropout rates were assessed. The court even criticized a defense witness who testified that the FST method was unreliable, on the grounds that the witness used likelihood ratios in her own work. People v. Rodriguez, Ind. No. 5471/2009, Decision and Order, Supreme Court, New York County, New York, May 1, 2012.

36. Robert Gavin, "Judge: Schenectady DNA Testimony Will Be Allowed," *Albany Times Union,* March 17, 2015. The *Albany Times Union* covered the case closely, including several reports on the TrueAllele hearings.

37. Robert Gavin, "DNA Technology Crucial in Murder Conviction of John Wakefield," *Albany Times Union,* March 20, 2015, http://www.timesunion.com/news/article/DNA-technology-crucial-in-murder -conviction-of-6149072.php; Robert Gavin, "DNA Expert Links Man to Schenectady Murder," *Albany Times Union,* March 17, 2015, http://www.timesunion.com/news/article/DNA-expert-links-man-to -Schenectady-murder-6141088.php.

38. State v. Wakefield, 2015 N.Y. Slip Op. 25037 (Supreme Court, Schenectady County, New York, February 9, 2015).

39. Robert Gavin, "Cybergenetics True Allele Casework DNA Study Is Winner in Cold Case Murder Conviction," *Albany Times Union,* March 31, 2015.

40. Brendan J. Lyons, "State Police Moves to Fire 15 Scientists in DNA Cheating Probe," *Albany Times Union,* April 22, 2015.

41. Hannah Kelly et al., "A Comparison of Statistical Models for the Analysis of Complex Forensic DNA Profiles," *Science and Justice* 54 (2014): 66.

42. Brendan J. Lyons, "Cheating Scandal Fouls State Police Test," *Albany Times Union*, January 17, 2015.

43. Brendan J. Lyons, "Scientists Suspended as State Police DNA Scandal Deepens," *Albany Times Union*, April 12, 2015.

44. Gill et al., "Recommendations on the Evaluation of STR Typing Results," 679–688.

45. Ibid.

46. L. Prieto et al., "Euroforgen-NoE Collaborative Exercise on LRmix to Demonstrate Standardization of the Interpretation of Complex DNA Profiles," *Forensic Science International: Genetics* 9 (2014): 47–54.

47. "Detenido tras confesar que mató a su pareja embarazada y arrojó el cadaver a un muladar," ABC .es, October 24, 2013, http://www.abc.es/local-castilla-mancha/20131024/abci-detenido-matar-pareja -cifuentes-201310241412.html.

48. Christopher D. Steele et al., "Verifying Likelihoods for Low Template DNA Profiles Using Multiple Replicates," *FSI: Genetics* 13 (November 2014): 82–89. Balding proposes that even noisy DNA results can be "more powerful than many traditional types of evidence, . . . as long as its strength is not overstated." David Balding, "Evaluation of Mixed-Source, Low-Template DNA Profiles in Forensic Science," *PNAS* 110, no. 13 (July 23, 2013): 122–141. The problem is, there is no reason to have such confidence in the ability of the criminal justice system to use DNA modestly and accurately; history suggests quite the opposite.

49. Hannah Kelly et al., "Comparison of Statistical Models."

CHAPTER 7

1. Transcript from In the Matter of the Application of the State of California for an Order, Cause No. MISC-001, Superior Court, Maricopa County, October 17, 2005 (J. James H. Keppel), 21–23.

2. Arizona criminalists, including Troyer herself, testified that some of the initial documents reporting her findings contained inaccurate estimates, but the corrections still placed the figures in astronomical terms. Ibid.

3. Erin Murphy, "The New Forensics: Criminal Justice, False Certainty, and the Second Generation of Scientific Evidence," *California Law Review* 95 (2007): 721, 782, and 262n.

4. Edward Ungvarsky, "What Does One in a Trillion Mean?" *GeneWatch* 20 (2007): 10–14. http:// www.wispd.org/attachments/article/244/What%20does%20One%20in%20a%20Trillion%20Mean .pdf.

5. Jason Felch and Maura Dolan, "FBI Resists Scrutiny of 'Matches,'" *L.A. Times*, July 20, 2008, http:// articles.latimes.com/2008/jul/20/local/me-dna20/2. Dr. Bieber also testified he had seen a ten-locus match, but it was the result of incest (the father was also an older brother).

6. Kathryn Troyer, Theresa Gilboy, and Brian Koeneman, "A Nine STR Locus Match Between Two Apparently Unrelated Individuals Using AmpF/STR Profiler Plus and Cofiler" (presented at International Symposium on Human Identification, 2001).

7. Erin Murphy, "The New Forensics: Criminal Justice, False Certainty, and the Second Generation of Scientific Evidence," *California Law Review* 95 (2007): 721.

8. Arizona Department of Public Safety, "9+ Locus Match Summary Report*," November 2, 2005.

9. Felch and Dolan, "FBI Resists Scrutiny."

10. Ibid.

11. Erin E. Murphy, "Databases, Doctrine and the Future of Constitutional Criminal Procedure," *Fordham Urban Law Journal* 37 (2010): 803. Fingerprints were first searched by computer as early as 1980, but that method was less sophisticated and efficient. http://www.fbi.gov/about-us/cjis/fingerprints _biometrics/iafis/iafis.

12. This is distinct from what is commonly called a keyboard search, which is a direct search against a database for a particular profile.

13. For a list of cases, see Andrea Roth, "Safety in Numbers? Deciding When DNA Alone Is Enough to Convict," *New York University Law Review*, 85 (2010): 1142–1144.

14. D. E. Krane et al., "Time for DNA Disclosure," *Science* 326, no. 5960 (December 17, 2009): 1631. I joined as a signatory to this letter.

15. Laurence D. Mueller, "Can Simple Population Genetic Models Reconcile Partial Match Frequencies Observed in Large Forensic Databases?" *Journal of Genetics* 87, no. 2 (2008): 101–108.

16. B. Budowle, F. S. Baechtel, and R. Chakraborty, "Partial Matches in Heterogeneous Offender Databases Do Not Call into Question the Validity of Random Match Probability Calculations," *International Journal of Legal Medicine* 123 (2009): 59–63.

17. Mueller, "Can Simple Population Genetic Models?"

18. Sarah M. Ruby, "Checking the Math: Government Secrecy and DNA Databases," *I/S: Journal of Law and Policy for the Information Society* 6 (2010): 259.

19. National Research Council, *The Evaluation of Forensic DNA Evidence* (Washington, DC: National Academy Press, 1996), 40, 134; FBI DNA Advisory Board, "Statistical and Population Genetics Issues Affecting the Evaluation of the Frequency of Occurrence of DNA Profiles Calculated from Pertinent Population Database(s)," Forensic Science Commission, February 23, 2000, http:// www.fbi.gov/hq/lab /fsc/backissu/july2000/dnastat.htm.

20. Roth, "Safety in Numbers?" 1179–1182; David H. Kaye, "Rounding Up the Usual Suspects: A Legal and Logical Analysis of DNA Trawling Cases," *North Carolina Law Review* 87 (2009): 425. Actually there is also a fourth approach, which would require corroborative testing of other loci. Ibid., 438, citing National Research Council, *DNA Technology in Forensic Science* (Washington, DC: National Academy Press, 1992), 124.

21. David J. Balding and Peter Donnelly, "Evaluating DNA Profile Evidence When the Suspect Is Identified Through a Database Search," *Journal of Forensic Science* 41 (1996): 603.

22. Kaye, "Rounding Up," 491–492.

23. David H. Kaye, "Case Comment—*People v. Nelson*: A Tale of Two Statistics," *Law Probability & Risk* 7 (2008): 256.

24. Roth, "Safety in Numbers?" 1179. This figure assumes a match probability of 1 in 1.1 million in a population of 2 million suspects (the rough-male, age-appropriate population in San Francisco at that time). Although some might be inclined to count Puckett as one of those two, and thus assume only one other match, one can explain two possible matches by noting that the rarity of a profile is independent of the fact that the profile has been observed. To use an example devised by Dr. Laurence Mueller, if you were asked the probability of a "heads" landing from ten coin flips, you would say 5 out of 10. If your first four flips land heads, and you were again asked the probability of a "heads" landing from the remaining six flips, you would not say 1 (sticking to your 5 out of 10, subtracting the four that happened). You would say 3 (half of the remaining six). That is because your observation (of the first four flips) does not affect the probability of observing the target (heads) in the remaining population, since those observations are independent of the first observation.

25. D. R. Hares, "Expanding the CODIS Core Loci in the United States," *Forensic Science International: Genetics* 6(1) (2012): e52–e54; D. R. Hares, "Addendum to Expanding the CODIS Core Loci in the United States," *Forensic Science International: Genetics*, 6, no. 5 (2012): e135.

26. ENFSI DNA Working Group, *DNA-Database Management: Review and Recommendations*, April 2014, http://www.enfsi.eu/sites/default/files/documents/enfsi_2014_document_on_dna-database _management_0.pdf.

27. Ibid. The presence of a significant number of relatives further exacerbates the likelihood of coincidental matches in large datasets.

28. Ibid., 87.

29. William C. Thompson, "The Myth of Infallibility," in *Genetic Explanations: Sense and Nonsense*, ed. Sheldon Krimsky and Jeremy Gruber (Cambridge, MA: Harvard University Press, 2013), 245.

30. Rebecca Fowler, "DNA, the Second Revolution," *The Guardian* (UK), April 26, 2003, http://www .theguardian.com/uk/2003/apr/27/ukcrime7.

31. Annie Sweeney and Frank Main, "Botched DNA Report Falsely Implicates Woman: Case Compels State to Change How It Reports Lab Findings," *Chicago Sun-Times*, November 8, 2004.

32. Thompson, "Myth of Infallibility," 245; Elizabeth Gibson, "Retest of DNA Clears Defendant of Charges," *Columbus Dispatch*, June 3, 2010, 01B.

33. William C. Thompson, "Tarnish on the 'Gold Standard': Understanding Recent Problems in Forensic DNA Testing," *The Champion*, January/February 2006, 9, 10, 13–14, 25, 28–29.

34. Appellant's Opening Brief, People v. Puckett, No. A121368 (First Appellate District, California Court of Appeal), 28.

35. Ibid.

36. Leila Schneps and Coralie Colmez, *Math on Trial: How Numbers Get Used and Abused in the Courtroom* (New York: Basic Books, 2013).

37. Kaye, "Rounding Up," 430–432 (summarizing cases of Jenkins, Nelson, and Johnson).

38. People v. Johnson, 43 Cal. Rptr.3d 587, 597 (Ca. Ct. App. 2006).

39. Kaye, "Rounding Up," 446.

40. Ibid., 452.

41. Roth, "Safety in Numbers?" 1144.

CHAPTER 8

1. David Millward, "Baby on Board Stickers 'Cause One in 20 Accidents,'" *The Telegraph*, October 11, 2012, http://www.telegraph.co.uk/motoring/news/9599881/Baby-on-board-stickers-cause-one-in-20 -accidents.html.

2. David H. Kaye, "Trawling DNA Databases for Partial Matches: What Is the FBI Afraid Of?" *Cornell Journal of Law and Public Policy* 19 (2009): 145, 157n69.

3. United States v. Trala, 162 F.Supp.2d 336 (D. Del. 2001); United States v. Morrow, 374 F.Supp.2d 51 (D. D.C. 2005) ("The testimony indicates that if an analyst follows the FBI protocol and uses properly calibrated instruments, there is essentially zero rate of error, i.e., obtaining a wrong result, within established measurement conditions."); United States v. Ewell, 252 F.Supp.2d 104 (D. N.J. 2003).

4. See, for example, State v. Jones, 922 P.2d 806 n.1 (Wash. 1996) (en banc); State v. Proctor, 595 S.E.2d 476 (S.C. 2004). In Proctor, the defendant sought proficiency-test information about the lab's DNA unit. In response, the lab produced an affidavit claiming analysts had "never made an incorrect 'match'"— essentially, a zero error rate. The defendant sought to probe that assertion, but the trial court denied further inquiry and the appellate court—while finding that denial, an error—upheld it as having not impeded the defendant's right to a fair trial. See generally J. J. Koehler, "On Conveying the Probative Value of DNA Evidence: Frequencies, Likelihood Ratios, and Error Rates," *University of Colorado Law Review* 67 (1996): 870n28.

5. William C. Thompson, "Tarnish on the 'Gold Standard': Understanding Recent Problems in Forensic DNA Testing," *The Champion*, January/February 2006, 10, 15.

6. Peter Gill, *Misleading DNA Evidence: Reasons for Miscarriages of Justice* (Oxford, UK: Academic Press, 2014), 59.

7. United States v. Trala, 162 F.Supp.2d 336 (D. Del. 2001); United States v. Ewell, 252 F.Supp.2d 104 (D. N.J. 2003); Roberts v. United States, 916 A.2d 922 (D.C. Ct. App. 2007); United States v. Lowe, 954 F. Supp. 401 (D. Mass. 1996). State v. Tester, 968 A.2d 895 (Vt. 2009).

8. See, for example, United States v. Beasley, 102 F.3d 1440 (8th Cir. 1996).

9. National Research Council, *The Evaluation of Forensic DNA Evidence* (Washington, DC: National Academy Press, 1996), 86.

10. Ibid. The report pointed out that a defendant can retest if there is a fear of error. But, of course, if early contamination occurred, or if the sample is too depleted, then retesting provides no remedy.

11. J. J. Koehler, "Matches and Statistics: Important Questions, Surprising Answers," *Judicature* 76, no. 5 (February–March 1993): 222.

12. For example, Roberts, 916 A.2d at 931.

13. United States v. Ewell, 252 F.Supp.2d 104 (D. N.J. 2003).

14. Some courts have even suggested that this constitutes inadmissible propensity evidence. But questions intended to probe the reliability of the expert's opinion and the expert's credibility are different in kind from the use of character evidence to suggest behavior in conformity therewith. First, the concern with typical character is that it is ancillary to credibility, and potentially distracting or inflammatory. But negligence or misconduct associated with an expert, in the context of exercises of that expertise, is central to questions regarding both the expert's believability and reliability. For general discussion of this issue, see George L. Blum, "Propriety of Questioning Expert Witness Regarding Specific Incidents or Allegations of Expert's Unprofessional Conduct or Professional Negligence," *American Law Reports*, 5th ed. 11 (2015).

15. Office of the Inspector General, State of New York, *Investigation into the Nassau County Police Department Forensic Evidence Bureau* (November 2011) 5, 133.

16. McDaniel v. Brown, 555 U.S. 1152 (2009).

17. Joint Appendix, Vol. II, McDaniel v. Brown, No. 08–559, 2009 WL 1229026 (May 1, 2009), 458.

18. Ibid. The transcript records Ms. Romero as saying 99.99967, but the exhibits and subsequent testimony suggest she actually said 99.999967.

19. Ibid., 460–461.

20. Ibid., 462.

21. Ibid.

22. Ibid., 730.

23. In fact, estimates suggest that 1 in 12 adults suffer from asthma; it is unclear how many regularly carry an inhaler.

24. Brief of 20 Scholars of Forensic Evidence as Amicus Curiae Supporting Respondents, McDaniel v. Brown, No. 08–559, 2009 WL 2247124, July 24, 2009, 3.

25. Joint Appendix, McDaniel v. Brown, 472. If the chances of a match were 1 in 6,500, then the probability of a match would be 0.015 percent, rather than 0.02 percent. This appears to have either been a small computational error of no significance or an instance of rounding off.

26. Ibid.

27. David H. Kaye and George F. Sensabaugh Jr., Federal Judicial Center, *Reference Guide on DNA Evidence, in Reference Manual on Scientific Evidence*, 2nd ed. (2000), 485, 539, http://www.fjc.gov/public/pdf.nsf/lookup/sciman00.pdf/$file/sciman00.pdf.

28. National Research Council, *Evaluation*, 133.

29. Nuffield Council on Bioethics, *The Forensic Use of Bioinformation: Ethical Issues* (2007): 68–72, available at http://www.nuffieldbioethics.org/ go/ourwork/bioinformationuse/publication_441.html.

30. William C. Thompson and Edward L. Schumann, "Interpretation of Statistical Evidence in Criminal Trials: The Prosecutor's Fallacy and the Defense Attorney's Fallacy," *Law and Human Behavior* 11, no. 3 (1987): 167. Some experts prefer to call this error the "fallacy of the transposed conditional," because it arises from transposing two conditional probabilities. The random match probability represents the conditional probability of a match *if* the person being tested is not the source; the source probability is the conditional probability that a person is the source *if* the person matches; see, for example, Ian W. Evett and Bruce S. Weir, *Interpreting DNA Evidence: Statistical Genetics for Forensic Scientists* (Sunderland, MA: Sinauer Associates, 1998), 30–32, 227.

31. National Research Council Committee on Identifying the Needs of the Forensic Science Community, *Strengthening Forensic Science in the United States: A Path Forward* (Washington, DC: National Academies Press, 2009), 21–22.

32. Andrea Roth, "Safety in Numbers? Deciding When DNA Alone Is Enough to Convict," *New York University Law Review* 85 (2010): 1151.

33. Ibid., 1152–1153.

34. Ibid.

35. Devlin's Angle, *Damned Lies* (blog), October 2006, https://www.maa.org/external_archive/devlin/devlin_10_06.html.

36. National Research Council, *Evaluation*, 194–202. For an explanation of this approach, see Keith Inman and Norah Rudin, *Principles and Practices of Criminalistics: The Profession of Forensic Science* (Boca Raton, FL: CRC Press, 2001); William C. Thompson and Simon A. Cole, "Psychological Aspects of Forensic Identification Evidence," in *Expert Psychological Testimony for the Courts*, ed. Mark Costanzo et al. (London, UK: Psychology Press, 2006), 31, 44–46.

37. John M. Butler, *Advanced Topics in Forensic DNA Typing: Interpretation* (Oxford, UK: Academic Press, 2014), 282, 297.

38. Testimony of this kind, known as individualization testimony, is controversial because it requires drawing an arbitrary line for how low the random match probability must be for the probability of finding another matching profile to be deemed effectively zero. Ibid., 298–300.

39. Ibid., 299.

40. Charles R. Nesson, "Reasonable Doubt and Permissive Inferences: The Value of Complexity," *Harvard Law Review* 92 (1979): 1187, 1192–1193; see also Laurence H. Tribe, "Trial by Mathematics: Precision and Ritual in the Legal Process," *Harvard Law Review* 84 (1971): 1329, 1372.

41. Leila Schneps and Coralie Colmez, *Math on Trial: How Numbers Get Used and Abused in the Courtroom* (New York: Basic Books, 2013), 101.

42. Ibid., 105.

43. Thomas Bayes, "An Essay Towards Solving a Problem in the Doctrine of Chances," *Philosophical Transactions of the Royal Society of London* 53 (1763): 370–418. For discussions about the application of Bayes's theorem in a legal context, see Tribe, "Trial by Mathematics"; Richard Lempert, "Modeling Relevance," *Michigan Law Review* 75 (1976–1977), 1021. In a typical case, jurors would attempt to quantify the prior probability—the probability that the defendant is guilty, based on all evidence other than the DNA match. Then the prior probability is multiplied by a likelihood ratio, typically the inverse of the RMP because it is the prosecutor's theory (that the defendant is the source, or "1") over the probability the match is just by chance.

44. Roth, "Safety in Numbers?" 1156. Studies consistently show that the form used to present probabilistic evidence affects verdicts. See, for example, Nicholas Scurich and Richard S. John, "Mock Jurors' Use of Error Rates in DNA Database Trawls," *Law and Human Behavior* 37, no. 6 (2013): 424–431.

45. Roth, "Safety in Numbers?" 1157.

CHAPTER 9

1. FBI Laboratory, National DNA Index System (NDIS) Operational Procedures Manual, Version 3, Effective January 1, 2015, 4.

2. See audit reports, collected at http://www.justice.gov/oig/reports/codis-ext.htm.

3. US Department of Justice, Office of the Inspector General, Audit Division, Audit of Compliance with Standards Governing Combined DNA System Activities at the Bexar County Criminal Investigation Laboratory, San Antonio, Texas, Audit Report GR-60–11–004 (November 2010).

4. Arkansas State Crime Lab in Little Rock, 2001 Audit; June 2009 audit of Tennessee Bureau of Investigation in Knoxville.

5. Federal Bureau of Investigation, Laboratory Services, CODIS Brochure, http://www.fbi.gov/about-us/lab/biometric-analysis/codis/codis_brochure.

6. Peter Jamison, "Secret Court Transcript Reveals Concerns About 'Deliberate Attempt' to Mislead Crime Lab Auditors," *San Francisco Weekly*, November 28, 2011, http://www.sfweekly.com/thesnitch/2011/11/28/secret-court-transcript-reveals-concerns-about-deliberate-attempt-to-mislead-crime-lab-auditors; Bicka Barlow, e-mail message to author, April 2, 2015.

7. Ibid.

8. Excerpt from Harmon memo, 6 (on file with author).

9. Transcript of People v. Mayfield, Reporter's Confidential Transcript on Appeal, No. 2429916 (Court of Appeal for the State of California, 1st App. Dist., September 21, 2011), 18.

10. Ibid., 9–10.

11. The hearing was held at attorney Barlow's request for disclosure of the memo in connection with another cold hit homicide in which Boland had conducted the testing. "Prosecutor Wants DNA Lab Memo Released," September 15, 2011, http://abclocal.go.com/story?section=news/local/san_francisco&id=8356294.

12. Transcript of People v. Mayfield, Reporter's Confidential Transcript on Appeal, No. 2429916 (Court of Appeal for the State of California, 1st App. Dist., September 21, 2011), 20.

13. Gerry Shih, "Pressure Mounts on Gascon to Release Crime Lab Memo," *Bay Citizen*, September 27, 2011, https://www.baycitizen.org/news/politics/pressure-mounts-gascon-release-crime-lab/?page=2; Ari Burack, "San Francisco Police, DNA Lab Slammed in Released Transcript," *San Francisco Examiner*, November 30, 2011, http://www.sfexaminer.com/sanfrancisco/san-francisco-police-dna-lab-slammed-in-released-transcript/Content?oid=2187143.

14. Transcript of jury trial proceedings in People v. Marco A. Hernandez, Court No. 12015380, December 31, 2014 (Superior Court, San Francisco, J. Angela M. Bradstreet), 46–47.

15. Ibid., 47.

16. Ibid., 49.

17. Transcript, January 8, 2015, 9.

18. Letter from Bicka Barlow to Greg Suhr, chief of police, "Re: Allegations of Serious Misconduct in the San Francisco Police Department Laboratory and the Paul Coverdell Forensic Sciences Improvement Grant Program," March 6, 2015.

19. Ibid.

20. Ibid.

21. Transcript of jury trial proceedings in People v. Marco A. Hernandez, Court No. 12015380, December 31, 2014 (Superior Court, San Francisco, J. Angela M. Bradstreet), 58, 75.

22. Letter from Bicka Barlow to Greg Suhr, chief of police, San Francisco Police Department, March 6, 2015.

23. Jaxon Van Derbeken, "Technician, Boss in SFPD Lab Scandal Flunked DNA Skills Exam," *San Francisco Chronicle*, March 31, 2015; Jaxon Van Derbeken, "DNA Lab Irregularities May Endanger SFPD Cases," *San Francisco Chronicle*, March 28, 2015, http://www.sfchronicle.com/crime/article/DNA-lab-irregularities-may-endanger-hundreds-of-6165643.php.

24. Memo from Eleanor Salmon, DNA technical leader, to John Sanchez, crime lab manager/QA manager, September 10, 2014 (on file with author).

25. Van Derbeken, "Technician, Boss."

26. Transcript of deposition of Susanne Brenneke, State v. Cecil McBenge, 11th Judicial Circuit Court of St. Charles County, Missouri, January 29, 2014, 89–92.

27. In the McBenge case, the problem again was a low-quality sample. Testing produced raw data with missing and questionably reliable portions. Because no single profile emerged clearly, the analyst instead experimented with different options, including through a "keyboard search"—a search that directly queries the database—as opposed to uploading a sample and then letting the system conduct its usual twice-weekly automatic search.

28. Transcript of deposition of Susanne Brenneke, State v. Cecil McBenge, 11th Judicial Circuit Court of St. Charles County, Missouri, January 29, 2014, 133–136.

29. 42 U.S.C. § 14132(b)(3).

30. FBI Laboratory, National DNA Index System (NDIS) Operational Procedures Manual, Version 3, Effective January 1, 2015, Part 6.6.1, 54.

31. Mont. Code Ann. § 44–6-106.

32. FBI Laboratory, NDIS Operational Procedures Manual, Part 3.2.3, 29.

33. Transcript of jury trial proceedings in People v. Marco A. Hernandez, Court No. 12015380, December 31, 2014 (Superior Court, San Francisco, J. Angela M. Bradstreet), 49.

34. People v. Douglas Brown, NA 036413, Superior Court of California, County of Los Angeles, Motion to Quash Subpoena Duces Tecum, November 21, 2002.

35. People v. Brown, 2004 WL 2958271 (Ca. Ct. App. 2004) (unpublished opinion).

36. People v. Douglas Brown, NA 036413, Superior Court of California, County of Los Angeles, Motion to Quash Subpoena Duces Tecum, November 21, 2002, 8.

37. Jason Kreag, "Letting Innocence Suffer: The Need for Defense Access to the Law Enforcement DNA Database," *Cardozo Law Review* 36:805, 822.

38. Rivera v. Mueller, 596 F.Supp.2d 1163 (N.D. Ill. 2009).

39. See 725 Ill. Comp. State. Ann. 5/116–5; Md. Code Ann. § 2–508(b); McKinney's N.Y. Crim. Proc. Law § 240.40(1)(c).

40. All states now grant courts explicit authority to order DNA testing in a case postconviction, to see whether the evidence matches the convicted person. But fewer states also explicitly authorize the court to order the government to conduct a database search of an unknown profile found in the evidence. See Colo. Rev. Stat. Ann. § 18–1–412(9); Ga. Code Ann. § 5–5–41(9); Miss. Code Ann. § 99–39–11(10); N.Y. C. P. L. § 440.30.1-a(c); N.C. Gen. Stat. Ann. § 15A-269 Ohio Rev. Code Ann. § 2953.74(E); Tex. Code. Crim. Proc. Ann. art. 64.035.

41. People v. Harvey Wright, 971 N.E.2d 549 (App. Ct. Ill. 2012).

CHAPTER 10

1. Brief for the Respondent Maryland v. King, No. 12–207, 2013 WL 315233, 9 (January 25, 2013); Harry Jaffe, "Truth and Consequences," *Washingtonian*, April 30, 2013, http://www.washingtonian.com /articles/people/truth-and-consequences/.

2. Ibid.; Brief for Respondent, Maryland v. King, 8n6 (citing North Carolina v. Alford, 400 U.S. 25 [1970], which permits a plea without admission of guilt).

3. Md. Code Ann., Pub. Safety § 2–504 (West 2015).

4. Ibid.

5. Opening Brief, Haskell v. Brown, No.10-15152, 2010 WL 767028 (9th Cir. 2010).

6. Haskell v. Harris, 669 F.3d 1049 (9th Cir. 2012).

7. Brief for Respondent, 9n2.

8. Jaffe, "Truth and Consequences."

9. Brief for the Respondent, Maryland v. King, 9–10.

10. King v. Maryland, 425 Md. 500, 594 (2012).

11. Maryland v. King, 133 S. Ct. 1, 2–3 (July 30, 2012); Order, Haskell v. Harris, D.C. No. 3:09–cv–04779–CRB (9th Cir. en banc November 13, 2012).

12. Other constitutional provisions might conceivably come into play, such as the Equal Protection Clause, the Fifth Amendment (although that typically applies only to testimonial evidence), or even some

idea of substantive due process. But given that the Fourth Amendment most directly restricts the policing power, it provides the likeliest source of restraint.

13. National Conference of State Legislatures, *Convicted Offenders Required to Submit DNA Samples* (2013), http://www.ncsl.org/Documents/cj/ConvictedOffendersDNALaws.pdf.

14. West's Louisiana Rev. Stat. Ann. §§ 15: 609, 603 (2014). Section 609 requires DNA sample for adults or juveniles arrested of "a felony or other specified offense." Section 603 lists "other specified offenses" as including battery of a school teacher, battery of a recreation athletic contest official, simple battery, and simple assault.

15. N.Y. Exec. Law § 995 (McKinney 2015); Wis. Stat. Ann. § 165.76 (West 2015) (mandating misdemeanor collection as of April 1, 2016).

16. Julie Samuels, Allison Dwyer, Robin Halberstadt, and Pamela Lachman, *Collecting DNA From Juveniles* (Urban Institute 2012), at http://www.urban.org/research/publication/collecting-dna-juveniles.

17. Transcript of Oral Argument, Maryland v. King, 133 S. Ct. 1958 (2013), No. 12–207, 34.

18. Maryland v. King, 133 S. Ct. 1958 (2013).

19. "Integrated Automated Fingerprint Identification System," Federal Bureau of Investigation, accessed May 16, 2015, http://www.fbi.gov/about-us/cjis/fingerprints_biometrics/iafis.

20. Federal Bureau of Investigation, *Monthly Fact Sheet* (March 2015), http://www.fbi.gov/about-us/cjis/fingerprints_biometrics/ngi/next-generation-identification-monthly-fact-sheet.

21. "Integrated Automated Fingerprint Identification System: Five Key Services," http://www.fbi.gov/about-us/cjis/fingerprints_biometrics/iafis/ngi_services.

22. "NIJ Award Detail: Methods for Obtaining STR Quality Touch DNA from Archived Fingerprints," Office of Justice Programs, accessed March 16, 2015, http://nij.gov/funding/awards/pages/award-detail.aspx?award=2014-DN-BX-K013.

23. National Conference of State Legislatures, *DNA Arrestee Laws*, accessed May 16, 2015, http://www.ncsl.org/Documents/cj/ArresteeDNALaws.pdf. That chart does not show Mississippi's or Rhode Island's laws, enacted in 2014. It also wrongly lists Oklahoma, Minnesota, and Vermont as allowing arrestee DNA sampling.

24. Katie Sepich Enhanced DNA Collection Act of 2012, Pub. L. No. 112-253, 126 Stat. 2407.

25. "Police Making Arrests 'Just to Gather DNA Samples,'" BBC News, November 24, 2009, http://news.bbc.co.uk/2/hi/uk_news/8375567.stm.

26. David N. Kelley and Sharon L. McCarthy, "The Report of the Crime Reporting Review Committee to Commissioner Raymond W. Kelly Concerning Compstat Auditing" (April 8, 2013), 42–43; Joseph Goldstein, "Audit of City Crime Statistics Finds Mistakes by Police," *New York Times*, July 2, 2013, http://www.nytimes.com/interactive/2013/07/03/nyregion/03crime-doc.html?ref=nyregion.

27. Office of Chief Medical Examiner, *OCME DNA Expungement Guidelines*, February 11, 2005 (noting that, when it receives court order of expungement, it "will implement only the particular action ordered by the court").

28. "Stop-and-Frisk Campaign: About the Issue," NY ACLU, accessed May 16, 2015, http://www.nyclu.org/issues/racial-justice/stop-and-frisk-practices.

29. Lynn Langton and Matthew Durose, *Police Behavior During Traffic and Street Stops, 2011*, Special Report (September 2013), http://www.bjs.gov/content/pub/pdf/pbtss11.pdf.

30. Shane Bauer, "The FBI Is Very Excited About This Machine That Scans Your DNA in 90 Minutes," *Mother Jones*, November 20, 2014, http://www.motherjones.com/politics/2014/11/rapid-dna-profiles-database-fbi-police.

31. Stevan Jovanovich et al., "Developmental Validation of a Fully Integrated Sample-to-Profile Rapid Human Identification System for Processing Single-Source Reference Buccal Samples," *Forensic Science International: Genetics* 16 (May 2015): 181–194.

32. Sean Allocca, "First Ever Rapid-DNA Profile Uploaded to NDIS," *Forensic Magazine*, May 7, 2015.

33. "Board of Directors," IntegenX, accessed August 14, 2014, http://integenx.com/board-of-directors/ (listing Joseph DiZinno and Louis Grever). DiZinno left IntegenX in 2014 to assume a senior role at American Systems, which provides identity intelligence services to the government.

34. Bauer, "The FBI Is Very Excited."

35. "Integrated Automated Fingerprint Identification System," http://www.fbi.gov/about-us/cjis/fingerprints_biometrics/iafis/iafis.

36. Jennifer Lynch, "FBI Plans to Have 52 Million Photos in its NGI Face Recognition Database by Next Year," Electronic Frontier Foundation, accessed May 16, 2015, https://www.eff.org/deeplinks/2014/04/fbi-plans-have-52-million-photos-its-ngi-face-recognition-database-next-year.

37. US Department of Justice, Federal Bureau of Investigation, "A Vision for DNA in the Booking Environment," Solicitation No. 1000, September 19, 2014, https://www.fbo.gov/?s=opportunity&mode=form&id=d9e73d3fcceb31671808af5a38be9da5&tab=core&_cview=0.

38. Elizabeth Jones and Wallace Wade, "'Spit and Acquit': Legal and Practical Ramifications of the DA's DNA Gathering Program," *Orange County Lawyer* 51 (September 2009): 18.

39. Yoohyun Jung, "TPD, Sheriff's Department Using 'Rapid DNA' Technology," *Arizona Daily Star*, March 20, 2015. The Richland County Sheriff's Department in Columbia, South Carolina, has also acquired a RapidHIT machine, which it uses for case work and known offender samples. *Validation and Incorporation of* RapidHIT *Technology into Routine Forensic DNA Casework*, http://www.keyforensic.co.uk/docs/WhitePaperRCApril15.pdf.

40. Stevan Jovanovich, *RapidHit Human Identification Systems*, http://biometrics.org/bc2012/presentations/DNA/Jovanovich.pdf.

41. Jovanovich et al., "Developmental Validation."

42. Haskell v. Harris, 745 F.3d 1269 (9th Cir. 2014).

43. State v. Medina, 102 A.3d 661 (Vt. 2014).

44. People v. Buza, 231 Cal. App. 4th 1446 (Ct. App. 1st Dist. Ca. 2014).

CHAPTER 11

1. Commonwealth v. Bly, 862 N.E.2d 341, 351–52 (Mass. 2007).

2. State v. Athan, 158 P.3d 27, 31 (Wash. 2007).

3. Amy Harmon, "Lawyers Fight DNA Samples Gained on Sly," *New York Times*, April 3, 2008, A1, http://www.nytimes.com/2008/04/03/science/03dna.html?pagewanted=all.

4. Ibid.

5. State v. Christian, No. 04–0900, 2006 WL 2419031, *1 (Iowa Ct. App. August 23, 2006).

6. People v. LaGuerre, 29 A.D.3d 820 (NY App. Div. 2006).

7. US v. Davis, 690 F.3d 226 (4th Cir. 2012).

8. Roy Wenzl, "When Your Father Is a Serial Killer, Forgiveness Is Not Tidy," *Wichita Eagle*, February 21, 2015, http://pubsys.kansas.com/static/BTK/index.html?Src=longreads.

9. Ellen Nakashima, "From DNA of Family, a Tool to Make Arrests," *Washington Post*, April 21, 2008, http://www.washingtonpost.com/wp-dyn/content/article/2008/04/20/AR2008042002388.html.

10. See, for example, People v. Thomas, 132 Cal. Rptr.3d 714 (Ca. Ct. App. 2012) (burglary cases).

11. Elizabeth E. Joh, "Reclaiming 'Abandoned' DNA: The Fourth Amendment and Genetic Privacy," *Northwestern University Law Review* 100, no. 2 (2006): 857, quoting Victor Weedn.

12. 99 A.3d 753 (Md. 2014), certiorari denied by 135 S. Ct. 1509 (March 2, 2015).

13. Joh, "Reclaiming 'Abandoned' DNA,' 865. But see State v. Reed, 182 N.C. App. 109 (2007) (finding expectation of privacy in cigarette left in home's patio area). For a nice compilation of cases, see the website of the Denver district attorney, http://www.denverda.org/DNA/Surreptitious_Collection_and_Abandoned_DNA_Cases.htm. For a general overview of the Fourth Amendment in this area, see Albert E. Scherr, "Genetic Privacy & The Fourth Amendment: Unregulated Surreptitious DNA Harvesting," *Georgia Law Review* 47 (2013): 445.

14. Emily Ramshaw, "DSHS Turned Over Hundreds of DNA Samples to Feds," *Texas Tribune*, February 22, 2010, http://www.texastribune.org/2010/02/22/dshs-turned-over-hundreds-of-dna-samples-to-feds.

15. Azeen Ghorayshi, "Most Parents Don't Know Their Babies' Blood Is Given to Scientists—But That May Change," *BuzzFeed*, March 17, 2015, http://www.buzzfeed.com/azeenghorayshi/most-parents-dont-know-their-babys-blood-is-given-to-scienti#.vsrGz3q95.

16. Elizabeth E. Joh, "DNA Theft: Recognizing the Crime of Nonconsensual Genetic Collection and Testing," *Boston University Law Review* 91 (2011): 667.

17. Andrew Martin, "The Prosecution's Case Against DNA," *New York Times Magazine*, November 25, 2011, http://www.nytimes.com/2011/11/27/magazine/dna-evidence-lake-county.html?pagewanted=8.

18. Heather Dewey-Hagborg, *Stranger Visions*, accessed May 16, 2015, http://www.deweyhagborg.com/strangervisions/about.html.

19. Joh, "DNA Theft," 686.

20. When laws applicable also to the employment context are included, the number rises to thirty-three. See Joh, "DNA Theft," 668n11.

21. Joh, "DNA Theft," 688–689.

22. New Museum Store, accessed May 16, 2015, http://www.newmuseumstore.org/browse.cfm/invisible/4,6471.html.

23. Complaint, Kohler v. Englade, No. CV03-857-D-M2, M. D. Md. Nov 14, 2003; Keith O'Brien, "Men Seek Return of DNA from Serial Killer Search: Some Claim Police Bullied Them for Swabs," *New Orleans Times-Picayune,* December 28, 2003.

24. Brett Martel, "SOU Serial Killer DNA, "*Associated Press,* May 30, 2003.

25. "Louisiana Police Demand DNA from White Drivers," *Washington Times,* January 14, 2003.

26. Mark Hansen, "DNA Dragnet," *ABA Journal,* May 1, 2004.

27. Kohler v. Englade, 470 F.3d 1104 (5th Cir. 2006). A similar thing happened in Maine, State v. Glover, 89 A.3d 1077 (Me. 2013) (finding error in admission of refusal to consent to request for DNA sample as evidence of consciousness of guilt).

28. For a partial list of cities, see Brief of Amicus Curiae Electronic Privacy Information Center, Kohler v. Englade, 2005 WL 6125030 (5th Cir. 2005). Voluntary contributors have later balked at the government's continued retention of the genetic sample after the case is closed. See, for example, Tim Potter and Stan Finger, "Motion Asks: What Happens to DNA?," *Wichita Eagle,* March 9, 2005.

29. Max Yavel, "Campus Escorts a Reminder of Last Fall's Anxiety at UF," *Gainesville Sun,* March 8, 2015, http://www.gainesville.com/article/20150308/ARTICLES/150309690?p=2&tc=pg; Sara Sidner and Ashley Fantz, "Police Hunt for University of Florida Attacker," CNN.com, September 8, 2014, http://www.cnn.com/2014/09/08/justice/florida-university-assaults/.

30. Sheldon Krimsky and Tania Simoncelli, *Genetic Justice: DNA Data Banks, Criminal Investigations, and Civil Liberties* (New York: Columbia University Press, 2011), 59.

31. David M. Halbfinger, "Police Dragnets for DNA Tests Draw Criticism," *New York Times,* January 4, 2003, http://www.nytimes.com/2003/01/04/us/police-dragnets-for-dna-tests-draw-criticism.html.

32. Jeffrey S. Grand, note, "The Blooding of America: Privacy and the DNA Dragnet," *Cardozo Law Review* 23 (2002): 2277.

33. John O. Savino and Brent E. Turvey, *Rape Investigation Handbook,* 2nd ed. (Oxford, UK: Academic Press, 2011), 354.

34. Ibid.

35. http://www.charlotteobserver.com/2015/01/06/5429683/nc-court-of-appeals-upholds-use.html#.VLVa8Vrfxtc.

36. Brief of Amicus Curiae Electronic Privacy Information Center.

37. http://newstandardnews.net/content/index.cfm/items/1044.

38. Seth, "The Slippery Slope: DNA Dragnets and DNA Samples from All Arrestees," *Plain Error* (blog), The Innocence Project of Florida, February 22, 2008, http://floridainnocence.org/content/?tag=dna-dragnet.

39. Peter J. Neufeld, codirector of the Innocence Project, member of New York State's Forensic Science Review Board, testimony at the Subcommittee on Crime, Terrorism, and Homeland Security (July 17, 2003).

40. Petitioner's Brief, Varriale v. Maryland, No. 85 (March 9, 2015). In Varriale's case, he was actually presented with and signed a consent form. Its language would reasonably be understood to mean that the DNA sample could be used in a future prosecution related to *that investigation*   not that it would be kept in perpetuity in a law enforcement database.

41. Maryland Code Regs. 29.05.01.04; 29.05.01.02(1) (2015).

42. Varriale v. State, 96 A 3d 793 (Md. Ct. Spec. Appeals 2014); but see Amato v. Dist. Attorney for Cape & Islands Dist., 80 Mass. App. Ct. 230, 235, 952 N.E.2d 400, 406 (2011).

43. See, for example, Joseph Goldstein, "Police Agencies Are Assembling Records of DNA," *New York Times,* June 12, 2013.

44. Stephen Mercer and Jessica Gable, "Shadow Dwellers: The Underregulated World of State and Local DNA Databases," *NYU Annual Survey of American Law* 69, (2014): 639.

45. Ian Duncan, "Maryland Police DNA Tactics Again at Issue in Top Courts," *Baltimore Sun,* April 10, 2014.

46. Goldstein, "Police Agencies."

47. Richard Willing, "Local DNA Labs Avoid State and U.S. Laws to Nab Criminals," *USA Today,* March 26, 2007.

48. People v. Hendrix, No. 3668-03 (Kings County, New York, 2004), as described in http://www.nyclu.org/case/people-v-hendrix-challenging-dna-database-maintained-nyc-chief-medical-examiner.

49. Memo from Paul D. Fuller, deputy county attorney (Monroe County) to Nancy A. Scibetta, assistant laboratory director, August 4, 2004 (on file with author).

50. Bert-Jaap Koops and Maurice H. M. Schellekens, "Forensic DNA Phenotyping: Regulatory Issues," *Columbia Science and Technology Law Review* 9 (2008):163. In a small-scale investigation in Britain, the correct surname could be "predicted" from DNA in 19 percent of the cases. If a surname is less common, this percentage is higher. The eighty least occurring surnames involved in the investigation were correctly predicted in 34 percent of the cases. Ibid.; see also Uta-Dorothee Immel et al., "Y-Chromosomal STR Haplotype Analysis Reveals Surname-Associated Strata in the East-German Population," *European Journal of Human Genetics* 14 (2006): 577, 580; Erin Murphy, "Relative Doubt: Familial Searches of DNA Databases," *Michigan Law Review* 109 (2010): 291.

51. "Couple Fights over Assets," *Burlington Times-News*, November 21, 2003.

52. Travis Fain, "DNA as Crime Prevention Tool Has Risks, Benefits," *News & Record (Greensboro)*, February 22, 2013.

53. Ibid.

54. Bill Berger et al., "LODIS, a New Investigative Tool: DNA Is Not Just for Court Evidence Anymore," *Police Chief Magazine*, April 2008, http://www.policechiefmagazine.org/magazine/index .cfm?fuseaction=display_arch&article_id=1465&issue_id=42008.

55. "Innovation in Solving Crime, DNA Is Not Just Court Evidence Anymore," accessed May 16, 2015, at http://icma.org/Documents/Document/Document/21010.

56. Berger, "LODIS."

57. Justice for All Act 2004, Pub. Law 108-405, § 203, 118 Stat. 2260.

58. "Innovation in Solving Crime."

59. Travis Fain, "Greensboro Police's DNA Lab Plan in Limbo," *News & Record (Greensboro)*, September 1, 2013, http://www.news-record.com/news/local_news/greensboro-police-s-dna-lab-plan-in-limbo /article_275905fc-12c2–11e3–95fa-001a4bcf6878.html.

60. https://business-bankruptcies.com/cases/dna-si-labs-inc.

61. "Palm Bay Police Nail Crooks with DNA Evidence," *Space Coast Daily*, February 25, 2014, http:// spacecoastdaily.com/2014/02/palm-bay-police-nail-crooks-with-dna-evidence/.

62. http://www.smallpondllc.com. Other services of this kind include BodeHits, http://www.bodetech .com/bodehits-putting-the-power-of-dna-in-your-hands/; Lodis Worldwide, http://lodisworldwide.com/; and Sorensen Forensic's LEAD, http://www.sorensonforensics.com/forensics-lab-forensic-dna-testing/dna -forensics-lab-news-forensic-lab-development/sorenson-forensics-launches-new-cloud-based-database-to -simplify-crime-scene-case-management-archival-of-dna-profiles.

63. http://www.smallpondllc.com.

64. "Over One Million Served," May 8, 2013, http://www.smallpondllc.com/NewsDetail.aspx?ID=14.

65. "IntegenX Announces First State-Wide Deployment of the RapidHIT System with SmallPond at Arizona Department of Public Safety," May 13, 2014, http://www.smallpondllc.com/NewsDetail .aspx?ID=25; "Revolutionary DNA Testing Instruments Now Available to DPS Detectives," May 13, 2014, http://www.azdps.gov/Media/News/View/?p=477.

66. 42 U.S.C. § 14132(2).

67. Alaska Stat. Ann. § 44.41.035(d) (West 2015); Wash Rev. Code Ann. § 43.43.758 (West 2015). Washington's law says no rogue local database can be established "before July 1, 1990," which leaves open whether such databases are allowed after that date.

68. N.Y. Exec. Law § 995-c (McKinney 2015). This law does provide for the removal and destruction of a sample collected either voluntarily or pursuant to court order in connection with a case later dismissed or acquitted. But that process requires court approval. It also is unclear whether the lab would interpret it as applying to local databases. On the one hand, the provision appears in the section of law covering the "State DNA Identification Index." On the other, the law itself says "any sample, analyses, or other documents relating to the DNA testing" should be expunged.

CHAPTER 12

1. James M. Curran and John S. Buckleton, "Effectiveness of Familial Searches," *Science and Justice* 84 (2008): 164.

2. Maura Dolan and Jason Felch, "Tracing a Crime Suspect Through a Relative," *L.A. Times*, November 25, 2008.

3. Ellen Nakashima, "From DNA of Family, a Tool to Make Arrests," *Washington Post*, April 21, 2008.

4. Ibid.

5. Dolan and Felch, "Tracing a Crime."

6. "Interim Plan for Release of Information in the Event of a 'Partial Match' at NDIS," CODIS Bulletin #BT072006, July 20, 2006.

7. California Department of Justice, Division of Law Enforcement, Information Bull. No. 2008-BFS-01, DNA Partial Match (Crime Scene DNA Profile to Offender) Policy (2008); see also Maura Dolan and Jason Felch, "California Takes Lead on DNA Crime-Fighting Technique," L.A. Times, April 26, 2008.

8. Jim Spellman, "Using Relative's DNA Cracks Crime, but Privacy Questions Raised," CNN.com, November 17, 2008.

9. Jianye Ge et al., "Comparisons of the Familial DNA Databases Searching Policies," Journal of Forensic Sciences 56, no. 6 (2011): 1451. These figures range widely from seven to sixteen alleles shared among siblings in some systems, or twelve to twenty-two using the CODIS loci.

10. David H. Kaye, "Trawling DNA Databases for Partial Matches: What Is FBI Afraid Of?" Cornell Journal of Law and Public Policy 19 (2009): 145; B. Budowle et al., "Partial Matches in Heterogeneous Offender Databases Do Not Call into Question the Validity of Random Match Probability Calculations," International Journal of Legal Medicine 123 (2009): 59.

11. Eva Steinberger and Gary Sims, "Finding Criminals Through the DNA of Their Relatives—Familial Searching of the California Offender DNA Database," Prosecutor's Brief 31 (2008): 28, 30; John M. Butler, Fundamentals of Forensic DNA Typing (Oxford, UK: Academic Press, 2009), 275.

12. Denver District Attorney Mitchell Morrissey has stated that he uses software explicitly designed for such searches. See http://projects.nfstc.org/postconviction/presentations/morrissey.pdf. It appears that he is referring to a program known as "DNA-View"—see http://dna-view.com/dnaview.htm—which was developed by a researcher. Morrissey claims that it can eliminate 90 percent of unrelated people.

13. "Recommendations from the SWGDAM Ad Hoc Working Group on Familial Searching," http://swgdam.org/SWGDAM%20Recs%20on%20Familial%20Searching%20APPROVED%2010072013 .pdf, table 1.

14. S. P. Myers et al., "Searching for First-Degree Relatives in California's Offender Database: Validation of a Likelihood Ratio-Based Approach," Forensic Science International 5, no. 5 (2011): 493.

15. Eric Duvall, "The Use of Familial DNA Searching as an Investigative Tool," Denver Police Department Crime Lab, at http://www.slideshare.net/Lifetech_HID/the-use-of-familial-dna-searching-as-an-investigative-tool-denver.

16. Reid et al. modeled familial searches using a likelihood ratio approach, and found that roughly 42 percent of full siblings matched on the first hit. Also, Reid et al. modeled a 12,929-person database with thirteen CODIS loci, and investigated 109 sibling pairs. Their finding is consistent with earlier studies by Frederick R. Bieber et al., "Finding Criminals Through DNA of Their Relatives," Science 312 (2006): 1315, 1315-1316, and T. Hicks et al., "Use of DNA Profiles for Investigation Using a Simulated National DNA Database. Part II. Statistical and Ethical Considerations on Familial Searching," Forensic Science International: Genetics (January 14, 2010). However, this finding depended on the use of the population-specific allele frequencies, which might not normally be known in advance and could be material in a diverse population. Accordingly, they concluded that "DNA profile data may not consistently produce enough useable leads to make it meaningful." T. M. Reid et al., "Use of Sibling Pairs to Determine the Familial Searching Efficiency of Forensic Databases," Forensic Science International: Genetics (2008): 340-342.

17. Studies show that, if the database does indeed contain a relative and the search threshold is set widely enough, it is 80 to 90 percent likely that a partial match search will include the relative in its results. Rori V. Rohlfs, Erin E. Murphy, Yun S. Song, and Montgomery Slatkin, "The Influence of Relatives on the Efficiency and Error Rate of Familial Searching," PLoS One 9, no. 1: 10.1371/annotation/2544c2e3 -0065-4d14-ab1c-3d3fcb0fee84. But studies also show that such a search is also likely to return a number of persons that are not in fact related to the source. Ibid.

18. Robin Williams and Paul Johnson, "Inclusiveness, Effectiveness and Intrusiveness: Issues in the Developing Uses of DNA Profiling in Support of Criminal Investigations," Journal of Law, Medicine, and Ethics 34 (2006): 234, 242. Kinship connections have, of course, also been used to establish identity in missing persons cases.

19. Ibid., 243. A year later, UK authorities conducted another high-profile familial search, this time successfully locating a lead and thereby apprehending a young man who threw a brick off of an overpass, causing the death of the driver after a heart attack. Sheldon Krimsky and Tania Simoncelli, Genetic Justice: DNA Data Banks, Criminal Investigations, and Civil Liberties (New York: Columbia University Press, 2011), 64.

20. Ibid.

21. Ibid.

22. "Interim Plan for Release." At the close of 2011, US representative Adam Schiff introduced a bill authorizing federal law enforcement to engage in familial searches, but it failed to garner support.

23. One recent article surveyed forty-seven states, and reported the practices of each. Natalie Ram, "Fortuity and Forensic Familial Identification," *Stanford Law Review* 63 (2011): 751.

24. Erin Murphy, "Relative Doubt: Familial Searches of DNA Databases," *Michigan Law Review* 109 (2010): 291, 302–303.

25. National Forensic Science Technology Center, "Calling All CODIS Lab Directors: Survey Coming Up," http://www.nfstc.org/calling-all-codis-lab-directors-survey-coming-up/; National Institute of Justice, "NIJ Award Detail: Understanding the Use and Efficacy of Moderate Stringency DNA Searches," Number 2014-IJ-CX-0005 (awarding $494,447 to the RAND Corporation for study).

26. Natalie Ram, "Interactive Map: State Policies for DNA Crime Databases Vary Widely," available at http://www.scienceprogress.org/2009/11/map-state-dna-policies/ (November 11, 2009).

27. http://www.fbi.gov/about-us/lab/biometric-analysis/codis/codis-and-ndis-fact-sheet, citing *Federal Register* 73, no. 238 (December 10, 2008), 74937.

28. "Recommendations from the SWGDAM."

29. Ibid.

30. Information bulletin from Attorney General Edmund G. Brown Jr., "DNA Partial Match (Crime Scene DNA Profile to Offender) Policy No. 2008-BFS-01" (April 24, 2008), available at http://www.dnaresource.com/documents/CAfamilialpolicy.pdf.

31. Colorado Bureau of Investigation, "DNA Familial Search Policy" (October 22, 2009), available at http://www.dnaresource.com/documents/ColoradoPolicy.pdf.

32. CODIS Advisory Board, Standard Operating Procedures: "Partial Matches and Familial Searches," DRN CO-04003A, April 24, 2012, http://www.denverda.org/DNA_Documents/Familial_DNA/Tx%20FS%20policy.pdf.

33. Commonwealth of Virginia, Department of Forensic Science, "Policy Relating to Acceptance of Cases for Performance of Familial DNA Searching" (March 9, 2011), available at http://www.dnaresource.com/documents/VirginiaPolicy.pdf.

34. SWGDAM, "Wyoming—Scientific Analysis on DNA Methods," July 2013 Report (Federal Training Center in Dumfries, Virginia), 3, http://swgdam.org/SWGDAM_July_2013_report.pdf.

35. The current iteration of the CODIS software does a poor job at identifying true leads in familial searches. Steinberger and Sims, "Finding Criminals," 28. That is because "CODIS looks for allele-sharing patterns based on the level of stringency specified in a search, and does not take into account the rarity in the population of a shared allele." Ibid.

36. Md. Code Ann., Pub. Safety § 2–506(d) (West 2010).

37. D.C. Code § 22–4151 (2010).

38. New York approved the release of partial matches, and a number of additional states have introduced legislation to allow it, most recently Minnesota and Pennsylvania. A lobbying group for forensic DNA companies has a website that catalogs published policies; see http://www.dnaresource.com/policycategories.html.

39. California, Washington, Oregon, Montana, Wyoming, Minnesota, Nebraska, Missouri, Oklahoma, Louisiana, Florida, Alabama, Connecticut, and North and South Carolina. Ibid.

40. Iowa, Wisconsin, Indiana, Ohio, Kentucky, and Maryland. Ibid.

41. Nevada, Utah, New Mexico, Georgia, Maine, Tennessee, Massachusetts, Rhode Island, Vermont, Michigan, and Alaska. Ibid.

42. "The Confession," *Dateline*, NBC, August 24, 2012.

43. Bryan Clark, "Mother, Son Hope 1996 Murder Conviction Will Be Overturned," KBOI2.com, December 1, 2014, http://www.kboi2.com/news/local/Mother-son-hope-1996-murder-conviction-will-be-overturned—284380391.html.

44. "Ancestry.com Enters DNA Genealogy Field Through Exclusive Partnership with Sorenson Genomics," press release, June 18, 2007, http://corporate.ancestry.com/press/press-releases/2007/06/ancestry.com-enters-dna-genealogy-field-through-exclusive-partnership-with-sorenson-genomics/.

45. Roberta Estes, "Is History Repeating Itself at Ancestry," *DNAeXplained—Genetic Genealogy* (blog), August 30, 2012, http://dna-explained.com/2012/08/30/is-history-repeating-itself-at-ancestry/.

46. http://dna.ancestry.com/.

47. However, some advocates of adoptee genetic testing to find biological relatives have criticized Ancestry's reporting methods. CeCe Moore, "AncestryDNA: Confusing Relationship Predictions

and Adoptees," *Your Genetic Genealogist* (blog), August 21, 2012, http://www.yourgeneticgenealogist.com/2012/08/ancestrydna-confusing-relationship.html.

48. Michael Martinez, "Man Discovers He Wasn't Kidnapped Baby; FBI Reopens 49-Year-Old Case," CNN.com, August 8, 2013.

49. Jim Mustian, "New Orleans Filmmaker Cleared in Cold-Case Murder; False Positive Highlights Limitations of Familial DNA Searching," *New Orleans Advocate*, March 12, 2015, http://www.the neworleansadvocate.com/news/11707192–123/new-orleans-filmmaker-cleared-in.

50. Ibid.

51. Mitchell R. Morrissey, debate, "The Constitutionality, Effectiveness, and Implications of Familial Searches, Criminal Justice in the Age of DNA," *Annual Survey of American Law* Symposium, New York University School of Law (February 22, 2013).

52. California Department of Justice, Office of the Attorney General, "BFS DNA Frequently Asked Questions: California's Familial Search Policy," http://oag.ca.gov/bfs/prop69/faqs.

53. Ellen Nakashima, "From DNA of Family, a Tool to Make Arrests," *Washington Post*, April 21, 2008, http://www.washingtonpost.com/wp-dyn/content/article/2008/04/20/AR2008042002388_3.html?sid=ST2008042100610.

54. National Institute of Science and Technology, "Biometrics," accessed May 16, 2015, http://www.nist.gov/oles/forensics/forensic-database-biometric-table.cfm.

55. Nakashima, "From DNA of Family."

56. Ibid.

57. Ibid.

58. Ibid.

59. Ibid.

60. Frederick R. Bieber, Charles H. Brenner, and David Lazer, "Finding Criminals Through DNA of Their Relatives," *Science* 312, no. 5778 (2006): 1316 (asserting that studies show a "strong probabilistic dependency between the chances of conviction of parents and their children, as well as among siblings").

61. Ibid.; "Recommendations from the SWGDAM."

62. In making their argument, Professors Bieber, Brenner, and Lazer cited two studies: a 2004 study in the *Journal of Child Psychology and Psychiatrics* and a Bureau of Justice statistical report. The latter source is fraught with problems. Most important, this study measured the percentage of *jail* inmates with prior incarcerated family members. But jail inmates include both nonconvicted and convicted persons; indeed, in the cited study, roughly 29.2 percent had never before been sentenced, and almost half of those appear to be in jail awaiting adjudication of their case. A sampling of jail inmates—even convicted ones—inevitably samples low-level offenders, because convicted serious offenders almost always are sentenced to state or federal prisons. Bureau of Justice Statistics, "Correctional Population in the United States, 1996," US Department of Justice (April 1999), 58, Table 4.11. The same study reported the percentage of convicted and unconvicted (typically awaiting trial) persons in the jails in 1996 as roughly fifty-fifty, Ibid., 73, Table 2.6. See generally Murphy, "Relative Doubt," 306–307.

63. Jack Leonard, "Authorities Missed a Chance to Catch Grim Sleeper Suspect," *L.A. Times*, July 15, 2010, http://articles.latimes.com/2010/jul/15/local/la-me-grim-sleeper-dna-20100715.

64. Henry T. Greely et al., "Family Ties: The Use of DNA Offender Databases to Catch Offenders' Kin," *Journal of Law, Medicine, and Ethics* 34 (2006): 255.

65. Bieber, "Finding Criminals,"; See generally Jennifer Mnookin, "The Perils of Expanding DNA Searches to Relatives," *UCLA Today*, July 5, 2008.

66. D. H. Kaye and Michael E. Smith, "DNA Identification Databases: Legality, Legitimacy, and the Case for Population-Wide Coverage," *Wisconsin Law Review* (2003), 413, 454. While this imbalance is somewhat lessened if misdemeanants and arrestees are included, there still exist stark disparities. Ibid., 456.

67. Thomas P. Bonczar, "Prevalence of Imprisonment in the U.S. Population, 1974–2001," Bureau of Justice Statistics, August 2003, available at www.ojp.usdoj.gov/bjs/abstract/piusp01.htm.

68. Committee on Causes and Consequences of High Rates of Incarceration, *The Growth of Incarceration in the United States*, ed. Jeremy Travis, Bruce Western, and Steve Redburn (2014), 91. For an argument that adding arrestees will have a slight leavening effect, because arrests are less racially skewed than convictions, see Kaye and Smith, "DNA Identification Databases," 454.

69. For example, one student note even argued that the impact was likely to be greatest for Hispanics, because they tend to have larger family structures. Daniel J. Grimm, "The Demographics of Genetic Surveillance: Familial DNA Testing and the Hispanic Community," *Columbia Law Review* 107 (2007): 1164.

70. Greely, "Family Ties."

71. Nakashima, "From DNA of Family." In order to estimate the impact on the African American community, Greely assumes that African Americans make up 40 percent of the DNA profiles in the database, even though they constitute only 13 percent of the population, and that each person in the database has on average five first-degree relatives. Greely, "Family Ties."

72. For instance, substantive due process privacy claims are difficult and disfavored, and procedural due process would require a positive entitlement of some kind.

73. Arlington Heights v. Metropolitan Housing Development Corp., 429 U.S. 252 (1977); Washington v. Davis, 426 U.S. 229 (1976).

74. Some may believe that police routinely make such assumptions—for instance, assuming without basis that the perpetrator of a crime is poor or male, and that such biases are to some extent unavoidable. But to formally enshrine them as formal protocol—to announce arbitrarily that the police will first investigate all poor people, or all men, before considering the possibility of a different kind of suspect—elevates a questionable but arguably inescapable reality to the status of officially endorsed practice.

75. City of Cleburne, Texas v. Cleburne Living Center, 473 U.S. 432 (1985).

76. Grutter v. Bollinger, 539 U.S. 306, 326 (2003). It might be argued that it does implicate the fundamental right to liberty and free association, or even some notion of a fundamental right to familial privacy; see, for example, U.S. Dept. of Agriculture v. Moreno, 413 U.S. 528 (1973); Moore v. City of East Cleveland, 431 U.S. 494 (1977).

77. See, for example, Anderson v. Commonwealth, 650 S.E.2d 702 (Va. 2007).

78. 547 U.S. 103 (2006).

79. Of course, one argument against this position might be to cite cases, such as Samson v. California 547 U.S. 843 (2006), that hold that probationers and parolees can be subjected to warrantless and suspicionless searches at any time. The authority to search may apply even in the event that the parolee shares a space with another person, waiving the constitutional right of the nonparolee home occupant. However, we cannot choose the persons with whom we share our genetic code. In some cases, a relative may have entirely disavowed the convicted offender, or not even know that person. Therefore, it seems indefensible to claim a voluntary relinquishment of privacy by the relative, on account of mere biology.

80. See, for example, Erin Murphy, "Paradigms of Restraint," *Duke Law Journal* 57 (2008): 1321, 1329–1330.

81. For instance, Justice Scalia (although writing for himself alone) has even stated that, in a case involving the drug testing of urine samples, "only one act . . . could conceivably be regarded as a search . . . the *taking* of the urine sample." Ferguson v. City of Charleston, 532 U.S. 67, 92 (2001) (Scalia, J., dissenting). Similarly, in another case, the DC Circuit held that "accessing the records stored in the CODIS database is not a 'search' for Fourth Amendment purposes. As the Supreme Court has held, the process of matching one piece of personal information against government records does not implicate the Fourth Amendment." Johnson v. Quander, 440 F.3d 489, 498 (D.C. Cir. 2006).

82. Erin E. Murphy, "Databases, Doctrine and the Future of Constitutional Criminal Procedure," *Fordham Urban Law Journal* 37 (2010): 803.

83. Ferguson, 532 U.S. 76 n.9; Chandler v. Miller, 520 U.S. 305 (1997); Vernonia School Dist. 47J v. Acton, 515 U.S. 646 (1995); Skinner v. Railway Labor Executives' Assn., 489 U.S. 602 (1989); Treasury Employees v. Von Raab, 489 U.S. 656 (1989).

84. See, for example, United States v. Weikert, 504 F.3d 1, 15–17 (1st Cir. 2007); see also United States v. Amerson, 483 F.3d 73 (2d Cir. 2007).

85. Transcript of Oral Argument, 16, Maryland v. King, 133 S. Ct. 1958 (2013) (No. 12-207).

86. United States v. Davis, 657 F.Supp.2d 630 (D. Ct. Md. September 15, 2009), aff'd by 690 F.3d 226 (4th Cir. 2012).

87. Federal Bureau of Investigation, "Frequently Asked Questions (FAQs) on the CODIS Program and the National DNA Index System," http://www.fbi.gov/about-us/lab/biometric-analysis/codis/codis -and-ndis-fact-sheet. There are two main reasons for this: (1) true siblings do not always share alleles at all thirteen CODIS loci; and (2) as offender DNA databases grow, the number of unrelated people that do share at least one allele at all loci increases rapidly.

88. Memorandum from Deputy Attorney General Michael Chamberlain, DNA Legal Unit to Attorney General Brown, California Department of Justice, "DNA Data Bank Program: Reporting 'Partial Matches' to Law Enforcement," (June 6, 2007), 3.

89. Rohlfs et al., "The Influence of Relatives"; Reid et al., "Use of Sibling Pairs"; Curran and Buckleton, "Effectiveness."

90. As of early 2011, Colorado had searched all its forensic unknowns, and made ten identifications resulting in one conviction. California had conducted thirteen searches, and made two arrests.

91. "Familial DNA Database Searches," accessed May 17, 2015, http://www.denverda.org/DNA /Familial_DNA_Database_Searches.htm. Indeed, as observed earlier, the three family search leads that caused Denver District Attorney Mitchell Morrissey, one of the most vocal proponents of familial search methods, to encourage the FBI rule change did not in the end pan out.

92. Federal Bureau of Investigation, "Familial Searching," accessed May 16, 2015, http://www.fbi.gov /about-us/lab/biometric-analysis/codis/familial-searching.

93. Erica Haimes, "Social and Ethical Issues in the Use of Familial Searching in Forensic Investigations: Insights from Family and Kinship Studies," *Journal of Law, Medicine, and Ethics* 34 (2006): 263, 269.

94. The frequency of misattributed paternity has proven difficult to measure, but studies suggest rates as low as 1 percent or as high as 30 percent in the population, though most hover in the 2 to 5 percent range. Bryan Sykes and Catherine Irven, "Surnames and the Y Chromosome," *American Journal of Human Genetics* 66 (2000): 1417.

CHAPTER 13

1. Cesare Lombroso, *L'Uomo Delinquente* (1876).

2. See, for example, Deborah W. Denno, "Human Biology and Criminal Responsibility: Free Will or Free Ride?," *University of Pennsylvania Law Review* 137 (1988): 615.

3. Paul Lombardo, "Medicine, Eugenics, and the Supreme Court: From Coercive Sterilization to Reproductive Freedom," *Journal of Contemporary Health Law and Policy* 3 (1996–1997): 1, 2–3.

4. H.F. 641 (Iowa 1913).

5. Transcript of oral argument in Circuit Court, Buck v. Bell, 274 U.S. 200 (1927), 32–34, available at http://readingroom.law.gsu.edu/buckvbell/31.

6. Buck v. Bell, 274 U.S. 200, 208 (1927).

7. 316 U.S. 535, 545 (1942).

8. Sterilization sanctions have not entirely abated. For example, see Associated Press, "Nashville Assistant DA Fired Amid Reports of Sterilization in Plea Deals," April 1, 2015 (reporting on cases involving Nashville DA and others, including 150 female inmates in California sterilized between 2006 and 2010).

9. For example, Elizabeth Fee, "Nineteenth Century Craniology," *Bulletin of History of Medicine* 53 (Fall 1979): 415, 418 (describing belief in "the real differences in the minds of men and women," in that "women's brains were analogous to those of animals: in them the organs of sense were overdeveloped to the detriment of the brain proper," and that the "type of the female skull approaches in many respects that of the infant, and still more that of the lower races").

10. Terence D. Keel, "Religion, Polygenism and the Early Science of Human Origins," *History of Human Science* 26 (2013): 4, 22 ("This group of scientific men took up a rigorous study of the various human populations across the globe, and worked collaboratively to develop the idea that racial variation stemmed from immutable physical differences passed down from one generation to the next and therefore the human races could not have shared an ancestor. For its time, polygenism was a true science and entailed a creative mix of scrupulous data collection about human population traits and novel theories about the deleterious consequences of racial mixing.")

11. William H. Sheldon, *The Varieties of Temperament* (1942).

12. See, for example, Daniel Goleman, "New Storm Brews on Whether Crime Has Roots in Genes," *New York Times*, September 15, 1992.

13. W. M. Court Brown, letter to the editor, "Sex Chromosomes and the Law," *The Lancet*, September 8, 1962, 508–509 ("I have been wondering for some time whether the legal authorities should not now give some consideration to the problem of the numbers of individuals in the population who either have a normal sex-chromosome constitution but one which is grossly at variance with their sexual phenotype, or have an abnormal sex-chromosome constitution. . . . If it is [likely that people with abnormal chromosomes may be 'predisposed to delinquency'], then the numbers of abnormal individuals in the general population are such that individuals with an abnormal sex-chromosome complement might constitute an appreciable proportion of those who repeatedly clash with the law.")

14. Theodore S. Hauschka et al., "An XYY Man with Progeny Indicating Familial Tendency to Non-disjunction," *American Journal of Human Genetics* 14 (March 1962): 1, 22, 27; J. Money et al., "47,XYY and 46,XY Males with Antisocial and/or Sex-Offending Behavior: Antiandrogen Therapy," *Psychoneuroendocrinology* 1 (1975): 165, 169–170.

15. Mary A. Tefler et al., "Incidence of Gross Chromosomal Errors among Tall Criminal American Males," *Science* 159 (March 15, 1968): 1249, 1250.

16. Ibid.

17. Richard D. Lyons, "Genetic Abnormality Is Linked to Crime: Genetics Linked to Violent Crimes," *New York Times*, April 21, 1968, 1–2.

18. Robert W. Stock, "The XYY and the Criminal," *New York Times*, October 20, 1968, SM30, SM90–97.

19. Ibid.; Charles E. Parker et al., "The XYY Syndrome," *American Journal of Medicine* 47 (November 1969): 801, 806.

20. See, for example, Money et al., "47,XYY and 46,XY Males," 165, 169–170.

21. Transcript of Oral Argument, 10, Maryland v. King, 133 S. Ct. 1958 (2013) (No. 12-207).

22. Ibid., 15.

23. Ibid., 16.

24. The origin of the phrase is typically ascribed to Susumu Ohno; see "So Much 'Junk' DNA in Our Genome," in *Evolution of Genetic Systems*, ed. H. H. Smith (New York: Gordon and Breach, 1972), 366–337, and was in use in the 1960s.

25. A. F. Palazzo and T. R. Gregory, "Case for Junk DNA," *PLoS Genetics* 10, no. 5 (May 8, 2014), http://www.plosgenetics.org/article/info%3Adoi%2F10.1371%2Fjournal.pgen.1004351#pgen.1004351 -ENCODE1.

26. Brief of "Genetics, Genomics and Forensic Science Researchers as Amici Curiae in Support of Neither Party," Maryland v. King, No. 122-207, 2012 WL 6762585, December 28, 2012, 19–20.

27. See for example, National Institute of Justice, $514,432 award to University of Colorado–Denver, "Genetic Analysis of Face Shape and Appearance" (2013), available at http://nij.gov/funding/awards/pages /award-detail.aspx?award=2013-DN-BX-K005.

28. Peter Aldhous, "Genetic Mugshot Recreates Faces from Nothing but DNA," *New Scientist*, March 20, 2014.

29. Kevin M. Beaver, *Intersection of Genes, the Environment, and Crime and Delinquency: A Longitudinal Study of Offending*, National Criminal Justice Reference Series (August 2010), available at https://www .ncjrs.gov/app/publications/abstract.aspx?id=253671.

30. See grant to University of Utah, "Genome-Wide Forensic DNA Analysis," 2012-DN-BX-K037.

31. See, for example, A. R. Sanders et al., "Genome-wise Scan Demonstrates Significant Linkage for Male Sexual Orientation," *Psychological Medicine* 45, no. 7 (2015): 1379–1388.

32. William Seltzer and Margo Anderson, "The Dark Side of Numbers: The Role of Population Data Systems in Human Rights Abuses," *Social Research* (Summer 2001).

33. Ibid., Table 1.

34. For a visual depiction of the process, see Heather Murphy, "I've Just Seen a (DNA-Generated) Face," *New York Times*, February 23, 2015, at http://www.nytimes.com/2015/02/24/science/dna-generated-faces .html.

35. Jam Kotenko, "Facebook Reveals We Load a Whopping 350 Million Photos to the Network Daily," *Digital Trends*, September 18, 2013.

36. Tony Frudakis, *Molecular Photofitting: Predicting Ancestry and Phenotype Using DNA* (Oxford, UK: Academic Press, 2007): 614. A second high-profile case involved the use of ancestry information to buttress the case against the suspected bombers of a Madrid commuter train. Christopher Phillips et al., "Ancestry Analysis in the 11-M Madrid Bomb Attack Investigation," *PLoS One*, 4, no. 8 (August 2009).

37. Frudakis, *Molecular Photofitting*, 599–605.

38. Ibid., 602.

39. Of course, not every genetic trait is this complex. For example, sickle-cell anemia is highly predictable because it depends on the variants of a single gene; one mutant copy and one normal copy manifests as resistance to malaria, whereas two mutant copies manifests as sickle-cell anemia. However, many phenotypic traits involve much more complex articulation. In light of this, two recent research trends have developed. First, the falling costs of whole-genome sequencing has led to the emergence of genome-wide association studies (GWAS), which are undertaken as a form of backward reasoning from a trait to possible involved genetic markers. Second, as researchers have learned that gene expression is not just a function of genetic sequence, but also points to other aspects of genetic function, a new field of epigenomics has emerged that studies such influences. See Adrian Bird, "Perceptions of Epigenetics," *Nature* 447 (May 24, 2007): 396; Bird describes epigenetics as "a potential antidote to genetic determinism" that has "a deliciously Lamarckian flavor."

40. See, for example, Mario F. Fraga et al., "Epigenetic Differences Arise During the Lifetime of Monozygotic Twins," *PNAS* 102, no. 30 (July 26, 2005): 10604; Albert H. C. Wong et al., "Phenotypic

Differences in Genetically Identical Organisms: The Epigenetic Perspective," *Human Molecular Genetics* 14 (2005): R-11.

41. Brendan Keating et al., "First All-in-One Diagnostic Tool for DNA Intelligence: Genome-Wide Inference of Biogeographic Ancestry, Appearance, Relatedness, and Sex with the Identitas V1 Forensic Chip," *International Journal of Legal Medicine* 127, no. 3 (November 13, 2012). The study was complicated by several factors; for instance, accuracy rates were likely lowered due to counted "misses" that were in fact the product of self-reports that might not match objective observation.

42. Wojciech Branicki et al., "Model-Based Prediction of Human Hair Color Using DNA Variants," *Human Genetics* 129 (2011): 443; Susan Walsh et al., "IrisPlex: A Sensitive DNA Tool for Accurate Prediction of Blue and Brown Eye Colour in the Absence of Ancestry Information," *Forensic Science International: Genetics* 5, no. 3 (2011): 170; Susan Walsh et al., "DNA-Based Eye Colour Prediction Across Europe with the IrisPlex System," *Forensic Science International: Genetics* 6, no. 3 (2012): 330; Susan Walsh et al., "The HIrisPlex System for Simultaneous Prediction of Hair and Eye Colour from DNA," *Forensic Science International: Genetics* 7, no. 1 (2013): 98.

43. Sven Bocklandt, "Epigenetic Predictor of Age," *PLoS ONE* 6, no. 6 (June 22, 2011): e14821; D. D. Zubakov et al., "Estimating Human Age from T-cell Rearrangements," *Current Biology* 20, no. 22 (2010). Interestingly, one of the genes used in the Bocklandt study has been shown to have a relationship to pancreatic cancer and Parkinson's disease.

44. P. Claes et al., "Modeling 3D Facial Shape from DNA," *PLoS Genetics* 10, no. 3 (2014); P. Claes, "Toward DNA-Based Facial Composites: Preliminary Results and Validation," *Forensic Science International: Genetics* 13 (2014): 208–214. Lavinia Paternoster et al., "Genome-Wide Association Study of Three-Dimensional Facial Morphology Identifies a Variant in PAX3 Associated with Nasion Position," *American Journal of Human Genetics* 90, no. 3 (2013): 478; Fan Liu et al., "A Genome-Wide Association Study Identifies Five Loci Influencing Facial Morphology in Europeans," *PLoS Genetics* 8, no. 9 (2012): e1002932.

45. Walsh, "HIrisPlex," 99. Studies suggest that heritability of some common traits ranges from 100 percent for such features as hair and eye color, bitter taste capacity, and tongue rolling, to around 50 percent for moles, migraine susceptibility, or finger ratios. Brendan Keating et al., "First All-in-One Diagnostic Tool for DNA Intelligence: Genome-Wide Inference of Biogeographic Ancestry, Appearance, Relatedness, and Sex with the Identitas v1 Forensic Chip," *International Journal of Legal Medicine* 127, no. 3 (2013): 559–572.

46. Benedikt Hallgrimsson et al., "Let's Face It—Complex Traits Are Just Not That Simple," *PLoS Genetics* 10, no. 11 (November 2014).

47. Ibid. (citing Liu et al., "A Genome-Wide Association Study").

48. Murphy, "I've Just Seen a (DNA-Generated) Face."

49. Erika Harrell, "Violent Victimization Committed by Strangers, 1993–2010," Bureau of Justice Statistics, December 2012, http://www.bjs.gov/content/pub/pdf/vvcs9310.pdf.

50. Matt Stroud, "The Most Advanced Police Sketch Ever Might Solve Cold Cases," *Verge*, July 20, 2014, http://www.theverge.com/2014/7/20/5916661/the-most-advanced-police-sketch-ever-might-solve-cold-cases.

51. Parabon NanoLabs, Snapshot, accessed May 17, 2015, http://snapshot.parabon-nanolabs.com.

52. Andrew Pollack, "Building a Face, and a Case, on DNA," *New York Times*, February 23, 2015.

53. Parabon NanoLabs, "Parabon Snapshot™ Puts a Face on Litterbugs," April 22, 2015, http://parabon-nanolabs.com/nanolabs/news-events/2015/04/snapshot-hkcleanup.html.

54. Melody Schreiber, "Police Turn to New DNA-Powered Technology in Hopes of Finding Killer," *Washington Post*, February 23, 2015, http://www.washingtonpost.com/national/health-science/new-technology-generates-photo-illustration-from-a-persons-dna/2015/02/23/4cf5248e-b85d-11e4-9423-f3d0a1ec335c_story.html.

55. JASON, The Mitre Corporation, *The $100 Genome: Implications for the DoD*, Report No. JSR-10–100 (December 2010), 43.

56. Ibid., 5–6.

57. Maryland v. King, No. 12–207, Oral Arg. Tr., 16 (February 26, 2013).

58. These traits are sometimes abbreviated as "EVCs," for externally visible characteristics. The EVC standard may be overinclusive; although it may be true that an externally visible trait is unlikely to reveal sensitive information about a person, this need not always be the case. At the minor end of the spectrum, genetic testing might reveal whether people have had plastic surgery, lie about their age, wear a hairpiece, or dye their hair. At the more intrusive end of the spectrum, it could reveal that someone has changed

genders, call parentage into question, or cloud a person's sense of self with conflicting information about ancestry. Consider that an entire television series is devoted to revealing confirming or disconfirming facts about ancestry. Lastly, externally visible traits may on occasion have genetic associations to sensitive information—imagine a gene for detached earlobes that turns out also to be predictive of Parkinson's.

59. Maryland v. King, 133 S. Ct. 1958, 1971–1972 (internal quotation omitted).

60. See generally Christopher Slobogin, *Proving the Unprovable: The Role of Law, Science and Speculation in Adjudicating Culpability and Dangerousness* (Oxford, UK: Oxford University Press, 2007), 106–109.

61. Manfred Kayser et al., "Y Chromosome STR Haplotypes and the Genetic Structure of U.S. Populations of African, European, and Hispanic Ancestry," *Genome Research* 13 (2003): 632 ("All U.S. samples used here . . . were provided to us by U.S. crime laboratories, with the exception of Louisiana and the Acadian samples.")

62. 42 U.S.C. § 14135a et seq (2015).

63. 42 U.S.C. § 14132(b)(3)(A) (2006).

64. In addition, these laws give law enforcement the authority to collect and test samples for inclusion in the *federal* database. They say nothing about samples collected for other reasons—such as to put in a state or local database, or to collect and test as a voluntary submission or a crime scene sample not uploaded to the database. 42 U.S.C. § 14135a(a)(1), § 14135a(b), (c)(2); § 14132, and § 14135e(a).

65. New Mexico Admin. Code § 10.14.200.11.

66. R.I. Gen. Laws § 12–1.5–10(5) (2007).

67. Wyo. Stat. Ann. § 7–19–404(c) (2007).

68. Ind. Code Ann. § 10–13–6–16 (West 2004).

69. M.C.L.A. § 28.175a.

70. Vt. Stat. Ann. tit. 20, § 1937(b).

71. S.D.C.L. § 23–5A-17.

72. West's RCWA § 43.43.753. Washington's statute provides a policy statement that declares that "the legislature further finds . . . Washington state patrol has no ability to predict genetic disease or predisposal to illness. Nonetheless, the legislature intends that biological samples collected . . . be used only for purposes related to criminal investigation, identification of human remains or missing persons, or improving the operation of the system. . . ." This language at least implicitly suggests that the "purposes" clause is limited to testing that does not reveal disease or illness.

73. U.C.A. § 53–10–406(1)(f).

74. F.S.A. § 943.325(13)(b).

75. Tex. Gov't Code Ann. § 411.143.

76. Ibid.

77. The United States is not alone in failing to anticipate, and therefore regulate, phenotypic testing of DNA samples. The laws of other countries have similar loopholes. In 2008, Dutch researchers Bert-Jaap Koops and Maurice Schellekens conducted a survey of positive law regulating forensic DNA phenotyping in eleven countries, using legal resources as well as qualitative assessments in the form of questionnaires sent to experts. Overall, they concluded that "[a]lmost all surveyed countries have some form of DNA legislation, but these laws are generally confined to traditional DNA forensics, that is, making DNA profiles or fingerprints from crime-scene material and comparing these to profiles stored in forensic DNA databases." Bert-Jaap Koops and Maurice H. M. Schellekens, "Forensic DNA Phenotyping: Regulatory Issues," *Columbia Science and Technology Law Review* 9 (2008): 166.

78. There is a debate in the literature as to the defensibility of a right not to know, versus that of informed consent. Compare David E. Ost, "The 'Right' Not to Know," *Journal of Medicine and Philosophy* 9 (1984): 301, with Mark Strasser, "Mill and the Right to Remain Uninformed," *Journal of Medicine and Philosophy* 11 (1986): 265.

79. In that case, closer scrutiny was needed in order to ensure the accuracy of the frequency tables used to assign meaning to a match. One study of African American, European American, and Hispanic haplotypes in the United States concluded that there was no significant variation among the frequency of observed haplotypes according to geography. East Coast populations genetically resemble West Coast, Midwestern, and southern populations. Manfred Kayser et al., "Y Chromosome STR Haplotypes and the Genetic Structure of U.S. Populations of African, European, and Hispanic Ancestry," *Genome Research* 13 (2003): 624. There is one exception: samples from Texas exhibit heterogeneity to the haplotypes of whites and Hispanics.

80. Koops and Schellekens, "Forensic DNA Phenotyping," 173, 190.

81. Frudakis, *Molecular Photofitting*, 603.

82. As it stands, that may not be an issue. See, for example, "People of the British Isles: Preliminary Analysis of Genotypes and Surnames in a UK-Control Population," *Journal of Human Genetics* 20, no. 2 (February 2012): 203–210.

83. Victoria Woollaston, "Forensic Experts Create E-fits from DNA: Traces at Crime Scenes Used to Build Face Shapes with Accuracy Eye and Skin Colors," *Daily Mail (UK)*, January 30, 2015, http://www .dailymail.co.uk/sciencetech/article-2932943/Forensic-experts-create-e-fits-DNA-Traces-crime-scenes -used-build-face-shapes-accurate-eye-skin-colours.html.

84. Jonathan Kahn, "Race, Genes, and Justice: A Call to Reform the Presentation of Forensic DNA Evidence in Criminal Trials," *Brooklyn Law Review* 74, no. 2 (2009): 325, 350, quoting sociologist Michael Omi as observing that "on the one hand, scientists routinely use racial categories in their research. . . . On the other hand, many scientists feel that racial classifications are meaningless and unscientific." Michael Omi, "Racial Identity and the State: The Dilemmas of Classification," *Law & Inequality: A Journal of Theory and Practice* 15 (1997): 7; Linda M. Hunt and Mary S. Megyesi, "The Ambiguous Meanings of the Racial/Ethnic Categories Routinely Used in Human Genetics Research," *Social Science & Medicine* 66, no. 2 (2008): 349–361.

85. See, for example, Dorothy E. Roberts, "Crime, Race, and Reproduction," *Tulane Law Review* 67 (1993): 1945.

86. For example, consider a study in the United Kingdom that investigated a genetic basis, among others, for observed higher rates of schizophrenia in a particular immigrant population. Although researchers have concluded that there was no genetic link, even preliminary findings to the contrary might be viewed as legitimating racist or biased policies of exclusion, and result in the stigmatization of certain groups with regard to housing, health care, employment, and the like. Rebecca Pinto et al., "Schizophrenia in Black Caribbeans Living in the UK: An Exploration of Underlying Causes of the High Incidence Rate," *British Journal of General Practice* 58, no. 551 (2008): 429.

87. Paul Dostie, "Case Number 03-0929: Murder in Mammoth Lakes," *Forensic Magazine*, January 6, 2007, http://www.forensicmag.com/articles/2007/01/case-number-03–0929-murder-mammoth-lakes; Douglas Page, "Four Years to Day One: A Saga of Science and Inquest," *Forensic Magazine*, January 6, 2007, http://www.forensicmag.com/articles/2007/01/four-years-day-one-saga-science-and-inquest.

88. Ibid.

89. See, for example, Dov Fox, "The Second Generation of Racial Profiling," *American Journal of Criminal Law* 38 (2010): 49, 77–78.

CHAPTER 14

1. "Twins' DNA Foils Police," *The Telegraph* (*London*), April 3, 2010, http://www.telegraph.co.uk/news /uknews/crime/7547964/Twins-DNA-foils-police.html.

2. State v. Toomes, 191 S.W.3d 122 (Tenn. Crim. App. 2015).

3. Bob McGovern, "DNA Twist Frees Rape Suspect—For Now," *Boston Herald*, May 1, 2014.

4. Eurofins, "New Genetic Tools for Differentiating 'Identical' Twins: Eurofins Develops First DNA Test for Forensic And Paternity Testing of Twins," December 10, 2013, http://www.eurofins.com/en /media-centre/press-releases/2013-12-10.aspx, citing Jacqueline Weber-Lehman, "Finding the Needle in the Haystack: Differentiating 'Identical' Twins in Paternity Testing and Forensics by Ultra-Deep Next Generation Sequencing," *Forensic Science International: Genetics* 9 (March 2014): 42–46.

5. Bob McGovern, "Dropping Charges Worth the Risk. Suspect Reindicted After New DNA Test," *Boston Herald*, September 12, 2014. In a different case, the Massachussetts high court held that a twin did not have to produce a DNA sample to authorities in the prosecution of his brother. *Commonwealth v. Kostka*, 31 N.E. 3d 116 (Mass. 2015).

6. Denise Lavoie, "Twin Convicted in Third Trial on Rape Charge," Associated Press, March 22, 2006.

7. "She's Her Own Twin," ABC News/Primetime, August 15, 2006, available at http://abcnews.go.com /Primetime/story?id=2315693.

8. N. Yu et al., "Disputed Maternity Leading to Identification of Tetragametic Chimerism," *New England Journal of Medicine* 346 (2002): 1545.

9. Pierre Grimal, *The Dictionary of Classical Mythology* (Hoboken, NJ: Wiley-Blackwell, 1996), 100, 143.

10. Lyn Gardner, "Chimera Review—DNA Drama Is All Head and No Heart," *The Guardian*, November 25, 2014, http://www.theguardian.com/stage/2014/nov/25/chimera-review-twin-genetics.

11. David H. Kaye, "Chimeric Criminals," *Minnesota Journal of Law, Science, and Technology* 14 (2013): 438.

12. Peter Aldhous, "Bone Marrow Donors Risk DNA Identity Mix-up," *New Scientist*, October 29, 2005, 11.

13. Mads Kamper-Jorgensen et al., "Male Microchimerism and Survival Among Women," *International Journal of Epidemiology* 43, no. 1 (2014): 168–173.

14. Zhen Yan, "Male Microchimerism in Women Without Sons: Quantitative Assessment and Correlation with Pregnancy History," *American Journal of Medicine* 118, no. 8 (August 2005): 899–906.

15. Vanessa Hua, "Your Baby's Leftover DNA Is Making You Stronger," *Atlantic*, October 20, 2014, http://www.theatlantic.com/health/archive/2014/10/your-babys-leftover-dna-is-making-you-stronger/381140/.

16. For example, one of the most popular such tests is known as "Harmony," http://www.ariosadx.com.

17. Kaye, "Chimeric Criminals," 7.

18. Ibid.

19. Catherine Arcabascio, "Chimeras: Double the DNA—Double the Fun for Crime Scene Investigators, Prosecutors, and Defense Attorneys," *Akron Law Review* 40 (2007): 443.

20. Kristen Chen et al., "Chimerism in Monochorionic Dizygotic Twins: Case Study and Review," *American Journal of Medical Genetics Part A* 161, no. 7 (2014): 1817.

21. Ibid.

22. Sheldon Krimsky and Tania Simoncelli, *Genetic Justice: DNA Data Banks, Criminal Investigations, and Civil Liberties* (New York: Columbia University Press, 2011), 303.

23. Kaye, "Chimeric Criminals," 9.

24. Steve Mills and Dan Hinkel, "Attorneys: Police Planted Blood on Juan Rivera's Shoes in Waukegan Slaying," *Chicago Tribune*, December 10, 2014, http://www.chicagotribune.com/news/local/breaking/ct-juan-rivera-shoes-met-20141210-story.html#page=1; Juan Rivera, The Innocence Project, accessed May 17, 2015, http://www.innocenceproject.org/Content/Juan_Rivera.php.

25. Andrew Martin, "Cops Turn to Roadblock in Hunt for Sitter's Killer," *Chicago Tribune*, August 26, 1992.

26. Stanley Holmes, "Waukegan Marchers Focus on Sex Assault," *Chicago Tribune*, September 26, 1992.

27. Andrew Martin et al., "Suspect Charged in Baby-sitter Killing," *Chicago Tribune*, October 31, 1992.

28. Jerry Thomas and Karen Brandon, "Rivera Loved Kids, Family Says," *Chicago Tribune*, November 3, 1992.

29. Ibid.

30. Jerry Thomas and Andrew Martin, "Electronic Monitoring No Cure-All for Crime," *Chicago Tribune*, November 16, 1992.

31. Andrew Martin, "Staker Family Sues County over Monitors," *Chicago Tribune*, February 1, 1994.

32. Robert Enstad, "Blood on Rivera Shoe Matched to Girl," *Chicago Tribune*, March 11, 1993.

33. Robert Enstad, "Judge Won't Order Inmate's Blood," *Chicago Tribune*, May 29, 1993.

34. Robert Enstad, "Contempt Charges Dropped in Baby-sitter Murder Case," *Chicago Tribune*, November 25, 1992.

35. Ibid.

36. Robert Enstad, "Public Defender Gets New Deputy," *Chicago Tribune*, March 23, 1993.

37. Andrew Martin, "The Prosecution's Case Against DNA," *New York Times Magazine*, November 25, 2011, http://www.nytimes.com/2011/11/27/magazine/dna-evidence-lake-county.html?pagewanted=all.

38. David Silverman, "Key Witness Recants in Staker Case," *Chicago Tribune*, October 2, 1993.

39. "Defendant's Cellmate Testifies of Confession to Sitter's Murder," *Chicago Tribune*, November 13, 1993.

40. People v. Rivera, 962 N.E.2d 53 (App. Ct. Ill. 2011).

41. Steve Mills and Dan Hinkel, "Attorneys: Police Planted Blood in Waukegan Slaying."

42. In a further twist, both samples matched a bloody board used to beat a man to death in 2000 while Rivera was incarcerated, which implied that the beating and Staker's killing might have been committed by the same person. Interestingly, it did not match the man convicted of the beating, who has claimed innocence. Steve Mills and Dan Hinkel, "DNA Links Murder and Rape of Holly Staker, 11, to Second Murder 8 Years Later," *Chicago Tribune*, June 10, 2014, http://articles.chicagotribune.com/2014-06-10/news/chi-dna-links-murder-and-rape-of-holly-staker-11-to-second-murder-8-years-later-20140610_1_holly-staker-dna-evidence-dna-match.

43. Paul Bibby, "Robert Xie Planned to Use DNA from Body to Clear Him of Lin Deaths, Trial Hears," *Sydney Morning Herald*, May 12, 2014, http://www.smh.com.au/nsw/robert-xie-planned-to-use-dna-from-body-to-clear-him-of-lin-deaths-trial-hears-20140512-zraaf.html.

44. Thyrie Bland, "Mobile County ADA on Tainted Sample: 'Somebody Dumped His DNA from Whatever Source in His Mouth,'" Alabama.com, November 20, 2014, http://www.al.com/news/mobile /index.ssf/2014/11/how_did_someone_elses_dna_get.html.

45. D. Frumkin et al., "Authentication of Forensic DNA Samples," *Forensic Science International: Genetics* 4, no. 2 (February 2010): 95–103, http://www.fsigenetics.com/article/S1872-4973(09)00099-4 /abstract.

46. Rebecca Dent, "The Detection and Characterization of Forensic DNA Profiles Manipulated by the Addition of PCR Amplicon" (master's thesis, Centre for Forensic Science, University of Western Australia, 2006); William C. Thompson, "The Myth of Infallibility," in *Genetic Explanations: Sense and Nonsense*, ed. Sheldon Krimsky and Jeremy Gruber (Cambridge, MA: Harvard University Press, 2013), 268.

47. Allen v. State, 103 A.3d 700, 705 (Md. 2014) (internal quotation marks omitted).

48. Ibid., 719 (citing Maryland Ann. Code, Pub. Safety § 2-508(b) [West 2015]).

49. Diggs & Allen v. State, 73 A.3d 306 (Md. Ct. Spec. App. 2013); Allen v. State, 103 A.3d 700 (Md. 2014).

50. Thompson, "Myth of Infallibility," 252.

51. See discussion in Chapter 11, and also http://deweyhagborg.com.

CHAPTER 15

1. Committee on Causes and Consequences of High Rates of Incarceration, *The Growth of Incarceration in the United States,* ed. Jeremy Travis, Bruce Western, and Steve Redburn (2014), 2.

2. Leah Sakala, "Breaking Down Mass Incarceration in the 2010 Census: State by State Incarceration Rates by Race/Ethnicity," Briefing, May 28, 2014, http://www.prisonpolicy.org/reports/rates.html. Human Rights Watch puts those figures at 478 white, 3,023 black for every 100,000 males in that group. Human Rights Watch, *Nation Behind Bars: A Human Rights Solution,* 4, http://www.hrw.org/sites/default/files /related_material/2014_US_Nation_Behind_Bars_0.pdf.

3. Ibid. (citing 53.4 percent of prisoners with a sentence of more than one year).

4. Ibid., 5.

5. *Growth of Incarceration,* 3.

6. Becky Pettit and Bruce Western, "Mass Imprisonment and the Life Course: Race and Class Inequality in U.S. Incarceration," *American Sociological Review* 69 (2004): 3.

7. See Samuel R. Gross and Michael Shaffer, *Exonerations in the United States, 1989 Through 2012* (June 2012), 49 https://www.law.umich.edu/special/exoneration/Documents/exonerations_us_1989_2012_full_ report.pdf

8. Toya Z. Like-Haislip and Karin Tusinski Miofsky, "Race, Ethnicity, Gender & Violent Victimization," *Race and Justice* 1, no. 3 (2011): 254–276.

9. See, for example, Harry G. Levine et al., "Drug Arrests and DNA: Building Jim Crow's Database," Council for Responsible Genetics Forum on Racial Justice Impacts of Forensic DNA Databases, June 19, 2008.

10. Sakala, "Breaking Down Mass Incarceration."

11. David H. Kaye and Michael E. Smith, "DNA Identification Databases: Legality, Legitimacy, and the Case for Population Wide Coverage," *Wisconsin Law Review* (2003): 459.

12. M. Rotenberg, and M. Ngo, Electronic Privacy Information Center, REAL ID Implementation Review: *Few Benefits, Staggering Costs: Analysis of the Department of Homeland Security's National ID Program,* May 2008, 4–5.

13. Hiibel v. Sixth Judicial District Court of Nevada, 542 U.S. 177 (2004); California v. Byers, 402 U.S. 424 (1971).

14. Michelle Alexander, *The New Jim Crow: Mass Incarceration in the Age of Colorblindness* (New York: The New Press, 2012), 132–135.

CHAPTER 16

1. Robin W. Cotton, "Introduction to Workshop" (presentation at International Symposium on Human Identification, Nashville, Tennessee, October 15, 2012).

2. Nick Swartell, "Pileup at the Morgue," *Cincinnati CityBeat,* December 17, 2014, http://citybeat.com /cincinnati/article-31775-pileup_at_the_morgue.html.

3. Matthew R. Durose, Kelly A. Walsh, and Andrea M. Burch, *Census of Publicly Funded Forensic Crime Laboratories, 2009* (Bureau of Justice Services, August 2012).

4. Rick Green, "Thousands of DNA Tests Are Not Being Performed in Oklahoma," *Oklahoman,* October 8, 2014, http://newsok.com/article/5349551.

5. Nathan James, *DNA Testing in Criminal Justice: Background, Current Law, Grants, and Issues* (Congressional Research Service, December 6, 2012), 9.

6. Mark Nelson, Ruby Chase, and Lindsay DePalma, *Making Sense of DNA Backlogs, 2012—Myths vs. Reality* (National Institute of Justice, December 2013), 3.

7. Federal Bureau of Investigation, *CODIS–NDIS Statistics,* http://www.fbi.gov/about-us/lab/biometric -analysis/codis/ndis-statistics (last visited May 18, 2015).

8. US Department of Justice, Federal Bureau of Investigation, *Crime in the United States,* Violent Crime Offense Figure: Five Year Trend 2006–2010, http://www.fbi.gov/about-us/cjis/ucr/crime-in-the-u.s/2010 /crime-in-the-u.s.-2010/violent-crime; http://www.disastercenter.com/crime/uscrime.htm.

9. The forensic database is cumulative; solved cases are not removed. James, *DNA Testing,* 6, Table 1.

10. This figure assumes 20 million violent crimes, times a 50 percent clearance rate, plus 136 million property crimes, times a 19 percent clearance rate, to get to 120 million unsolved offenses.

11. Joseph Peterson et al., *Final Report: The Role and Impact of Forensic Evidence in the Criminal Justice Process,* National Institute of Justice, 2010, 8, https://www.ncjrs.gov/pdffiles1/nij/grants/231977.pdf. To be fair, Peterson's data came from 2003, because the team wanted to give enough time for cases to have completed the criminal justice process. But other studies, such as those by Strom and McEwen discussed in this chapter, appear to corroborate these findings.

12. A separate study reported similar numbers. In Denver, for example, forensic evidence was recovered in 95.5 percent of homicides and 52 percent of sexual assaults, but only 5.1 percent of assaults, 7.4 percent of robberies, and 15.7 percent of burglaries. Note that 74.6 percent of homicides and 50.2 percent of rapes had biological evidence, but less than 5 percent of other cases did. Tom McEwen, *The Role and Impact of Forensic Evidence in the Criminal Justice System* (December 13, 2010).

13. Kevin J. Strom et al., *The 2007 Survey of Law Enforcement Forensic Evidence Processing,* Final Report (US Department of Justice: October 2009), 3–1.

14. Brian A. Reaves, *Hiring and Retention of State and Local Law Enforcement Officers, 2008—Statistical Tables* (Bureau of Justice Statistics, October 2012), http://www.bjs.gov/content/pub/pdf/hrslleo08st.pdf; Brian A. Reaves, *Census of State and Local Law Enforcement Agencies, 2008* (Bureau of Justice Statistics, July 2011), http://www.bjs.gov/content/pub/pdf/csllea08.pdf.

15. National Research Council Committee on Identifying the Needs of the Forensic Science Community, *Strengthening Forensic Science in the United States: A Path Forward* (Washington, DC: National Academies Press, 2009), 2–2.

16. Strom et al., *2007 Survey,* 3–2, https://www.ncjrs.gov/pdffiles1/nij/grants/228415.pdf.

17. Ibid., 4–2.

18. John K. Roman et al., *The DNA Field Experiment: Cost Effectiveness Analysis of the Use of DNA in the Investigation of High-Volume Crimes* (Urban Institute, April 2008), 4.

19. Matthew Gabriel, Cherisse Boland, and Cydne Holt, "Beyond the Cold Hit: Measuring the Impact of the National DNA Data Bank on Public Safety at the City and County Level," *Journal of Law, Medicine, and Ethics* (Summer 2010): 396.

20. In addition to the studies cited in the text, two GeneWatch reports advised that after a certain point, crime scene samples, not known profiles, drive the efficacy of the database. Human Genetics Commission, *Nothing to Hide, Nothing to Fear?* (November 2009), available at http://www.statewatch.org/news/2009 /nov/uk-dna-human-genetics-commission.pdf; memorandum submitted by GeneWatch UK, *Home Affairs Committee, The National DNA Database (House of Commons), Eighth Report,* 2009–10, HC 222-II (U.K.), available at http://www.publications.parliament.uk/pa/cm200910/cmselect/cmhaff/222 /222ii.pdf; GeneWatch UK, *National DNA Database: Submission to the Home Affairs Committee* (January 2010), available at http://www.genewatch.org/uploads/f03c6d66a9b354535738483c1c3d49e4/.GWsub _Jan10.doc.

21. Jeremiah Goulka et al., *RAND Center on Quality Policing, Toward a Comparison of DNA Profiling and Databases in the United States and England* (2010).

22. S. and Marper v. The United Kingdom (2008) ECHR 1581.

23. Home Office (UK), National DNA Database Strategy Board, *Annual Report,* 2013–14.

24. Ibid.

25. Brief of 20 Scholars of Forensic Evidence as Amicus Curiae Supporting Respondents, McDaniel v. Brown, No. 08–559, 2009 WL 2247124, July 24, 2009, 8.

26. Filipe Santos et al., "Forensic DNA Databases in European Countries: Is Size Linked to Performance?," *Life Sciences, Society and Policy* 9, no. 1 (2013): 12.

27. Victor Toom, "Forensic DNA Databases in England and the Netherlands: Governance, Structure and Performance Compared," *New Genetics and Society* 31 (2012): 311.

28. "Lawmaker: Backlog Delays Expansion of Vermont DNA Database," WCAX.com, February 15, 2015. http://www.wcax.com/story/28093047/lawmaker-backlog-delays-expansion-of-vermont-dna-database.

29. Brief of 20 Scholars, 11–13.

30. Specifically, the Paul Coverdell Forensic Sciences Improvement Grant Program; see https://www .cfda.gov/index?s=program&mode=form&tab=core&id=04caa46b1bb259fc354051d39ab17250, and the Debbie Smith Backlog Reduction Program, 42 U.S.C. § 14135 (2014).

31. David A. Graham, "Rapists Go Free While Rape Kits Go Untested," *Atlantic*, February 24, 2015, http://www.theatlantic.com/national/archive/2015/02/how-many-crimes-could-clearing-the-rape-kit -backlog-stop/385943/.

32. Sean Allocca, "Why Backlogged Kits Are a Public Safety Problem," *Forensic Magazine*, April 10, 2015.

33. http://www.endthebacklog.org/detroit-0.

34. Graham, "Rapists Go Free."

35. Katherine Driessen, "While Some Rape Kits Sat Untested, Suspects Committed More Assaults," *Houston Chronicle*, February 23, 2015, http://www.chron.com/news/houston-texas/houston/article/While -some-rape-kits-sat-untested-suspects-6097408.php.

36. Erik Eckholm, "No Longer Ignored, Evidence Solves Rape Cases Years Later," *New York Times*, August 2, 2014, http://www.nytimes.com/2014/08/03/us/victims-pressure-cities-to-test-old-rape-kits .html?_r=0.

37. Associated Press, "Ohio AG: More than 5,600 Rape Kits Tested for DNA," WKBN27, December 6, 2014, http://wkbn.com/2014/12/06/ohio-ag-more-than-5600-rape-kits-tested-for-dna/.

38. Rachel Dissell, "Rape Kit Testing Projects Could 'Revolutionize' Future Sexual Assault Investigations, Prosecutor Says," *Plain Dealer (Cleveland)*, October 20, 2014, http://www.cleveland.com/court-justice /index.ssf/2014/10/prosecutor_rape_kit_testing_pr.html.

39. Rachel Dissell, "Serial Rapists Responsible for at Least 600 Attacks Linked to Untested Evidence, Authorities Believe," *Plain Dealer (Cleveland)*, March 21, 2015, at http://www.cleveland.com/rape-kits /index.ssf/2015/03/authorities_believe_serial_rap.html.

40. Rachel Dissell, "With New Law, Ohio Continues Trend Toward National Leadership on Rape Kit Testing," *Plain Dealer (Cleveland)*, December 19, 2014, http://www.cleveland.com/court-justice/index .ssf/2014/12/with_new_law_ohio_continuos_tr.html.

41. The White House, Office of the Press Secretary, press release, "Fact Sheet: Investments to Reduce the National Rape Kit Backlog and Combat Violence Against Women," March 16, 2015, https://www .whitehouse.gov/the-press-office/2015/03/16/fact-sheet-investments-reduce-national-rape-kit-backlog -and-combat-violen&.

42. Sean Allocca, "Can $41 Million Even Dent the Backlog?" *Forensic Magazine*, March 18, 2015, http://www.forensicmag.com/articles/2015/03/can-41-million-even-dent-backlog.

43. Tresa Baldas, "Fund-Raising Campaign Aims at Solving Detroit Rape Cases," *Detroit Free Press*, January 6, 2015, http://www.freep.com/story/news/local/michigan/detroit/2015/01/06/rape-kit-fund -raiser/21330399/.

44. Roman, *Field Experiment*; Jennifer J. Raymond, "Trace DNA Success Rates Relating to Volume Crime Offences," *Forensic Science International: Genetics* 2 (2009): 136; Shannon Prather, "DNA Forensics Helping Crack More Property Crimes," *Star Tribune*, December 20, 2014, http://www.startribune.com /local/north/286468711.html.

45. Chuck Heurich, "Making Sense of DNA Backlogs" (presentation at International Symposium on Human Identification, Phoenix, Arizona, October 1, 2014).

46. P. Gill et al., "DNA Commission of the International Society of Forensic Genetics: Recommendations on the Evaluation of STR Typing Results that May Include Drop-out and/or Drop-in Using Probabilistic Methods," *Forensic Science International: Genetics* 6 (2010): 680.

47. Strom et al., *2007 Survey*, 3.2.4.

48. Peter Dujardin and Ashley K. Speed, "Man Convicted in 36-Year-Old Williamsburg Rape," *Daily Press*, October 12, 2014, http://articles.dailypress.com/2014–10–12/news/dp-nws-crime -notebook-1012–20141012_1_mary-jane-burton-york-county-man-apartment.

49. The Innocence Project, "How Is Your State Doing?," http://www.innocenceproject.org/how-is-your -state-doing.

50. Technical Working Group on Biological Evidence Preservation, *The Biological Evidence Preservation Handbook*, NIST (April 2013).

51. Examples include Colorado, Colo. Revised Stat. Ann. § 18–1-1101 et seq.; Wisconsin, Wisc. Stat. Ann. § 968.205; and a law recently signed by the governor of Washington.

52. Federal Bureau of Investigation, "CODIS—NDIS Statistics," http://www.fbi.gov/about-us/lab/biometric-analysis/codis/ndis-statistics.

53. Frederick R. Bieber, "Turning Base Hits into Earned Runs: Improving the Effectiveness of Forensic DNA Data Bank Programs," *Journal of Law, Medicine, and Ethics* 34, no. 2 (2006): 227.

54. Matthew R. Durose, Kelly A. Walsh, and Andrea M. Burch, *Census of Publicly Funded Forensic Crime Laboratories, 2009* (Bureau of Justice Services, August 2012), 7.

55. California Department of Justice, Division of Law Enforcement, *Annual Report 2009–10*, 19–20 (describing CHOP program), http://oag.ca.gov/sites/all/files/agweb/pdfs/publications/09–10_DLE_ANNUAL_REPORT.pdf.

56. Gabriel, et al., "Beyond the Cold Hit," 409n41.

57. For instance, the Katie Sepich Enhanced DNA Collection Act, signed by the president in 2013, provides financial support and incentives to states to implement arrestee DNA collection laws.

58. Eric Lander, "DNA Fingerprinting on Trial," *Nature* 339 (1989): 501, 505.

59. For example, in April 2015 the ANSI-ASQ National Accreditation Board suspended the Washington, DC, Forensic Crime Lab due to findings that DNA analysts were "not competent and were using inadequate procedures." Keith L. Alexander, "National Accreditation Board Suspends All DNA Testing at D.C. Crime Lab," *Washington Post*, April 27, 2015. Yet a search of that lab on the accreditor's website listed the agency's status as "accredited," http://search.anab.org/search-accredited-companies.aspx?, accessed May 14, 2015.

60. Paul Coverdell National Forensic Sciences Improvement Act of 2000, Pub. L. No. 106–561, 114 Stat. 2787 (codified at 42 U.S. Code § 3797j et seq.). The act is named after the late senator Paul Coverdell, who first introduced similar legislation in 1999 but died suddenly before its passage. Prior to its passage, limited funding for laboratory improvements was available through programs such as the Byrne grants, Omnibus Crime Control, and Safe Streets Act of 1968, Pub. L. No. 90–351, § 401.

61. Oversight of the Department of Justice's Forensic Grant Programs: Hearing Before the S. Comm. on the Judiciary, 110th Cong. (2008) (statement of Glenn A. Fine, inspector general, US Department of Justice), 6.

62. US Department of Justice, National Commission on Forensic Science, Work Products, accessed May 17, 2015, http://www.justice.gov/ncfs/work-products.

63. Audit Division, Office of the Inspector General, US Department of Justice, *U.S. Department of Justice Audit of the National Institute of Justice's Practices for Awarding Grants and Contracts in Fiscal Years 2005 through 2007* (September 2009), http://www.justice.gov/oig/reports/OJP/a0938.pdf.

64. Letter from Jed S. Rakoff to fellow commissioners, January 28, 2015 (on file with author).

65. David Kaye, *The Double Helix and the Law of Evidence* (Cambridge, MA: Harvard University Press, 2011), 257.

66. Roger Koppl and Meghan Sacks, "The Criminal Justice System Creates Incentives for False Conviction," *Criminal Justice Ethics* 32, no. 2 (2013): 126, 146–147, citing laws in eighteen states.

67. Kansas Stat. Ann. 28–176 (2014).

68. DNA Resource, accessed May 17, 2015, http://www.dnaresource.com/policy.html.

69. Ibid. (listing Alabama, Arizona, California, Colorado, Indiana, Missouri, New Jersey, and North Carolina).

70. Justice Policy Institute, *System Overload: The Costs of Under-Resourcing Public Defense*, July 2011, 2.

71. Gretchen Engel, "North Carolina's Crime Lab Scandal Remains Unaddressed," NC Policy Watch, September 24, 2013, http://www.ncpolicywatch.com/2013/09/24/north-carolinas-crime-lab-scandal-remains-unaddressed/.

72. *The Mismatch Between 21st Century Forensic Evidence and Our Antiquated Criminal Justice System*, S. Calif. L. Rev. 87 (2014): 113–120.

73. Ibid.

74. Transcript of Oral Argument, Bullcoming v. New Mexico, No. 09–10876, US Supreme Court, March 2, 2011, 37.

75. Williams v. Illinois, 132 S. Ct. 2221 (2012).

76. United States v. Luke, 69 M.J. 309, 313 (Ct. App. Armed Forces 2011); Office of the Inspector General, United States Department of Defense, "Review of DoD Response to Noncompliant Crime Laboratory Analyses," Report No. DODIG-2013–033 (January 23, 2013), 6.

77. Koppl and Sacks, "The Criminal Justice System," 126; Marisa Taylor and Michael Doyle, "Army Slow to Act as Crime-Lab Worker Falsified, Botched Tests," *McClatchy DC*, March 20, 2011, http://www.mcclatchydc.com/2011/03/20/110551_army-slow-to-act-as-crime-lab.html?rh=1#storylink=cpy.

78. Office of the Inspector General, "Review of DOD," 15.

79. Michael Doyle and Marisa Taylor, "Discredited Army Analyst Built His Career Around Crime Lab," *McClatchy DC*, March 20, 2011, http://www.mcclatchydc.com/2011/03/20/110549/discredited-army-analyst-built.html.

80. Derek Gilna, "Misconduct at U.S. Army Lab Taints Hundreds of Military Prosecutions," *Prison Legal News*, December 2012, 26, https://www.prisonlegalnews.org/news/2012/dec/15/misconduct-at-us-army-lab-taints-hundreds-of-military-prosecutions/; Marisa Taylor and Michael Doyle, "More Errors Surface at Military Crime Labs as Senate Seeks Inquiry," *McClatchy DC*, May 15, 2011, http://www.mcclatchydc.com/2011/05/15/114221/more-errors-surface-at-military.html#storylink=cpy.

81. Michael Doyle and Marisa Taylor, "Crime-lab Worker's Errors Cast Doubt on Military Verdicts," *McClatchy DC*, March 20, 2011, http://www.mcclatchydc.com/2011/03/20/110548/crime-lab-workers-errors-cast.html.

82. Ibid.; Office of the Inspector General, "Review of DOD," 4.

83. Brent E. Turvey and Craig M. Cooley, *Miscarriages of Justice: Actual Innocence, Forensic Evidence, and the Law* (Oxford, UK: Academic Press, 2014), 187–188.

84. Derek Gilna, "Misconduct at U.S. Army Lab."

85. Office of the Inspector General, "Review of DOD," 1.

86. Ibid.

87. Ibid; Taylor and Doyle, "Army Slow."

88. House v. United States, 99 Fed. Cl. 342 (2011); Harris v. United States, 102 Fed. Cl. 390 (2011).

89. The National Registry of Exonerations, A Project of the University of Michigan Law School, Roger House, accessed May 17, 2015, https://www.law.umich.edu/special/exoneration/Pages/casedetail.aspx?caseid=3308.

90. "U.S. Army Criminal Investigation Command Responses to McClatchy Questions," *McClatchy DC*, accessed May 17, 2015, http://www.mcclatchydc.com/static/pdf/Doyle forensics/Doyle-CID-questions.pdf.

91. Ibid.

92. United States v. Luke, 69 M.J. 309 (C.A.A.F. 2011); see also Luke v. United States, 942 F.Supp.2d 154 (D.D.C. 2013); Doughty v. United States, No. NMCCA 9900437, 2013 WL 3242797 (N-M. Ct. Crim. App. June 27, 2013); Ohio v. Ellison, 1 N.E. 3d 824 (Ct. App. Ohio 8th D. 2013).

93. Doyle and Taylor, "Crime-lab Worker's Errors."

94. See generally Michael Nasser Petegorsky, note, "Plea Bargaining in the Dark: The Duty to Disclose Exculpatory Brady Evidence During Plea Bargaining," *Fordham Law Review* 81 (2013): 3599.

95. Buffey v. Ballard, 2012 WL 2675332 (N D W Va 2012) (unreported opinion), and http://www.innocenceproject.org/cases-false-imprisonment/joseph-buffey.

96. David Gutman, "With New DNA Evidence, Appeal to the Supreme Court in Clarksburg Rape Case," *West Virginia Gazette*, December 6, 2014.

97. West Virginia Rule of Criminal Procedure, 16.

98. John M. Butler, *Perspectives on the Future: What Have We Learned and Where We Need to Go* (presentation at International Symposium on Human Identification, Nashville, Tennessee, October 15, 2012).

99. N.Y.C., N.Y., Admin. Code §§ 17–207, 17–208 (adopted September 12, 2013).

100. Jennifer N. Mellon, notes, "Manufacturing Convictions: Why Defendants Are Entitled to the Data Underlying Forensic DNA Kits," *Duke Law Journal* 51 (2001): 1097.

101. Michael Morton Act, 2013 Tex. Sess. Law Serv. Chap. 49 (S.B.1611), 83rd Leg., 2013 Regular Session. Michael Morton's story is beautifully recounted in two pieces in the *Texas Monthly*: Pamela Colloff, "The Innocent Man, Part One," *Texas Monthly*, November 2012, and "The Innocent Man, Part Two," *Texas Monthly*, December 2012.

102. "Judge Finds That Anderson Hid Evidence in Morton Murder Trial," *Statesman (Austin)*, April 19, 2013.

103. Vernon's Ann. Texas Code Crim. Proc. Art. 39.14.

104. American Bar Association, *Standards on DNA Evidence*, 3rd ed. (2007), http://www.americanbar.org/publications/criminal_justice_section_archive/crimjust_standards_dnaevidence.html.

105. John M. Butler, *Advanced Topics in Forensic DNA Typing: Interpretation* (Oxford, UK: Academic Press, 2014), 304.

106. Forensic Resources: North Carolina Office of Indigent Defense Services, accessed May 17, 2015, http://www.ncids.com/forensic/.

107. Jonathan Simon, *Governing Through Crime: How the War on Crime Transformed American Democracy and Created a Culture of Fear* (Oxford, UK: Oxford University Press, 2007).

108. Winston v. Lee, 470 U.S. 753 (1985); Rochin v. California, 342 U.S. 165 (1952).

109. Mincey v. Arizona, 437 U.S. 385 (1978).

110. Riley v. California, 134 S. Ct. 2473 (2014).

111. Ibid., 2489.

112. Maryland v. King, 133 S. Ct. 1958, 1968–69, 1972 (2013).

113. Riley, 134 S. Ct. at 2484.

APPENDIX

1. John M. Butler, *Introduction to Interpretation Issues* (presentation in Mixture Interpretation Webcast, National Institute of Standards and Technology, April 12, 2013), http://www.cstl.nist.gov/strbase/training/MixtureWebcast/2_InterpretationFundamentals-Butler.pdf.

2. Scientific Working Group on DNA Analysis Methods, *Guidelines for STR Enhanced Detection Methods* (2014), 3.

3. Martin Enserink, "FBI's Top Scientist Takes the Lead in Forensic Biology," *Science* 300, no. 5616 (April 4, 2003): 41–43.

4. Bruce Budowle et al., *Forensic Science International: Genetics Supplement Series* 2, no. 1 (2009): 551.

5. *Forensic Science International: Genetics* 5 (2011): 1–15.

6. Scientific Working Group on DNA Analysis Methods, *SWGDAM Guidelines for STR Enhanced Detection Methods*, http://swgdam.org/SWGDAM%20EDMI%20Guidelines%20(Final%20APPROVED%200717 2014).pdf.

7. Kelly S. Grisedale and Angela van Daal, "Comparison of STR Profiling from Low Template DNA Extracts With and Without the Consensus Profiling Method," *Investigative Genetics* 3, no. 1 (2012): 14.

INDEX

ERIN E. MURPHY is a professor at NYU School of Law and an expert in DNA forensics. She is a graduate of Harvard Law School. In addition to scholarly journals, her writing has appeared in *Scientific American*, the *New York Times*, *USA Today*, *Slate*, the *San Francisco Chronicle*, and the *Huffington Post*. Follow her on Twitter @ErinMurphysLaw.

The Nation Institute

Founded in 2000, **Nation Books** has become a leading voice in American independent publishing. The inspiration for the imprint came from the *Nation* magazine, the oldest independent and continuously published weekly magazine of politics and culture in the United States.

The imprint's mission is to produce authoritative books that break new ground and shed light on current social and political issues. We publish established authors who are leaders in their area of expertise, and endeavor to cultivate a new generation of emerging and talented writers. With each of our books we aim to positively affect cultural and political discourse.

Nation Books is a project of The Nation Institute, a nonprofit media center dedicated to strengthening the independent press and advancing social justice and civil rights. The Nation Institute is home to a dynamic range of programs: the award-winning Investigative Fund, which supports ground-breaking investigative journalism; the widely read and syndicated website TomDispatch; the Victor S. Navasky Internship Program in conjunction with the *Nation* magazine; and Journalism Fellowships that support up to 25 high-profile reporters every year.

For more information on Nation Books, The Nation Institute, and the *Nation* magazine, please visit:

www.nationbooks.org

www.nationinstitute.org

www.thenation.com

www.facebook.com/nationbooks.ny

Twitter: @nationbooks

11/15